WAGING WAR *on* COMPLEXITY COSTS

RESHAPE YOUR COST STRUCTURE, FREE UP CASH FLOWS, AND BOOST PRODUCTIVITY BY ATTACKING PROCESS, PRODUCT, AND ORGANIZATIONAL COMPLEXITY

STEPHEN A. WILSON

COAUTHOR OF **CONQUERING COMPLEXITY IN YOUR BUSINESS**

AND ANDREI PERUMAL

New York Chicago San Francisco Lisbon London Madrid Mexico City
Milan New Delhi San Juan Seoul Singapore Sydney Toronto

The McGraw-Hill Companies

1 2 3 4 5 6 7 8 9 10 11 12 13 14 15 16 17 18 19 20 21 FGR/FGR 0 9

ISBN 978-0-07-163913-2
MHID 0-07-163913-6

Contents

Part II—Know Thine Enemy: The Faces of Complexity and Implications for Battle

Part III—Battle Strategies to Eliminate Complexity Costs

Part IV—Defense Strategies to Keep Complexity Costs at Bay

Addenda

About the Authors

Stephen A. Wilson is Managing Director of WilsonPerumal, the strategy and operations management consultancy. He is co-author of *Conquering Complexity in your Business* and a contributing author of *Fast Innovation*, both published by McGraw Hill. He has a decade of experience advising senior clients in the U.S. and Europe on issues relating to operations and strategy. Previously, Mr. Wilson was a Principal with George Group Consulting and has experience with Marakon Associates. His education includes an MBA from The Wharton School at the University of Pennsylvania.

Andrei Perumal is Managing Director of WilsonPerumal, the strategy and operations management consultancy. He works with CEOs, executive teams, and government leaders to help them solve challenging problems with a focus on integrating strategy, operations and organization. Previously, Mr. Perumal was with Bain & Company and was part of the leadership team at George Group Consulting. He also served as an officer in the US Navy, worked in industry as an engineer and as director of strategic operations for a financial services firm. He has a BS in Aeronautical and Astronautical Engineering from the Massachusetts Institute of Technology and is a graduate of the US Navy's Nuclear Power Program.

Acknowledgments

We'd like to extend our heartfelt thanks to our colleagues and friends for their unending support of us in the writing of this book. In particular, we'd like to thank our colleagues at WilsonPerumal: Brian Hefner for his thoughtful comments and significant contribution to the manuscript; and Dr. Nick Vikitset, for his analytical support and for his pioneering work in developing the equations for calculating optimal batch sizes. It is no small task to review a manuscript, and to do so is a real act of friendship: our gratitude to Jason Santamaria, David Kim and Andy Bonney. A big thank you to the entire team at McGraw-Hill: to our editor, Knox Huston, for his ongoing guidance and support, and to Mary Glenn, Editorial Director, for her encouragement and sponsorship of the project. We also especially thank Sue Reynard, for her expertise, focus, and passion in shaping, editing, and producing the book. Also, our deep appreciation goes to our publicist, Barbara Cave Henricks.

Finally, a special thanks to our families, for their encouragement and understanding of the long hours and all-consuming focus that the book has demanded.

The Authors

FOREWORD

Why This, Why Now

Boldness has genius, power, and magic in it.

— Goethe

Turbulent times expose weakness and opportunity in equal measure. For businesses today, this is particularly true: As revenues shrank with the sudden contraction in demand, costs remained. The downturn not only exposed the magnitude of previously hidden costs but also revealed their true nature. For the past two decades the pursuit of growth has created massive complexity in companies, and with it, massive complexity costs. The only good news about this weakness is that your competitors may be carrying as much or more complexity cost as you are—and hence the opportunity: Learn how to effectively remove complexity, and you can regain competitive footing by creating a cost advantage over your competitors.

There's definitely an edge to be had: Few companies have earnestly tackled the issue of complexity costs. They may view their complexity as an intractable problem. Many do not fully appreciate the size of the prize that can be won by engaging in this war. But as we will explain later, **complexity costs are the biggest single determinant of your cost-competitiveness.** So while some may be tempted to batten down the hatches and wait for smoother waters, we'd suggest you instead take bold action and let others drift. After the storm has passed, your efforts will have placed you in new harbors.

Five years ago, few could have predicted the dire straits we now find ourselves in. But even then, certain CEOs had correctly tagged complexity and particularly the costs of complexity as the enemies of profits and performance. In my 2004 book *Conquering Complexity in Your Business*, I detailed how some of these companies had chosen to wrestle with the problems of product and service complexity. But fast-forward to today and the world is a very different place. The issue has evolved and the stakes are much higher.

- **The magnitude of the problem is far broader and far deeper.** The market contraction has exposed complexity costs as sharp liabilities that need to be dealt with. A vast number of firms have seen demand for their goods and services fall away, while the associated costs remain. Furthermore, their ability to "absorb" complexity, waste, and inefficiencies has been impeded. Few economists think this downturn is a blip. Companies will need to manage the cash crisis in the near term but also adapt to new sets of competitors, new customer expectations, and new levels of long-term demand. In fact, the degree to which companies can (a) examine which parts of their business align with or support customer preference—not yesterday's preference, but tomorrow's, and (b) deal effectively with those parts that do not (the liabilities) will determine their trajectory into the future. The implication is that while many companies may have nibbled at this issue in the past, addressing it squarely head-on is now a requirement.

- **The nature of the problem has changed.** Variety in products and services is still a major contributor to complexity costs. But in today's world, to make a significant and lasting reduction in cost, companies must also address the complexity in the underlying processes and organizational structures. Simply slashing SKUs or eliminating service options is no longer sufficient, nor necessarily the right response. The new war on complexity costs requires a shift in approach and new strategies that reflect this deeper understanding of the types of complexity and their origins and interactions.
- **The time frame for driving results is compressing.** It used to be that companies could afford to take six months or longer just to understand the problem. That is no longer feasible. Companies are racing each other to understand the implications of what the Wal-Mart CEO calls the "new normal"[i] of consumer behaviors and take effective action. The upside of turbulence? The competitive landscape shifts, and new winners emerge. But delay can put you at the back of the pack.

In short, companies need pragmatic and fast approaches to attacking complexity costs, not academic distractions that generate a lot of activity but few tangible results. They need actionable insights, quickly, so they don't end up investing in new systems or elaborate activity-based costing techniques that themselves become activity traps.

This book is a response to these changes and an attempt to answer the common questions asked by executives, such as,

- What's the business and financial case for removing complexity costs?
- How do I identify the biggest opportunities? Are there big costs I can remove fast?
- How do I remove these costs from my organization?
- Once I've taken out complexity costs, how can I keep them out?
- Where do I start?

The goal of this book is to help you improve the short-term *and* long-term health of your organization by shedding complexity costs, whether they are associated with your products and services, your processes, or your organizational structure. We will walk you through examples that demonstrate just how big the prize is and show you how to calculate the opportunity for your own company. We will discuss the misconceptions about the sources of complexity and explain the interactions that make conquering complexity so difficult (which will demonstrate why the more common tactics used today often fail in the long run). And we will provide clear strategies that can make an immediate impact on your bottom line as well as prepare your company for healthy growth.

Seizing the Opportunity

Traditionally, one of the biggest obstacles to winning the war on complexity costs is surmounting internal barriers, creating the momentum within the organization to break past legacy beliefs. We have seen many CEOs struggle heroically in the past to communicate the urgency of change in their organizations in a bid to steel their teams to break past existing orthodoxies that are out of tune with the market.

That is not required today; CEOs seeking a burning platform to mobilize change now have it in spades.

While this is a testing time for many, it also represents a transformational opportunity. "I am an optimist. It does not seem too much use being anything else," said Winston Churchill.[ii] We concur: Beware the grim tidings of soothsayers, fortune-tellers, and economists, but be ready to act and seize the opportunity that the moment presents.

Leaders who declare a *War on Complexity Costs* will find many willing recruits inside their organization, as it turns an economic reality for surviving today into a battle cry for thriving tomorrow.

Stephen A. Wilson,
September 2009

Preface Endnotes

[i] Mike Duke, CEO of Wal-Mart, speaking at the 2009 annual shareholders meeting.

[ii] Lord Mayor's banquet, London, November 9, 1954.

Part I

A Call to Arms:

The Imperative for Action

CHAPTER 1

The Imperative for Waging This War

(And the Need for Better Battle Strategies)

We're surrounded. That simplifies the problem.
— *General Lewis B. "Chesty" Puller, U.S. Marine Corps*

A few years ago, Procter & Gamble reduced product cost by more than $2/case over a three-year period as a result of a program of simplification and standardization, accounting for nearly $3 billion in savings. An additional $1 billion was generated through the closure of 10 plants as a result of the simplification. Its margins over that period increased from 6.4% to 9.5%.

Similarly, Motorola generated savings of $2.6 billion in operating and material costs in two years of a "War on Complexity," at the same time reducing inventory by $1.4 billion and capacity by 40% as fewer factories and distribution centers were needed.

These cost reductions were all made before the current economic downturn savaged revenues. The implication is even in boom times there was opportunity. But now that "*the list of bad news is almost endless*" (as *The Economist Intelligence Unit* put it), the opportunity, and challenge, has been magnified manyfold.

Early in 2009, *The Economist* forecasted the worst global GDP performance since the end of the Second World War. Global in nature, pan-industry, and to all indications sustained, this contraction is not only putting immediate cost pressures on companies, but also threatening to reshape the economic landscape in ways that may last a decade or more. To what exactly, no one knows. But as the landscape changes, so too must companies.

The contraction marks a sharp divide between the last decade and the next. Companies over the past decade were part of a rising tide that floated all boats, growing and expanding in sync with the consumer. They rushed to market with new products and line extensions, expanded into adjacent markets and services, and grew rapidly into new geographies driven by steadily growing consumer demand.

Consider, for example, the trajectory of many food retailers in the past decade and the demands of growth, as they…

- Expanded into new formats, from the traditional grocery store format to variants including city center stores and the out-of-town megastores
- Stretched their processes and supply chain to handle an explosion in new ranges, both inside existing grocery categories and beyond—into hardware, clothing, and electronics (in fact, many stores now carry more than 100,000 SKUs in diverse categories)
- Grew their organizations to expand into new geographies, from home base countries to high-growth markets in China, India, and elsewhere

The consumer packaged goods companies, as suppliers to these retailers, have kept apace, launching a volley of new products: new versions of Oreo cookies, an aisle of potato chips, hundreds of types of toothpaste. The retailers, the consumer goods companies, and *their* suppliers have all rightly rushed to meet consumer demand, but not without considerable adjustment.

Think about the impact of all that change on the supply chain that "grew up" over many years getting cans of soups from the supplier to the shelf edge. That same supply chain now has to also support flat-screen TVs… now extend across multiple countries… now support different format stores, and on and on.

You may not be in the business of retailing soup or flat-screen TVs, but chances are your business has gone through similar changes. You have seen your range of products and services expand to meet the growing diversity of customer demands. Your internal processes, organizational structures, and technology have likewise grown in complexity. Your business has stretched and rapidly grown to meet a decade of growth but has left in its wake an enormous burden of complexity costs.

A "product" by any other name

A core principle of this book is to simplify things as much as possible. Therefore, we use the term "product" and "product complexity" to represent the complexity in the portfolio of offerings that you put before your customers, whether these offerings are products or services. Clearly there are some differences between service complexity and product complexity. A prime difference is the fact that service complexity is often rife because of its ability to lurk unnoticed. A warehouse full of spare parts because of product proliferation is a very visible manifestation of complexity. But a bulging portfolio of banking products may go unnoticed under the radar. We will continue to spell out some of those nuances in the book. But to keep things simple, we will refer to customer-facing complexity as product complexity, as shorthand.

An Island of Profit in a Sea of Cost

As the P&G and Motorola stories illustrate, the prize for cutting complexity costs can be substantial. At a general level, we've found that it's **possible for companies to reduce costs by 15% to 30% in significant portions of their business by waging war on complexity costs.**

How is this possible? Consider how profit is usually concentrated within a company. A so-called Whale Curve (Figure 1) demonstrates this effect, plotting a company's cumulative profit as a function of products ranked by their profitability. (There are a variety of Whale Curves, each showing cumulative profits against various drivers, such as products, customers, and revenue.)

What does the Whale Curve tell us? Often the most profitable 20% to 30% of products generate **more than 300% of the profits** in a company.[1] Because actual profits can't exceed 100% of the total, the **remaining 70% to 80% *lose* 200% of the profits:** they are tied to assets, processes, products, and customer groups that are disproportionate drivers of cost in your organization.

Figure 1: The Whale Curve

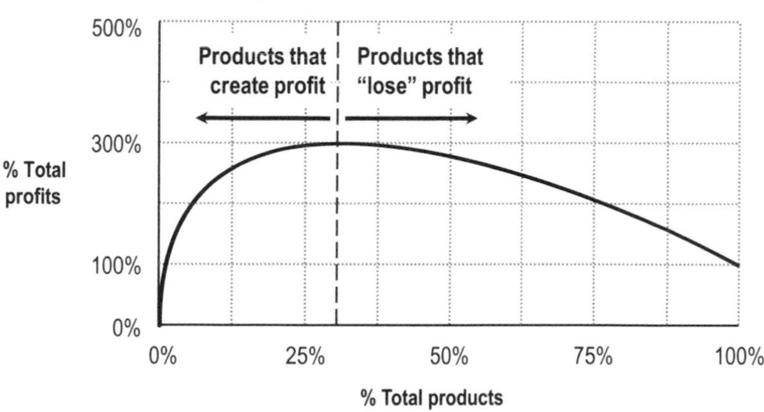

The Whale Curve is a provocative representation of profit concentration, and it provides a tantalizing reflection of the possibilities. What would your organization look like if you could somehow shed the 80% of products that were sapping profit? (We will later discuss how process and organizational complexity affect the Whale Curve.) A prerequisite to shed that excess baggage is to understand how your product line creates or "loses" profits by undertaking a profitability study. However, the results often jar with commonly held assumptions. In his book *The 80/20 Principle*, Richard Koch reports, "*Routinely, executives who commission product-line profitability exercises often do refuse to believe the results when first presented with them.*" And even if they believe that 80% of their products are "profit losers," they often shy away from dealing with that portion of the product line. The executives' rationale, Koch maintains, is that it is impossible to remove the 80% of corresponding overhead in any sensible time frame. Therefore, only the most horribly unprofitable business is removed. Koch further says,

> *Yet all this is a dreadful compromise.... The truth is that the unprofitable business is so unprofitable because it requires the overheads and because having so many different chunks of business makes the organization horrendously complicated. It is equally true that the very profitable business does not require the overheads, or only a very small portion of them.*

It is difficult for many—despite the data—to accept the impact of complexity on the overall health of the organization, particularly given the fact that complexity does not announce itself with fanfare. Rather, it creeps in decision by decision, each choice adding costs that are hidden from traditional accounting methods. Worse still, its effects are geometric: a small expansion in a product or service line affects not just the offering of the delivery process but also everything else that goes into creating and supporting that process—inventory, instructions, overhead, and more.

Consider a familiar business strategy of the past decade: consumer goods companies proliferating line extensions as a way to secure customer niche segments, steal share, or in response to customer requests. What has been the impact on revenue and costs? The first thing to understand with line extensions is that they rarely increase demand. As a study pointed out, "People do not eat or drink more, wash their hair more, or brush their teeth more frequently simply because they have more products from which to choose."[2] What happens frequently is a cannibalization of one product by another.

On the cost side, the news is rarely better: Line extensions require increases in marketing expenditure, product development, production, and packaging as new manufacturing lines are required. New warehouses and sometimes new factories are needed. Transportation costs increase, not only with increased volumes going to stores but also with fewer and fewer full pallets being loaded onto trucks. Administration and overhead costs increase as new product managers are brought in to manage the expanding portfolio. The result as cited in the above study: **the unit costs for multi-item lines can be 25% to 45% higher than the theoretical cost of producing only the most popular item in the line**. (We will reveal the math behind the proliferation costs in Part II.)

Decomplexity Case Study

Let's consider a concrete example of complexity creep and what one company did to address it. Toblerone is the iconic candy bar with the distinctive triangular shape (meant to echo the Matterhorn in the Swiss Alps). As often happens, complexity within the brand line occurred as the result of many incremental decisions, all made with the best of intentions. Since its creation 100 years ago, the Toblerone bar has grown in popularity and availability. Slightly different versions were launched in neighboring geographies, requiring the support of additional processes and organizations.

In short, the growth created a web of complexity. To turn this around, Kraft (which now owns the brand) launched a "decomplexity" effort, which promoted three strategic goals for the company: help drive growth, improve consumer satisfaction, and drive out costs and assets. The Toblerone effort is summarized in Table A.

Kraft saw benefits in two types of cost:

1) **Reduced material costs**, from savings in raw materials, ingredients, packaging, formats, and SKUs

2) **Reduced process costs**, including savings in R&D, procurement, conversion, logistics, marketing, sales, and administration.

Table A: Kraft's Toblerone Decomplexity Initiative

From...	To...
9 plants in 9 countries	1 plant
Multiple dimensions	Unified dimensions*
Numerous recipes	Common recipe
One language per package	Language clusters
Seasonal packaging	Standard w/ promotional sleeve
Country-specific or regional sourcing	Global sourcing

**While all Toblerone bars were a similar triangular shape, there were slight variations in the dimensions of the bar.*

Kraft estimated that the result was an ongoing pre-tax cost benefit of $400 million per year.[3] With a focus on sustainable productivity improvements, Kraft used decomplexity as an enabler to efficiently attain global scale and develop functional excellence. The company understood that a focus on eliminating the bad complexity costs was good for the shareholder and good for the customer.

Why Companies Lose the War or Avoid It Altogether

We've now seen three examples—P&G, Motorola, and Kraft—of companies that have made significant progress in cutting costs via complexity reduction. And we're now in a climate that demands meaningful action on costs. So the question arises as to why more companies have not taken action.

Clearly companies everywhere are looking at costs. But traditional corporate approaches inspire little confidence. A recent study reported that fewer than half of all the companies launching cost-reduction programs actually realized benefits, and even then the benefits were short lived.[4] Only 10% of the companies were able to sustain the cost reductions through year 3. Executives have their own opinions as to why things go awry; we have heard the following:

> *"The cost program focused on the wrong areas."*
> *"It sacrificed long-term value for short-term benefits."*
> *"It didn't go beyond the low-hanging fruit."*

Part of the trouble is that companies are not in business to cut costs, nor should they be. For the consumer products company, the source of competitive strength lies in getting compelling new products to market fast; for the retailer, it is keeping shelves stocked with customers' favorites; for the industrial goods manufacturer, it is keeping quality high and lead times short. In short, cost-reduction efforts for most companies are not a core competence. Such tactics are one-time events, forced by external circumstances, focused on short-term results. This may be why so few cost-reduction initiatives deliver what's required of them or help truly transform the cost position of the company. (See "Deep Dive #2: Assessing Your Company's Cost-Cutting IQ" for further discussion of this topic.)

But all that said, our takeaway is the following: **Cost-reduction approaches that didn't work before won't work any better now just because the need is greater.**

It is our assertion that the best path to restructuring your costs is by attacking product, process, and organizational complexity. But although the issue of complexity costs is increasingly transparent, many shy away from attacking the issue as a more strategic and effective path to cost reduction. Why does such a large and attainable prize go unclaimed?

1) **No one has quantified the size of the prize—so attacking complexity as a root cause has not been made a priority.** Financial systems and processes are ill equipped to quantify, or even flag, the costs of complexity, which is why many of these costs stay hidden from executive line of sight. But even when leadership recognizes the symptoms, they have difficulty placing a dollar value on what it's worth to address complexity. This is a major hurdle when it comes to deploying real resources and investment to wage the war on complexity costs. Thus, such initiatives often fail to get traction, overshadowed by alternative initiatives that are less profitable but more easily quantified. (The ineffectiveness of GAAP in capturing complexity costs has been widely explored elsewhere[5]; we won't belabor the point here.)

2) **Companies are put off by the scale and nature of the problem itself.** Even for those executives who recognize the issue and the opportunity, it can seem at the outset an intimidating mountain to climb. There are many interactions between products, processes, and organizational structures that extend beyond the normal functional structures in corporations for "getting things done." Cross-functional efforts, by definition, require coordination across functions to work. Given the nature of complexity, it is not surprising that many efforts that start out with ambitious goals are reduced to piecemeal solutions.

3) **Companies need better battle strategies.** Even companies that understand the financial prize on the table, and are looking to take this on, need battle plans that account for the nature of complexity, which can extract meaningful benefits quickly without quagmiring them in endless analyses and frustrating sets of interdependencies. (In Parts II and III, we will explain the nature of unlocking complexity costs and provide specific battle strategies you can use.)

To close these gaps, we are writing this book. We will explain how to size the prize, scope your efforts, and extract the benefits to successfully take cost out of your organization.

The Art of Complexity Warfare

We recently met with the CEO of a Midwest industrial equipment manufacturer. The company had correctly diagnosed complexity as an issue and formed an internal team to reduce product variations by 40%. The team had worked diligently toward this goal and eventually achieved this reduction. But the CEO was puzzled: Despite the efforts and investment in the team, there was no improvement in the bottom line. How could they cut the product offerings like this without seeing a reduction in costs?

Unfortunately, this scenario is not uncommon. For while few companies can stick with the "do nothing" strategy, the "just do something" strategy can be just as ineffective, absent an understanding of what it takes to extract the full benefits of complexity reduction.

To meet the task before us, then, we need a different approach—different, and better, battle strategies that can help companies like this manufacturer better quantify, locate, and purge complexity costs. We need to *think* differently about how we approach the challenge.

There are six key principles that inform the art of complexity warfare:

- **Principle 1:** There is good complexity and bad complexity (reduce the bad and make the good less expensive to deliver)

- **Principle 2:** Complexity is a multi-dimensional issue (and must be viewed as such to be understood in its fullness)
- **Principle 3**: Piecemeal approaches will not move the needle on cost reduction (don't nibble at the edges of the issue)
- **Principle 4**: Unlocking the benefits requires "concurrent actions"
- **Principle 5:** Complexity costs "creep in" incrementally, but you need to remove them in chunks
- **Principle 6:** This need not be a long, academic exercise

Principle 1: There is good and bad complexity

Companies are reacting to new levels of demand and assessing what the future may hold. In a *Wall Street Journal* article from April 2009, executives discussed concerns that "shrunken nest eggs—along with an overhang of home foreclosures, personal bankruptcies and credit card debt—may cause shoppers to tighten the purse strings indefinitely."[6]

Mike McCallister, CEO of Humana, one of the United States' largest publicly traded health benefits providers, said,

> *The real trick there is to separate the good complexity from the bad complexity.*
>
> *If you're going to respond to consumers and try to meet them where they are, it will generate some complexity, but try to stay away from what's not important and what consumers won't pay for.*
>
> *I think we in the industry allow our complexity to be the wrong kind at the wrong place.... We're early in figuring out exactly what complexity we're going to be able to manage and put in front of consumers directly.... We'll have to see how that plays out. I think the complexity that we manage, tolerate, and make good at the consumer level has big potential. Ongoing complexity in the back office from an old model is absolutely non-value-add.*

Customer demand is part of the equation, and companies will have to adjust to new levels of demand. But as Humana CEO McCallister points out, we also need to establish a much deeper understanding of how complexity is impacting our organization and what it is costing us, both from a financial perspective and in terms of productivity.

The fact that some complexity is good means you can't just focus on eliminating SKUs, parts, vendors, dealers, and so on. While this is an important component of controlling costs, it is only half the answer. Reducing complexity costs is not just about *reducing the amount of complexity* in your business. It is also about reducing the cost of delivering complexity—**making complexity less expensive.** This means a two-pronged approach:

1st Prong: Reduce the overall amount of complexity in the business by removing complexity that adds disproportionately large costs to the business

2nd Prong: Reduce the cost impact of each "unit" of complexity on the business by becoming much better at managing and delivering it

Figure 2: A Two-Pronged Assault on Cost

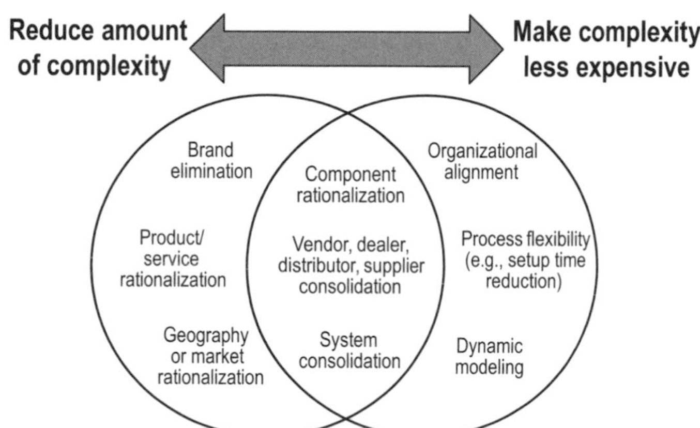

Waging the war on complexity costs requires a two-pronged attack to reduce the amount of complexity in the business while also making complexity less expensive. You achieve the latter by improving how the company manages and delivers complexity. Cost-reduction actions, examples of which are shown in the Venn diagram above, tend to fall across the spectrum between these two approaches.

The mix of the two prongs in the approaches will vary according to your business and to the opportunity. But it is usually a mix of both, rarely one or the other. Why? Because in many if not most business sectors, cutting product complexity is necessary but insufficient to remain competitive. For one thing, customers are demanding more products and services—at a lower cost but with improved service levels. To keep up requires becoming much better at delivering complexity—and better translates to lower cost. And if you can't do it, your competitors will. For another, a lot of slack has crept into processes over time, which imposes its own costs. So even in situations where the customer values the variety and is willing to pay for it, there are often opportunities in the supporting processes.

Principle 2: Complexity is a multi-dimensional issue

Complexity is a systemic problem, one that is dispersed in origin and affects everything inside the system. It is the result of the interactions of many different parties—and to compound the problem, like pollution, the effects are hard to see and track. Therefore, the approach to tackle this also needs to have a systemic—or integrated—perspective.

For example, suppose you make what seems to be a rational choice to add new varieties to a product line or add new options to a service. Consider first just the more **visible costs** of complexity:

- Variable costs increase as more staff is required to handle new products and services, more production time is needed, and inventories rise owing to increased material goods or the IT applications become more complicated to support additional options.
- Increased complexity brings step-change increases in brand management costs and marketing support. New fixed costs are required.
- Product complexity bequeaths what we term process complexity—new administrative processes and production processes needed to provide the increased variety—which in turn engenders increased organizational complexity, as functions flex to cope with new levels of variety and variation.

This all amounts to a leap in costs that can destroy profitability. Further, consider the more **hidden costs** of complexity:

- Production and delivery lines see diminished capacity and increases in waste and yield problems as a result of complexity.
- New functions sprout simply to work around the complexity; expeditors are dispatched to track down orders lost in the noise.
- Worst of all, at some point, complexity creates "a fog." At this point, there is no standard process: Every order is treated as a one-off; scale economies are destroyed; and costs rise further. Consider the industrial giant with 2 million parts in its database. "We have so many parts, all with different numbers, while in fact many are the same," said a VP associated with the company, "but we just don't know which is which. It's easier to create a new part than track down an existing one through the system."

The model we've found most useful for understanding the "complexity of complexity" is to think about the impact in three dimensions:

1) **Product complexity:** the variety of products and services you offer
2) **Process complexity:** the non-value-add activity required to deliver product complexity, including duplication, coordination, rework, and complexity-related work-arounds

3) **Organizational complexity:** the demands placed on your organizational structures (staffing, assets, policies, metrics, etc.) to support the delivery of the complexity to the customer

Understanding these dimensions—and, more importantly, how they interact with each other—is key to developing appropriate battle strategies. For now, suffice it to say that **it's the multi-dimensional nature of complexity that has thwarted many traditional cost-cutting approaches**. Trying to cut product complexity (eliminating product or service options or brands, for example) without *also* tackling the associated process or organizational complexity will have a limited effect.

Principle 3: Piecemeal approaches will not move the needle on cost reduction

In "peacetime," it is not uncommon to see a large and diverse set of cost-reduction programs across an organization. In our experience, most of these nibble at the edges of cost management and do not address some of the core structural issues.

In "wartime," we cannot afford that approach; in fact the need for step-change cost reductions represents an opportunity. As the Whale Curve and the 80/20 principle showed, "Big results require big ambitions," using the words of Greek philosopher Heraclitus. It is as true today as it was in 500 BCE (see sidebar "Cut by half," next page). As the saying goes, if nothing changes… nothing changes! For a company to find and sustain significant improvements in its cost structure, it needs to make some big changes in the way things are done. A cost-reduction strategy that focuses on doing the same things the same way but cheaper is likely to lead to disappointing results.

Consider a lesson from Toyota, as described in *The Toyota Product Development System*:

> *During its global CCC21 initiative, for example, Toyota asked its suppliers to reduce the price charged Toyota by 30% for the next new model. This sounds like an impossible goal, especially given suppliers' tight profit margins. But Toyota never just dumps a demand on suppliers; it makes a request and then works with the supplier to achieve what is needed….*
>
> *As Darrel Sterzinger, general manager of engineering design chassis at Toyota Technical Center, explained:*
>
> *"A true North American supplier cannot imagine 30 percent—it boggles the mind. But when I sit down with them and explain Toyota's thinking, they can understand the purpose of it. It is not the 30 percent we are thinking about. It is a new way of doing business."*

Cut by half

In his book *Cost Half,*[7] author Toshio Suzue describes how he recommends companies push past existing paradigms to uncover opportunities through a series of "cut by half" questions:

- How can we cut the number of parts by half?
- How can we cut the number of production processes by half?
- How can we shrink development lead time by half?

Why half? Because, Suzue asserts, "when cost-cutting activities are based on a goal such as a mere 10% or 20% reduction in costs, people tend to come up with small, incremental cost-cutting ideas and are always conscious of the constraints involved.

Principle 4: Unlocking the benefits requires "concurrent actions"

Given the systemic nature of complexity, unlocking the benefits requires a coordinated combination of actions. To achieve big savings, you need to understand how the three dimensions of complexity (process, product, and organizational) work to trap costs in the business. And then you need to attack complexity with an integrated campaign targeted at a combination of dimensions.

For example, consider the pharmaceutical company that was looking to reduce its factory footprint and distribution network. As it examined the various factors involved, such as geography, channels, portfolio, and volumes, the focus soon became how to best rationalize the footprint *assuming the same or near same portfolio of products*. This is a decision trap: assuming an element is fixed and designing around it. The fact is—to revert to the Whale Curve for a moment—no company aspires to a long "profit-losing" arc in their curve, and no company would fund a production and distribution footprint to support this portion of the product line. For the pharmaceutical company, this is an opportunity to assess how the product line is defining the footprint and rethink where it wants to be.

A global industrial goods company had a different dilemma: it knew its product range was hopelessly bloated. As the executive considered what it would mean to make big cuts in its offerings, the team quickly got nervous at the prospect of many of its factories sitting idle with lower capacity utilization but the same overhead.

Both teams discovered that looking at the factory footprint *and* product portfolio in concert leads to whole new vistas of opportunity, as they would be putting in play the very factors that tend to limit impact. The big savings come from unlocking these interdependencies, which is why we assess complexity in terms of interactions between products, the processes that deliver those products, and the organizational structures (work practices, capabilities, staffing levels, etc.) needed to operate the process.

Principle 5: Complexity costs "creep in" incrementally, but you need to remove them in chunks

Consider a typical product portfolio. Over a number of years, a portfolio has grown bloated with line extensions, new products, and new brands. These additions pile on top of the existing portfolio. You are left with a sprawling portfolio that is the result of hundreds of isolated decisions. The answer is not to trim the bottom 5% of SKUs. That will do little to free up capacity, cost, and focus. Only when you can cut deep enough to cut a brand, close a warehouse, or cease a productivity-draining process will you see substantive cost savings.

The takeaway is that when addressing complexity costs, recognize that there are **pivot points** at which fixed or semi-fixed costs are released. These points represent the staircase of cost targets that can release substantive costs.

Moreover, *the likelihood that you will reach these pivot points by chance is low,* as it often requires a coordinated combination of actions that stretches across process, product, and organizational dimensions. For example, we have seen successful cases where companies have evaluated their asset base and their portfolio simultaneously in a way that helped release "step-change" costs from the organization in a way that was congruent with their strategy. Elsewhere, companies have avoided the common pitfall in SKU reductions of cutting too shallow because of perceived constraints.

Thinking in these terms will change your focus: Traditionally, most companies focus cost efforts on variable costs; however, the biggest cost opportunities often lie in shedding fixed costs. Thus, when you shift from thinking about short-term gains to finding a cost breakpoint that will provide a bigger and longer-lasting shift in your cost basis, you are more likely to look for fixed costs that can be shed, and *the onus on variable costs is less on cost reduction in its own right and more on productivity enhancement that will help you release chunks of cost.*

Principle 6: This need not be a long, academic exercise

Throughout your efforts, we urge you to focus on leveraging 80/20 thinking (see sidebar, next page). Taking out complexity costs does not and should not be a long, academic exercise. Ensure that you are not embarking on a months-long program that is long on analysis but short on insights. It is important to get a more grounded view of the drivers of complexity cost, but a broader view with less detail is more important than deep-diving into any one area. Do enough to develop a battle strategy, and constantly ask yourself, *What do I need to know to move forward on this?* In our experience, it is possible to quickly develop hypotheses as to the drivers of complexity cost, which can then be validated, and this is a much faster approach than an exhaustive, bottom-up approach.

80/20 costing

As an example of what we mean by 80/20 thinking, consider how companies approach the issue of accurate costing. For many companies, getting an accurate view of complexity costs often gets lost between two extremes: launching an all-out activity-based costing effort or doing nothing. We'd recommend a different path: make the 20% of adjustments that provide 80% of the answer. Understand where the big chunks of cost are and how they should be allocated to get you to a more accurate view of costing without being bound to a full activity-based costing (ABC) effort. Also leverage key rules of thumb.

For example, consider how, all else being equal, the ratio of inventory costs between two products is proportional to the square root of the ratio of their demand. This rule of thumb is nearly as easy to apply as the peanut butter approach (where inventory costs are spread evenly across products on a per-unit or percentage-of-cost basis) but provides a significantly better estimate of actual cost by product. (We will discuss the analytics behinds this rule in Chapter 10.)

What's behind this? Consider how in calculating standard costs, most companies spread inventory costs (the cost for the warehouse, for example) evenly across the number of units that pass through the warehouse. Each unit is burdened with an equal share of the pie. But this is just as wrong as allocating inventory costs evenly between product lines, regardless of their volume. In a typical supply chain, lower volume products enjoy fewer inventory turns; hence, each low-volume item spends more time in the warehouse. It makes sense then to burden lower-volume products with a greater portion of inventory costs per unit. But how much more? The rule of thumb tells us how much. Not knowing this, most companies continue to use the straightforward but wrong peanut butter approach and miss the opportunity to get quickly to a better grasp of true costs.

The Opportunity: Big gains, with speed

Complexity cost is the elephant in the room, and no one is quite sure what to do about it. In this book we tell you what you need to know to be able to confront the issue head-on. We do not suggest that complexity can and should be tackled only through huge, transformation-like efforts. But neither do you want to fritter your time, energy, and resources on attacking individual symptoms.

As you'll discover in the following chapters, it is possible to take targeted actions to achieve both financial and performance benefits and create virtuous cycles of improvement (see sidebar "Forging a new path," p. 18). The key is to structure the effort in a way that will allow you to make substantive improvements at a rapid pace while avoiding the trap of diluting your efforts. Behind this is the philosophical acknowledgment that winning the war on complexity costs can be difficult but will be ultimately rewarding, and this is vastly superior to a path that is easy but futile. There are no silver bullets, but there are actions of high leverage.

The shift in the competitive landscape—and the threat and opportunity that implies—is strengthening the resolve of many. Our advice is to use the momentum of the crisis! Strong performers will use a downturn to shed poorly performing assets, renew a sense of urgency and purpose in the business, and think about preparing for growth around the corner. A recent article in *The Economist*, "Swinging the Axe," says, "Many bosses admit that the crisis is giving them a chance to restructure their firms in ways that they should have done before, but found a hard sell when things were going well."

The willingness to follow through on major decisions is a prerequisite for success in the war on complexity costs. All the analysis and insight in the world on how to best drive rapid improvements to a company's cost base are fruitless if the will for action is lacking. Now is the time for action, without delay, for we know that...

Things may come to those who wait, but only the things left by those who hustle.[8]

Chapter 1 Endnotes

[1] Cited in Sievanen, Suomala, and Paranko, *Activity-Based Costing and Product Profitability* (Tampere, Finland: Institute of Industrial Management, Tampere University of Technology, Finland).

[2] John A. Quelch and David Kenny, "Extend Profits, Not Product Lines," *Harvard Business Review*, Sep/Oct (1994).

[3] "Kraft: Driving Out Costs and Assets," Investor presentation, Franz-Josef Vogelsang, Executive Vice President, Global Supply Chain, July 19, 2004.

[4] McKinsey & Company.

[5] Michael L, George, Stephen A. Wilson, *Conquering Complexity in Your Business* (New York: McGraw-Hill, 2004).

[6] "Food Firms Cook Up Ways to Combat Rare Sales Slump," *The Wall Street Journal*, April 22 (2009).

[7] Toshio Suzue, *Cost Half: The Method for Radical Cost Reduction* (New York: Productivity Press, 2002).

[8] Abraham Lincoln.

Forging a new path

We have developed a new path for waging war on complexity costs based on the principles outlined here. Each of these pieces will be covered in much more detail in later chapters, and the structure of this book reflects the path you will need to forge. Later chapters of this book will spell out detailed analyses and decisions your management team will need to make to achieve the type of step-change complexity savings we've described in this chapter. At a broad-brush level, the path forward is...

1. **Make the case, and quantify the benefits.** We will show you how to estimate the size of the prize for your company based on the specifics of your business. For many companies, this has been a "holy grail" of sorts: the ability to quantify the cost of complexity. This knowledge enables you to launch your efforts and frame the ambition of the effort. Chapters 4 and 5 will describe the method you can use to accomplish this goal.
2. **Identify the key levers for big gains.** The biggest drivers of complexity cost lie in the interaction between different types of complexity (e.g., how added service options affect the processes used to deliver the service). Part II will identify where some of the biggest costs lie, and will enable you to start identifying your key areas of opportunity.
3. **Extract the big costs quickly.** The focus of this book is to help you find big opportunities and to do so quickly. In Part III we will share some specific battle strategies to incorporate into your campaign.
4. **Keep the bad costs out.** Complexity is insidious because it creeps in under the radar of most business metrics and systems. To avoid the reemergence of complexity costs into your business, you need leverage methods for preventing complexity creep in the first place. We'll cover those strategies in Part IV.

DEEP DIVE #1

What Winning Looks Like

Cash Flows, Profits, and Performance

Given its capacity for reshaping your cost structure, freeing up cash flows, and boosting productivity, Waging War on Complexity Costs is worth elevating to the top of your management agenda. We'll go into detail later in the book, but we estimate that attacking complexity correctly results in cost reductions of 15% to 30% in significant portions of a business.[9] (If companies were able to eliminate all non-value-add complexity costs, this percentage would be even higher. The approach we advocate, however, gets companies to quickly take a meaningful chunk out of a large pie rather than spend months and months trying to exhaustively purge all non-value-add costs, an effort that typically fails anyway.)

You've already seen one example of what winning the war looks like in the story of how Kraft was able to announce a pre-tax cost benefit of $400 million per year in its Toblerone business alone as a result of its decomplexity initiative, which was a mixture of SKU reduction, product harmonization, and supply chain simplification.

So where, you might ask, do these gains come from? When all is said and done, can you expect something similar from your efforts? More specifically, where and how will you see benefits in your financial statements and key performance metrics? To help answer this questions, following is a case study that is an amalgamation of recent examples that we'll use to explore a recognizable and probably familiar situation.

The CEO of Complexity Products, Inc., is under fire to cut costs, quickly. Cash flows are tight, sales are down in the last quarter. Three of the plants are deemed "focused factories" and have low utilization. The other two are mixed-mode plants and are maxed out to the extent that they have to outsource some production to experienced contract manufacturers. The product portfolio is looking bloated, and customer satisfaction is at an all-time low because of long lead times and poor on-time delivery. Worse, the recent downturn has exposed the company's high-cost structure as a competitive liability: competitors have reduced their prices to levels that the company cannot match in a bid to win share in a generally flat market. The executive team is facing a perfect storm.

It caused many to wonder, *How did we get here?* In fact, looking back, it was possible to see how costs had crept in.

From a top-line perspective, the last several years had been tremendous for Complexity Products, Inc. Revenues had grown approximately 25% from three years ago on a motivated sales team and a volley of new products launched with fanfare. But the pursuit of growth had brought with it growing complexity—in the product portfolio, in the organizational structures, and in the processes—that had gradually revealed itself in the financial statements as increasing costs. In fact, as the CEO studied the financials, comparing the current situation to one right before the growth initiatives, it was not a pretty picture (see Table B).

Table B: Income Statement (in $000s)

	3 Years Ago	Current Situation
Total revenue	5,350,000	6,700,000
Cost of goods	2,300,000	3,000,000
Gross profit	3,050,000	3,700,000
Operating expenses		
R&D	4,600	7,100
SGA	2,500,000	3,250,000
Depreciation	100,000	200,000
Operating income	445,400	242,900
Less interest expense	147,000	226,000
Less taxes	107,000	6,100
Net income	191,400	10,800

Table B, cont.: Common Size Comparison (% of revenue)

	3 Years Ago	Current Situation
Total revenue	100.0%	100.0%
Cost of goods	43.0%	44.8%
Gross profit	57.0%	55.2%
Operating expenses		
R&D	0.1%	0.1%
SGA	46.7%	48.5%
Depreciation	1.9%	3.0%
Operating income	8.3%	3.6%
Less interest expense	2.7%	3.4%
Less taxes	2.0%	0.1%
Net income	3.6%	0.2%

The good news was that Complexity Products, Inc.'s larger investments in R&D five years ago were finally paying off: revenues were up 25%. But that growth came at a price. While the CEO expected some increase in costs, he did not expect to see them increase as a percentage of revenue, affecting margins at every level of the income statement. Cost of goods sold (COGS) increased almost 2 percentage points, reducing gross margins by the same amount. The CEO quickly thought of two reasons for this: (1) efficiencies in the plants were declining because of increased changeover times, and (2) he recently had to outsource some volume to contract manufacturers, costing him some margin transfer. The last issue really irked the CEO because the company had to outsource its cash cow product while some of its other specialized plants were underutilized.

Selling, marketing, and general and administrative expenses were also up. Selling expenses as a percentage of revenue rose as the mix changed and reps responded to incentives to sell new (lower-margin) products to new accounts. Marketing expenses exploded over the past few years in line with the product portfolio expansion. Fixed general and administrative (G&A) expenses climbed on new operations launched in Asia and Europe to include regional procurement and finance organizations.

The balance sheet indicated a similar downhill trend. Most noticeable was how inventories and accounts receivable were now unacceptably high, seemingly a losing situation at every plant. Those plants that were underutilized had too much finished goods inventory sitting on shelves, to the extent that the CEO had had to invest in a small satellite warehouse close to one of the facilities, affecting fixed assets. Raw materials were the issue at the plants suffering most from long lead times and late deliveries. The two plants in this situation were suffering from the classic bullwhip effect with raw materials buyers "hedging" against stock-outs by buying raw materials in larger quantities. The result: raw materials piling up in the aisles of the factories.

Additionally, trailers full of raw materials were positioned outside the receiving dock, essentially serving as temporary warehouses. Receivables were starting to see a hit because of customers holding back payments in protest to late orders and long lead times. In total, most of the key levers of the balance sheet were going opposite to what the CEO desired—inventories higher, receivables growing, and even increases in property, plant, and equipment. The CEO kept his eye on two key financial metrics in his business:

1) Inventory turns, a leading indicator of the size of costs

2) Return on invested capital (ROIC), an overall measure of the value his business was creating

Given the current situation, he was not surprised by the results against both financial metrics. Inventory turns went from an average 9.2 three years ago to a worse 7.5 today. And the company's ROIC was down by more than half (from over 14% to 6%), not even covering its cost of capital. Not surprisingly, the share price had decreased, even with the dramatic growth in revenue, especially for this industry.

Table C: Financial Metrics

	3 Years Ago	Current Situation
Inventory turnover	9.2	7.5
Invested capital	$ 1,978,130	$ 2,509,449
NOPLAT	$ 285,689	$ 155,226
ROIC	14.4%	6.2%

Operationally, what disturbed the CEO more than anything was how late deliveries were affecting the company's core customers, those who consistently ordered the "bread and butter" products in large volumes. As a result, the people growing most dissatisfied with the company's performance were its most profitable customers. This trend was not exactly new to the CEO; in the past 18 months he had launched half a dozen initiatives focused on addressing key operational issues and an expense reduction program. But they had barely made a dent. It was time for more robust action.

Resolution

The CEO decided that Complexity Products, Inc., needed to "change the way we do business and emerge more competitive for the future." He set a cost-reduction target of $1 billion, knowing that even then he was "leaving money on the table." But he wanted to move at lightning speed: take out big costs fast to drive up profit margins. To ensure that this happened, he gave day-to-day responsibility for managing the work to the COO. It was designed as a three-phase effort:

- Phase 1 was a rapid diagnostic to validate key cost levers
- Phase 2 was a concurrent attack on asset complexity and product complexity
- Phase 3 was focused on attacking process complexity through process stratification, process improvement initiatives in key areas, and the launch of process governance

From the financial situation described above, it was no surprise that the primary cost levers were COGS (primarily labor), SG&A (sales, general, and administrative expenses), and inventory. To understand what exactly was driving those costs, the team made strong links between a host of products and their impact on key processes and assets, specifically long lead times and low utilization. Primarily responsible were low-volume products ordered with erratic frequency and in highly variable quantities. Other drivers included some more customized products as well as legacy products that had been on the chopping block for as long as anyone could remember.

After making the link between products and operational effects on assets and processes, the team discovered deeper connections surrounding trends around specific regions and customers. Surprisingly, one entire region and a handful of customers were entirely unprofitable when factoring in the complexity-related cost impact on other products, customers, and regions.

Given the holistic picture that the team constructed, it became much easier for the CEO and senior leadership to make broad-based changes, starting with eliminating unprofitable products and then reducing the overall asset footprint of the company's operations. Taking those actions put the company in a position to optimize plant loading for the remaining products and plants, getting back to competitive lead times and overall cost structure. The following are some highlights of the effort:

- The company decided to no longer serve one entire region and its associated customers.
- The portfolio was thinned by 45%. Additionally, three brands were identified for sale.
- As a result of the reduction in products, the remaining product volume would be manufactured from a base of four factories instead of five. There was also the closure of one fully operational warehouse and one overflow satellite warehouse.
- The remaining volume was reallocated to the remaining plants, optimizing capacity, distribution costs, and inventory levels.

The changes improved the income statement, inventory, and ROIC (see Table D, next page, for the results). The margins were much healthier across the board: gross margins up 5 percentage points, SG&A down by almost $750 million, increasing operating margins by 13 percentage points. The impact of reduced inventory levels (turns increase to 12) and PPE (property, plant, and equipment) compounded the positive effects of the income statement, raising ROIC to 36%, levels not seen since almost 15 years ago, and marking Complexity Products as a clear leader in the industry.

Revenues picked up with strength with the improvements in service levels. On-time deliveries improved to 98%. The highest in the industry historically hovered around 90%; this level of performance was a competitive advantage (two quarters on, revenue growth had picked up to around $6.5 billion once the majority of the improvements had been implemented).

Table D: Income Statement (*in 000s*)

	3 Years Ago	Before Changes	After Changes
Total revenue	5,350,000	6,700,000	6,000,000
Cost of goods	2,300,000	3,000,000	2,400,000
Gross profit	3,050,000	3,700,000	3,600,000
Operating expenses			
R&D	4,600	7,100	4,500
SGA	2,500,000	3,250,000	2,500,000
Depreciation	100,000	200,000	90,000
Operating income	445,400	242,900	1,005,500
Less interest expense	147,000	226,000	130,000
Less taxes	107,000	6,100	315,180
Net income	191,400	10,800	560,320

Table D, cont.: Common Size Comparison (*% of revenue*)

	3 Years Ago	Before Changes	After Changes
Total revenue	100.0%	100.0%	100.0%
Cost of goods	43.0%	44.8%	40.0%
Gross profit	57.0%	55.2%	60.0%
Operating expenses			
R&D	0.1%	0.1%	0.1%
SGA	46.7%	48.5%	41.7%
Depreciation	1.9%	3.0%	1.5%
Operating income	8.3%	3.6%	16.8%
Less interest expense	2.7%	3.4%	2.2%
Less taxes	2.0%	0.1%	5.3%
Net income	3.6%	0.2%	9.3%

The impact of the effort surprised even the CEO; it not only reshaped the company's cost structure but also galvanized his team and prepared the company for taking share from competitors.

To grow revenues, cut complexity

The fear of impacting revenues is one of the biggest reasons that companies don't reduce complexity. But in fact, in our experience, when you cut complexity you will see your revenues grow. The reason: complexity consumes precious resources and in return delivers below-average results—marginal SKUs, me-too products, and the waste of process and organizational complexity.

Complexity also can impact the key customer metrics that define performance in the customers' eyes. Complex portfolios can be hard for customers to deal with and can lead to late orders, long lead times, and quality issues. To put it another way, by trying to hang on to all your complexity, you are likely trading off focus, cost-effectiveness, and performance in a bid for breadth. How would customers evaluate that balance?

When Motorola Computer Group (MCG) considered massively reducing its portfolio as part of a turnaround, the objections did not emanate from customers but from employees worried about customers. In fact the customers were fine with the changes, as it enabled MCG to improve quality and ratchet up on-time delivery from 70% to 78%.[10] The result: Customer satisfaction leaped from 27% to 55% in just a year. And revenues increased by 25% despite reducing the product portfolio by 40% over the same time period.

Deep Dive #1 Endnotes

9 WilsonPerumal estimate. "Study of 20 Global Companies Estimated 25% to 35% of Costs to Be Complexity Driven"; Pieter Klaas Jagersma, "Hidden Cost of Doing Business,"*Business Strategy Series* Vol. 9, No. 5, pp. 238-242. Pieter Klaas Jagersma is a professor of international business at Nyenrode University, Breukelen, The Netherlands.

10 Michael L. George, James Works, Kimberly Watson-Hemphill. *Fast Innovation* (New York: McGraw Hill, 2005).

CHAPTER 2

The Nature of Complexity

(And What It Means for Your Business)

The greatest challenge to any thinker is stating the problem in a way that will allow a solution.

— *Bertrand Russell*

The secret to successfully attacking complexity costs, to paraphrase Bertrand Russell, is framing the problem in a way that will permit you to succeed. To do this requires an understanding of the nature of complexity itself—not to engender an academic discussion but to help you correctly scope and select your targets and to know what will and will not work in your efforts to take out cost. In this chapter, we will explore the true nature of complexity, explain why many past solutions have failed to live up to expectations, and show why the solutions we propose are more effective. We'll start by discussing the three distinct types of complexity, then look at the interactions of these types (which is often where the hidden costs reside) and the symptoms you may see in your business, and finally describe the implications for attacking complexity and taking out its costs.

The Three Types of Complexity

When businesses talk about "reducing complexity," they usually mean that they're going to cut product variety or eliminate service options. The focus of the action is on the **products** or services of the business. But complexity also creeps into the **processes** used to design, create, and support those offerings and in the **organizations** (people, structures, assets) needed to execute those processes. Let's first define these types of complexity, starting with product complexity.

1. Product (and Service) Complexity

Product complexity describes the variety of and within the products or services you offer your customers, be it banking services or frozen pizzas, hydraulic pumps or CAT scans.

Not enough variety will leave a company struggling to compete, but too much variety will saddle a company with cost, impairing its ability to deliver and in some cases frustrating its customers with *too much* choice. All variety adds costs to a business, but not all of it is sufficiently valued by customers. "Differentiation that does not drive customer preference is a liability," said Geoffrey Moore, author of *Crossing the Chasm*. Put another way, variety in your products that offers customers something they are willing to pay for is good complexity; variety that they won't pay for—or won't pay enough for—is bad complexity.

But while "good" and "bad" complexity are easy to define in theory, in practice it has been difficult for companies to identify just *how much* variety is too much. Given that tendency, it is perhaps no surprise that the dominant anxiety is fear of having too little, which is fertile ground for complexity to grow unabated (whether in a quest to grow revenue or as the byproduct of acquisitions). But the costs of too much variety can no longer be ignored.

The Impact of Product Complexity

Few companies know how much "bad" product complexity is costing them until they eliminate it. Jostens, whose products include caps and gowns for graduation ceremonies, realized the need for SKU rationalization when they began to see issues in inventory costs, quality levels, and production flexibility resulting from what was then more than 85,000 SKUs.[11] As Jostens discovered, SKU complexity increases manufacturing and supply chain costs and reduces forecasting accuracy, which in turn leads to excessive inventories and transportation costs.

Through techniques that reduced the number of product options, Jostens kept customers happy while cutting SKUs by 85% (down to 12,000). Inventories were cut in half, from $40 to $20 million. Moreover, the reduction in complexity enabled Jostens to rationalize fixed costs by outsourcing the manufacturing of 98% of its gowns, gaining it 10 points on gross margin.

In short, bad product complexity (meaning anything your customers do not value enough to provide an adequate return) represents an obvious target that companies can and should go after.

For some companies, the symptoms of product complexity are tangible to the point where they can't help but trip over them. If your warehouse resembles the cavernous vault of treasures at the end of the movie *Raiders of the Lost Ark*, you know you have bad product complexity.

For example, Porsche CEO Wendelin Wiedeking has been an outspoken advocate on the need to battle complexity: "We have to eliminate as much as possible."[12] When he was confronted by mountains of inventory, he grabbed a circular saw, walked down the parts aisle and sawed off the metal shelving![13] (Think the staff got the message?)[14]

Service companies and service operations in general are not confronted by visible product complexity in quite the same way: there's no warehouse to walk through nor metal shelving to saw through. As a result, complexity is often more widespread in service industries. Worse, because the effects of complexity are invisible, many transactional operations give the illusion that their complexity is free. Of course, it is not; it surfaces in reduced service levels, lower productivity, and higher non-value-add costs. This book will enable you to focus first on quantifying some of those hidden costs, shining a bright light on the problem and the magnitude of the opportunity whether the issue is in physical products or services.

The internal and external components of product complexity

The term "complexity" is often associated with the range and variety of offerings (the products and services) that a company offers to customers. This is "external product complexity"—so-called because it is the complexity presented to the customer. (Customers may feel the impacts of other forms of complexity, but it's external product complexity they see and typically the only type they value.)

But follow the pipeline backward and you can see that *external* product complexity often generates *internal* product complexity—the number of parts, specifications, instructions, options, inputs, etc., used to deliver external product complexity to the customer.

Clearly, greater internal complexity can add to product/service cost and make delivering external complexity more expensive. Our goal in this book is to help you identify the external product complexity that is "good"—meaning it generates sufficient return—and help you think about ways to minimize the internal complexity needed to deliver what customers want.

2. Process Complexity

Process complexity is the number of processes, process steps, handoffs, etc. involved in executing and delivering its products. Bad process complexity looks like duplication, rework, and complexity-related work-arounds.

A decade ago, check processing in a bank was a relatively simple, linear process. The cashed check went through an assembly-line process: from proofing and encoding to balancing to sorting and reconciliation. This enabled scale economies and low unit costs. Since then, however, there has been an explosion in channel and product variety, leading to a far more convoluted process. No longer just the domain of the traditional checking account, checks are now attached to money market accounts, credit cards, and brokerage accounts. They can be deposited at ATMs, by merchants, and electronically. The increase in options has also led to an increase in fraud, requiring new process steps as a defense.

The proliferation of channels, options, inputs, and outputs means that the simple process of a decade ago is now a complex web. The coordination costs, the duplications costs, waste from processes unable to cope with the new complexity—these costs are the result of myriad interactions, visible at a macro level but difficult to pinpoint at a line-item level.

The demands of variety on a firm's processes have stretched them to the breaking point: "Heroic activities" required to support an increasing variety of products and channels have become the new standard operating procedures. The scale benefits have been erased, and in some cases outweighed, by complexity costs.

Global expansion, process fragmentation, outsourcing, product proliferation, and migration from product-centric environments to service-centric environments all compound the overall levels of process complexity.

Is process complexity just process waste?

Followers of Lean may be thinking that our definition of process complexity sounds like what they learned as "process waste" or "process non-value-add." Both terms refer to work that you want to remove from your organization because it is not valued by customers.

While at a technical-level complexity costs are not necessarily synonymous with non-value-add (NVA) costs, complexity is what drives NVA costs to be very large. This is why we can, at a practical level, treat complexity costs and NVA costs as equivalent.

If your goal is to eliminate what are likely very large complexity-related costs, it is better to assume all the waste in your processes is the result of complexity, as opposed to getting into an academic debate about what is NVA cost versus complexity cost. (We will discuss this in more detail in Chapter 4.)

The Impact of Process Complexity

Process complexity can consume a disproportionate amount of time and costs, otherwise deployed to customer-facing activities. And it has increased at a geometric rate to the point that process complexity often constitutes greater than 50% of all activities.[15]

Unfortunately, though the cost of process complexity is substantial, it is *disaggregated* across an organization, meaning it often lies hidden and outside the range of normal cost-reduction initiatives. You won't recognize the cost of excess process complexity in traditional accounting figures.

However, there are ways to identify process complexity, which we'll get to in a later chapter. The good news is that when you learn how to target and remove process complexity, the effects can be felt almost immediately on cash flows. (It's usually possible to change a process almost overnight, whereas changes to product or service lines or operational structures take time.) And, therefore, tackling process complexity and its linkages to offering and organizational impacts will take center stage in our recommendations for making rapid progress in the war on complexity costs.

3. Organizational Complexity

Organizational complexity is the number of facilities, assets, functional entities, organizational units, systems, etc., involved in executing the processes of a company. If bad process complexity is the disarray in how your product or service is conveyed to the customer, bad organizational complexity is the disarray in the elements of the firm that support that conveyance. Not surprisingly, organizational complexity has grown at the same pace as process complexity.

Think about how your own company's product and service lines have changed in the past decade. Think about all the extra steps, work-arounds, and rework loops that comprise your processes today. Now think about everything you've had to put in place—more people, more IT, more organizational structures and functional supports, more rules, more metrics—all to support the product and process complexity.

But managing growth while keeping organizational complexity at bay is critical given the increase in organizational collaboration via network orchestration (see Chapter 3, "The Rise and Rise of Process and Organizational Complexity"). Michael Dell, CEO of Dell, described his company's ability to orchestrate a network as

> *...a key part of why rivals have had great difficulty competing with Dell.... The way the information from the customer flows all the way through manufacturing to our customers... the kind of coordination of information that used to be possible only in vertically integrated companies.*

The Impact of Organizational Complexity

Organizational complexity results in a number of key issues:

- **Trapped costs and stranded assets:** functions and organizations that evolve organically end up with elements misaligned with the key core processes supporting the business's strategy and generate and effectively trap chunks of non-value-add cost inside the organization, for example, a sales organization supporting a product line that is now largely commoditized

- **Poor performance:** structure impedes performance as organizational complexity creates an "inward focus" as opposed to an outward, customer focus

- **Lack of information flow:** myriad functions, systems, and fiefdoms create lack of information flow, preventing top performance and feedback loops for performance improvements
- **Lack of accountability:** with organizational complexity, we often find a lack of "process ownership" or general accountability

A Three-Dimensional View of Complexity

We have introduced each type of complexity individually—for simplicity. The fact is, though, that the three types of complexity are interwoven and interdependent. As introduced in Chapter 1, your ability to identify and remove complexity costs will be shaped in large part by your understanding of how these dimensions interact in your business.

For example, as anyone who has ever attempted to reduce complexity costs will know, *the issues lie at the intersection of these dimensions;* adding an SKU has the impact of not only directly adding costs, such as inventory costs associated with the new item, but also indirectly adding cost to each of the products already delivered through the same value stream. This happens because the additional product impacts the process that delivers it, which in turn impacts the other products the process delivers. When the retailer started carrying flat-screen TVs (a low-volume item), it did not anticipate the additional costs that would be accrued to cans of baked beans (a high-volume item) because of the impact on the supply chain. (More on this in Part II.)

The key point is that **attacking a single dimension** (for example, product complexity) **is meaningless unless you are attacking it in the context of a second dimension** (for example, the process complexity caused by the SKU proliferation).

The Complexity Cube

In reality, each type of complexity impacts the others. From a practical standpoint, therefore, it makes more sense to think of product, process, and organizational complexity as dimensions of the Complexity Cube (see Figure 3). Complexity may reside on the axis of the cube, but its costs reside on the faces of and within the cube (see Figure 4).

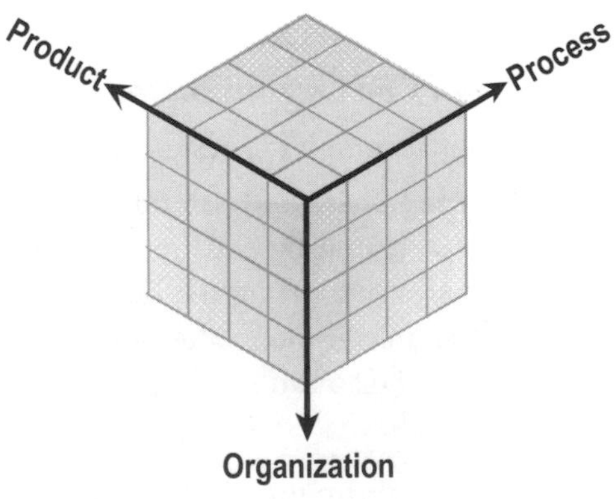

Figure 3: Complexity Cube

The cube illustrates the geometric nature of complexity costs: how your products interact with your processes or your organization, for example, is what drives complexity costs. Conversely, trying to attack product complexity without understanding how it interacts with the organization and processes is ineffective.

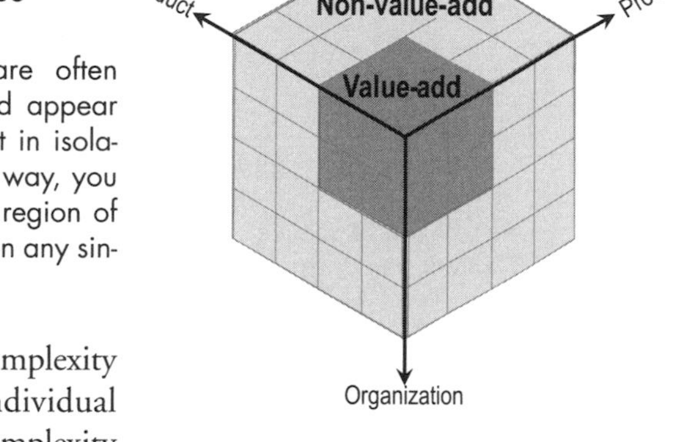

Figure 4: Costs on the Complexity Cube

Non-value-add costs are often much larger than would appear by examining one facet in isolation. Looked at another way, you can't eliminate the vast region of NVA costs by focusing on any single dimension alone.

Typical efforts to attack complexity usually focus on an individual dimension. But because complexity costs are multiplicative between the dimensions, looking at only a single dimension of complexity underestimates complexity costs.

Those multi-dimensional impacts explain why you can't just attack any single dimension of complexity if you want to have big (and lasting) impact. For example, an equipment manufacturer that made a move to eliminate a lot of offering complexity (slashing variety in the products) could not reap the full benefits. Why? Because everything put in place to support that product complexity—the additional warehouse space, the extra processes, the workarounds, the staff—was left in place. The effort was centered on reducing product complexity, but because they had failed to see how some of the costs were rooted in interactions with the company's processes and organizational structure, the costs remained.

The Geometric Nature of Complexity Costs

As illustrated with the Complexity Cube, the most defining characteristic of complexity costs, and the most important for you to grasp as you wage the war, is that *complexity costs grow geometrically with complexity.* Complexity costs do not just rise *in proportion* to the amount of complexity in the business, whether product, process, or organizational complexity; they rise *exponentially* with greater levels of complexity. The effects are geometric, not linear (see Figure 5).

Figure 5: Complexity Costs Rise Exponentially

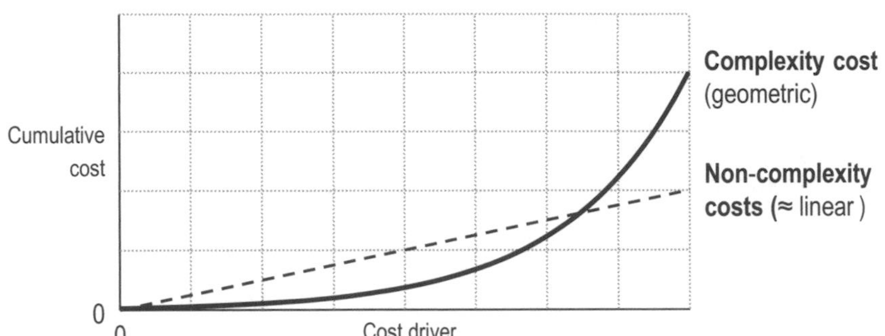

The geometric nature of complexity cost growth separates it from other forms of cost. For complexity costs (and non-complexity costs), the incremental cost is simply the slope of the line. For non-complexity costs, the slope is roughly the same along the entire line, so the incremental cost is relatively independent of the place along the line. This is not so for complexity costs, where the incremental cost depends on the place along the line or the total amount of complexity that exists.

Geometric growth is what sets complexity costs apart from other costs (which usually grow proportionally to their driver of cost or slightly less than proportional if scale benefits exist) and is why traditional approaches are ill equipped for attacking complexity costs. With linear costs, the cost of an incremental item doesn't depend on the total amount of items or costs before it. Therefore, costs can easily be assigned to a specific item. But with geometric costs, the cost of an incremental item depends on the total amount of items—the total complexity—before it. This exponential effect not only explains why complexity costs

Complexity versus complexity costs

It is important to be clear on the distinction between what we mean by complexity and what we mean by complexity costs. Complexity is simply the number of different things, whether product components, process steps, or organizational units. As such, complexity can be either good or bad. But while all complexity adds costs (for each item itself and from the interactions between items), not all the costs of that complexity are complexity costs. For example, while product complexity refers to the overall number of products, not all product costs are complexity costs.

Rather, complexity costs are the costs to deliver items not valued by customers (e.g., unwanted features) as well as the "interaction" costs that exist between items. Complexity costs, therefore, are all non-value-add and are driven by the overall number of items—the overall level of complexity. So, while complexity is simply the number of things, complexity costs are the non-value-add costs associated with having a number of things.

can grow to be so large but also alludes to how to best go after it—with a strategy that accounts for geometric effects by seeking out the pivot points that release substantial costs.

It is this characteristic of complexity costs—its geometric growth—that explains the shape of the Whale Curve. As more complexity is added, costs grow geometrically to the point that they overcome the value offered by additional complexity. (See Figure 6.)

Figure 6: The Impact of Complexity Costs on the Shape of the Whale Curve

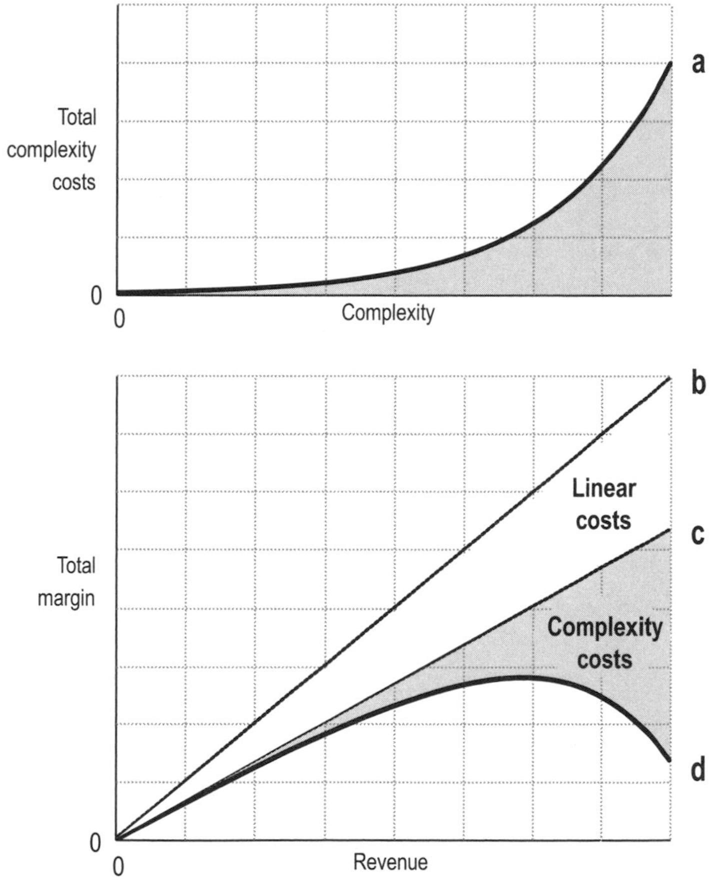

Complexity costs grow geometrically with increasing complexity, as shown in **curve a** in the upper chart. If there were no costs at all, then margin would grow linearly with revenue, as shown in **line b** in the lower chart. Subtracting linear costs, such as raw materials, direct conversion costs, etc., from line b results in **line c** (a hypothetical margin line if no complexity costs were to exist). Subtracting complexity costs, which grow geometrically, from line c results in **line d**, known commonly as the Whale Curve, which is what companies actually experience.

How complexity costs compound

As you can tell, complexity costs compound on multiple levels and over time:

- **Along any single dimension:** As product lines expand, the portion of costs due to interactions between products grows geometrically. And this doesn't just apply to the products. "Complexity… is a 'cube' function," said Lee Coulter, former senior vice president of Kraft's Global Shared Services Group. "If I have 10 applications, I may be able to manage them all. If I have 100 applications, managing them is not simply 10 times the complexity—it's more like 30 times the complexity."[16]
- **Between dimensions:** The overall level of complexity costs isn't simply the sum of the costs along the individual dimensions but rather the product of those costs, as is clearly evident in the Complexity Cube. Hence, non-value-add costs are often much larger than would appear by examining any single dimension in isolation, which is one reason the complexity growth can go unnoticed.
- **Over time:** The compounding nature of complexity, at all levels, means that complexity costs are prone to geometric growth over time. Don't miss the importance here. This means that complexity costs can become significant very fast, with important implications for how they must be attacked and defended against. James Martin, in his book *The Meaning of the 21st Century*, explains, "Geometric growth is the mathematical phenomenon that causes many aspects of our world to become catastrophes with astonishing suddenness." This tendency is characteristic of complex systems.

Implications for Waging the War

To review, we have shown that

1) Complexity exists along multiple dimensions (product, process, and organization)

2) Complexity costs result from the interactions between these dimensions

3) Complexity costs grow geometrically

These ideas are fundamental to complexity and bear significant impact on how you attack complexity and take out its costs. They are, therefore, central to framing the effort in a way that will allow success.

Given how we frame complexity—to paraphrase Einstein, as simple as possible but no simpler—let's discuss the principles for attacking complexity. In practice, systemic solutions benefit from an approach that can be described like this:

Attain a broad understanding, then take focused actions.[17]

Why this approach? Systemic issues, by definition, affect the whole of a system. The starting point, therefore, is to ground any efforts in an integrated view of the business. This does not and should not translate to an exhaustive diagnosis of each part of the operation but rather an understanding of how the different pieces interact. At this stage, completeness is more important than precision. The key is to identify the linkages and trade-offs, often hidden, that connect the different parts of the business.

In the spirit of quickly taking ground, it is important to go after the right chunks. This requires focus but yields enormous dividends. Just as complexity grows geometrically, the converse is also true: Attack the right levers and the benefits are disproportionate to the effort.

In light of this, how do you make rapid progress against complexity in your business? We'll provide details in later chapters, but here is a quick overview.

1) **Understand that you cannot attack just a single dimension of complexity.** While complexity can be measured along a single dimension—the number of products, for example—*complexity costs do not reside along individual dimensions*. From a cost perspective, product complexity, for example, is meaningful only with respect to the associated organizational and process-related complexity it engenders. Efforts targeted at a single dimension recognize neither the nature of complexity nor the source of its costs. Such efforts—for example, SKU rationalization efforts that don't recognize the interactions between products and the processes that deliver them—will deliver inferior results because they leave the sources of cost untouched.

2) **That said, recognize you don't need to attack the whole cube at once.** Just as attacking a single dimension will fall short, attacking the issue as a whole (in our language, trying to attack all sides of the cube at the same time) can be daunting in scope and impractical in action. Many efforts are stymied by trying to attack the whole problem at once. Fortunately, there is a middle path. Progress is best made in terms of both speed and impact by concentrating efforts on attacking one of the three faces of the Complexity Cube (where two dimensions interact: product-process, process-organization, or product-organization).

3) **Pick the right face of the Complexity Cube to start.** Each face represents a key area of interactions—for example, your company may be struggling with common issues that relate to *process-product interactions*, such as SKU proliferation or process performance issues. Or the complexity issues may center on *process-organization interactions*, such as functional silos. Or you may have a lot of cost trapped in *product-organization interactions,* such as a bloated asset footprint and network. (We will describe each set of interactions in Part II and give specific strategies related to the faces in Part III.) But the point is it is likely that complexity is manifesting on one face more than the others—and that is

where the biggest cost-reduction opportunities probably lie, representing a good starting point for attacking complexity and removing its costs. Picking the right face will streamline efforts to gain benefits quickly. Picking the wrong face may make attacking complexity a long slog with little reward.

4) **Shift between the faces as you wage the war.** What does the systemic nature of complexity mean for your choice of tactics *once the battle has begun*? The answer is that while it is better to identify a single face to start with (or key set of interactions that are currently the biggest drivers of complexity cost), once you begin, you will likely discover new insights and information that will change the battle plan. For example, a pharmaceutical company started their efforts on the **Organization/Product** face (misalignment between plants, capacity, and products), but as the work moved forward, it became clear that a number of contributing issues were rooted on the **Process/Organization** face; specifically, organizational silos were affecting the plant loading process. To fix the problem required an understanding of their **Product/Process** interactions: how could they best optimize their capacity given the complexity of the offering and performance levels of their processes? It is this combination of very deliberate prioritization, focus, *and* flexibility that will help you get to releasing big costs quickly.

In summary, while it is common to discuss complexity in terms of product complexity, process complexity, or organizational complexity, that is not where complexity costs manifest in a real-life situation. Consider the situations in your own company.

Complexity Costs' Impact on Profitability in a Downturn

By understanding how complexity costs define the shape of the Whale Curve and how the Whale Curve shifts, we can also gain greater insight into how revenue contraction in the current downturn is affecting the profitability of many firms, especially those that are holding on to their product, process, or organizational complexity.

Keeping complexity in the face of revenue contraction concentrates the cost of that complexity over less revenue (see top chart in Figure 7, next page), making complexity "more expensive" and magnifying its impact on the Whale Curve (see bottom chart). The result is that the Whale Curve doesn't simply scale down proportionally with revenue loss but rather moves decidedly downward, with devastating impact on profitability (an unfortunate reality that General Motors, with its large number of brands, models, dealerships, etc., experienced over years of revenue contraction in its North American operations).

A common reaction is to launch cost-cutting efforts that relieve some pressure but don't address the fundamental structure of the issue.

Figure 7: The Impact of Revenue Contraction on Profit (with same level of complexity)

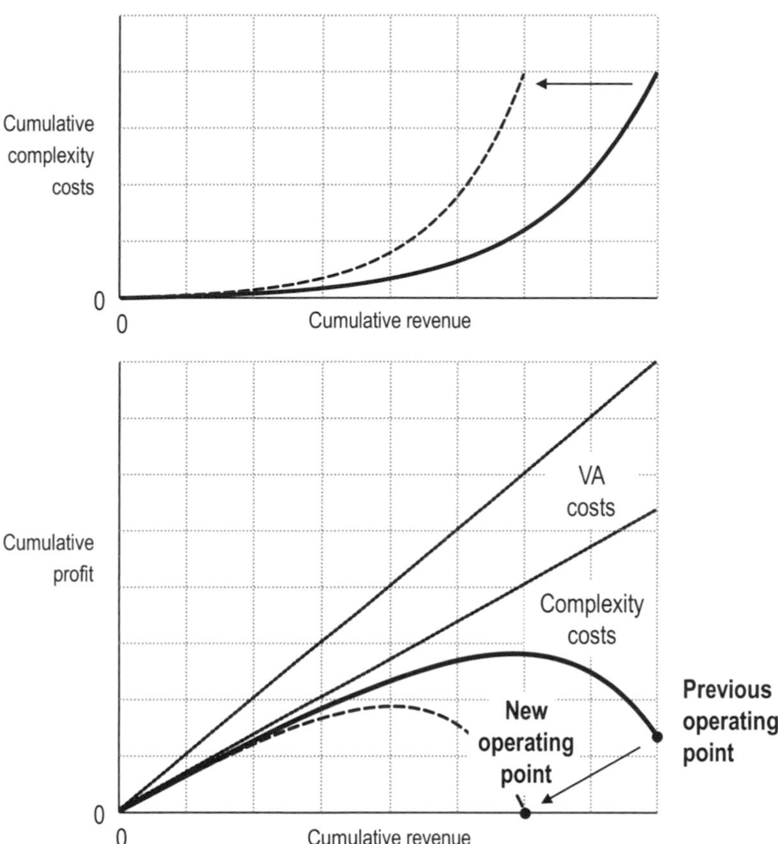

Contraction without releasing complexity concentrates complexity costs within less revenue. In this illustration, because of complexity costs a 25% contraction in revenue completely eliminates all profit (even with a corresponding 25% reduction in the value-add linear costs). The larger the portion of NVA costs to begin with, the more extreme is this effect.

Preview: Taking out complexity costs

Understanding the nature of complexity doesn't just affect where you attack complexity but also how best to go after removing its costs.

A company's Whale Curve typically shows significant cost reduction and profit improvement opportunity. But this invariably underestimates the potential cost savings and overestimates the potential impact on revenue.

The most effective way to take out large chunks of cost is not only by removing complexity to move to a better place on the curve but also by **changing the shape of the curve**—*shifting it upward and to the right* (see Figure 8).

Figure 8: Reshaping the Whale Curve

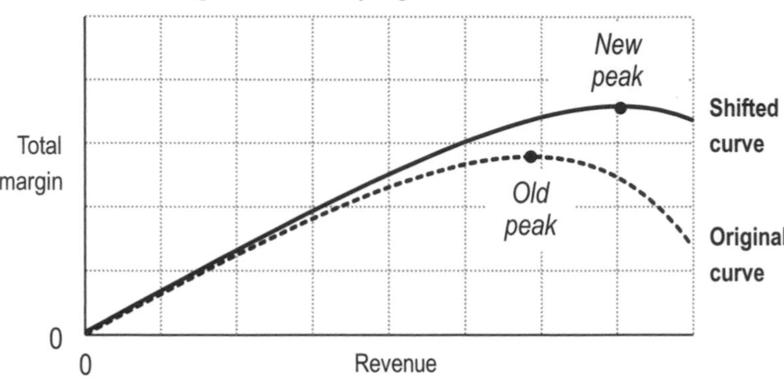

Shifting the Whale Curve upward and to the right also moves its peak upward and to the right, resulting in greater cost-reduction opportunity (and margin improvement) with less potential revenue loss.

The shape of the Whale Curve results from the geometric nature of complexity costs. By attacking the faces of the Complexity Cube, you can alter your complexity cost curve and shift your Whale Curve.

The battle strategies for taking out complexity costs that you'll find later in this book can all be categorized across the following:

1) **Removing complexity to obtain a better position on the Whale Curve** (removing the bad complexity that destroys value)

2) **Removing complexity to change the shape of the Whale Curve** (capturing the same or more revenue with less complexity by ensuring that each product offers incremental revenue, effectively making complexity less expensive)

3) **Becoming much better at delivering complexity to change the shape of the Whale Curve** (making complexity less expensive by becoming more efficient in processes and organizational structures)

Efforts aimed at only the first item above will leave tremendous benefit on the table while skewing the focus unnecessarily toward SKU reduction programs. More on this later.

Moving Forward with a Fuller Understanding

Complexity and its costs seem to pile up quickly in our organizations. And now we know that the "piling up" is not a simple linear effect; it is a geometric, exponential effect. The math isn't 10 + 10 + 10 = 30. It's more like 10 x 10 x 10 = 1000. As we'll discuss later in the book, this understanding will enable you to take a more nuanced and effective approach to removing its costs. ***You will have more options, more battle strategies for waging war on complexity costs!***

A fuller view enables you to get big costs out faster because it frames the problem as it really is, in its fullness, and, therefore, points you to the levers of meaningful change, as opposed to being trapped within a narrow slice of the problem. You will learn not just how to take out bad complexity but also how to capitalize on the significant impact from converting bad complexity to good and making the good even better. You'll see later in the book that this combination of actions and impact, taken within the context of a much fuller view of complexity and a deeper understanding of its interactions, will equip you to successfully wage this war.

Chapter 2 Endnotes

[11] Case study reported in "Corporate Executive Board's Report on Controlling SKU Proliferation" (October 2002).

[12] Pieter Klaas Jagersma, "The Hidden Cost of Doing Business." *Business Strategy Series* Vol 9, No. 5, pp. 238-242.

[13] The turnaround of Porsche by CEO Wendelin Wiedeking was centered on reducing complexity costs and associated processes. He targeted a 30% improvement in productivity and cost in three years. He killed the front-engine 928 and the less expensive 968, so that all that remained was the 911. He attacked wasteful processes and the manifestations of bad complexity.

[14] Alex Taylor III, "Porsche's Risky Recipe: Wendelin Wiedeking Has Produced Higher Profits for 9 Straight Years. But Will the Spicy New Cayenne SUV Give Tradition-Minded Customers Heartburn?" *Fortune*, February 17 (2003).

[15] WilsonPerumal estimate based on experience with unimproved processes.

[16] Speaking at GMA/FPA Executive Conference, *Greenbriar* (2007).

[17] Authors' note: Many companies get this backward. They diagnose individual pieces and then take broad, sweeping, and unfortunately somewhat blunt actions.

CHAPTER 3

The Rise and Rise of Process and Organization Complexity

The essential point to grasp is that in dealing with capitalism we are dealing with an evolutionary process.

— *Joseph A. Schumpeter*[18]

I will build a car for the great multitude. It will be constructed of the best materials, by the best men to be hired, after the simplest designs that modern engineering can devise. But it will be low in price that no man making a good salary will be unable to own one.[19]

So said Henry Ford, announcing his intentions for the Model T, which famously came in any color that a customer wanted "as long as it is black." It was a move that confounded his sales team, who were convinced he was killing the business.[20] It was also a move that enabled him to capture half the automobile market by 1914, just six years after the first car came off the line.

The great innovation behind the Model T—and what enabled volume at low cost—was the assembly line. It transformed industry but extended far beyond manufacturing into services and transactional arenas. The idea of moving products through standard processes for the pursuit of scale economics came to define the operations of product and service firms throughout the 1900s.

A century on from the introduction of the famous Model T, the world has changed in ways that Ford would have struggled to imagine. In *Chasing the Rabbit*, author Steven J. Spear describes the contrast this way:

> *In the past, simple science often meant simple systems, whether those systems were the physical products that people used or the systems of work (the organizations or the processes) that generated those products. There were few pieces; their relationship tended to be linear and predictable—one thing leading logically to the next.*

> *We are in a much different situation today. Scientific progress has led to products and services that have better performance but are far more complex, requiring the integration of an increasing number of specialties that are linked to each other in far more convoluted ways.*

The processes tied to these specialties are dependent on each other in ever more convoluted ways. As process complexity has risen, so too has organizational complexity, as functions, organizational structures, and IT systems struggle to support countless process interfaces. Worse, process and organizational complexity have fed on each other: new market opportunities have stretched processes and organizational structures to deliver more than they are capable of, which generated work-arounds and other forms of process complexity, which, in turn, generated organizational complexity and made it more and more difficult to "see" any process end-to-end. (See Figure 9.)

Figure 9: The Compounding of Organization and Process Complexity

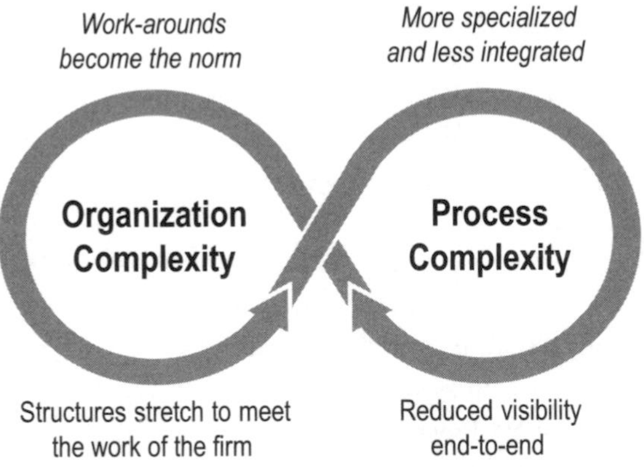

Traditionally, complexity reduction efforts have centered on product complexity, which as we now know represents just one dimension of complexity costs. But attacking complexity costs *without* a thorough understanding and examination of the two additional dimensions is akin to fighting with one arm tied behind your back. Moreover, **unless we understand why companies are prone to process and organizational complexity, we will never be able to keep complexity costs at bay.** By examining why companies have seen a surge in process and organizational complexity, we will gather insights into how to most effectively adapt our organizations to deal with its onslaught.

To better understand the dynamics of the issues, it helps to explore the evolution of process and organizational complexity.

The Three Waves of Process Architecture

The scale economics that enabled Ford's success has been complicated by new waves of change. Changes in customer demographics and tastes have led to an explosion of product and service complexity. Changes in technology have enabled greater speed but have also created a need for tighter integration. At the same time, fundamental changes in the global marketplace now offer the potential to leverage the best process capabilities the world has to offer, but they require orchestration.

When looked at through a historical lens, it's easy to pick out three distinct trends in what organizations demand of their processes (Figure 10):

1st Wave: The pursuit of **volume**

2nd Wave: The pursuit of **variety**

3rd Wave: The pursuit of **velocity**

Figure 10: Volume, Variety, and Velocity

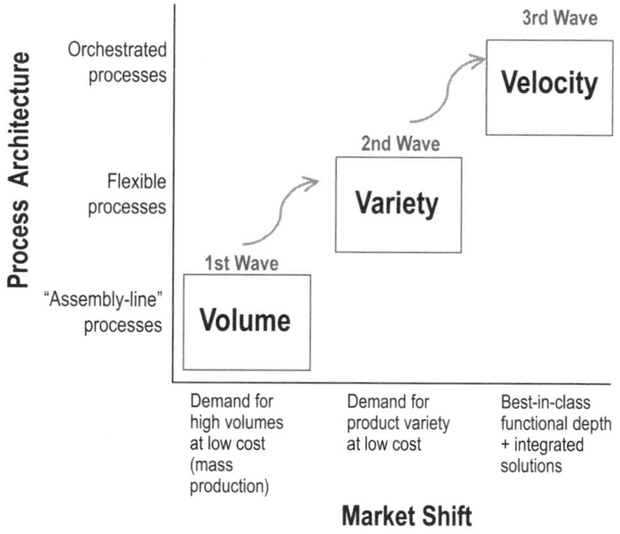

Companies have responded to changes in technology and markets to pursue new opportunities, reflected in three "waves" of process architecture.

The 1st Wave: The pursuit of volume at low cost

Before Henry Ford's development of the assembly line and the Model T, cars were the domain of the wealthy. Slow to make and prohibitively expensive, they were individually built by teams of craftsmen and skilled workers and marketed as "pleasure cars," with a focus on luxury features. The assembly-line process enabled volume at lower costs and democratized car ownership, propelling Ford to market leadership.

Ford himself gave an analogy: axe handles, which when produced by machine cost a few cents and were all of a consistent quality. It was progress on the prior situation:

> *In a little dark shop on a side street an old man had labored for years making axe handles. Out of seasoned hickory he fashioned them, with the help of a drawshave, a chisel, and a supply of sand paper. His average was eight handles a week, for which he received a dollar and a half each. And some of these were unsaleable.*

From axe handles to automobiles to insurance claims, the switch to the assembly-line paradigm was a pivot point for industry. Since that time, assembly-line process architecture has been a sensible choice for firms looking to take advantage of scale. The pursuit of scale to reduce unit costs has been particularly important given companies' need to take on fixed costs in IT, in assets, in organizational growth. This model was successful for much of the 20th century.

Assembly-line thinking led to a wave of process standardization and automation, which decreased transaction costs even further. Industrial companies, financial services, consumer goods suppliers—all saw benefits from scale economics, the result of large volumes of identical or very similar products or transactions going through an assembly-line style process.

But the benefits of scale depended on homogeneity of demand.[21] And as we all know, homogeneity is a rare commodity these days. As companies began tapping into customers' desire for increasing variety, operations and processes were woefully inadequate.

It is hard to overemphasize the avalanche of complexity that has hit many firms. Product complexity has piled up because of trends in microsegmentation and shorter product life cycles. More and more sectors find themselves struggling with lower volumes of a greater variety of products.

Moreover, the impact of complexity is multiplicative in nature: Recall the Toblerone bar, produced in different shapes with different recipes with different packaging. The pileup of configurations had greatly increased inventory levels and decreased productivity.

But it was not just that customers were demanding more complexity but also that companies were reacting to the demand in ways that were counterproductive. Unsure about *what* to offer, they proliferated wildly, launching variety on to the market to see what worked—oftentimes labeling this strategy as "innovation." Sometimes, this proliferation was driven by internal metrics, as competing internal groups effectively engaged in a battle that did nothing but cannibalize their company's own sales and increase net costs.

Though this proliferation was often done in the *name* of the customer, the reasons for it frequently had nothing to do with customers, and the ensuing complexity many times led to negative reactions. In *The Economist Intelligence Unit* report titled "Managing the Challenge of Product Proliferation," a survey of executives revealed that "just over 60% of respondents say that they release products in response to the actions of competitors—despite the fact that less than 20% of revenue is generated" from products launched on this basis.

In short, the *processes* of many firms today are still designed around a plain vanilla offering of *products*. Yet few firms can survive, let alone thrive, on sales of one flavor. And when they react, they place themselves in a situation where **high-variety/low-volume products** go through a **process designed for low-variety/high-volume.** The result is rework, work-arounds, increased coordination costs, and complexity, all of which erode the benefits of mass production.

The 2nd Wave: The pursuit of variety

When your goal is to produce a lot of a few things, you need rigid processes following a limited set of standard procedures if you want to lower costs and improve speed. The opposite is true once the processes have to handle constant variety; now the need is for process flexibility. For many companies, "variety through flexibility" is today's biggest challenge: they have expanded their offerings to accommodate market demands for variety, but frequently little has been done to prepare internal processes and operations for the new demands placed on them. In a McKinsey study, 47% of executives rated increasing product and service complexity as having the most influence on supply chain strategy (the top answer), whereas only 35% said that their company had taken action on addressing complexity-related issues.[22]

Let's consider an example. Traditionally, the call center at a health insurer passed all enrollment requests that fell outside the "standard" benefits configuration to a separate department that helped with "custom" requests. All fine and good—apart from the fact that 95% of its volume fell into the latter bucket! This custom path, as you might expect, was more expensive, time consuming, and error prone.

What did this indicate? Was it that all these customers were really seeking custom plans and that there was very little commonality among them? Was this good complexity that customers truly valued? Or was it something else?

In fact, the problem with "custom" requests was really an operational issue: the health insurer's definitions of what was originally considered standard or custom masked the fact that there were several new benefit configurations that were high volume, low variation. These were unrecognized high movers. In short, some of the "custom" requests were really reflecting a new standard, yet they were mixed in with the truly custom orders. The new high-volume but nonstandard configurations were treated as "one-offs" time and time again.

This situation is not unusual. It's symptomatic of a broader issue: having realized tremendous cost benefits from driving standard products through a single process, companies have continued to act on the same principle. When variety increases—triggering process issues—the right response would be to study the process problems, determine the root causes, and develop new procedures (much as the health insurer did). But for many companies, the increase in variety has simply led to an increase in rework and ad hoc work-arounds: a state of affairs we label "accidental process design."

Of course, no one would explicitly design a process with rework loops, random work-arounds, and the need for costly coordination; but in essence this is what occurs. Many organizations possess a high tolerance for the process complexity that is a direct result of variety-channel misalignment. Steven J. Spear calls it the "basic pathology of complex systems.... In low-velocity organizations, people suppress those indications that the work processes are inadequate and have to be modified." The *noise* of the system—the ongoing signals that something is wrong—is rarely documented or quantified, and those signals are even less frequently aggregated so they can be studied.

The usual response is a temporary fix, or perhaps heroic firefighting. You may see the same piece of paper circulate, seeking 25 different signatures; or you may be investing in expediting to figure out *Just where is that order?* It is all non-value-add work that has sprung up as a result of this high-variety/low-volume phenomenon. The correct response is flexibility. In the case of the health insurer, that meant

- **Triaging the separate requests into different channels.** This enabled higher levels of service at lower cost by ensuring the more standard requests got though the process quickly without being blocked by the truly custom requests.
- **Applying Lean techniques to reduce waste in processes.**
- **Managing the number of options so that processes were not overwhelmed by "random" variety.** Originally, customers were essentially encouraged to choose nonstandard options because the standard options offered by the firm did not meet their needs.

If you have seen an inordinate increase in the variety of goods and services in the past decade, or if your industry has been singled out for its levels of innovation, or if your company has embraced a focus on customer centricity, it is highly possible that the capabilities of your processes are unable to keep pace with the demands on your product variety. Developing flexibility in response to these pressures is a topic we'll cover in depth later in the book (see sidebar for preview).

Battle strategies to enable the pursuit of variety

There are some effective strategies for building organizational flexibility that will let you deliver greater variety without incurring a complexity penalty. We'll cover each in some detail in Part III. Here is a quick preview:

Having a process that is too rigid—too tied into procedures designed for a narrow set of offerings—is what leads to work-arounds. **Flexibility** in processes acknowledges the multiplicity of demands placed on them, and rather than try to reduce the "product" complexity, it reduces the cost to deliver that complexity. Central to this is the application of Lean to enable low-cost complexity. (See Chapter 13, "Enabling Variety with Lean Processes.")

The second key strategy recognizes that process flexibility via Lean can only get you so far. It is impossible and also unhealthy to drive toward offering infinite variety to the market. Therefore, you need to **rebalance your portfolio**. (See Chapters 9 and 10 on Portfolio Optimization.)

The third, and least used, strategy is one that bridges the first and the second. **Process segmentation** brackets products and services based on their similarity and the impact each has on the processes themselves. Structuring processes and production or delivery schedules around similarities allows the organization to be better prepared to introduce new variety demanded by the market. (See Chapter 14, "Process Segmentation: Minimizing the Effects of Variety.")

The 3rd Wave: The pursuit of velocity through process orchestration

As we have said, adapting their operations to accommodate requisite variety is where many (if not most) firms find themselves today. But while they play catch-up to this key capability, the acceleration of globalization has launched a whole new range of opportunities requiring brand new capabilities.

Tom Friedman, in his book *The World Is Flat*, begins with a chapter titled "While I Was Sleeping." He recounts the "flattening" of the world through a convergence of the personal computer and email (which democratized the tools for content creation), fiber optic cable (which connected that content to the rest of the world), and workflow software (which enabled collaboration on digital content between workers no matter where they were). All of that happened, says Friedman, while he was consumed covering post-9/11 events. But the impact of this great convergence, he observed, was (and is) having significant consequences for business:

> *Companies that have managed to survive and grow today... are the ones that recognize—faster than their competitors—everything new that the flattening of the world enables... and are the first to develop strategies to exploit the new possibilities and to cope with the new requirements.*

In their book *Competing in a Flat World*, Victor K. Fung and William K. Fung (of global sourcing company Li & Fung) and Wharton professor Jerry Wind discuss the implications of flattening. They write, "Henry Ford's factory was built on the principle of *division* of labor. The new principle was *dispersion* of labor." They continue,

> *Companies realized that the supply chain could be broken up and spread across the globe. They could do more than source products or components from other parts of the world. They could put stages of the supply chain in different parts of the world and coordinate them centrally. This meant breaking up the processes of the supply chain, farming them out to different companies in different locations, and then managing these dispersed processes.*

Michael Dell recalled how Dell developed based on similar notions:

> *As a small startup, Dell couldn't afford to create every piece of the value chain. But more to the point, why should we want to? We concluded we'd be better off leveraging the investments others have made and focusing on delivering solutions and systems to customers.*

For Dell, working within a network was less expensive, and it allowed them to focus on where they could add value. It also made them quick, able to respond to customer demand with faster and faster lead times. And it made them agile; they could respond to the shifts in market quicker than competitors and without being weighed down by their existing assets.

This ability to respond quickly is increasingly important if you believe that the pace of change is increasing. A company that *participates* in a value chain will react to a shift in the marketplace by redesigning the network—shuffling the pieces and emerging with the right supply chain to deliver what customers want, when they want it. A company that *owns* the entire value chain will react, too, but whatever action it takes is balanced by its need to feed the rest of the supply chain: *I can switch to a new product, but what do I do with my factories?*

The dilemma is this: As a result of the flattening that Tom Friedman writes about, a company's *opportunity* to reinvent itself has dramatically increased. This is the pursuit of velocity. But equally true, a company's *need* to continually reinvent itself has also increased, as the market takes advantage of the opportunities before it.

In other words, as players pursue velocity, the game changes for all players, meaning that playing the game of network and process orchestration will become mandatory in certain industries. But successful orchestration requires different skill sets than exist in most companies today, such as managing more interfaces and using empowerment vs. control. (See Figure 11.) Failure to recognize this last fact will lead to enormous process and organizational complexity.

Figure 11: Decision Tree

Is pace of creative destruction increasing?
YES
NO
Do you embrace network orchestration?
Business as usual
YES
NO
Do you possess orchestration capabilities?
Cost and agility disadvantage
YES
NO
You are ready to compete
High process complexity
Key questions
Positive or neutral outcome
Negative outcome

In the age of process and network orchestration, a company's ability to succeed depends on whether it participates and how well it participates. Companies are likely going to see increasing levels of process orchestration in their industry, mandating new capabilities if they want to stay competitive.

The gales of creative destruction

Austrian American economist Joseph A. Schumpeter referred to capitalism as the "gales of creative destruction." He wrote,

> *Most new firms are founded with an idea and for a definite purpose. The life goes out of them when that idea or purpose has been fulfilled or has become obsolete or even if, without having become obsolete, it has ceased to be new. That is the fundamental reason why firms do not exist forever. Many of them are, of course, failures from the start. Like human beings, firms are constantly being born that cannot live. Others may meet... death from accident or illness. Still others die a "natural" death, as men die of old age. And the "natural" cause, in the case of firms, is precisely their inability to keep up the pace in innovating which they themselves had been instrumental in setting in the time of their vigor.*

The analogy to life and death is appropriate, as indications are that life spans for firms are decreasing. Figure 12 illustrates this idea. Looking at membership on the Dow Jones Industrial Average (DJIA) as a proxy for "life span," we can see the rapid decline over the past 30 years.

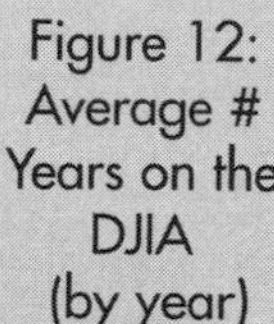
Figure 12: Average # Years on the DJIA (by year)

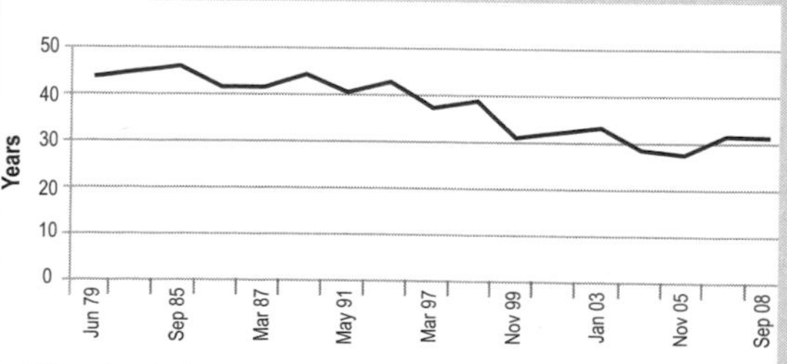

As the graph shows, duration on the DJIA is getting shorter and shorter. As the pace of creative destruction increases, a company's ability to completely reinvent itself will be what distinguishes those that endure from those that don't.

It is a shift in mindset to think in terms of positioning your company as an orchestrator of supply chain players rather than of being a player yourself. Yet some industries such as retail were early adopters of network orchestration. Fung and Fung cite Les Wexner, former CEO of retailer The Limited, as one of the first to realize that his company was not competing against its suppliers—and so the traditional adversarial relationships were gone—nor was it competing against other companies. He realized that it was now a matter of networks competing against other networks.[23]

Global sourcing titan Li & Fung, by its own definition, is a network orchestrator in the purest form. The company owns no factories and employs no factory workers. It started as a trading broker in Canton, China, in 1906 and in the ensuing century grew into an exporter, then a multinational corporation, then finally into its role as an orchestrator. It now orchestrates 8,300 suppliers in more than 40 countries to produce more than $8 billion in garments, consumer goods, and toys. They describe what this means in practice:

> *If an order for 100,000 dress shirts comes into Li & Fung today for a delivery date four months from now, the best set of suppliers for filling this order with the right quality in the right time frame will be drawn from the broader network. But if the same order comes in a month from now for the same delivery date, it likely will be delivered by a different supply chain that can respond faster.*
>
> *The world changes a lot in a month. Customer expectations change. Supplier capacity changes. The best supply chain for each given order will be created individually based on the order itself.*

Li & Fung represent one end of the spectrum when it comes to process and network orchestration. The degree of process orchestration will vary by company. But during the next decade, most companies will need to become process orchestrators to some degree. Why?

- **Increased specialization.** As new technologies emerge and our dependence on them increases, the need for deep specialization also rises. With globalization—and a broader playing field—the likelihood that the best capabilities for every part of the value chain resides within your company becomes lower and lower.
- **Lower costs.** By orchestrating across a network, a company can access lower costs in the value chain if it allows each stage to structure in a cost efficient manner and leverage economies of scale where possible. Empty capacity becomes someone else's problem.
- **Increasing need for self-reinvention.** Given the accelerating pace of creative destruction, firms will realize that continual reexamination of

their business model is a means to remain focused on the customer and be able to quickly adapt and move in new directions.

This pursuit of velocity creates new opportunities and puts new pressures on organizations. An orchestra produces beautiful music when the individual musicians, all masters of their instruments, play in synchronicity. But to achieve that you need a conductor, an emerging role for many companies. Fung and Fung state that the network orchestrator "plays three primary roles related to the focus, management and value creation of the firm or network":

Orchestration Role 1: Design and manage networks

This first capability is creating the network from which supply chains will be drawn. Many companies are on this path already. In its *Manufacturing Outlook for 2009*, research group Manufacturing Insights discussed the trend toward contract manufacturing and what it means going forward.[24] The group cites the craft brewing industry "where brands originally only made locally enjoy broader distribution by contracting with other craft brewers to produce their recipe in local markets. This pooling of manufacturing resources may prove itself to be applicable to many other vertical subsegments within manufacturing."

This trend, they suggested, will produce "tighter linkages with manufacturing partners around the world and a willingness to produce other companies' products within their own plants. The overall effect will be higher utilization of manufacturing assets worldwide, greater flexibility in responding to demand, and significant new challenges in managing the execution."

It is worth pointing out that a move toward networking is more than an acceleration away from vertical integration in industries, where companies outsourced processes to value-chain partners (via generally stable relationships). With a broader playing field and better technology, orchestration focuses on leveraging the best set of participants from the network at any one time. Orchestration of variable networks requires different skills than managing a constant supply chain does.

Orchestration Role 2: Emphasize empowerment rather than control

By definition, orchestrators do not own the means of production, so different forms of leadership and control are required. Yes, rewards are still important, as are standards and compliance. But excelling at orchestration is also about empowering the suppliers and value-chain partners to act entrepreneurially. When a 1997 fire in a brake maker's plant left Toyota without a critical component, the company was in danger of losing $40 million a day in profits.[25] What might have been a crisis, however, was quickly averted by the actions of its suppliers. While the original supplier (Aisin Seiki) had previously provided 99% of a brake component, just two days after the fire, 36 of Toyota's other suppliers (supported by 150 subcontractors) had put in place lines producing batches of the critical valve. What was remarkable—and a testament to the strength and resilience of a network—was that this was a largely self-organized effort with companies that generally had no previous experience with the P-valves used in braking systems.

Orchestration Role 3: Create value through integration

Like the orchestration of networks, integration represents a shift in mindset from a focus on specialization (keeping out rivals and even partners and fighting for a larger piece of a smaller pie) to a focus on integration (working with partners to attain a perhaps smaller piece of a potentially much larger pie)—a net gain overall. Integration doesn't just mean making links across a network; it means ensuring that your own company, within its four walls, is integrated across functions. Indeed this is a prerequisite for creating value through integration.

In *The Wall Street Journal*, Andy Grove, former CEO of Intel, asked what the U.S. automobile industry[26] could learn from Silicon Valley.[27] As a starting point, he recalled how in the 1980s, as a vertically integrated industry, the computer industry was focused on producing large, expensive mainframes. But with the emergence of the PC, the industry was transformed. "The entire industry began to rely on common hardware elements (microprocessors) and packaged software; selling was handed off to third parties." The result, he said, was a much more dynamic and thriving industry, where old participants faded away and new types of companies emerged.

Fast-forward to today, and he asks whether electric cars will become the PC of the auto industry. (Note: while the United States is focused on preserving jobs in the existing structure, China is placing a different bet, taking the lead on battery technology in hopes of capturing the new market.)

> *The car industry today is as vertical as the computer industry was before the PC. However, the simplicity of the electric car combined with the standardization of certain components may cause the automobile industry to shift to a horizontal structure. The internet is already emerging as a key marketing medium for automobiles and is easily adaptable to a horizontal structure.*

Migration to horizontal structures is a step toward orchestration. So it is critical to recognize when such transformations take place.

In Grove's perspective, transformation occurs only when a number of factors align, "such as a change in consumer demand, a shift of parts of the major supply chain from one country to another, and the emergence of key technological changes." In our view, there are few organizations that would not recognize these factors as increasingly important to their business. This is why orchestration, and improving orchestration capabilities, is critical.

But Grove warns that many have a "difficult time accepting that the future will be vastly different from the present because they rose to power in the old business environment. They excelled in the old environment and didn't acquire skills necessary to operate in the new."

Conclusion

Capitalism, as "gales of creative destruction" economist Schumpeter points out, never stands still. And with each new innovation and market shift, companies face new opportunities and new challenges. As we've discussed in this chapter, when companies seize new market opportunities without the requisite process discipline, flexibility, and capability, the result is process and organizational complexity.

Schumpeter framed capitalism as an "evolutionary process." And we have seen considerable change. Companies pursued volume and scale economics through assembly-line processes, then found—or are finding—their operations stretched by the demands of variety. Some developed flexible processes to accommodate product and service variety, then saw—or are seeing—their entire industry pursue velocity through greater levels of orchestration, which put different pressures on their processes.

In short, the pace of change in technology and markets has exceeded companies' process mastery, creating process complexity, as summarized in Figure 13 (next page).

Trends over the past century have not created a linear path. Many companies find themselves spread across all parts of this spectrum. One division may be able to carve off low-variety volume to gain scale economies while another division is becoming an orchestrator. The key is to monitor the alignment between the market demands and your process capabilities. The alternative is the downside of mismanaged process and organizational complexity.

So while you focus on slashing complexity costs, assess the health of your processes and organization and consider whether you are ready for a new wave of change.

Figure 13: Process Complexity Accompanies the Pursuit of Variety and Velocity

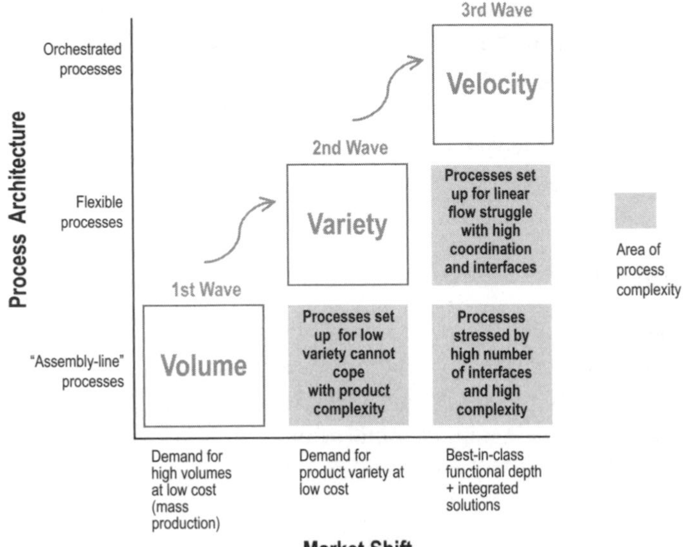

When the pace of change in technology and markets exceeds the capabilities of processes, companies suffer the consequences of process complexity (the shaded boxes). What follows is a period of "catch-up" so that a company's market response is supported by its execution capabilities.

Chapter 3 Endnotes

18 *Capitalism, Socialism, and Democracy*, 3rd ed. (New York: Harper and Brothers, 1950 [1942]).

19 *My Life and Work—An Autobiography of Henry Ford* [1922] (New York: Classic House Books, 2009).

20 Ford writes in his autobiography, "The selling people could not of course see the advantages that a single model would bring about in production. More than that, they did not particularly care."

21 In fact, Ford's refusal to offer a variety of cars led to tremendous market share loss—about 20% by the outbreak of World War II. His stubbornness was rooted in his pre–Model T experimentation and his belief that variety led to massive production disadvantages. He didn't see the potential for a variety of finished goods using standard parts.

22 "Managing Global Supply Chains," *The McKinsey Quarterly*, July (2008).

23 As reported in *Competing in a Flat World* (Upper Saddle River, NJ: Wharton School of Publishing, 2008).

24 Bob Parker, vice president of research at Manufacturing Insights. "Manufacturing Outlook for 2009, Buckle Up, It Could Be a Bumpy Ride," *IndustryWeek*, Feb. 3, 2009.

25 Steven Spear, *Chasing the Rabbit* (New York: McGraw-Hill, 2009).

26 And, by extension, the U.S. government, which owns large stakes in the U.S. auto industry. "Imagine if in the middle of the computer transformation the Reagan administration worried about the upheaval and tried to rescue this vital industry by making huge investments in leading mainframe companies. The purpose of such investments would have been to protect the viability of these companies. The effect, however, would have been to put the brakes on transformation and all but ensure that the U.S. would lose its leadership role."

27 Andrew S. Grove. "What Detroit Can Learn from Silicon Valley," *The Wall Street Journal*, July 13, 2009.

DEEP DIVE #2

Assessing Your Company's Cost-Cutting IQ

[As] part of the company's intensified efforts to live on a shoestring budget as it operates on $4 billion in federal loans, Chrysler... removed 40,000 of the 80,000 light bulbs at its headquarters.[28]

A company's actions in bad times can often reflect its culture in good times: if the DNA is short-term oriented, then short-term actions are likely. That is not a given, but a number of elements combine to create norms: metrics, culture, organizational history, a pattern of management, and so on. What we find is that as companies evaluate their options for cost reduction, their breadth and shape tend to reflect those norms—a company's Cost-Cutting IQ. By assessing your company's Cost-Cutting IQ, you'll be forewarned to your own company's biases. And as they say, forewarned is forearmed.

The Cost-Reduction Pitfalls

We define Cost-Cutting IQ in terms of a company's ability to avoid a set of common pitfalls:

Pitfall #1: Not really changing how work gets done

Pitfall #2: Cutting too shallow to achieve cost breakpoints

Pitfall #3: Using financial statements as a map (as opposed to a barometer)

Pitfall #4: Working with too much or too little data

Pitfall #5: Cutting the drivers of long-term value

Pitfall #6: Avoiding the tough calls

In a sense, these pitfalls are the alternatives to what we propose as the most effective, most strategic approach to resetting cost levels in an organization. They are well intentioned, and often partially successful. But they can also misfire and leave money—or opportunity—on the table. As you read through the following descriptions, ask yourself whether your company is susceptible to that pitfall or if you have the right operating principles to avoid it.

Pitfall #1: Not really changing how work gets done

Another way to describe this pitfall is that companies are betting on across-the-board cost reductions by function in hopes of dramatically changing their cost base. Does it work? Most companies find the answer to be no.

The Wall Street Journal reported that chip-maker ON Semiconductor Corp. was cutting costs through "broad-based trimming," which allowed executives the opportunity to keep their options open amid uncertain business conditions. [29] The CFO is reported as saying, "If you want to do it all through layoffs, then you have to decide ahead of the game what your future business is going to be." But right now, that's "a difficult call to make."

It's a typical approach, setting a mandate for 10% cost reductions for every department or function. And it has its advantages. It is directive—everyone understands the targets and metrics—and it is measurable. Moreover, as an approach it sits easily within existing structures. In other words, as a cost-cutting strategy, it is one of the easiest to deploy.

Unfortunately, while this type of approach can be useful in triggering greater scrutiny in ongoing *cost control*, it is unlikely to do more than nibble at the edges of the more substantive issue, which is fundamentally changing your cost structure.

The basic issue is that costs are output measures. They reflect performance after the fact. If you want to radically impact costs, you have to attack the inputs, the factors that are generating those costs. For example, many efforts to reduce product complexity costs are centered on making changes in operations. But downstream functions such as operations are driven by upstream decisions. Sales and marketing functions, for example, effectively determine the complexity that the operations function is trying to manage. That means the causes and the effects of complexity live in different parts of the business.

A side issue here is that if all the functions in a company are simultaneously optimizing their own budgets, the company as a whole will have suboptimal results. In retailing, for example, silo-mentality cost cutting could lead distribution hubs to push stock out of their warehouses and into stores, even if the products in question were not in demand. That kind of inventory shifting so the warehouse looks more productive just leads to crammed spaces and other operational issues for the stores—and thus increased waste as a whole for the organization.

The second problem with across-the-board percentage cuts is that you are capping the opportunities at levels that are likely too low. Functions have assigned budgets in sync with their purviews. Asking for functional cuts not only ignores the fact that the causal drivers of complexity within each function are external to those function but also reinforces silo behaviors. A CEO for a large retailer once told us, "If I ask for a 50% cost reduction, I have a chance of getting it because everyone has to work together to rethink how it works. If I ask for a 15% cost reduction, people will wall up and then tell me it's impossible." The bigger opportunities are generally buried in the processes and infrastructure that span two or more functional areas, but pursuing these bigger opportunities falls by the wayside when functional goals cause functional leaders to focus inward rather than looking across the organization.

In practice, what we see is a more fundamental issue emerging with the cuts-across-the-board approach: it consumes the focus and energy of the organization and precludes leaders from implementing broader, more significant action.

The usual suspects

In the WilsonPerumal cost survey "Navigating through Turbulence," we examined which avenues companies were pursuing to cut costs. We found that the stalwarts of cost reduction were once again at the top of the list: The most popular cost-reduction tool was "process optimization," with 82% of respondents checking that approach; 76% of respondents reported hiring freezes, 62% reported vendor or supplier consolidation, and 60% reported spending freezes.

What cost levers is the organization pulling to achieve its objectives? Figure 14 summarizes the results from our survey.

Figure 14: Cost Levers

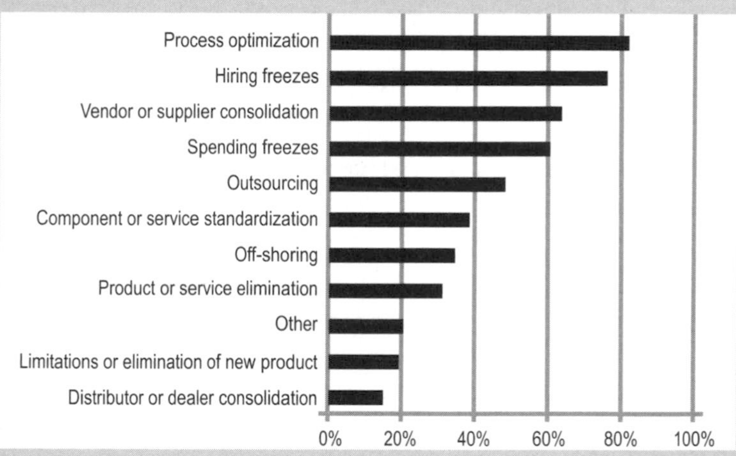

Undoubtedly, process optimization is a valuable lever that can generate large savings. But given the magnitude of cost targets participants reported and the focus on reshaping cost structures, the fact that only 30% reported product or service elimination as a key lever for cost reduction means that many companies are deferring (or simply avoiding) product line decisions.

There are many reasons why that would be so. For one, cutting product or service lines can be difficult decisions, particularly when companies are unclear about what to cut and what to keep. Also, some companies will be tempted to delay in hopes of "keeping options open." This, though, is a costly strategy, as we have found that bloated product and service portfolios can be the single biggest determinant of cost-competitiveness.

Most companies today need a slimmer profile, but the belt-tightening actions should be viewed as part of the more structural, impactful cost-based adjustments discussed in this book. The danger is that belt tightening is sometimes the "do nothing" option masquerading as action.

Pitfall #2: Cutting too shallow to reach cost breakpoints

In a bid to keep the effort manageable, companies attack a symptom, not a cause. Companies are launching initiatives without a good understanding of the link between the sources and the impact of complexity and its costs. They, therefore, anchor their attention on the most obvious symptoms.

It reminds us of the story about the old man losing his watch, who chose to look by the streetlamp because "that was where there was light." Attacking only complexity symptoms that are "in the light" is an ineffective strategy. It is unfortunate, for example, when companies confine their efforts to a trim of the bottom 5% of SKUs by sales or cut back on one type of service option and are then surprised by the superficial results. Just trimming the obvious symptoms is easy but often unproductive. It doesn't really change how work gets done (Pitfall #1), and it misses the opportunities to make cuts that will have a deep and lasting effect on balance sheets and financial statements. Upfront understanding of the key levers behind complexity costs is critical to (a) realizing substantive cost savings, and (b) ensuring that costs don't creep back in.

Pitfall #3: Using financial statements as a map (as opposed to a barometer)

When making decisions about cuts, a natural instinct is to start with what you can see. When dealing with cost, "what you can see" usually means financial statements, tangible items such as functional budgets. While standard financial numbers can provide clues to the opportunities available for cutting costs, no financial report does justice to the true size of the opportunity. In short, financial statements are better used as a barometer of financial health than as a treasure map that you hope will have a giant "X" pointing to the hidden cache.

As with Pitfall #1, limiting yourself to what you see on a standard financial report is another way to inadvertently put a cap on your potential savings. You have to go beyond financial statements to get your organization aligned to the size of the opportunity—a critical first step in creating the willpower to take significant action. (See Chapters 4 and 5 on how to estimate the size of your complexity prize.)

For those of you who are familiar with standard process improvement methods, a simple example may be useful. In a production process that has a total lead time of 100 days, it would not be unusual to find that no more than 10 of those days are spent on value-add activities (work that the customer values and will pay for); the remaining 90 days are consumed by non-value-add work. Traditional quality improvement activities focus on making improvements to the value-add time—helping the line work get faster so that the 10 days become 8 days. But Lean would suggest a different path: focus on reducing the 90 days. Make a 20% gain in the 10 value-add days, and you still have a process that takes 98 days. Make a 20% gain in reducing the 90 non-value-add days, and you have a process that takes 82 days.

The same principle applies here: cutting the visible costs that you'll see on a financial statement is like trimming a portion of the 10 days. Do that, and you're missing the much bigger target out there.

Pitfall #4: Working with too much or too little data

In *The Marine Corps Way*, the authors describe the "80 Percent Rule… which states that delaying any decision so that it can be made with more than 80 percent of the information is hesitation."[30] As companies try to assess their options for cutting complexity costs, they will often fall into two potential information traps:

1) Act without a preponderance of good information and assert that it's too complicated to figure out. We call this the information vacuum. The fallacy embedded here is the "we can't get it all, so we won't get anything" mentality: the belief that good information is either impossible to get or so expensive it is not worth getting. And for some companies, the lack of what is perceived as sufficient data is an excuse for inaction. (In fact, for the types of decisions we are talking about, having exhaustive, precise, detailed data is not only unnecessary, it is a fantasy.)

2) Identify a small portion of the problem and analyze it to death. You'll know the label for this problem: analysis paralysis. One of the repercussions of complexity is impaired information flow; and poor information flow creates more complexity. So complexity begets complexity, which leaves the company feeling helpless in its bid to systematically understand, reduce, and control that complexity—all of which results in fewer and fewer people understanding how it all ties together. The fallacy here is the belief that decisions can be made on complexity costs only after a detailed review of every product, every process, every margin. The bigger problem here is one of scoping: often, the tendency is to reduce the scope of what's being studied to ensure that the rigor of the analysis is supportable. What you're doing is compromising the size of the pie to preserve granularity. We recommend the converse: given the compounding nature of complexity, focus on assessing a broader scope (that encompasses the compounding interactions) and accept less granularity.

Pitfall #5: Cutting the drivers of long-term value

For many R&D and marketing departments these are tough times. Under intense cost pressures, many companies are cutting back on areas that they consider investments and deferrable. These make soft targets, but injudicious cutting in such areas can leave a company much worse off as they emerge from the downturn.

In fact, one of the key lessons from the dot-com bust in 2000 is that companies, as they take radical cost-cutting measures, need to protect the sources of revenue that will help them emerge as the economic difficulties fade. For many companies, that means keeping R&D spending intact.

The difference in outcomes can be stark: Consider the case of two technology giants. According to *The Wall Street Journal*, Apple increased R&D spending 42% between 1999 and 2002 even as revenue fell 6%.[31] Out of this investment came the iPod and later the iPhone. Motorola slashed R&D spending by 13% in 2002. The RAZR cell phone was the last notable product launch for the company. The difference shows up in share price history (Figure 15).

Figure 15: Apple and Motorola Stock Performance (1999–2009)

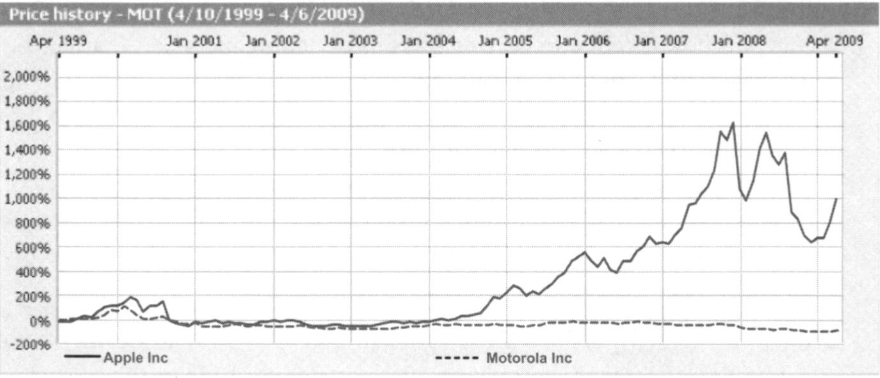

Of course, increasing R&D spending, or even just preserving it, is easier said than done when a company is 100% focused on cost reduction.

Glassmaker Corning Inc. is maintaining a longer-term mindset by placing R&D inside what it calls "rings of defense." The idea is simple: make R&D the *last* in line for cuts. Corning has already shut factories, laid off workers, and released contract workers, but has thus far preserved R&D spending despite revenue declines of 31% in the fourth quarter of 2008.

"That's a change from the last downturn," *The Wall Street Journal* reported, "when [Corning] responded... by cutting R&D spending nearly in half between 2001 and 2004."

Xerox has adopted a similar strategy. "I know from experience one of the biggest mistakes that can be made right now is to slash investments in innovation," said Anne Mulcahy, current chairman and former CEO of Xerox. "And by innovation, I don't just mean product research and development. It can also be innovating in new markets, launching new businesses, and even disruptive innovation in work processes."[32] Mulcahy, who engineered the Xerox turnaround earlier this decade, gives this piece of advice: "In the cost-cutting discussions we're having right now—and there are many—I remind my team that the next generation of technology and services will be born out of decisions we make at this unique moment in time."

Pitfall #6: Avoiding the tough calls

It is not unusual for companies to undertake an exercise to identify complexity-related issues but then delay decision making or fail to act because of organizational inertia. Leaders will have the resolve to take action only if complexity reduction is tied directly to explicit benefits.

After the analysis is complete and the cost opportunity is identified, the focus should shift to extracting the savings. Assuming that you have designed a better way of doing things that results in less cost, fewer resources, and/or lighter assets, the key is to ensure that the organization doesn't simply move resources around but actually removes costs.

Companies also postpone tough decisions in the hope that a silver bullet solution will arrive. As Ralph Peters put it in *Never Quit the Fight*,

> *Along with impatience, a great American weakness is our belief that every problem has a straightforward solution, if only we can figure it out. Especially in complex endeavors... this search for a silver bullet hampers our efforts.*

It is perhaps an unpopular message—that the productive path forward is difficult although manageable—but it is surely better than pretending otherwise. The search for silver bullets is nowhere more apparent than in IT systems. We have seen many organizations approach new ERP (enterprise resource planning) systems as a panacea for too much complexity in their business, apparently on the premise that "with this system we can now support near-infinite variety." But as you now know, the compounding impact of complexity quickly limits the flexibility of an organization.

As we'll cover in more detail later in the book, a better alternative to searching for silver bullets is to understand the root issues inflating costs in your business and to take coordinated actions across a number of points of high leverage.

Assessing Your Company's Cost-Cutting Biases

As you consider to what degree your own company falls into these six pitfalls, the right perspective is to see your assessment not as a static picture but as a baseline for launching your war on complexity costs. Assessing how your company will normally approach cost-cutting initiatives provides you valuable insights into how to best position, launch, and execute your program of cost reduction.

Deep Dive #2 Endnotes

28 Jewel Gopwani, "Chrysler Cuts Back on Clocks and More," *Detroit Free Press*, February 17 (2009).

29 Cari Tuna, "Searching for More Tools to Trim Costs, Companies, Seeking to Limit Layoffs and Preserve Talent, Cut Salaries, Hours and Benefits," *The Wall Street Journal*, February 23 (2009).

30 Jason A. Santamaria, Vincent Martino, and Eric K. Clemons, *The Marine Corps Way: Using Maneuver Warfare to Lead a Winning Organization* (New York: McGraw-Hill, 2004).

31 Justin Scheck and Paul Glader. "R&D Spending Holds Steady in Slump," *The Wall Street Journal*, April 6 (2009).

32 *Fortune*, May 4 (2009).

Chapter 4

Sizing Up the Prize, Part 1

The Fundamentals of Making the Financial Case

It ain't what you don't know that gets you;
it's the things you know that ain't so.

— *Mark Twain*

When companies embark on cost-reduction initiatives with such ineffective approaches as those outlined in the preceding Deep Dive, they vastly underestimate the potential benefits, further debilitating efforts. Most executives understand that complexity is extracting a price from the organization: They can feel the pain daily and observe the symptoms' impact. However, converting that gut instinct to a value proposition is much harder.

A business will always carry some complexity cost, no matter how well structured or high performing. The fundamental question is how much complexity cost you can eliminate without harming the short- or long-term potential of your business. To answer that question, it helps to establish a total "theoretical" cost of the complexity in your business, because doing so frames your efforts against the "art of the possible." Then you can look at the *possible* through the lens of the *practical*: what's achievable as a realistic prize. This is a good place to be: driving to short-run savings but armed with a grounded perspective of the nature and competitiveness of your cost position.

In short, executives must define a value proposition that spells out the size of the prize for their business by asking ***What is complexity costing me?*** Within this question are really two different questions: ***What is the total cost of complexity in the business?*** and, more important, ***How much can be removed (and removed quickly)?*** The answers will not only provide the impetus for taking action *now* but also help you make informed decisions about the scope and timing of your efforts as you move forward. In this chapter and the next, we will lay out the path to defining your own value proposition:

- This chapter will discuss the fundamentals of making the financial case and some of the key pitfalls
- Chapter 5 will describe our methodology for "sizing the prize"

Making the Financial Case to Focus the Organization

In most organizations, attaching a financial figure to the impact—and, therefore, opportunity—is a requirement for action. Eric Fidoten, a consumer goods supply chain executive with 25 years of experience, claims that quickly identifying the ballpark opportunity is critical to getting executive engagement and organizational momentum. *"If you can understand what the prize is, then that can get the organization aligned,"* he says.

Indeed, leaders who have successfully driven out complexity costs have been conspicuous for how much they have communicated the "entitlement" goal (how much savings the company is entitled to get from complexity reduction). The number you put to your opportunity needs to reflect a reachable goal. So whatever the rallying cry, ensure it is rooted in the real opportunity.

Given this need, it is perhaps no surprise that the biggest pitfall in trying to quantify complexity costs is over-engineering and overcomplicating the effort. Instead, to cut to the chase, what matters for most companies is answering two critical questions:

- What is the magnitude of the opportunity in going after complexity costs?
- Where should it fit on our management agenda?

We recommend that you *quickly identify the ballpark size of the prize.* That will allow you to engage the organization in committing to the effort.

You'll need to resist the temptation to embark on a bottom-up detailed summation of non-value-add costs, which may quickly unravel into an activity trap. We have seen it happen: A company wishes to remove complexity and first asks the question *What is it worth?* But the subsequent activity is focused on locating and adding up a thousand instances of "complexity cost"—a time-consuming and inaccurate approach that eventually stymies the whole effort.

Our approach will guide you past these landmines, so you can start taking immediate steps toward transforming your cost base.

Why Companies Struggle to Size the Prize

Many companies attempt to size the prize, but most hit stumbling blocks. Two key reasons are the following:

Reason 1: Financial systems don't capture "emergent" costs

Complexity costs are difficult to measure, by definition, because they are an *emergent* property of a complex system; they emerge from the relatively simple interactions of a large number of many items but do not "belong" to any individual item. In his book *Systems Thinking, Managing Chaos and Complexity*, Jamshid Gharajedaghi points out that "emergent properties cannot be measured directly; one can measure only their manifestations."

The problem is that conventional accounting methods cannot accommodate emergent costs. Traditional approaches categorize costs by department (sales, R&D), type of expense (labor, raw materials), entity (store, region), or how it scales (fixed vs. variable), among other breakdowns. This forces you to assign complexity-related costs to individual items and to report variances from the budget by function, business unit, or company. But complexity costs don't derive from items individually; neither do traditional accounting methods capture the unintended consequences or help you capture how complexity creeps into the "white spaces."

Reason 2: Quantifying complexity requires a fundamentally different approach to how companies generally quantify things

In most of our everyday lives, we are to used getting the total size of something by measuring the pieces and adding up the numbers. Surely if we want to estimate total complexity costs, the best approach would be to add up all the little pieces of costs that exist in the company, right? A + B = C.

And if that gets too complicated, the natural instinct is to divide it into ever-smaller pieces: $A_1 + A_2 + A_3 + \ldots$ = Total A costs.

But this kind of reductionist approach doesn't work with complexity. Complexity is fundamentally different from other things we measure because it gets harder to see the closer we get. Although complexity seems visible in aggregate, in pieces it is fleeting, Like fog, complexity seems to disappear the closer we get to it.

This is a fundamentally different view of costs—just ask any finance organization. Traditional finance approaches are influenced by the "add up the pieces" mentality described above: categorize costs by department (sales, R&D), type of expense (labor, raw materials), entity (store, region), or how it scales (fixed vs. variable), among other breakdowns, then add it all together.

But to quantify complexity costs, we must turn things around. We must stand back and take a more complete view. We must favor wholeness over an unfruitful quest for detailed precision. In applying traditional costing approaches to complexity, the quest for precision (with its focus on individual pieces) yields results that are actually *less precise in total.* So in wrestling with quantifying complexity costs, you're not facing a trade-off between the level of effort and the precision of result, as is the case with many other endeavors. You're facing a situation where a reductionist approach is both *more effort* and *less precise* in total.

Fundamentals for Quantifying the Cost

Before we lay out the mechanics for our approach, it is important to discuss key fundamental ideas that are central to our approach.

Fundamental 1: Why you can treat complexity costs as non-value-add costs and vice versa

How do we define complexity costs?

> *Complexity costs are those costs in a business associated with having too many parts, products, services, systems, processes, business lines, plants, stores, vendors, customers, organization functions, relationships, and so on, or the costs of the consequential interactions between these elements. They can take the form of inventory, obsolescence, lost capacity, decreased productivity, and growing overheads, among other things.*

It may be intuitive to many when we say that *all complexity costs are non-value-add costs*. Complexity costs do not add value directly to the product or service provided to a customer; therefore, by definition, they are non-value-add. They may be costs that accrue in the pursuit of customer benefit. Or it may be that they creep in for no good reason except that the fog of complexity has impeded decision making, data, and visibility, separating actions from consequences. Either way, they are non-value-add.

So for complexity-costing purposes, we separate all costs into one of two buckets: those that are value-add to the customer, and the typically much larger portion that are non-value-add to the customer. Lean focuses on removing time spent on NVA activities (NVA time) from individual processes to reduce waste and improve lead times. In this way, while improving process performance, Lean indirectly, albeit intentionally, reduces costs in individual processes. What is different here is applying the value-add versus non-value-add categorization directly to cost and to do so not at an individual process level but at an aggregate, whole-firm level.

So complexity costs are non-value-add, but we would also assert that the reverse is true: **for all practical purposes, you can treat all non-value-add costs as complexity costs.** This may seem quite a leap, so we will dive into this assertion a little further. First, it is important to clarify that "non-value-add" doesn't necessarily mean "not important." Many necessary parts of the business (such as sales, R&D, and finance) are NVA to the consumer but are clearly critical to the business (these types of costs are often termed "business-value-add"). The importance here isn't to eliminate these costs but rather to expose the growth of complexity behind these costs.

Second, while at a technical level, complexity costs are not necessarily synonymous with NVA costs, *complexity is what drives NVA costs to be very large.* This is why we can, **at a practical level, treat complexity costs and NVA costs as equivalent.**

Granted, if NVA costs are relatively small, then complexity must be low, and the difference between true complexity costs and NVA costs may potentially be significant. Think, for example, of the sales organization for a simple one-product company. There may be significant NVA cost in the sales process that has nothing to do with product complexity (since there isn't any). In such a case, NVA costs overall may be a relatively small portion of total costs, but complexity costs would be even smaller.

But now consider a sales organization where there are 1,000 variants of 100 different core services. In that case, there will likely be very large NVA costs in the sale processes driven by that complexity. Thus if NVA costs are very large, they are large due to complexity. In that case, the vast majority of NVA costs are complexity costs, and NVA costs are a good proxy for complexity costs. This is summarized like this:

If NVA costs are small ⇨ Complexity costs < NVA costs

If NVA costs are large ⇨ Complexity costs ≈ NVA costs

To put it another way, if complexity is significant, then NVA costs are large, and if NVA costs are large, then they are a reasonable proxy for complexity costs:

If complexity is significant ⇨ NVA will be large ⇨ $\text{Cost}_{\text{CMP}} \approx \text{Cost}_{\text{NVA}}$

We assume that those reading this book strongly suspect they have a complexity issue and have large NVA costs. If you fall into that category, you can move forward confident with the assumption that complexity costs and NVA costs are equivalent for the purposes of estimating the size of the prize.

Fundamental 2: Why we classify complexity as "good" or "bad" and costs as VA or NVA

A second foundation for quantifying complexity costs is an important distinction: the categorization of good versus bad complexity is very different from that between value-add (VA) and NVA costs (see Figure 16, next page).

Remember that the real cost of complexity isn't just the cost of the complexity that is determined to be bad (e.g., unprofitable products, customers, or business units). Rather, there are complexity costs (NVA) within nearly everything a company does and offers—even its very profitable products.

To mark this distinction, we recommend the following: while complexity can be termed "good" or "bad" (reflecting the net contribution to profit), costs

Figure 16: VA/NVA Cost Categorization versus Good/Bad Complexity Categorization

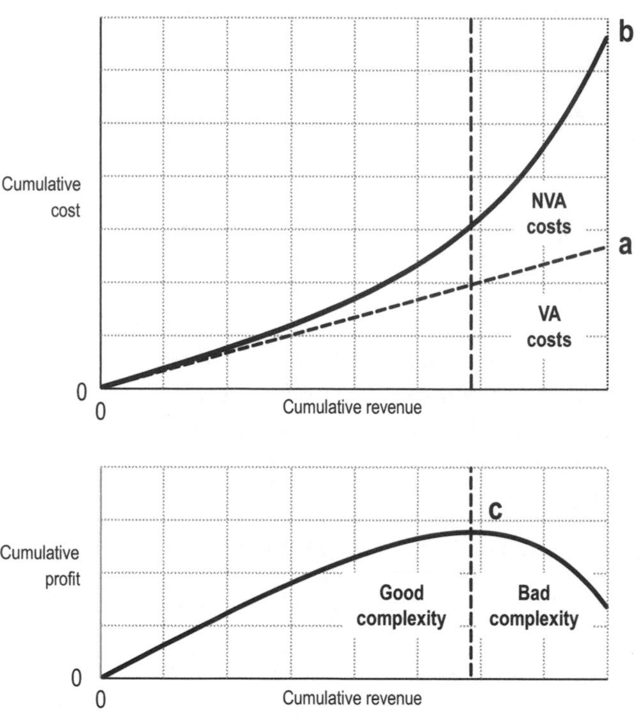

The value-add (VA) versus non-value-add (NVA) **cost** categorization is very different from the categorization of good versus bad **complexity** (and its impact on cumulative profit). VA costs *per unit* largely do not vary with the increased complexity (hence the linearity of **line a** in the upper graph). NVA costs, on the other hand, tend to grow geometrically with increased complexity **(line b)**. At some point (**c**), the growth in NVA costs overcomes *incremental* revenue, which is when *cumulative* profit declines. Complexity past that point is bad complexity. While NVA costs are concentrated in bad complexity, they also depress the profits of good complexity.

---

are better thought of as value-add or non-value-add. Complexity costs, therefore, are not just the costs of delivering bad complexity but rather the costs across the portfolio and throughout the business that result from all the complexity in the business. As we've asserted elsewhere, these costs grow geometrically with increasing levels of complexity. Attacking complexity costs is, therefore, a combination of removing bad complexity (i.e., having less complexity) as well as removing NVA costs across *all* complexity, both good and bad (i.e., making complexity less expensive).

Fundamental 3: Why we approach the problem top down, not bottom up

In Deep Dive #2, we talked about the pitfalls companies fall into when they attack only the most obvious complexity systems or when they attempt to quantify complexity costs in detail. This is where many efforts come undone. How can we best capture the systemic costs related to complexity?

It can be daunting to think about quantifying NVA costs from the bottom up, summing all the NVA costs throughout the business. NVA costs tend to grow, in part, because they are not as visible as VA costs. NVA costs, while all too real, are hidden in traditional accounting methods—often in overhead—making it difficult to find and impractical to quantify.

For all the reasons outlined previously in this book—the systemic and emergent nature of complexity, the interactive and compound nature of its costs—our approach to estimating the size of a complexity prize is the exact opposite of the bottom-up approach. Rather than try to add NVA costs bottom up, we suggest you **determine NVA costs top down by calculating VA costs directly and subtracting them from your total costs.** (By definition, VA plus NVA costs equal the overall cost base; so subtracting VA costs from total costs will give you an estimate of NVA costs.)

This is easily visualized with the Complexity Cube. Rather than calculating the less tangible non-value-add portion of the cube, you need to calculate only the more tangible portion of the cube and subtract it from the total (see Figure 17).

Figure 17: Calculating NVA Costs

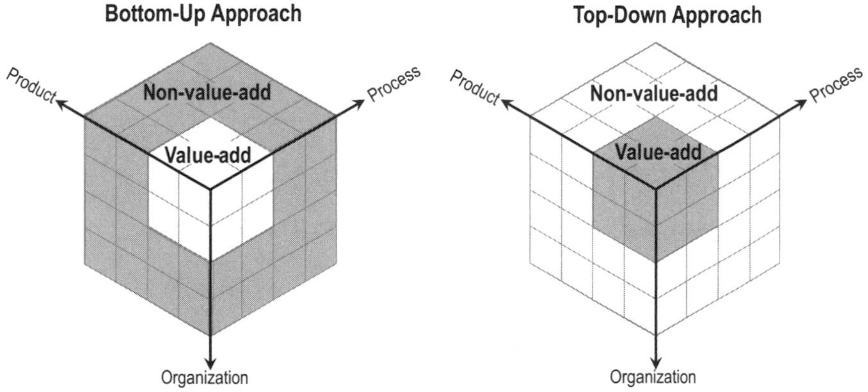

Mathematically, this is shown simply as

$$\text{NVA costs} + \text{VA costs} = \text{Total cost}$$

$$\text{NVA costs} = \text{Total cost} - \text{VA costs}$$

This approach for quantifying NVA costs is not only simpler than the bottom-up approach but also more effective, because VA costs are much easier to find and more readily quantified.

Fundamental 4: Why we want to assess the costs associated with process and organizational complexity, not just product complexity

Without a doubt, product and service complexity inflate the cost structure of many firms today. But as we showed in Chapters 2 and 3, there are big prizes elsewhere linked to process and organizational complexity. Many firms may have relatively little product complexity, but their processes and organizational structures are a web. Therefore, it is important that in sizing up the prize, you consider all three dimensions: product, process, and organizational complexity. Otherwise, you will underestimate the opportunity, skew efforts toward SKU reduction, and radically reduce your options.

Fundamental 5: Why we take a two-pronged approach (looking for ways to remove some complexity and make what remains less expensive)

We have framed the war on complexity costs as a two-pronged effort. The principle is that you need to not only *remove* complexity but also make the remaining complexity *less expensive* to deliver. Going after both of those goals is what will determine the true size of the prize for your company. And it is our contention that having a better handle on that prize will drive you to better battle strategies and open your mind to opportunities you hadn't previously considered.

From Fundamentals to Method: An introduction to the triangulation approach to sizing the prize

The preceding section spelled out five ways our method for estimating just how much you stand to gain with a properly scoped complexity war differs from traditional approaches. Here's a quick recap:

- Our method equates complexity costs with non-value-add costs
- It focuses on differentiating good versus bad complexity (using data on VA vs. NVA costs as inputs)
- It is top down (estimating overall complexity costs instead of summing up individual costs)

- It incorporates costs associated with all three dimensions of complexity
- It incorporates the idea that you'll need to wage a two-pronged war on complexity costs (removing some costs directly and making any remaining complexity less expensive)

These fundamentals come together in a method we call **triangulation**:

- We start by **bounding the issue**: performing three specific calculations that define the limits of just how much complexity cost is available for cutting
- Then we **triangulate** on those three points to select a **target prize**

In short, we will show you how to use data on overall VA costs and total costs, and your Whale Curve, to find the boundaries of the playing field within which your complexity cost prize exists. Then we show how to pick a point within that area that represents a good stretch but not impossible target for your business.

Using this method requires gaining a deeper understanding of what is happening to your revenue: how value-add and NVA costs are consuming it and how much profit is left over, and how this varies over your revenue. Essentially, you need to move from a singular view of revenue (your company makes X profit on Y revenue) to a much more multifaceted view, similar to that shown in Figure 18. (Recall the drivers of the shape of the Whale Curve, which we introduced in Chapter 2.)

Figure 18: A Multifaceted View of Revenue and How It Is Consumed

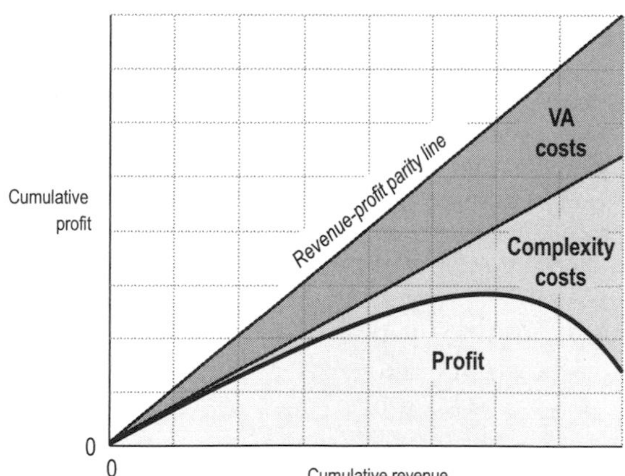

The revenue-profit parity line is simply the revenue line against the profit axis—or, in other words, the line against which costs are removed to get profit (i.e., if there were no costs, then profit would equal revenue). It is a theoretical line that defines a boundary. Subtracting VA costs and NVA costs (complexity costs) produces the Whale Curve line, which shows how cumulative profit usually grows and then falls with greater revenue.

Even a rough depiction like Figure 18 will add tremendous clarity. Against this backdrop, we can begin to estimate the size of the prize represented by **a higher-profit/lower-cost operating point** on the revenue-profit chart than what you have today.

Notice that the profit curve in Figure 18, which shows how cumulative profit grows and falls with greater revenue, is the now familiar Whale Curve (in this case, it is a Revenue Whale Curve; see sidebar, p. 78). Figure 19 shows visually the combined impact on the Whale Curve of our two-pronged approach. *Removing* complexity moves you to a better (i.e., higher) point on the Whale Curve; making complexity *less expensive* shifts the curve itself.

Figure 19: Visualizing the Two-Pronged Approach to Removing Complexity Costs

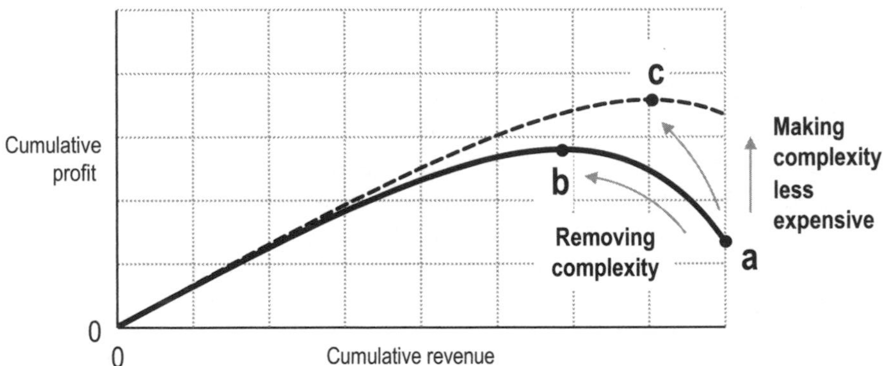

Point a is the company's current revenue-profit operating point. Removing complexity moves the operating point up and to the left along the Whale Curve toward **point b**, the curve's peak profit point. Making complexity less expensive moves the operating point upward and shifts the Whale Curve up and to the right (dashed line). By taking both actions, the company can achieve an operating point, **point c**, above and to the right of **point b**, resulting in greater profit improvement/cost reduction with less potential revenue loss than just removing complexity alone would.

Importantly, this means that the peak of the Whale Curve doesn't represent an upper bound for the size of the prize; rather, *with a two-pronged attack on complexity costs, the peak of the Whale Curve becomes the lower bound for the size of the prize.*

Therefore, the prize lies within an area extending up and to the right of the peak of your Whale Curve. This playing field (see Figure 20, next page), if you will, is defined by three points that are somewhat straightforward to determine:

Point 1: Your current revenue-profit operating point

Point 2: The peak profit point along your current Whale Curve (lower bound)

Point 3: The total cost of complexity, which when added to your current operating point defines a theoretical point representing removal of all complexity costs (upper bound)

(This last point represents the upper bound, a maximum but unattainable point for the size of the prize—although unattainable, it is still an important point for triangulation.)

Figure 20: Defining the Size-of-the-Prize Playing Field by Triangulation

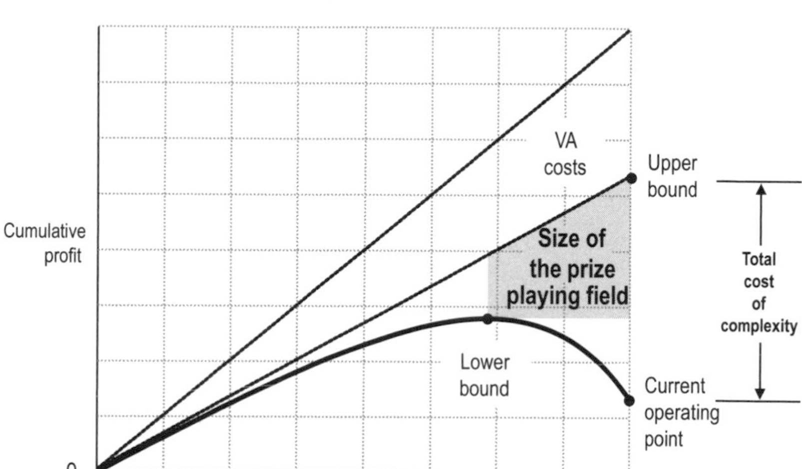

By both removing complexity and making it less expensive, you obtain a revenue-profit operating point above and to the right of the peak profit point of your original "whale" (within the shaded area of the chart). The amount of complexity costs you can remove from your business—the "size of the prize"—is represented by a targeted operating point somewhere within this shaded area. We can define this playing field by determining the peak of your current Whale Curve (the lower bound) and the total cost of complexity in your business (the upper bound).

The next question is where within this playing field can you go? How far *up and to the right* of your original operating point? The answer depends on how far you can stretch your Whale Curve, and that in turn depends on how much better you can get at delivering, managing, and operating in the face of complexity, that is, making complexity less expensive.

For example, Figure 21 (see next page) shows the impact on the Whale Curve from making complexity 35% less expensive, meaning that at a given level of revenue, total NVA costs are 35% less. The size of the prize is the peak of this "stretch" curve. The more you can stretch your Whale Curve, the greater the size of the prize.

Figure 21: Triangulation upon the Size of the Prize
(35% stretch example)

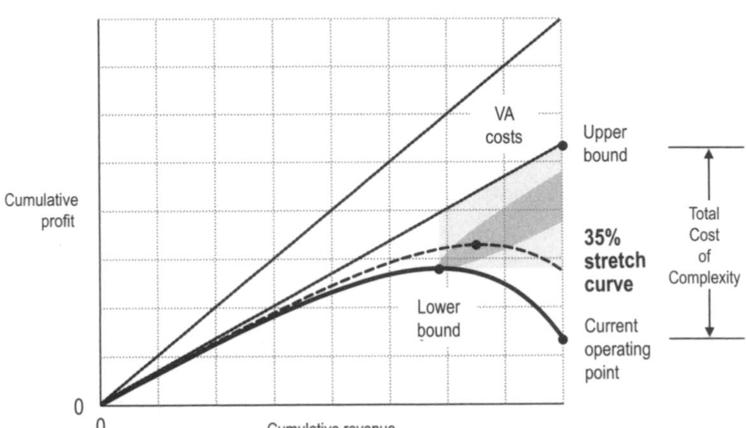

This example shows a "35% stretch" Whale Curve (dashed line) corresponding to making complexity 35% less expensive (meaning that for a given level of revenue there is 35% less NVA costs). The peak of the stretch curve corresponds to the size of the prize. Given the nature of how the Whale Curve stretches, we can define a narrower area within the playing field within which a targeted new revenue-profit operating point is more likely to reside (the darker shaded portion of the size-of-the prize playing field).

Notice that, given *how* the Whale Curve stretches, we can identify a narrower portion of the playing field within which the target revenue-profit operating

The revenue Whale Curve

A Whale Curve conveys how profits are concentrated around particular drivers: SKUs, regions, customers, etc. Hence, there are many types of Whale Curves you can create (each showing cumulative profit vs. a specific driver ranked by profitability).

But in the end, companies are concerned about revenue and especially so when it comes to complexity reduction, for example, how much revenue is put at risk by reducing complexity costs (although it is our contention, as pointed out earlier, that complexity reduction usually drives revenue growth). Therefore, the dominant Whale Curve is the Revenue Whale Curve, which shows cumulative profit versus cumulative revenue.

While there can be many drivers for profit concentration, the Revenue Whale Curve provides the top-line summary. All other possible Whale Curves are incorporated within it. Therefore, although other Whale Curves can be very informative, especially for helping target specific concentrations of cost, we will proceed with the Revenue Whale Curve, showing how profits and costs are concentrated on revenue.

point will likely be located (shown as the darker shaded portion on Figure 21). Your job will be to determine that point, and we will help you do this with more detailed instructions in the next chapter. (There is certainly judgment involved here, but with this method it is judgment from a defined point toward a defined maximum. The remainder of this book will help you estimate how much you can stretch.)

Conclusion

Odds are that if your business has tackled complexity and its costs before, it did it with a bottom-up approach. As you've now seen, that approach will make you underestimate the size of the prize, which may either lead you to avoid tackling the issue (because you don't perceive the payoff as that great) or allow you to be content with mediocre results.

Getting a realistic estimate of the prize will help you create the energy needed to tackle complexity and make sure you push for the biggest possible payoff. In the next chapter, we'll describe a methodology, step-by-step, that incorporates the principles outlined above. That way you, too, can launch your own war on complexity costs.

Chapter 5

Sizing Up the Prize, Part 2

The Methodology for Quantifying Complexity Costs

Make us to choose the harder right instead of the easier wrong, and never be content with a half truth when the whole can be won.

– *Col. C. E. Wheat*

As you can probably tell by now, estimating the size of the prize is not an exact science. The steps for sizing the prize can be carried out to various degrees of detail. Greater detail will lead to greater precision of the answer but will also yield diminishing returns, consuming more time and effort. It is up to you and your organization to determine what the right level of detail is for you, given the quality of your data, the culture of your company, your bandwidth for this effort, and the urgency of your situation.

Based on the discussion in Chapter 4, our recommended approach for determining the size of the prize for any organization starts with its current revenue and profit figures, followed by three steps (also summarized graphically in Figure 22, next page):

Step 1: Determine the lower bound (the peak profit of the starting Whale Curve)

Step 2: Determine the upper bound (the theoretical peak if *all* complexity costs were removed)

Step 3: Select a stretch target within the defined playing field

To help you, we will point out some key considerations and some shortcuts. But we urge you to keep one critical point in mind: **it is far better to make it all the way through the three steps than to be precise in any one step.** Therefore, start with the full picture in mind—even with a very approximate answer—and then ask yourself where you can add better detail. You decide how much time you have and how precise your answer must be. But working through the three steps, whatever the level of rigor, will provide you with a much better answer than would any other approach in the same period of time.

Figure 22: Summary of the Three-Step Process for Sizing the Prize

Start:

Start with your current revenue-margin operating point

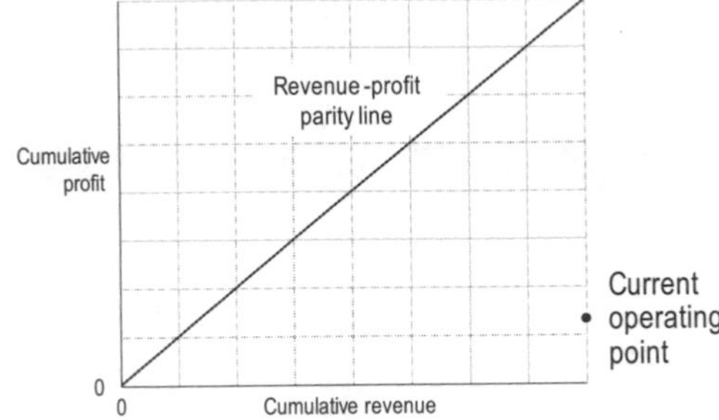

Step 1:

Plot your Whale Curve and identify its peak margin point *(this will be the lower bound of the size of the prize)*

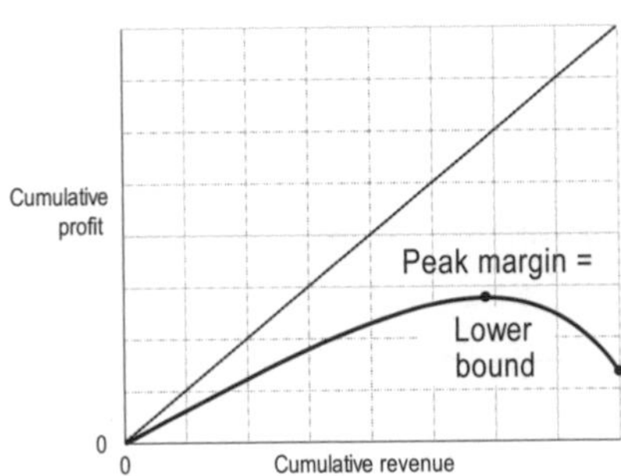

Step 2:

Determine the total cost of complexity and plot the upper bound

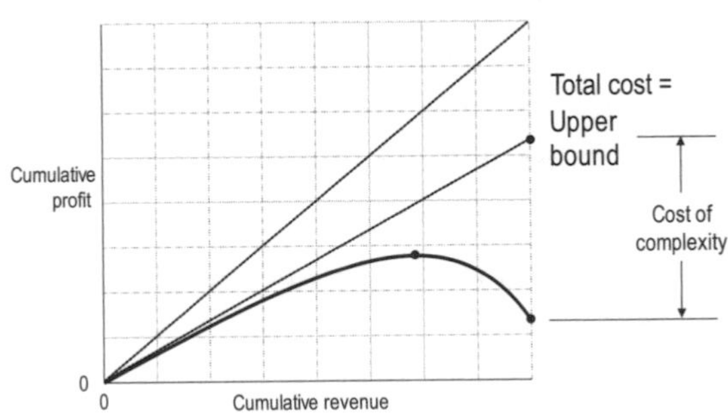

Start 3:

Estimate how much you can stretch your Whale Curve *(this is how to select a target operating point)*

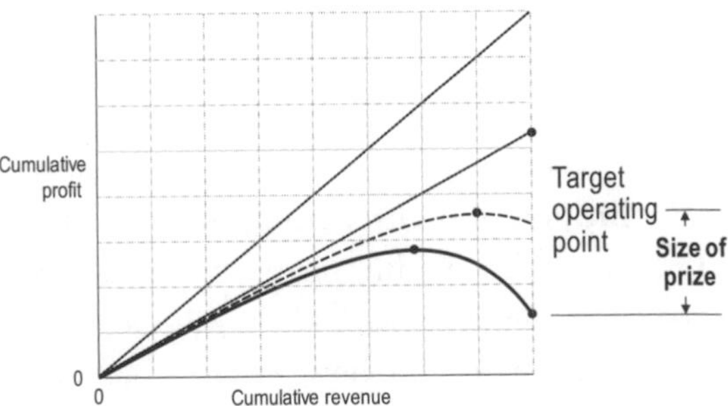

What follows is a more detailed explanation of these steps. We'll then show you an example and wrap up the chapter with a discussion of how to use the result to help you imagine new possibilities for your company.

Start with a good answer, then make it better

We call this the "1-day/1-week/1-month answer" approach. If you had to answer this question in 1 day, how would you do it? Our recommendation is to finish this three-step process by the end of the day using available information and estimates where you don't have information. While this will result in a certainly questionable answer, it would be much better than spending a day performing detailed analysis around a small piece of the problem.

Next, consider what you would do better if you had a week to determine the size of the prize; what part of the analysis would you do with greater rigor? And so on. This gets you to an answer quickly and then improves that answer over time. Once it is good enough, move on.

This approach keeps you focused on analysis that adds necessary detail to the answer and, therefore, streamlines your efforts toward finding a good enough number for the size of the prize. In other words, start with a complete answer (i.e., the three-step process) and then add detail to get a better answer. Completion is understanding, whereas detail is precision. Starting with precision before understanding can lead to wasting a great deal of time and effort on less important analysis, resulting in a lot of information but no answer.

With that in mind, immediately after reading this chapter (and all the more so after the rest of this book), we encourage you to use the three-step process to quickly estimate the size of your prize (though you may not want to share it with anyone just yet). If you don't feel comfortable with your information, then force yourself to make assumptions. Now ask yourself, Why don't you believe your answer? The answer to that question tells you where you need to conduct more analysis.

Step 1: Calculate the lower bound

Your lower bound is simply the peak profit point on your Whale Curve, so to determine your lower bound you must start by constructing your Whale Curve.

To construct your Whale Curve, we recommend starting with data that you have, however insufficient, and then making focused adjustments to make the curve good enough to give you a reasonable lower bound for our purposes.

This usually means starting with what we call a "simple" Whale Curve, one based on your standard margin data, however imperfect. Start with the most profitable revenue dollar, add the next most profitable, and so on to determine the peak point on the curve (this may be by product, by customer, by region or segment, or some matrix of these—you decide what is most relevant and revealing).

Though imperfect, the simple Whale Curve can be telling. It can show concentration of costs and can be useful for identifying areas of complexity reduction opportunity—and it is very easy to construct. However, this simple curve is usually insufficient because it invariably underestimates the opportunity. Standard cost and margin figures reflect corporate decisions regarding allocation of overhead, which almost always underrepresent the impact of complexity—and the benefit from removing it.

For example, most companies apply overhead like a tax, spreading it evenly across products, regions, customers, etc., per unit or as a percentage of cost or revenue. But small volume and more complex items usually consume much greater portions of overhead, or shared costs, per unit than do larger volume or less complex items (by items we mean products, customers, regions, business units, etc.).

Similarly, when companies try to develop fully loaded cost figures, they typically use some rule of thumb to "gross up" costs to cover SG&A. For example, if SG&A costs equal 55% of overall COGS, then the fully loaded cost for an item is simply its portion of COGS plus 55%. But on a per unit basis, low-volume items typically consume more SG&A costs than do high-volume items.

In both cases, whether allocating overhead to determine gross margins or SG&A costs to determine operating profits, larger volume items are usually over-costed while smaller-volume items are under-costed. Therefore, to get a much more accurate Whale Curve, you must correct for these "peanut butter spread" methods for allocating overhead and SG&A costs (see sidebar).

The need to adjust costs

Typical accounting methods for allocating costs spread overhead evenly across products, segments, regions, etc. based on typical revenue or unit volume. This is an accounting view. An operations view shows that overhead is not incurred evenly but rather is concentrated in certain areas. For example, in Chapter 6, you'll find a description of how low-volume products and products with high variation in demand consume disproportionate levels of overhead.

Take the overhead costs of a warehouse spread over several product lines. High-volume products are typically produced much more frequently and spend much less time in the warehouse than low-volume products do. So it is the latter products, the ones with low sales volume, that comprise the greater part of the inventory sitting in a warehouse—meaning they take up disproportionate warehouse capacity per unit. An accounting view that divides inventory or warehouse costs equally per unit does not reflect the reality of having low sales volumes taking up warehouse space. An operations view shifts the warehouse costs to the low-volume items.

Taking an 80/20 approach, the inventory costs for the highest volume products might be shifted to the lowest volume ones. While this may not be precise, it is more accurate.

Complexity-adjusted costing typical involves correcting for overhead allocations through a combination of adjustments across three categories:

- **Broad-brush corrections across large chunks of the portfolio** (products, customers, segments, dealers, etc.) or the entire portfolio itself, using various rules of thumb that represent a large improvement over the peanut butter spread rule of thumb. (For example, we will show later that inventory costs, rather than fitting a peanut butter spread, usually vary with the square root of volume, meaning, other things being equal, a product with 4 times the volume of another will in total have twice the inventory costs—or half the inventory costs per unit.)
- **Adjustments targeted at a small portion of the portfolio** (a single item or family of items) due to cost impacts unique to that portion of the portfolio. For example, consider the nutritionals company that had one product with a 4-day setup time (due to cleaning requirements for just that product) compared to a 10–15 hour setup time for all its other products. The company should consider manually adjusting the spread of plant overhead costs for this particular item.
- **Adjustments targeted at a specific area of costs** if that area is significant and the costs do not fit a rule of thumb or standard method. For example, consider the chemical company whose R&D costs to maintain its products were significant and varied across its products in a manner that wasn't adequately captured by any rule of thumb.

The exact nature of the corrections will depend in large part on the nature of your business and how your costs are actually allocated. The basic principle is that you want to look at costs and ask whether their allocation reflects the reality of how costs are incurred in your business—that is, you need to take an operations rather than an accounting view. (Part II of this book will dive deeper into the interactions across the Complexity Cube and will shed light on many of the areas in which to best correct for these "misallocations.")

Remember, too, that our goal is to get a reasonably good estimate and one much better than your standard costing data, though not necessarily a precise answer. Don't waste time trying to make sure all your non-value-add costs are accurately distributed. Rather, focus on the few large cost categories that account for the majority of the cost differences (what we call 80/20 costing).

Step 2: Calculate the upper bound

The upper bound of the playing field is the theoretical total cost of complexity in your business. It represents removal of *all* complexity costs. While this is certainly unattainable (as it would require removal of all complexity, which, in addition to being impractical, would make you uncompetitive), knowing the total costs of complexity to your business is useful for providing both a boundary for this size-of-the-prize triangulation procedure and a baseline to compare progress as complexity costs start to drop.

As we discussed earlier, it is reasonable to treat non-value-add costs and complexity costs as one and the same. Therefore, to calculate the upper bound—the theoretical cost of complexity—we determine the total non-value-add costs in the company. As we explained in Chapter 4, rather than try to add NVA costs bottom up, determine NVA top down by calculating VA costs directly and subtracting them from your total costs.

Let's consider a simple product example. For a given item (a TV, a bottle of water, a pen), the VA costs of the item are simply the cost of the raw materials in the item plus the direct cost to convert the raw materials into the product.

All other costs (e.g., design, marketing, sales, distribution, maintenance, inventory, waste) are NVA from the consumers' point of view. This is very different from the "standard cost" of an item, which is typically loaded with an often significant allocation of NVA costs.

Determining raw materials costs should be rather straightforward. A little more difficult is putting a number to conversion costs. The time spent on the manufacturing line actually converting the raw materials or components into the finished product is VA. The time spent changing over or setting up the line to produce the product is not; neither is planned or unplanned downtime. Separating manufacturing costs into value-add and non-value-add requires some analysis, but a reasonably good estimate can be obtained fairly easily.

The total value-add cost for a product-only company is the VA cost per item times the volume delivered of that item summed across all products. For the product-only company, this is the overall measure of the costs directly attributable to the value delivered to the consumer. However, we recognize that few companies are product only; most have some component of services delivered with their products, and many companies provide only services. Estimating value-add costs is harder in these cases, but it can be done (see sidebar).

Once you have that number, you just subtract it from your total costs. The result is your estimate of total NVA costs (which we are using as our proxy for complexity costs, for reasons discussed in Chapter 4, p. 70).

Step 3: Pick a stretch target

Now you will have three points of reference and can triangulate between them:

1) The original revenue-profit operating point (end point of the Whale Curve)

2) The peak of a complexity-adjusted Whale Curve (the floor or lower bound)

Summing value-add costs in a service company

VA cost may not be as tangible in a service company as in a product company, but we can take the same approach in breaking down what is and what isn't value-add to the consumer. First, in any company, there are a host of functions that are necessary for the company to function but are not involved directly with delivering the service to the consumer. The costs of all those enabling functions are NVA to the customer even though they are VA to the business (remember that NVA doesn't necessarily mean "not important"). This quickly and significantly narrows down where we are looking to find VA costs.

Similar to conversion costs for a product company, the VA cost is only that cost associated directly with the activities that comprise the service being delivered to the consumer. This requires a bit more discernment into what value-add activities are than on a manufacturing line. Take a tax preparer. The time spent advertising, hiring employees, and training is not value-add. Neither is the time producing reports or adding up sales numbers. *Only the time actually spent preparing a customer's tax return is value-add to the consumer.* The time booting up the tax software is not. Typically, from the eyes of the customer, management is NVA.

Just as we noted in the main text, the goal here is to get a reasonable estimate of NVA versus VA cost only for those resources involved in directly providing the service to the customer. Keep in mind that, for many companies, the larger driver of what are VA versus NVA costs is the delineation of what resources are involved in delivering the service and what activities actually constitute the service. Often, the more minor driver is the estimated allocation of resources time between activities.

3) An estimate of the total NVA costs in the business (the ceiling or upper bound)

The issue now is how much you can shift your Whale Curve. Essentially, how much less expensive can you make complexity to your organization? In terms of the profit versus revenue graphs shown earlier, that will mean moving the "peak profit" up and to the right (you get not only more revenue but also more cumulative profit from that revenue).

Shifting the curve brings us back to the two-pronged approach: removing some complexity and making the rest less expensive to deliver. How do you accomplish the latter? There are two ways:

1) **Improve how your business operates in the face of complexity and is able to deliver it.** By improving processes, work practices, organizational structures, systems, and even culture, you can make complexity less expensive to your organization. How much better can your company operate? By understanding the interactions that will be outlined in Part

II and the battle strategies that will be described in Part III, you will be much better equipped to answer this.

2) **Spread the costs over more revenue.** Either increase revenue for the same amount of complexity or reduce complexity while keeping revenue (having the opposite effect of holding on to complexity during a revenue contraction). For example, if you are able to remove complexity (remove a product, close a channel, etc.) but shift much of its revenue to other items, you will increase the revenue over which the remaining complexity is spread and, therefore, shift your Whale Curve. This can be a powerful lever for removing complexity costs.

It is important to understand and assess the impact of reducing the complexity in the portfolio versus focusing on making the existing complexity less expensive or, more likely, a combination of the two.

You can visualize the opportunity from cutting complexity in your current Whale Curve: imagine chopping off the tail of the curve (plus making other strategic cuts we'll discuss in Part II). In doing so, you'll minimize the amount of profit-losing complexity (the drop-off) that occurs to the right of the peak. And you can envision the impact of making complexity less expensive—which is reflected on the Whale Curve by stretching it so that the peak is higher and to the right—effectively minimizing the amount of profit-losing complexity.

For many firms, a sensible anchor point will be closer to the peak of your current Whale Curve—that is, setting a smaller "stretch" goal. They may recognize that the biggest sources of complexity cost are related to their product and service proliferation (it's the products/services beyond the peak of the Whale Curve that introduce huge elements of cost), yet there is little opportunity for shifting revenue to remaining products. They may have a relatively simple organization structure and not too much in the way of process issues.

Many other firms could quite logically pick an anchor nearer to the NVA cost ceiling, which translates as "much bigger cuts in complexity costs." This is reasonable in companies with a lot of process and organizational complexity driving costs or a lot of revenue substitutability between products, or both. Pushing the target closer to the ceiling also makes sense if your assessment of the situation leads you to believe that the ability to deliver complexity cheaply will be a critical capability in your industry.

Some management teams will be tempted to ignore the "eliminate complexity" part of this equation and try to push to the very top of the ceiling in making complexity less expensive: "We want to keep everything we've got but do it cheaper." We understand and can sympathize with the desire to avoid making difficult decisions about what to cut from a portfolio. But as we have emphasized throughout the book, you can't push efforts at making complexity very far unless you also trim the portfolio (and vice versa). The two issues are interlinked.

> **Revenue substitutability**
>
> Revenue substitutability means the likelihood that customers will shift their purchase dollars to other products/services in your portfolio if a particular product or service is cut. Obviously, finding a product with high revenue substitutability makes it a likely target for elimination, because in doing so you can simplify your portfolio (and lose the associated complexity costs) without losing the revenue it generates.

Just how close can you get to the ceiling? You can never get to the top. There will always be some level of non-value-add cost in the business, because no organization will ever be 100% efficient. But it is important to know the ceiling—not so you will reach it, but so you will move ever closer.

This is an iterative process and it does not have to be exact, but simply going through the approach will drive debate around what needs to happen to reach desired cost levels. How far can you stretch?

Parts II and III will give you the necessary perspectives and battle strategies to make a good estimate of your organization's ability to stretch. For now, however, consider the following rules of thumb (see Figure 23):

10% stretch: For most organizations, even those with relatively developed processes and little revenue substitutability, a 10% stretch is within reach. A significant amount of NVA cost creeps in with a large portfolio even if the company has strong process and organizational discipline.

30% stretch: For larger organizations with many (unimproved) legacy processes and significant product complexity *or* significant revenue substitutability, a 30% stretch is ambitious but appropriate.

50% stretch: For more extreme cases, significant complexity issues in your processes and organization and significant revenue substitutability might combine to make as much as a 50% stretch possible.

Figure 23: "Stretch" Rules of Thumb

Revenue substitutability	Process/Organization complexity: Low	Process/Organization complexity: High
High	20% – 40%	30% – 50%
Low	10% – 30%	20% – 40%

Companies with little Process/Organization complexity and lower revenue substitutability (i.e., less than half of the revenue of deleted products, channels, etc. would be expected to transfer to remaining products, channels, etc.) may expect to stretch their Whale Curve by between 10% and 30%. Companies with a large amount of Process/Organization complexity or high revenue substitutability should expect a 20% to 40% stretch. Companies with both high Process/Organization complexity and high revenue substitutability can expect between a 30% and 50% stretch.

"Sizing the Prize" Example

Company XYZ has revenue of $10 billion and 8% operating profit. Its total cost base is, therefore, $9.2 billion. The company's CEO suspects there is too much complexity in the business—across all dimensions (product, process, and organization)—and asks his CFO to determine what the size of the prize might be from waging a war on complexity costs.

To get going, the CFO first creates a Whale Curve using product revenue and standard margin and cost data (see Figure 24 and Figure 25). The curve shows that 55% of the company's products (accounting for 88% of its revenue) delivers 140% of its total profit, with the remaining 45% of its products being unprofitable. But the standard cost and margin figures reflect broad peanut butter allocations of overhead and other NVA costs—generally adding too much cost to higher-volume, more profitable products and too little to lower-volume, less profitable products.

Figure 24: Example Product-Profit Whale Curve

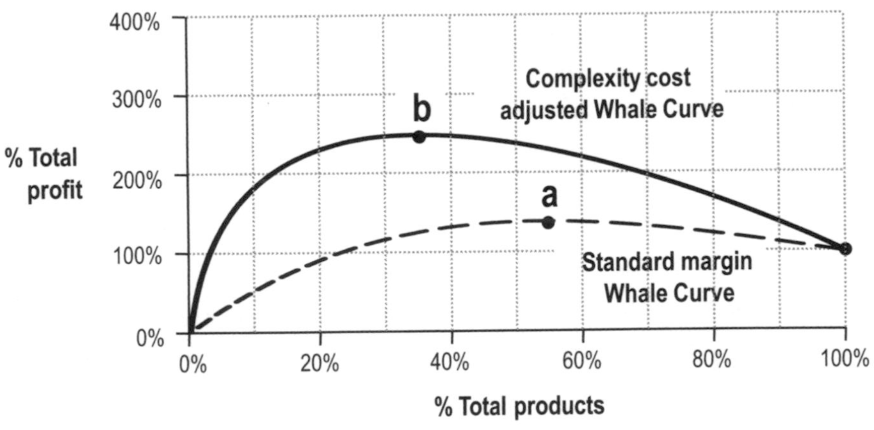

The Whale Curve built from standard margin data shows that only 55% of products are profitable, accounting for 140% of total profit (**point a**), with the remaining 45% of products destroying 40% of total profit. However, as is often the case, by spreading overhead evenly across products the standard margin figures underrepresent the true cost of lower-volume products and overrepresent that of higher-volume products. Adjusting for these costs results in the complexity-adjusted Whale Curve, the peak of which (**point b**) shows that only 35% of products are truly profitable, accounting for 250% of total profits.

Figure 25: Example Revenue-Profit Whale Curve

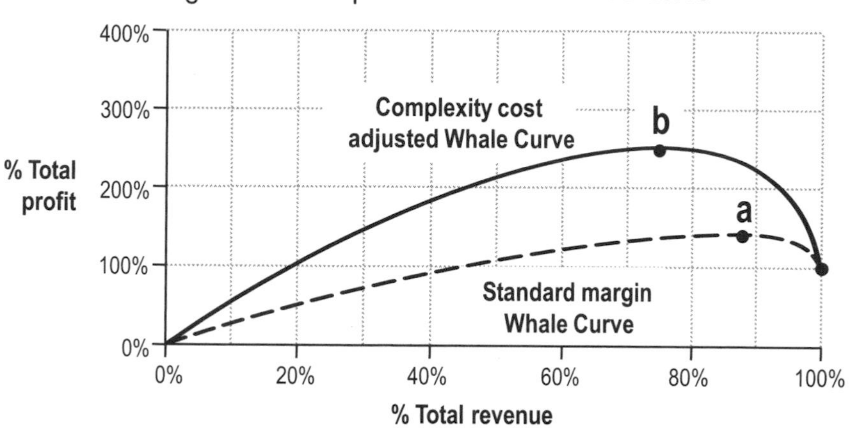

This chart translates Company XYZ's *product*-profit Whale Curve into a *revenue*-profit Whale Curve. The standard margin Whale Curve suggests that 88% of revenue is profitable revenue (**point a**), with 12% of revenue-destroying profit; but by accounting for true drivers of NVA costs, the complexity-adjusted Whale Curve shows that 25% of revenue is actually profit destroying (**point b**).

However, by taking an 80/20 approach to reallocating the larger categories of NVA costs (in this case, primarily plant overhead and SG&A costs) based on the true drivers of these costs, the CFO found that closer to only 35% of the company's products are profitable—accounting for 75% of revenue and *250% of the company's overall profit.*

This sets the lower bound for the size of the prize: a 250% increase in operating profit, from $0.8 billion to $2.0 billion, coupled with a 25% drop in revenue, from $10 billion to $7.5 billion (this corresponds to a rise in operating income from 8% to almost 27%). While this is certainly significant cost reduction and profit improvement, it comes with a large loss in revenue and leaves further cost-reduction opportunity on the table.

The next step is to establish the upper bound. The CFO determines that of its $9.2 billion total cost base, roughly half are NVA costs. Clearly, it's impossible to remove all NVA costs, but this is a useful reference point for triangulating on the size of the prize.

With these points the senior executive team is able to triangulate on a new target revenue-profit operating point and establish the size of the prize. After assessing the company's performance against the interactions on the three faces of the Complexity Cube and after reviewing the battle strategies for removing complexity costs, the executive team estimates that it can make its complexity 30% less expensive (i.e., it can remove almost a third of the waste associated with complexity). It is easy at this point to plot the "30% stretch" curve, which represents shifting each point of the Whale Curve 30% of the way from its current position to the upper bound line. You can do the math in an Excel spreadsheet or, as we've done, plot the new curve (see Figure 26).

Figure 26: Graphic Model for Sizing the Prize

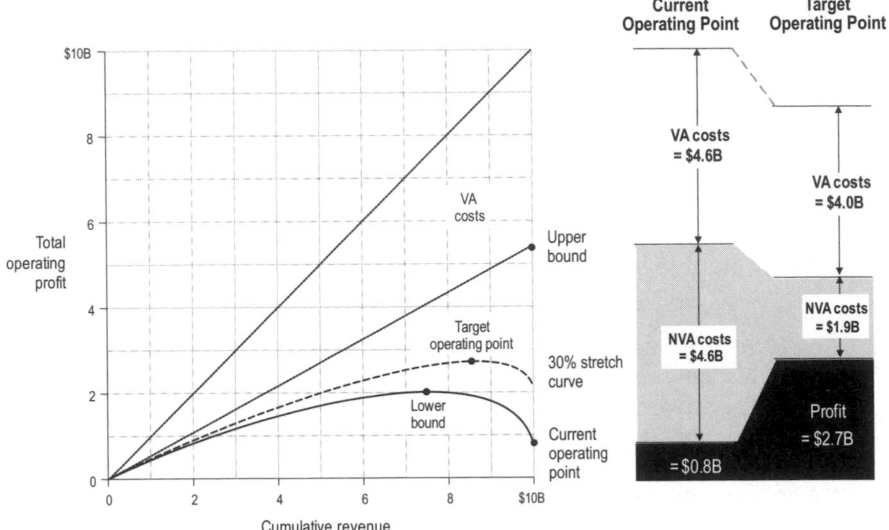

Table E: Sizing the Prize Calculations

	Current operating point	Removing complexity *alone* (lower bound)	Making complexity less expensive *alone*	***Both* actions** (target operating point)
Revenue	$10.0B	$7.5B	$10.0B	$8.6B
Total cost base	$9.2B	$5.5B	$7.8B	$5.9B
Operating profit ($)	$0.8B	$2.0B	$2.2B	$2.7B
Operating profit (%)	8%	26.7%	21.8%	31.5%
Cost savings ($)*	N/A	$1.2B	$1.4B	$1.9B
Cost savings (%)	N/A	13.0%	15.0%	20.9%

** Equals increase in operating profit. Does not include decrease in cost base simply due to reduction in revenue.*

The target operating point (the peak of the shifted curve and the "size of the prize") represents almost a $2 billion increase in operating profit (a 20% cost reduction on the $10 billion business). Other figures are shown in Table E, above.

Next: Re-imagine your business

Working through the steps above provides you with an understanding of the amount of NVA cost in the business, a deeper appreciation of how profit is concentrated in your business, a number of initial clues as to the drivers of cost in your business, and a revised set of financial statements for a less complex version of your business. This number is what your business could be: the gap between that and the current costs is the size of the prize.

The biggest benefit of sizing the prize is that it can force you to re-imagine what your business could be in the future with less complexity—and with an improved ability to operate in the face of and to deliver complexity.

Think about what your product portfolio and your organization would need to look like to generate the kinds of numbers associated with your stretch target. Now consider what would be required to support the business.

- Who are your customers, and what is their demand?
- What would your production and distribution footprint look like?
- What processes are still required? How are they different from today?
- What would that mean for labor, overhead, and capital?

These and other questions will shape the parameters for a re-imagined cost structure.

This process of identifying costs associated with a "peak profit" portfolio itself has important side benefits: initial insights into the key cost drivers and potential avenues for cost reduction. As you ponder what it would take to support a less complex business, it is only natural to wonder why the current state has the excess costs that it does.

You may take further steps to calibrate the number. But remember the purpose here is to identify the grounded but aspirational size of the prize that warrants this topic a place on the CEO agenda.

The work to attain the size of the prize then begins—using the clues and motivation from this process, as you develop a detailed battle plan.

What the CEO Needs to Know

This chapter has laid out the methodology for sizing the prize. Our approach recognizes that until companies have a sense of the magnitude of the opportunity, the issue does not get elevated to the top of the management agenda. Therefore, the key is to **quickly and relatively easily** get a sense of the size of the opportunity.

We believe that it's a critical first step to putting some bounds around the size of the issue.

Moreover, we'd encourage every CEO, CFO, COO, and senior executive to seek out answers to the key questions that will dictate the appetite for change:

- How much complexity cost is in our organization? (the total cost of complexity)
- How much of this can or should we target to take out? (the size of the prize)
- Where are the major opportunities for claiming these cost benefits?

The goal here is to recognize that this issue is one that cannot be ignored nor addressed with low ambition. The words of a famous Italian ring as true today as they did 500 years ago:

> *The greatest danger for most of us is not that our aim is too high and we miss it, but that it is too low and we reach it.*[33]

Chapter 5 Endnotes

33 Michelangelo.

Part II

Know Thine Enemy

The Faces of Complexity and Implications for Battle

Introduction to Part II

The secret of all victory lies in the organization of the nonobvious.
— Marcus Aurelius, Roman emperor and philosopher

In Part I, we laid out the imperative for waging war on complexity costs. If you worked through estimating the size of the prize for your business, you may have already developed some initial thoughts about where and how complexity is affecting your business. In Part II, we will help you further identify the biggest areas of opportunity by assessing common sets of symptoms and what that means for where you should start. We will delve more deeply into understanding how the product, process, and organization dimensions of complexity interact to create costs; we will analyze what that tells us about the best battle strategies for reducing those costs.

The interactions between the dimensions form the **faces** of the Complexity Cube we introduced in Chapter 2. Each face—each set of interactions—creates a different set of issues that as a whole add up to a powerful enemy. We've given these faces special labels that reflect their relationship to complexity, as shown in Figure 27, and we will cover each of the three faces in separate chapters:

Figure 27: The Faces of Complexity

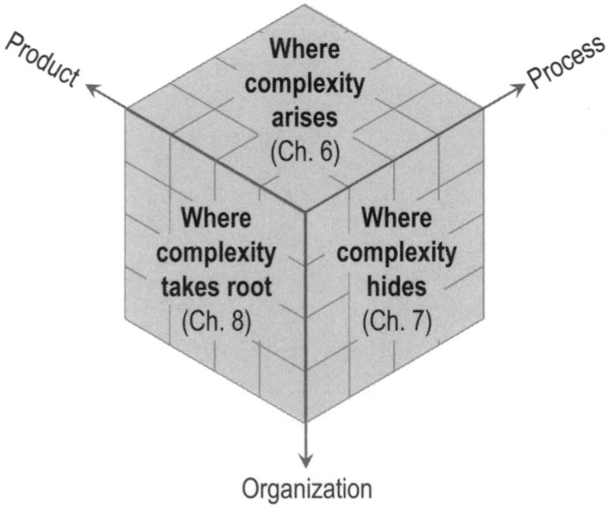

- Chapter 6 will discuss the **Product/Process face—where complexity most often arises:** Complexity often originates with the addition of new products or product variants. Whether based on customer need or not, increased variety in products and services can significantly affect the processes needed to provide those products.

- Chapter 7 will cover the **Process/Organization face—where complexity typically hides:** As we noted in Part I, the impact and costs of complexity are systemic; they spread across your processes and the organizational structures needed to support those processes. But typical accounting practices cannot tease out what parts of process and organizational costs are due to complexity, so they lie hidden within traditional financial statements. And it is very difficult to attack something you cannot see.
- Chapter 8 will dive into the **Organization/Product face—where complexity takes root:** To support the increased variety in products and services, and the processes producing those offerings, organizational structures are created, functions are staffed, factories and depots are built, and so on. While product portfolios can in theory flux very quickly in response to customer feedback and insights, the supporting organizational elements tend to drag. Put another way, once complexity has crept into this face, it can be hard to remove. That's why we call this the face where complexity takes root, where the issues tend to solidify and remain trapped.

In sum, complexity arises on the Product/Process face, where process issues and ill-defined customer needs can lead to overproliferation of products and services. That problem is compounded on the Process/Organization face, where complexity lies hidden in the weeds of procedures and structures, undetected by traditional financial accounting. The problem is compounded further as complexity takes root on the Organization/Product face, solidifying and remaining trapped. There is very little defense anywhere in here against increasing complexity.

The net result for many companies is that once complexity is introduced, it gets "absorbed" into the organization and eventually takes root—a one-way street. It is possible to reverse that trend, but only through a deep understanding of complexity dynamics, how they are influencing your organization today, and what that means in terms of battle strategies most likely to generate results in reducing complexity costs.

The fact that each dimension interacts with the others is why we emphasized the need for multi-dimensional action in Part I. For example, while product or service complexity is an issue for many firms, they can extract full benefit only by considering the issue in the context of processes or organizational elements (such as assets put in place to support the creation and delivery of complexity). So while it is tempting to reduce the issue of complexity costs to the *axes* of the cube—to treat each type of complexity separately—you must realize that the real issues and opportunities reside on the *faces* of the cube.

In the following chapters, we will examine each face of the Complexity Cube and describe the following:

- **Common symptoms.** Understanding how the interactions manifest themselves will help you begin to recognize the biggest opportunities for your organization. When launching your campaign, it helps to focus first on the face (the set of interactions) that reflect your biggest issues, though your efforts may end up touching the other faces as well.
- **Major interactions.** The dimensions of complexity interact in unique ways. It is critical to understand the dynamics and interactions that characterize each face to understand how best to formulate your response and where best to begin.
- **Key implications for battle.** Given these interactions, what are the implications for battle? What do you need to keep in mind when going after complexity costs on a particular face? For example, organizational and product complexity have a tendency to trap each other; what does that imply for uprooting complexity costs on that face?
- **Recommended high-value battle strategies.** Which battle strategies are best suited for attacking complexity costs on a particular face? Details of the commonly used strategies will be given in Part III. In Part II, we will show the links between the interactions and the best strategies for tackling them.

By reading Part II, therefore, we hope you will gain a deeper understanding of the nature of complexity and specifically how the dimensions of complexity interact to create costs. You will become more aware of common symptoms of complexity problems and from these be able to start evaluating which face of complexity represents your priority target. Lastly, you will be able to start assessing the best approaches for attacking complexity in your organization.

DEEP DIVE #3

The Juice Dilemma

A Case Study on How a Larger Portfolio Can Lead to Smaller Profits

The rest of Part II discusses the different faces of complexity—the interactions between products, processes, and organizational elements. But before going there, let's first anchor on what those interactions look and feel like in the real world. This Deep Dive provides a case study to demonstrate what we mean by interactions between dimensions of complexity.

The chapter walks through the story of the fictional Morley Farms, a producer of organic juices that is considering expanding its product line. Though we've set up Morley Farms as a rather simple business, the case study is based on real interactions. It illustrates how adding product variety can deteriorate profitability and process performance, even if it increases revenues at the same time. We will dive right into describing Morley Farms and its business environment, discuss the impact of adding varieties to its product line, and show how an understanding of the impact of complexity can alter fundamental business decisions and strategies. At the end of the case, we highlight further implications on product lifecycle management, process flexibility, and investments of capital in capacity.

Background on Morley Farms

Morley Farms, Inc., is a small, family-owned business that presses, bottles, and sells award-winning organic juices. It has a small but cohesive management team. Ben Williams, who founded and still owns most of the company, serves as the company's president and general manager of its only plant. The rest of Morley's management team consists of its operations manager and its sales and marketing manager.

Morley Farms currently produces just three types of juice: cherry, blueberry, and raspberry. Morley sells its juices directly to local stores for $100 a crate. It makes 20% gross margins on each of its three juices. Its total product costs, therefore, are $80 per crate, broken down as follows:

Table F: Initial Cost per Unit

Raw materials costs ($/crate)	**$28**
Conversion costs ($/crate)	**$50**
Finished goods inventory costs ($/crate)	**$2**
Total cost per unit ($/crate)	**$80**

- **Raw materials costs** include the costs of all the ingredients (the fruit, water, organic sugar, etc.), disposal of waste products (fruit remains), and packaging (bottles, labels, crating). Raw materials costs are equal across the juices.
- **Conversion costs** include all the costs Morley Farms incurs to convert the raw materials into a packaged product ready for sale. This includes labor, utilities, consumables (e.g., lubricants, cleaning agents), and allocated equipment and facilities costs for pressing, processing, bottling, and packaging. Labor is the dominant conversion cost, and the same labor is required whether the employees are producing product or changing over the line. Further, other conversion costs correlate with labor costs, meaning that if labor doubles then we can assume that conversion costs also double.
- **Finished goods (FG) inventory costs** include storage and handling costs and any capital charge for tying up working capital. Overall FG inventory costs are proportional to overall average inventory levels; that is, if inventory is doubled then inventory costs are too. (For simplicity, we will ignore raw materials inventory costs.)

On its single production line, Morley produces a run of each of the three juices each day, so its **cycle time interval** (CTI)—the time from when it starts making a given juice to when it starts making it again—is 24 hours. For simplicity we will assume that Morley operates 24 hours a day, 7 days a week, and that there is neither equipment breakdown nor downtime needed for maintenance. (While these are certainly unrealistic assumptions, being more realistic here would only complicate the math later and does not affect the complexity principles at work or invalidate the conclusions; so we hope you will forgive these simplifying assumptions.)

It takes line operators 1 hour to change the line from producing one type of juice to producing another (setup time = 1 hour). Because Morley produces a run of each of its three juices each day, 3 hours out of every 24 (or 12.5%) are lost to setups. The remainder of the time is spent producing product.

One final assumption we need to point out: Morley's inventory profile for each of its three juices resembles a classic sawtooth profile, where product is consumed at a steady rate between new batches (see Figure 28). While this would likely not be the case (product would likely be consumed in clumps, such as truckloads of product being shipped out), it is a reasonable simplifying assumption for this analysis.

Figure 28: Cherry, Blueberry, and Raspberry Inventory Profiles

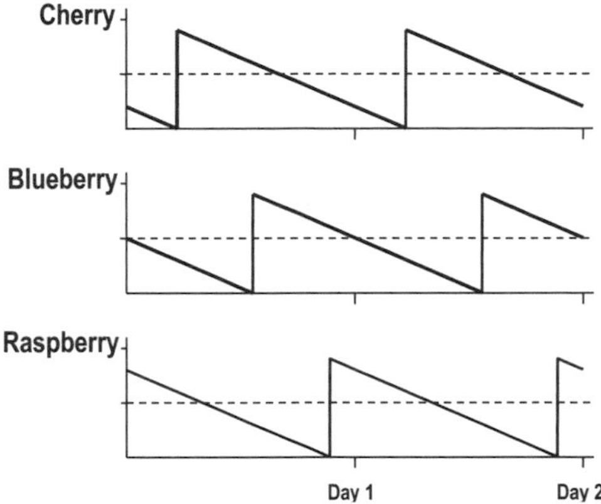

Morley Farms produces a production run of each of its three juices each day. Demand is steady, and to simplify the analysis, we will assume the inventory profile of each juice resembles the classic sawtooth pattern.

This, then, is the base case:

- three juices
- 24-hour cycle time
- $80 unit cost
- 20% gross margin

The Opportunity

After rigorous market research involving both its customers (local stores) and its end consumers, Morley's sales and marketing manager recommends to the rest of the management team that the company also offer pomegranate and blackberry juices. Her research shows that although there would be some cannibalization of existing sales, overall sales volume would increase by 10%; and since the new juices would also be sold for $100/crate, revenues would increase by 10% as well.

The key question facing Ben Williams is whether to offer the two new juice varieties. There is no capital available for investment in new plants, production lines, or additional equipment. Morley has already worked hard to reduce its setup time to an hour, and the management team is sure that further reductions are not possible given their equipment. On the other hand, an additional 10% in sales and revenue is certainly attractive, and Ben is confident that they can squeeze another 10% of volume out of the plant.

The Analysis

While the research shows that adding pomegranate and blackberry juices would raise the top line by 10%—and within the scope of this case, the market research is assumed correct—Ben knows that the key question concerns the impact to the bottom line. To help answer this question, Ben asks his operations manager, Daniel, to determine what the impact would be on operations and to Morley's overall cost per unit from adding pomegranate and blackberry juices to their portfolio.

Impact on Operations

What is the impact on operations from adding two more juices and 10% more volume? To answer this question, Daniel considers the impact on each portion of the unit cost bar (raw materials, conversion costs, and FG inventory costs).

Raw materials costs are the easiest for Daniel to analyze. Given the earlier assumptions and constraints, he determines that they are equal, at $28 per crate, across all the juices whether making three different juices or five. Conversion and FG inventory costs require more analysis, and to do this Daniel finds it helpful to think through a few different approaches:

1) What would happen if they tried to fit in the two additional juice varieties **without changing the CTI** (meaning that each juice would be produced once every 24 hours)?

2) What would happen if they focused instead on **maintaining time lost to setup at 12.5%**? (Per the constraints we laid out, they cannot reduce setup time, so that would mean they could do only three changeovers a day and, therefore, could *not* produce all five juices in any 24-hour period.)

3) How could this work if they drove for the **10% additional volume**?

Here is Daniel's analysis of those three scenarios (the results are summarized in a Table H on p. 106).

Scenario 1: Same cycle time interval

First, Daniel considers the impact on operations from producing a run of each of the five juices each day. He realizes

- Time lost to setup would increase from 3 hours to 5 hours, or from 12.5% to just over 20% of the time
- More time setting up means less time producing
- Greater setup cost and lower production volume would undoubtedly increase conversion costs per unit

Furthermore, reducing the portion of time spent producing *goes in the opposite direction from increasing production volume 10%*—meaning this scenario is a nonstarter.

Scenario 2: Same time lost to setup

Next, Daniel considers how Morley Farms could produce each of the 5 juices—with their combined 5 hours of setup per cycle—while keeping the portion of time lost to setup the same as that in the base case (12.5%). After a little thought, he realizes that with setup time fixed, the only way to keep the portion of time lost to setup at 12.5% is to **increase the CTI to 40 hours**, meaning that a production run of each juice will be made once every 40-hour period (5 hours is one-eighth, or 12.5%, of 40 hours). Another way to look at this is to look at the time lost to setup as a fraction:

$$\text{Portion of time lost to setup} = \frac{\text{Time lost to setups during one cycle}}{\text{Cycle time interval}}$$

Because he can't reduce the numerator (each setup is fixed at 1 hour), Daniel correctly determines that his only alternative is to increase the denominator, the CTI.

On reflection, he also realizes that by setting the portion of time lost to setup equal to that of the base case, conversion costs per unit would also be equal to that of the base case. But when he considers the impact on inventory costs and on the line's ability to deliver 10% additional volume, he realizes those effects may be a deal breaker:

- With a sawtooth inventory profile, average inventory levels are proportional to batch size (Chapter 6 contains an explanation of why this is so)
- Because the plant would still average 3 production runs each day, and each production run would still average about 7 hours, **batch sizes would be about the same as in the base case**
- Therefore, inventory levels would also be about the same as in the base case *per product*
- But because there are now two additional products, **inventory levels will increase by about two-thirds**

Daniel becomes more disappointed when he realizes that since the portion of time lost to setup is the same as that in the base case, the portion of time spent producing would also be the same, and the production volume would, therefore, be no different from in the base case. **That means this scenario is also a nonstarter.** Because Morley Farms must make 10% more volume, another approach is needed.

Scenario 3: Increase production time (and, therefore, volume) by 10%

Daniel now feels that he has a pretty good grip on the dynamics between setup times, CTI, production volume, and inventory. He decides to begin with the requirement for making 10% more volume. Because the production rate is fixed (per the constraints of this case), it is clear that to produce 10% more volume, the plant must produce 10% more of the time.

In the base case, 12.5% of the time is changing over the line and 87.5% is spent producing. To produce 10% more volume, the time spent producing must be increased from 87.5% to 96.25% (87.5% multiplied by 1.1). This leaves only 3.75% of the time for setup.

Base case 87.5% of time is production

+ 10% = 87.5 × 1.1 = 96.25% production time

Conclusion: 100% – 96.25% = 3.75% *(time available for setup)*

To have 5 hours of setup be only 3.75% of the cycle, Daniel calculates that the CTI must be increased well beyond 24 hours (base case) or even 40 hours (scenario 2) to 5.5 days:

Base case: 3 hours of setup = 12.5% of 24 hours

+ 10% volume scenario: 5 hours of setup has to equal 3.75% of X number of hours

(5 hours/X hours) × 100 = 3.75%

X = (5/3.75) × 100 ≈ 133.3 hours ≈ 5.5 days

While this seems like a rather large answer to Daniel, he realizes that cutting the time lost to setup by 3 or 4 times (from 12.5% to 3.75%) requires that he increase the cycle time over which the setups are spread by 3 or 4 times (from 40 hours to 5.5 days).

Daniel is relieved to determine that the plant is able to make the two additional juice varieties and produce 10% more volume. Also, since the portion of time lost to setup would decrease, conversion costs per unit would also decrease. (Because the overall labor costs would remain unchanged, conversion costs in total would be unchanged; but since these costs would be spread over 10% more volume, conversion costs *per unit* would drop by about 10%.)

The only downside appears to be that **inventory costs per unit increase proportionally to CTI.** Compared to the base case, inventory costs would be 5.5 times that of the base case. While Daniel is disappointed with that news, this is the only scenario that delivers the additional varieties *and* the additional volume.

Daniel sums up his findings for scenario 3:

- Raw materials costs per unit remains unchanged at $28 per crate
- Conversion costs per unit drop by 10% from $50 to $45 per crate
- But FG inventory costs, while small before, rise 5.5 times from $2 to $11 per crate—an increase of $9 per crate

In all, Daniel finds that adding the pomegranate and blackberry varieties increases overall product costs from $80 to $84 per unit, an increase of 5%, for all juice varieties. The full results of his analysis for all three scenarios are shown in Table H, next page.

Impact on Morley Farms

Ben, of course, is disappointed to hear from Daniel that adding the two new juices and delivering 10% more volume will increase cost per unit by 5%. He wonders if adding the two new juice flavors will be good for the company. The question he must now think through is whether the company should take a 5% increase in its cost per unit to make 10% more revenue.

At first, this doesn't sound too bad, but Ben is smart enough to realize that he can't directly compare the incremental *unit* cost figure with the incremental revenue figure (the first figure is per unit, and the number of units will be increasing; the second figure is a total).

Rather than overcomplicating this, Ben decides to consider a simple "before" and "after" case (Table G). In doing so he determines, a little surprisingly, that adding the two additional juices, while increasing revenue, will actually deliver *less* total profit to Morley Farms:

- For every 10 units sold "before," the company would now sell 11
- Revenue will indeed go up, but because of the increase in unit cost, *unit margins will drop from $20 to $16*

Table G: Gross Margin with Two More Products

	Before	After
Number of units sold:	10	11
Total revenue (@ $100/unit)	$1,000	$1,100
Gross margin per unit:	$20	$16
Total gross margin:	$200	$176

Conclusion: Ben would rather make $20 on each of 10 crates for a total $200, than make $16 on each of 11 crates for a total of $176.

Reflecting on this outcome, Ben realizes that the more informative metric is the **decrease in gross margin per unit** (rather than the increase in unit cost). Adding the pomegranate and blackberry juices would drop gross margin per unit from $20 to $16—*a 20% drop*. When reframed this way, it is clear to Ben that he wouldn't take a 20% drop in gross margin per unit to sell 10% more units. (As a side note: Clearly, by looking at the right metrics the answer

Table H: Impact on Process Performance and Product Cost per Unit of Increasing Juice Varieties

Item	Base case	**Scenario #1:** Cycle interval the same *(nonviable)*	**Scenario #2:** % time lost to setup held constant *(nonviable)*	**Scenario #3:** Increase production time **(viable)**
Number of juice varieties	3	5	5	5
Cycle time interval (CTI)	24 hrs	24 hrs	40 hrs	5.5 days
Portion of time lost to setup	12.5%	20.8%	12.5%	3.75%
Portion of time spent in production	87.5%	79.2%	87.5%	96.25%
Production volume (indexed to base case)	1.00	0.90	1.00	1.10
Overall average inventory level (indexed to base case)	1.00	0.90	1.67	6.1
Average inventory level per unit produced (indexed to base case)	1.00	1.00	1.67	5.5
Raw materials cost per unit	$28	$28	$28	$28
Conversion cost per unit	$50	$55	$50	$45
FG inventory cost per unit	$2	$2	$3	$11
Total product cost per unit	$80	$85	$81	$84

This table compares scenarios for making all five juice varieties against the base case. Scenarios #1 and #2 are helpful to understand the dynamics involved but turn out not to be viable options because they don't deliver 10% more production volume. Scenario #3 delivers the 10% volume increase while producing the two new varieties and the three existing varieties but **results in a 5% increase in unit cost for all juice varieties.**

becomes much clearer, but complexity makes it more difficult, rather than less, to identify the right metrics).

Ben is not quite ready to give up. He is a bit perplexed that adding varieties and growing sales would not just yield diminishing returns but actually diminish overall returns to the company. Indeed, sales volume would increase, and the incremental sales would still be at a profit. But then he realizes that although the additional units sold would each be profitable, *adding the new varieties would take away a portion of the profit from each of the larger volume of existing sales.* More specifically, adding the two varieties would take away $40 of margin for every existing 10 crates sold, only to add $16 of margin back in on the 11th, incremental crate sold.

Ben decides to hold off adding pomegranate and blackberry juices to Morley Farms' product portfolio but also decides to pull together his management team to better understand these dynamics and the implications for his company.

Further Insights from Morley Farms

Do the results of the analysis mean that the desire to add new varieties was misguided? And what about the market research that showed a real customer demand for the new juices? The answers to these questions raise some important implications for product lifecycle management, process flexibility, and capital investment.

Product Lifecycle Management

Are pomegranate and blackberry juices duds that the company should avoid? Not necessarily. The market research showed that there was certainly pull in the marketplace—at least enough to raise overall sales volume by 10%. Rather, the analysis in this case focused on the *overall number of juice varieties*, not on any specific combination of varieties. It showed that given Morley Farms' process capabilities and constraints around capital investment, producing five varieties instead of three would be unwise for them. Offering three varieties is better for the company, in terms of its bottom line, *but the analysis didn't identify which three are best.*

All Morley knows at this point is adding the two new juice varieties added costs to the existing flavors. The converse is also true: *the presence of the existing flavors made adding the new ones more costly.* If any existing flavors were in the declining part of their lifecycle, it might be better for Morley to replace them with the new flavors. But they are trapped by conventional business practices where declining products are kept in the portfolio, making it more difficult for new products to join the portfolio without eroding value. The implication is that *companies must be diligent about pruning their portfolio to allow new products to be more successful.*

A second important implication for product lifecycle management involves how costs are allocated among products. As this case shows, and as we've pointed out elsewhere in this book, many costs exist between products—they result only from having a *combination* of products. Here, adding pomegranate and blackberry varieties added $4 per crate to the cost of the cherry, blueberry, and raspberry varieties.

You may make very different portfolio decisions depending on how *covariance* cost is allocated to old products, allocated to new products, or split in some way between them. At Morley, increasing the number of varieties from 3 to 5 adds $4 per crate for all juices, which raises the issue of whether that cost, totaled across all crates, should be assigned entirely to just the new varieties, assigned to just the existing varieties, or shared across all varieties.

Our view is that, generally, these costs should be shifted to products approaching the end of their lifetime (this is the cost to the business, but borne on the rest of the portfolio, from keeping old products around). But this requires having a very clear view of your product lifecycle and where your products are along it. (We will discuss this in more detail in Chapters 9 and 10 on Portfolio Optimization.)

Those of us who speak of allocating complexity costs and of complexity-adjusted costs usually point out the disproportionate cost differences between high- and low-volume products. While that certainly is true, you should not make a decision about what products to keep or cut solely on that basis. Eliminating a product with great promise at the beginning of its lifecycle simply because it has low volume and because complexity-adjusted costs show it to currently be margin poor would be a bad management decision. That would be a choice based on a static view of the organization, which fails to consider a product's future performance. (That's why we recommend that companies develop a more dynamic view of their portfolios and customer needs and incorporate not just what is going on today but also likely future scenarios.)

Process Flexibility

Another perspective to consider here is how traditional applications of Lean, with its focus on setup time reduction, would have attempted to resolve the situation. In this case, we constrained setup times (the dominant metric of process flexibility) to 1 hour. Consider how different this case would have been if setup times could have been reduced from 60 down to 30 minutes. Although we won't redo the analysis here (we'll leave that for our more intense readers), be assured that **setup times of 30 minutes would have reversed the answer!** With 30-minute setups, offering the five varieties instead of the original three delivers more overall margin dollars to the company.

Shorter setup times mean more flexible processes. More flexible processes mean lower cost impact from additional variety. While highlighting the significant impact of *product variety* on process performance, this case underscores rather than detracts from Lean's focus on setup time reduction. (We will discuss this in more detail in Chapter 13, "Enabling Variety with Lean Processes.")

Capital Investment

Let's briefly consider the implications on capital investment. For the sake of simplicity, we excluded the option of adding capacity. It should be clear that given Morley Farms' process capabilities, rather than simply choosing to *not* add the additional juice varieties and gain an additional 10% of revenue, the company should explore opportunities to increase capacity—possibly through targeted capital investment. (But carefully—adding equipment and building new facilities to handle additional product complexity is one of the ways that complexity becomes rooted in a business, the topic we'll discuss in Chapter 8.)

Without understanding the dynamics between setup times, CTI, production volumes, and inventory, it would be difficult, if not impossible, to know where best to target investment, for example, at equipment to reduce setup time, increase line speed, or simply add capacity (more of the same) to the line.

This also plays out on a larger scale. Understanding these dynamics is central to making any decisions regarding investments in capacity, whether specific pieces of equipment or whole plants.

Conclusion

In this simplified case, we saw Ben and his team develop a very good understanding of the complexity dynamics in Morley Farms' operation. But this was a very simple case, with one plant, one production line, and only three products going to five. In real companies with thousands of products facing the addition of hundreds more that often are produced across global supply chains, these dynamics can be very difficult indeed to see. This is why many companies, lured by the potential of revenue growth (like Morley), will add products in good faith. And although some companies will see revenues increase, many find in the end that they suffer a hit to profitability.

Rarely will companies perform the type of thorough analysis that Morley Farms did and have the kind of facts that would show the better choice was to *not* add products or varieties, because doing so would destroy margin.

The broader insight is this: **these dynamics are real whether companies acknowledge and understand them or not!** Our purpose in discussing the interactions in the following pages is to make the issue of removing complexity not more complex but less so. By understanding how the dimensions of complexity interact, you can identify the biggest driver of issues and target your efforts. Knowing what you are looking for is an important first step.

CHAPTER 6

Where Complexity Arises

The Product/Process Face

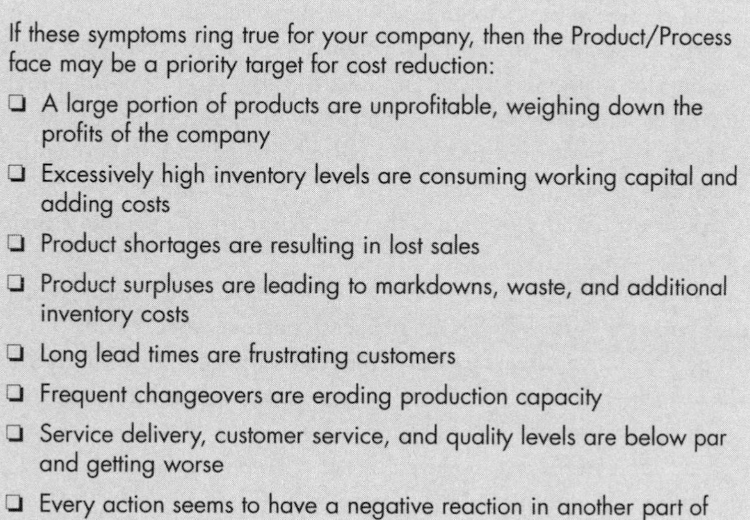

If these symptoms ring true for your company, then the Product/Process face may be a priority target for cost reduction:

- ❑ A large portion of products are unprofitable, weighing down the profits of the company
- ❑ Excessively high inventory levels are consuming working capital and adding costs
- ❑ Product shortages are resulting in lost sales
- ❑ Product surpluses are leading to markdowns, waste, and additional inventory costs
- ❑ Long lead times are frustrating customers
- ❑ Frequent changeovers are eroding production capacity
- ❑ Service delivery, customer service, and quality levels are below par and getting worse
- ❑ Every action seems to have a negative reaction in another part of your operations

Anyone seeking a clear example of Product/Process complexity needs look no further than the supply chain. Wharton professor Marshall L. Fisher has said, "Never has so much technology and brainpower been applied to improving supply chain performance." But he also claimed, "The performance of many supply chains has never been worse,"[34] with many suffering the symptoms listed above.

A *Harvard Business Review* study found that "Despite the increased efficiency of many companies' supply chains, the percentage of products that were marked down in the United Sates rose from less than 10% in 1980 to more than 30% in 2000, and surveys show that consumer satisfaction with product availability fell sharply during the same period."[35]

Why are such issues still so common despite investments in capabilities, in programs, and in technologies such as electronic data interchange? According to Fisher, "the root cause is a mismatch between the type of product and type of supply chain"—a symptom of complexity. And it's getting no better. A recent study reported that "Supply chain risk is rising sharply. The increasing complexity of products and services tops the list of global factors that executives say most influence their supply chain strategies."[36]

As product complexity grows, it strains the processes of a business. When the pain becomes too great, some companies react with product/SKU rationalization or component standardization initiatives. Unfortunately, such efforts usually focus on the product dimension alone. Likewise, attempting to solve the issues by launching process improvement efforts that do not address the variety of items going *through* the process—which ultimately is driven by the product dimension—will also leave opportunity on the table.

But what does poor process performance look like? Typically, a mixture of excessive handoffs, poor coordination, and numerous work-around loops, and high levels of rework driving a combination of long lead times, excessive work-in-process (WIP), poor productivity, impaired quality, and high inventories. All of this ties up working capital and adds costs. And although these costs are the result of poor process performance, they are borne by the products the process delivers.

Product profitability and process performance are, therefore, inextricably linked. **Product variety affects process performance, and, conversely, process performance affects product profitability.** This means that the cost of a product is not an intrinsic property of the product itself, not simply the result of product design alone. More correctly, *the cost of a product is also determined by the performance of the process or processes that deliver it.* (While this may sound like common sense, product profitability is too often judged in isolation of the processes that deliver it.)

We can go an important step further: **the cost of a product is the result of the processes that deliver it *and* everything else going through the same processes.** Product complexity impacts process performance, which in turn impacts the cost of all products delivered by that process.

Therefore, adding a new product doesn't just add the cost of the new product itself, it also *adds some cost, however small, to each of the existing products traveling through the same processes* (as was demonstrated in the preceding Deep Dive, where adding two more varieties to the production line increased the unit cost of the existing varieties by 5%). Conversely, SKU rationalizations, when well executed, not only release the costs associated directly with the deleted products but also improve the overall cost levels of the remaining items because of improved process performance.

The key takeaway is that while most approaches to products and processes are quite static in nature, in reality theirs is a very dynamic relationship. This face is where complexity most often arises—in the additional products or variations added to a portfolio and the impact on the processes needed to provide those products or varieties. Companies impede the effectiveness of their own processes by adding more products or varieties than they take away, and the affected processes limit the profitability of a burgeoning portfolio.

Common Symptoms of Product/Process Complexity

What does complexity on the Product/Process face look like? The answers are myriad, but here are some of the most common symptoms we see:

- **A large portion of products are unprofitable, weighing down the profits of the company.** Whether through unrestrained new product development, overresponsiveness to customer requests, unconsolidated acquisitions, or simply a dominant focus on sales and revenue before profit, the product portfolio has proliferated to the point that the company now has too many overlapping and/or one-off offerings. There are many low-volume SKUs eating up capacity and organizational energy. Processes are strained and their performance has declined. Standard margin figures may mask the extent of the problem, but it is clear that as the portfolio has grown, profitability has eroded (the cost base has risen faster than revenue).

- **Excessively high inventory levels are consuming working capital and adding costs.** As product complexity has grown, inventories have piled up, straining cash flow and depressing return on invested capital (ROIC). Finished goods inventories (in make-to-stock [MTS] firms) and raw materials inventories have ballooned. The amount of WIP may be astonishing, and the issue shows no sign of relief. As inventories have grown, so too have obsolescence and possibly spoilage.

- **There are product shortages due to strained capacity resulting in lost sales.** With such a large portfolio, product shortages are on the rise. Products begin to compete with each other for availability, and there is not enough capacity to go around. With many small-volume products, the impact of demand fluctuations on your operations is magnified. MTS operations inadvertently shift toward de facto make-to-order (MTO) operations, but many customers are not willing to wait.

- **Product surpluses are leading to markdowns, waste, and additional inventory costs.** With so many products in the portfolio, demand is cut up into ever-finer segments, making it more difficult to match supply to demand. The result is shortages in some areas and surpluses in other areas. To move these surpluses, companies mark down prices.

- **Long lead times are frustrating customers.** Product variety is straining production processes and scheduling. With more products to fit into the production schedule, each product is made less often and customers may have to wait for the next production run to get what they want. As WIP has grown, so too have lead times. (Remember Little's Law: Lead time equals WIP divided by completion rate. Add more WIP and you get longer lead times, assuming that the completion rate stays constant.) Customers for whom lead time is a key buying factor may be defecting to your competitors. As a defensive move, some MTO operations begin holding inventory and shift toward MTS operations.

- **Long and frequent changeovers are eroding production capacity.** As the number of products has grown, production runs have became smaller, with manufacturing plants now spending a greater portion of their time changing over the production lines. Plants built for large-volume, low-variety production are taxed with low-volume, high-variety product lines. Manufacturing suffers.
- **Service delivery, customer service, and quality levels are not meeting customers' expectations, and the situation is getting worse, not better.** The operation is strained with the variety it must deliver, and cracks begin to show. On-time delivery, first-order fulfillment rates, and quality levels suffer. The sales force may be overwhelmed with the breadth of the product portfolio it must represent and may focus on only portions of it—negating some of the benefits of variety. At this critical time, the operation may become even less responsive to customer issues. Brand suffers. Customers go elsewhere.
- **Every action seems to have a negative reaction in another part of your operations.** These problems are all intertwined, and solutions compete with each other. There seems to be no way to take action to improve performance in one area (either inventory, lead time, product availability, capacity, customer service, or quality levels), without sacrificing performance in another. Lacking breathing room in its operations, the company focuses on just the most immediate issues despite longer-term effects (the proverbial "wolf closest to the stagecoach").

You may not be experiencing all of these symptoms, but if some of them sound familiar then you may be suffering from interactions on the Product/Process face of the Complexity Cube.

Major Interactions on the Product/Process Face

That product complexity strains processes is true whether changing over a production line or requiring salespeople to recall information across a wide range of offerings. However, for simplicity, in much of our discussion below we will use a make-to-stock manufacturing example.

In a production plant, there is a dynamic relationship between product complexity, production capacity, inventory levels, and lead time. Increased product complexity (meaning a greater number of products flowing through the manufacturing and supply chain process) will drive reduced production capacity, increased inventory levels, lengthened lead times, or some combination of these; how much so is determined in large part by the setup time, or flexibility, of the accompanying processes. How a company operates its manufacturing base (plant loading, productions scheduling, etc.) determines where the negative impact of its product variety will be felt: on capacity, volume, or lead time. (The astute company understands this, and will operate so as to direct the negative impacts to the areas where the impact will be least costly to the company.)

To show why this is so, we will describe the impact of six Product/Process interactions (these dynamics are interlinked, but for clarity we will address each one individually):

1) Increased product variety increases inventory levels (and lead times) in a linear relationship [p. 116]
2) Increased product variety erodes production capacity (in a big way) [p. 118]
3) Low-volume products have a nonlinear impact on inventory and capacity [p. 121]
4) Demand variation magnifies the impact of product variety [p. 122]
5) Setup times limit a process's ability to deliver product complexity [p. 124]
6) A process designed for product simplicity breaks down under product variety [p. 125]

The first four interactions address the impact of product complexity on process performance: Interactions 1 and 2 describe fundamental impacts of product variety on inventory levels, lead times, and production capacity. (We lump inventory and lead time together because the nature of the impact on them is essentially similar.) Interactions 3 and 4 describe two important product characteristics (low volume and variation in demand) that exacerbate the impacts described in Interactions 1 and 2.

The explanatory detail behind interactions 1 through 4 is rather technical. We have provided a detailed analysis for interaction 1 and summary analyses for the other interactions. (Additional detail for those interactions is in Appendix B.) In interactions 5 and 6, we turn things around to describe the impact of key process characteristics on a process's ability to deliver variety and, therefore, on product profitability.

Interaction 1: Increased product variety increases inventory levels (and lead times) in a linear relationship

One of the rules of complexity is that **overall inventory levels grow proportionally with the number of products.**[37] The implication is that the more finitely you cut up your demand across products, the greater your overall inventory levels will be, as shown in Figure 29.

Figure 29: Impact on Inventory from Spreading a Given Demand Equally across a Greater Number of Products

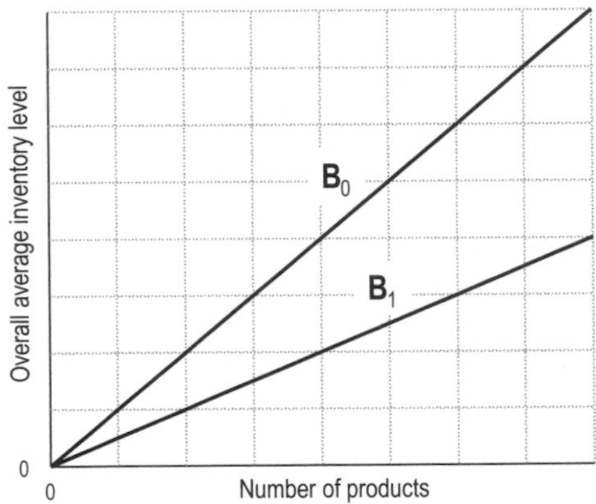

For the same level of overall demand spread evenly across a number of products, the overall inventory level grows proportionally with the number of products. The slope of this relationship is the batch size (B). Smaller batch sizes result in lower overall levels of inventory, but the relationship between inventory and number of products is still proportional. In this example batch size B_1 is half that of B_0. (JIT or "just-in-time" practices minimize inventory levels by effectively minimizing the batch size.)

Of course, there are many things companies can do to minimize their inventory levels. They can produce in smaller batches, but that eats up production capacity. They can try to shift the burden of inventory to their customers, but this isn't always possible. They can establish JIT relationships with their suppliers, but this isn't without investment and risk.

All these measures should be pursued to better manage inventory levels, but they do not change the core relationship governing how inventory levels scale with product variety—which is approximately linear. That is why doubling product complexity will lead to a doubling of inventory levels, at a minimum, all else being equal. And given that lead times are governed by the amount of work-in-process inside the process, we would expect to see the lead times double also.

This relationship is the crux of why inventory levels at many companies have grown significantly—to the point where they are exhausting working capital. Inventory levels are driven by the batch size and the number of products or components, and this relationship holds true whether we are talking about FG (finished goods) or raw materials.

Analysis of Interaction 1

To show why these claims are true, let's start by examining what happens with inventory. Inventory is a buffer. Its purpose is to allow demand to be met while waiting for new materials or products to be produced or delivered.

Assuming steady demand for or consumption of a given product (let's call it Flavor A), the level of inventory over time will typically resemble the profile of a saw—the so-called sawtooth profile (see Figure 30).

Figure 30: Sawtooth Inventory Profile

Inventory level

B

$\bar{I}$ = ½B

a b c d

Time

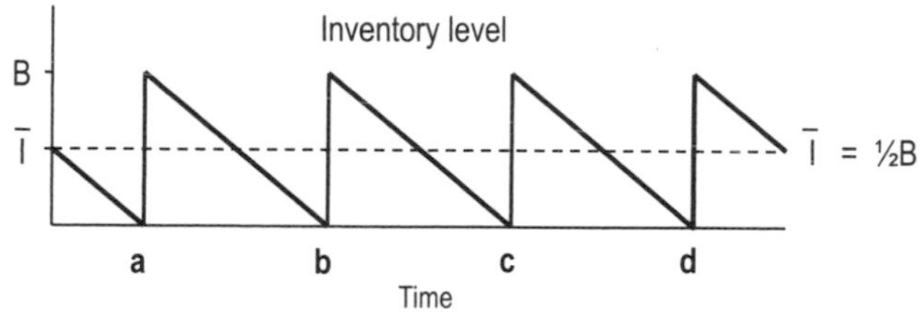

At times *a*, *b*, *c*, and *d*, a new batch of product is completed or delivered, and the inventory level jumps up in a stepwise fashion by an amount equal to the batch size. With steady demand or consumption, the inventory level declines linearly until the next batch is produced or delivered. With a sawtooth inventory profile, the average inventory level (I) is simply half the batch size (B). (For simplicity, this figure does not include safety stock. We'll get to that point later.)

At times *a*, *b*, *c*, and *d* in the figure, a new batch of Flavor A arrives, and its inventory level jumps up, in stepwise fashion, by an amount equal to the amount produced or delivered. (We will call this the **batch size**, which is the same as *campaign length* for continuous flow operations.) The inventory then decreases linearly, because of steady demand, until the next batch arrives or is produced. This is true whether we are talking about items on the retail shelf, finished goods in the warehouse, or raw materials in the stockroom.

To simplify this discussion, if we assume perfectly reliable production in addition to perfectly steady demand, we can ignore safety stock for the moment. The average inventory level for Flavor A is then simply half its batch size (mathphiles might remember that the area of a triangle is one-half its height times its base).

Now consider the impact of spreading the same level of *overall* demand and production volume evenly across two flavors instead of just one. (Although the reason for adding another flavor would likely be to increase demand, there is often much cannibalization. So for the sake of simplicity, and to focus on the impact on inventory, we will assume overall demand is unchanged.) Rather than making or receiving Flavor A at times *a*, *b*, *c*, and *d*, production now alternates between Flavor A and Flavor B. Flavor A is produced or received half as often (at times *a* and *c*), and it is consumed half as slowly. However, although production and demand for Flavor A is now half of what is was, **its average inventory level remains unchanged.** Why? Average inventory level still equals half its batch size, and although batches of Flavor A are now produced or received half as often, the *size* of each batch is unchanged; so the average inventory level remains unchanged.

We must also consider Flavor B, whose inventory profile looks just like Flavor A's except that it is shifted in time, being produced or received at times *b* and *d*. Its average inventory level is equal to half its batch size, and its batch size is equal to that of Flavor A (since their demands are equal). And since the overall average inventory level is simply the sum of that of Flavors A and B, *the overall average inventory level with two flavors is twice that with just one* (see Figure 31, next page, and the accompanying equations).

In this rather basic example, even though overall demand didn't change, overall inventory levels doubled as the number of flavors doubled, bringing us back to the opening statement in this section: overall inventory levels grow proportionally with the number of products. In other words, you can't add to your portfolio without also adding to inventory, which increases non-value-add (NVA) costs to your operations. That fact of nature doesn't argue against adding to your portfolio. It argues that you should be very careful when you do, investigate whether you can make cuts to the portfolio so overall inventory levels don't have to rise, and always consider the full impact on costs.

Interaction 2: Increased product variety erodes production capacity (in a big way)

Product variety has grown significantly over the past decade, often after the plants and facilities that deliver it were built. These plants, designed to handle high-volume, low-variety production, have seen their production capacity erode over the years in the face of an ever-growing variety of products (this erosion is often masked, or counterbalanced, by capacity improvement from improved operating practices and capital investment).

In the previous interaction, we showed how inventory levels are proportional to batch sizes. Companies can reduce inventory levels by running smaller and more frequent batches, but this eats up production capacity. Inventory level and

Figure 31: Comparison of One-Product and Two-Product Inventory Profiles

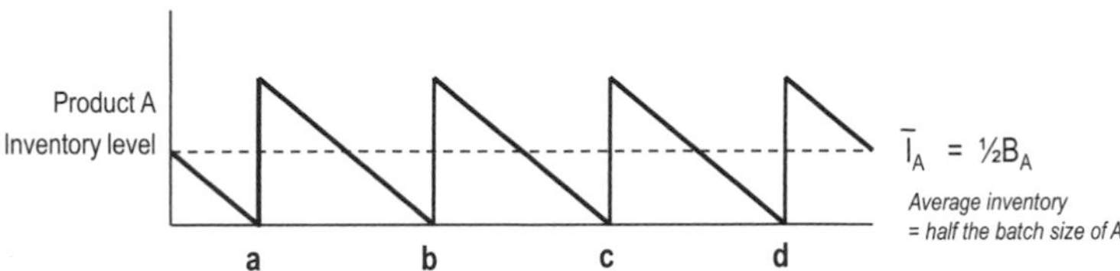

Two-product

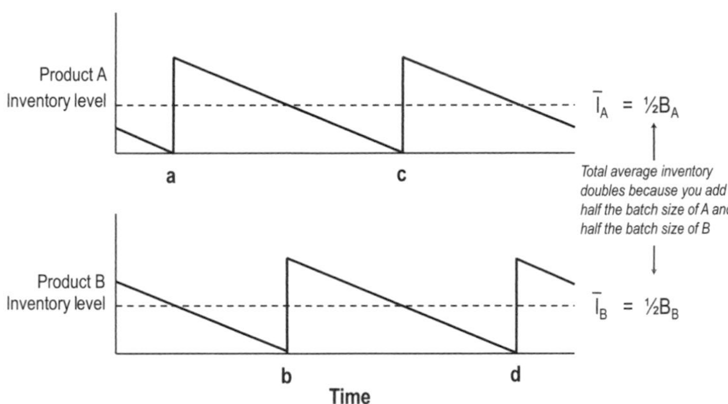

$$\begin{aligned}\bar{I}_2 &= \bar{I}_A + \bar{I}_B \\ &= ½B_A + ½B_B \\ &= 2 * ½B_A \quad \{\text{since } B_B = B_A\} \\ &= 2 * \bar{I}_1 \quad \{\text{since } I_1 = I_A = ½B_A\}\end{aligned}$$

In one-product production, Product A is produced at times *a*, *b*, *c*, and *d*, and the average inventory level is equal to half the batch size. With two-product production, Product A is produced at times *a* and *c* and Product B at times *b* and *d*. If the same overall demand is now split evenly across the two products, the inventory profile for each will change at half the rate as in the one-product case, **but the batch sizes will be unchanged.** The average inventory level for *each* product will therefore equal the original level for Product A in the one-product case, meaning the **overall average inventory level for the two products together will be twice that seen in the one-product case.**

production capacity are, therefore, inversely related: a lower level of overall inventory requires a lower level of overall production volume, or, alternatively, greater production volume requires greater inventory.

Increased product variety puts pressure on both inventory and capacity—resulting in either greater inventory (as described in Interaction 1) or reduced capacity, or a combination of both. Going back to the previous interaction, we kept overall demand constant when discussing the impact of product variety on inventory levels. Alternatively, by keeping inventory levels constant in the face of greater product variety, we can show **that overall production capacity decreases as product variety increases** (see Figure 32).

Figure 32: Impact of Product Complexity on Overall Production Volume (for a constant level of inventory)

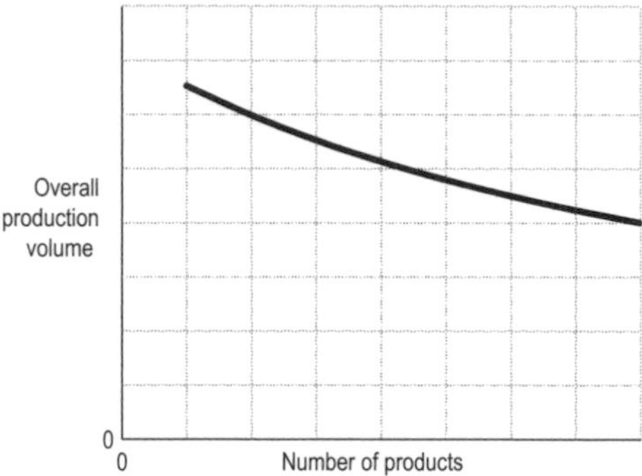

Production volume is inversely related to production complexity (number of products). Spreading production across a greater number of products reduces overall production volume (for a constant level of overall inventory).

Analysis of Interaction 2

Consider the infant formula market. In the 1950s the market saw little variety, with each manufacturer providing a single milk-based product (for example, Similac from Ross Laboratories and Enfamil from Mead Johnson). Today, each manufacturer has numerous products with the addition of lactose-free, organic, and soy varieties, among others. And typically, all these varieties are made in the same plant, requiring frequent and extensive changeovers, dedicated equipment, and much more complicated demand forecasting and production scheduling.

Adding products to a production process adds changeovers (the action of changing the line from making one product to another). Time spent on changeovers (also called setup time) is clearly non-value-add to the consumer. Typically, the greater the variety of products, the greater the number and frequency of changeovers, and the greater the portion of potential production time (capacity) that is lost.

Appendix B will explain why in more detail, but as Figure 32 shows, **production capacity decreases with an increasing number of products** (with the level of overall inventory held constant). Or flipping that statement, **increased product complexity erodes capacity.**

This effect can play out with real-world significance. In Chapter 16 we will show the example of a pharmaceutical company that had focused rather relentlessly over the years on minimizing inventory levels (a seemingly very good thing to do), while their product line had continued to grow. Capacity eroded steadily—unnoticed, because of process and organizational interactions that we will discuss in the next chapter—until the point that the company was forced to outsource a growing portion of its production volume to a third-party manufacturer at a significant premium to fill its capacity shortfall. The downside was that the value of the lost production was worth 15 times more to the company than its savings in inventory.

Interaction 3: Low-volume products have a nonlinear impact on inventory and capacity

On a per-unit basis, **low-volume products consume more capacity and/or result in greater inventory than do higher-volume products.** Most accounting systems, however, spread these costs in a peanut butter fashion, often by number of units, which is why low-volume products are almost invariably under-costed—and their true impact on the balance sheet is disguised.

Analysis of Interaction 3

So far in the examples we've provided, we've assumed that demand and production volume were split evenly over all products. This was a helpful, simplifying assumption to allow us to better understand the dynamics in the previous examples, but reality is a little messier. A discussion of product and process interactions would be inadequate without addressing low-volume offerings.

The fact that low-volume products have a disproportionate effect on inventory and capacity is evident from simply considering these scenarios:

- If produced at the same frequency as higher-volume products, low-volume products will incur the same number of changeovers and, therefore, consume the same amount of "lost" production capacity.
- If produced in the same size batches as higher-volume products, the inventory level of the low-volume product will be equal to that of the higher-volume product.

In either case—whether the same capacity erosion or the same inventory level—the impact is spread over a smaller volume. (See Appendix B for a more detailed explanation of why this is so.)

Why traditional batch-sizing methods fall short

Although plant operators understand that low-volume products should be produced less frequently than high-volume products, the more difficult question is, how much less frequently?

Production frequency is determined by batch size, but traditional methods for batch sizing fall short of specifying the optimal combination of batch sizes across products to minimize inventory and lead time for a given mix and level of demand. Consider these common methods:

- Economic order quantity (EOQ)—sets the batch size for each product to minimize inventory holding costs and ordering costs for the particular product
- Setup-to-run time ratio—sets the batch size for each product based on its setup time according to some ratio (for example 10 hours of production for every 1 hour of setup)
- Activity-based costing (ABC) stratification—stratifies products based on volume or other criteria, and A products are made more frequently (e.g., weekly), whereas C products are made less frequently (e.g., annually)

But each of these methods considers each product individually, not in relation to all other products. The result is that the individual batch size determinations, when aggregated across all products, can result in a production schedule that the plant doesn't have the capacity to meet or that leaves capacity unused. This is capacity that could have been used for more changeovers, which would have resulted in more frequent and smaller batches and thus lower lead time and less inventory.

Optimal batch sizes, that is, batch sizes that minimize lead time and inventory for a given demand and production capacity, can be determined only by considering all products in conjunction. This can be done using the Optimal Batch Size Equation presented in Appendix A.

Interaction 4: Demand variation magnifies the impacts of product variety

We have also assumed in our examples that demand was perfectly steady over time. This is very rarely the case. In almost all cases, demand for a particular product will vary over time. Whether that demand variation significantly affects your operations depends in part on how complex your portfolio is. If you have a relative simple portfolio, variation in demand may not have a sizeable impact on complexity costs. But if you have a lot of product variety, the effect of demand variation will be greatly magnified.

What we also know is that **variety brings variation.** When the number of products is increased, the variation in demand also increases, which means the cost of complexity will rise rapidly.

Analysis of Interaction 4

The impact of demand variation is most directly seen on the need for safety stock (the portion of inventory that we have ignored so far). Safety stock is additional inventory used as a buffer against running out of the inventory item when demand is uneven; i.e., it is that portion of inventory that is needed to cover variation.

Figure 33 shows various levels of total safety stock (as a percentage of the total monthly demand) as a function of the number of products for various levels of variation. For any number of products, **the level of safety stock rises proportionally with the level of variability in demand** (the latter indicated by a factor known as COV, or coefficient of variation).[38]

Figure 33: Total Safety Stock as a Function of Product Variety for Different Levels of Demand Variation

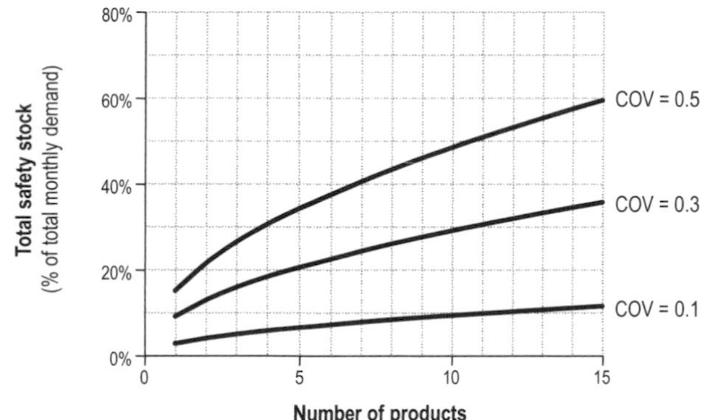

Total safety stock increases with both the number of products and variation of demand. The total safety stock level is shown as a percentage of the total monthly demand. Variation, indicated by the COV, shows how much demand levels vary compared to the overall average level. A COV of 0.1 means that demand is relatively steady; a COV of 0.5 means demand varies widely. (In this analysis, demand is divided evenly across products.)

The number of products and the level of variation combine to determine the necessary level of safety stock. In the example shown in Figure 33, when the demand variation is relatively low (COV = 0.1), increasing the number of products from 1 to 15 only increases total safety stock from 3% to 12% of total monthly demand. In contrast, increasing the number of products from 1 to 15 when the demand variation is relatively high (COV = 0.5) increases total safety stock from 16% to 60% of total monthly demand.

However, **low-volume products generally suffer from much greater demand variation than do high-volume products.** Larger volumes are usually spread over a greater number of orders or customers and often have larger, more stable individual order volumes. A small change, such as loss or delay of an order, or reduction in order volume can have a small effect when spread over a large volume. But when concentrated over a smaller volume, the percent "variation" is much greater.

Looking again at Figure 33, this means that increasing from 1 to 15 products may more closely resemble increasing safety stock from 3% (COV of 0.1) to 60% (COV of 0.5) of monthly demand. (Variation has the same impact on lead time in the MTO environment as it does on inventory in the MTS environment.)

Interaction 5: Setup times limit a process's ability to deliver product complexity

If you have only one product flowing through a process, there is no need to switch between offerings and, therefore, no time lost to changeovers (also known as setup time). As soon as you add a second offering running through the same process, there will be setup time when you switch from one product to the other.

Imagine an ideal world where setup time was zero. In that Utopia, there would be no penalty in productivity for running multiple products through the process. But as we all know, that Utopia doesn't exist. Setup takes time, and the longer the time, the bigger the penalty we pay for having variety in a process. Conversely, the closer we can come to having zero setup time, the smaller the penalty we pay for product complexity.

The key factor affecting just how much product complexity affects processes is the flexibility and robustness of the processes themselves: **more-flexible processes are able to support much greater variety flowing through them than are less flexible processes.** Product complexity determines how much strain is placed on processes, but setup time determines how well those processes can handle the strain.

Analysis of Interaction 5

You might recall this lesson from the Morley Farms' story in Deep Dive #3. In the original scenario, we set changeover time at 1 hour, and the impact of adding two more products increased cumulative changeover time so much that the costs of the added complexity more than offset the potential gains in revenue. However, the situation would have been reversed if they had been able to cut setup times to just 30 minutes. The cost incurred by adding two more products would *not* have offset the additional profit.

Why was that so? In each of the preceding interactions, we showed how product complexity impacts some key process metrics (inventory, lead time, capacity, and consumption). The greatest driver of process flexibility is the length of setup times. Therefore, a process with shorter setup times will be able to support a greater amount of variety. Take inventory for example. We have shown that inventory levels are proportional to batch sizes, but batch sizes are proportional to setup time. (See sidebar on batch size on p. 242 for an explanation.) This means that by cutting setup time in half, you can reduce by half the impact of product complexity on inventory (see left chart of Figure 34).

Or take capacity erosion. We showed that as the number of products increases, so does the time lost to setups and, therefore, the time available for production. But the amount of time that is lost to setups is affected by the length of the setups themselves. (Longer setups mean higher setup-to-run ratios, and higher setup-to-run ratios mean more capacity is consumed.) By cutting setup time in half, you can reduce by half the impact of product complexity in production capacity (see right chart of Figure 34).

Figure 34: Effect of Setup Time on the Impact of Product Complexity

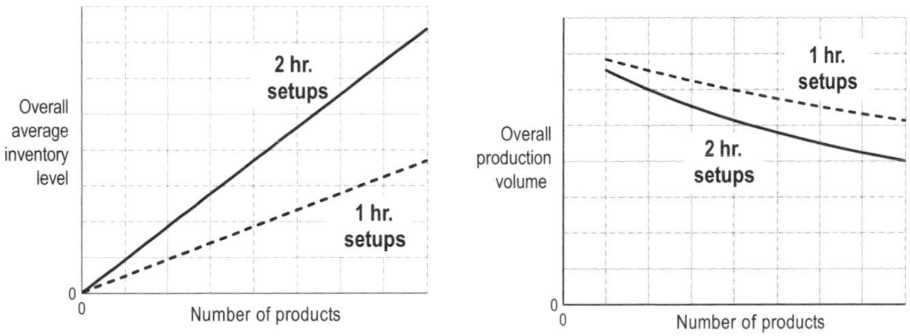

Reducing setup time makes a process better able to support variety. Cutting setup times in half (for example, from 2 hours to 1 hour) means that a process can support twice the number of products. Conversely, for the same number of products, smaller setup times can mean less inventory and/or greater production volume. (Note: The relationships shown assume products of equal volume.)

More generally, a doubling of setup times across products doubles the impacts of greater product complexity. Conversely, a halving of setup time cuts in half the impacts of product complexity on inventory, lead time, and capacity. In other words, *by cutting setup times in half, you can effectively double the number of products that a process can support* (for the same level of inventory, lead time, and production volume). We discuss setup time reduction on p. 243.

Interaction 6: A process designed for product simplicity breaks down under product variety

In the lifecycle of a company, most processes take shape at a time when the product portfolio is very simple, perhaps just a few offerings. What happens, then, when processes established during a time of simplicity are loaded with product variety? Typically, the result is *process* complexity: work-around loops, rework, exceptions, one-off handling, and so forth. The standard process is replaced with a complex web of activity. Indeed, it can become difficult to identify a standard process. In this environment, the efficiency of the process drops, and lead times can grow astonishingly long, driving excessive non-value-add time and WIP. (We discussed this phenomenon in Chapter 3.)

Key Implications for Battle

Being forewarned about Product/Process interactions is being forearmed. What do the interactions tell us regarding how to approach this issue? Here are five implications for attacking complexity costs on this face:

1) Adjust for the true drivers of cost

2) Remove product variety to make what remains even better

3) Remove both unprofitable products and those that cannibalize more than grow revenue

Mental setup time

Setup time is not just an issue for production plants. Service organizations suffer from setup time just as much as manufacturing plants. Anytime time, effort, or resources are involved in switching between different types of tasks, whether between different products on a production line or different services provided to a customer, setup is involved.

Researchers are discovering the phenomenon of mental setup time—with which we are all personally familiar. Mental setup is the time and effort it takes to shift from concentrating on one item to a different item. If the number of items (aka, complexity) is great or the frequency of switching is high (aka, small batch sizes), then the resulting stress and loss of effectiveness can be significant.

In his 2007 *Atlantic* article "The Autumn of Multitaskers,"[39] Walter Kirn states

> *Multitasking messes with the brain in several ways. At the most basic level, the mental balancing acts that it requires—the constant switching and pivoting—energize regions of the brain that specialize in visual processing and physical coordination and simultaneously appear to shortchange some of the higher areas related to memory and learning... studies find that multitasking boosts the level of stress-related hormones such as cortisol and adrenaline and wears down our systems through biochemical friction, prematurely aging us. In the short term, the confusion, fatigue, and chaos merely hamper our ability to focus and analyze, but in the long term, they may cause it to atrophy.*

4) Structure your processes with requisite variety in mind
5) Consider your company's ability to deliver complexity when determining the right level of complexity for your portfolio

1) Adjust for the True Drivers of Cost

The first, and perhaps most obvious, takeaway from understanding the interactions on the Product/Process face is that low-volume products as well as products with high variation in demand are almost always under-costed. (Conversely, high-volume products and products with little to no demand variation are almost always over-costed.) We've shown that low-volume and high variation products consume more overhead and erode more capacity per unit; yet traditional costing methods rarely account for the impact of small volume and almost never consider variation. Therefore, to properly identify true product profitability—that is, which products are creating and which are destroying value—requires correcting for these costs. (Making this worse is that low-volume products tend to also be the ones that suffer most from high variation in demand.)

2) Remove Product Variety to Make What Remains Even Better

Remember that adding variety to a process adds strain to the process, which in turn adds costs to everything going through that process. The profitability of a product is the result of the processes that delivers it *as well as the variety of everything else going through the same processes.* Removing product variety that doesn't create value (i.e., bad complexity) removes strain from your processes, improves process performance, and reduces the cost of the products that remain—making your good complexity even better.

3) Remove Both Unprofitable Products and Those That Cannibalize More than Grow Revenue

Adding product variety doesn't just add more products, it often splits up existing revenue over more products, making your products lower volume (and we've shown that lower-volume products are more costly per unit). By smartly removing certain products—those that cannibalize rather than grow revenue—you can make the products that remain higher volume and, therefore, even lower cost, not only moving you toward the peak of your Whale Curve but also shifting your Whale Curve by making the complexity that remains less expensive.

4) Structure Your Processes with Requisite Variety in Mind

Many processes today are subject to much greater variety than that for which they were designed. When there is a mismatch between the design of a process and the variety to which it is subject, process performance will be affected. As you take action on complexity costs and focus on restructuring processes, a key input to this process will be an understanding of the requisite variety the redesigned process will have to support.

5) Consider Your Company's Ability to Deliver Complexity When Determining the Right Level of Complexity for Your Portfolio

The right level of complexity to offer in your portfolio doesn't depend just on what your competitors are doing or what the market values, but also on how well you can deliver any complexity. This depends on your scale and your process capabilities (greater scale means you can spread your complexity over greater revenue, and better process capabilities means that complexity will cost you less, meaning you can afford more). Offering too much given your size and capability can saddle your entire portfolio with cost, whereas offering too little can neglect value in the marketplace. The key indicator behind what is too much or too little is your own profitability.

Recommended High-Value Battle Strategies

We have laid out in this chapter some of the key considerations for attacking this face of complexity. Part III will demonstrate a number of specific methodologies—battle strategies—that we recommend for removing complexity costs.

If the symptoms of this face ring true for you, note the chapters highlighted below for specific battle strategies for attacking complexity costs on this face. Start by reading the Introduction to Part III, "Taking Ground." Then the following chapters will offer the highest leverage for attacking Product/Process complexity:

- Chapters 9 and 10 on Portfolio Optimization offer a definitive and step-by-step approach to SKU reduction (i.e., reducing external product complexity)
- Chapter 12, "Component Rationalization and Vendor Consolidation," addresses reducing internal product complexity
- For reasons that will be addressed in Chapter 8, it makes sense to pair Chapters 9, 10, or 12 with Chapter 11, "Network and Footprint Consolidation" to maximize the benefits from removing product complexity

- Chapter 13, "Enabling Variety with Lean Processes" and Chapter 14, "Process Segmentation: Minimizing the Effects of Variety" address how to maximize your processes ability to handle product complexity
- Lastly, Chapter 16, "Dynamic Operations: Optimizing Complexity Trade-offs" includes a detailed example for optimizing capacity, inventory, and distribution cost trade-offs to minimize complexity costs for a given level of product complexity and process flexibility

Conclusion

In a 2009 WilsonPerumal cost-reduction survey, a full 82% of respondents reported they were pursuing process optimization as a means of cost reduction, yet only 30% reported that they were looking at product or service elimination. However, as we've discussed, the variety of products flowing through a process has a significant impact on the performance of the process itself. In fact, **the variety of products flowing through a process can be the single largest limiter of process performance.** This means that a process cannot be properly evaluated independently from the product complexity to which it is subject.

It also signals broader possibilities. Consider the financial services firm that said they used complexity like a "strategic weapon"; they explained that they knew they could deliver portfolio complexity less expensively than their competitors and they knew their competitors would follow. They intentionally brought a large amount of complexity to the marketplace and watched their competitors "implode" on unsustainable complexity costs. While certainly aggressive, this company had an astute view of complexity, its impacts, and their ability to deliver it as compared to their competitors.

Chapter 6 Endnotes

[34]Marshal L. Fisher, "What Is the Right Supply Chain for Your Product?" *Harvard Business Review*, March-April 1997, pp. 105–116.

[35] Cited in Knowledge@Wharton, "Special Report, Creating the Optimal Supply Chain" (The Boston Consulting Group).

[36] "Managing Global Supply Chains," *McKinsey Quarterly*, July 2008.

[37] For demand spread evenly across products.

[38] Standard deviation of demand over the mean demand level by product.

[39] Walter Kirn, "The Autumn of Multitaskers," *The Atlantic*, November 2007.

Chapter 7

Where Complexity Hides

The Process/Organization Face

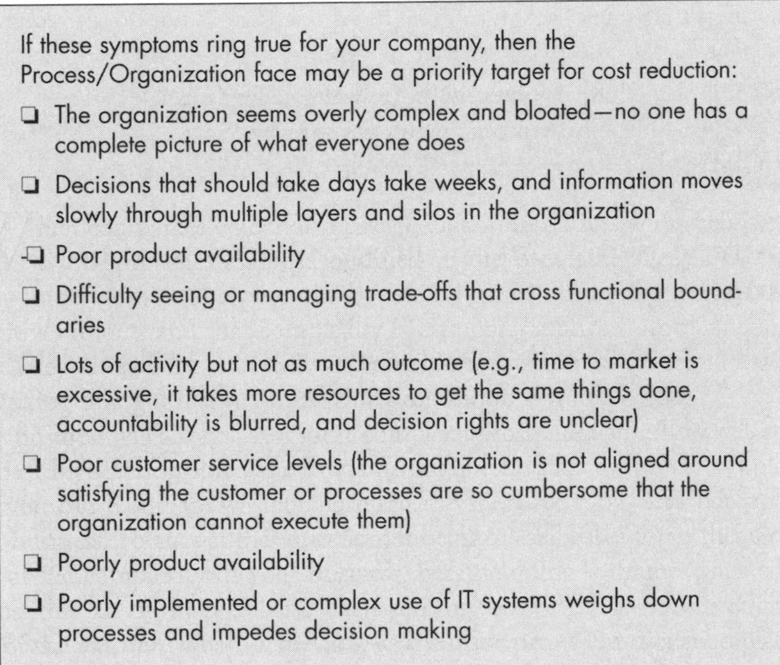

If these symptoms ring true for your company, then the Process/Organization face may be a priority target for cost reduction:

- ❑ The organization seems overly complex and bloated—no one has a complete picture of what everyone does
- ❑ Decisions that should take days take weeks, and information moves slowly through multiple layers and silos in the organization
- ❑ Poor product availability
- ❑ Difficulty seeing or managing trade-offs that cross functional boundaries
- ❑ Lots of activity but not as much outcome (e.g., time to market is excessive, it takes more resources to get the same things done, accountability is blurred, and decision rights are unclear)
- ❑ Poor customer service levels (the organization is not aligned around satisfying the customer or processes are so cumbersome that the organization cannot execute them)
- ❑ Poorly product availability
- ❑ Poorly implemented or complex use of IT systems weighs down processes and impedes decision making

A major snack foods company was organized by regions and had separate innovation teams working to develop new products to increase market share. But there were problems: as a result of the regional fiefdoms, each area duplicated management, processes, and inventories. And in the area of innovation, teams ended up competing against each other as a result of the siloed culture. The result was the launching of rival (but woefully similar) products on the market. As a whole, costs were bloated to noncompetitive levels, and new products were cannibalizing each other.

Similarly in the early 1990s, Xerox was struggling as a highly matrixed company, organized by product, geography, and segments, and bloated with ineffective processes. According to CEO Anne Mulcahy, "It was a nightmare. You couldn't find anybody who had clear responsibility for anything."[40]

If the *Product/Process* face is where complexity most tangibly arises, the *Process/Organization* face is where it most clearly hides. This face of the Complexity Cube comprises interactions between how a company delivers its work (its processes) and how it structures and deploys its resources against those processes (its organization). But because processes are fragmented between functions and functions are divided into silos, it is extremely difficult to see how these dimensions are affecting each other. For example, breaking up a process into manageable pieces makes it more easily administered across functions. But it also means no single person can see the whole process; nor does anyone have a grasp of all the resource deployed to support a given process. That makes seeing and managing Process/Organization complexity very difficult.

Issues on the Process/Organization face, in fact, are often the least recognized, most frequent, and hardest for companies to handle.

Common Symptoms of Process/Organization Complexity

How do interactions on the Process/Organization face manifest? At its worst, they create an **absence of coherence:** There is a lack of alignment between functions, goals, initiatives, resources, and so on. Portions of the organization and its processes work against each other. Even if there is a common goal, there remains a large disconnect between that goal and the specific actions taken by specific functions at specific points in the process, which is often described as an *inability to execute*. But what does a lack of coherence look like? Common symptoms include the following:

- **The organization seems overly complex and bloated; no one has a complete picture of what each group does.** Unfortunately, the reaction to many Process/Organization symptoms is to add more resources, often resulting in even more activity and more silos. It can reach the point where no one has a firm grasp on how all the pieces need to come together so that the organization can achieve its mission. No one sees all of the complexity, and when that happens, complexity can easily multiply unseen.

- **Decisions that should take days take weeks, and information flows slowly through multiple layers and silos in the organization.** This delay is often the result of an overly complex organization structure based on products or markets or a mix of both—potentially with low accountability, because of the gap between decision and actions. Overhead costs include areas that are nobody's responsibility; simple decisions are deferred. And the net result is long and winding information flows and decision making through consensus or decision stalemates, as functional fiefdoms exert themselves.

- **Seeing or managing trade-offs that cross functional boundaries is difficult.** Numerous functional and decision-making silos make it difficult to see, much less manage, linkages between silos. The organization becomes a composite of individual parts, each operating from its own view. Without a broader view, issues that span across boundaries are often not recognized and are sometimes ignored. The organization suffers from unintended consequences and out-of-balance trade-offs. (For example, in Chapter 16 we will show in detail how a company's focus on inventory reduction led to a master production schedule that resulted in smaller production batches, which inadvertently drove down production capacity. But because of Process/Organization complexity, the capacity effects were not foreseen.)
- **There is lots of activity but not much outcome (e.g., time to market is excessive, it takes more and more resources to get the same things done, accountability is blurry, and decision rights are unclear).** Process/Organization interactions create many activity traps. People are overloaded with "work." But there is no line of sight to what really matters, no mechanism for evaluating the value of that work against organizational and customer priorities. And as more and more people do more and more things, work that really matters takes longer to get done (because less important work is clogging the highways). Focus shifts to how much people are doing or how many projects are being worked, rather than what impact is being achieved. Given how difficult it can be to drive projects to closure in this environment, managers are reluctant to stop any initiatives. Rather, they mistakenly take the shotgun approach: the best way to get something done is to do many things. There is no means for prioritization. The volume of activity can begin to grow on itself as more work is needed to manage more and more activity—"fake" work abounds.
- **There are poor customer service levels (the organization is not aligned around satisfying the customer, or processes are so cumbersome that the organization cannot execute them).** Numerous hand-offs, excessive queues, and work-around loops disrupt process flow, significantly lengthening lead times and limiting responsiveness. Often, the burden for process and organizational complexity is inadvertently shifted to the customer, with poor results for both the customer and the company (for example, consider poor customer service experiences where customers are left to navigate through a complex and frustrating organi-

zation, or health insurance application processes where the customer must provide the same information many times).

- **Poor product availability arises as a result of poor supply chain coordination.** Because of poor coordination across supply chain participants, the supply chain struggles with getting the right product in the right place at the right time. It may be able to deliver when things are working well, but when conditions change (in the level or pattern of demand or supply, for instance) it is slow or unable to react. Because the processes and the organizational structures that support them are treated as individual pieces rather than an integrated whole, it is a struggle to balance work across the value chain and achieve high levels of execution.
- **Poorly implemented or complex use of IT systems weighs down processes and impedes decision making.** IT systems are sometimes viewed as the silver bullet to process and organizational complexity. But while IT systems can help well-run organizations operate better, they seldom turn a poor operation around. Rather, poor processes become hardcoded into the IT systems, which just adds to the complexity of an operation.

You may have noticed that this list of common symptoms seems very different from those of the previous chapter. With only a few exceptions, the symptoms on this face tend to be much more difficult to measure than those on the Product/Process face. Inventory, lead time, and production volume are very tangible measures that are typically tracked as a matter of course. It is much harder to measure symptoms such as *inability to manage trade-offs*, *impeded decision flows*, or *cumbersome systems*. But although less tangible, these impacts are no less real.

Major Interactions on the Process/Organization Face

Interactions on the Process/Organization face are less direct, more difficult to quantify, and more varied than those on the Product/Process face described in the last chapter. Part of the reason is that processes and organizational structures are very much intertwined. The interactions on this face seem almost as varied as companies themselves. But we have seen commonalities between these interactions and are able to group most of them within a few categories:

1) "Exceptions" become the rule, driving process and organizational complexity [p. 135]
2) Process and organization interactions mask the linkages across the company [p. 135]

3) High resource utilization and high process variation combine to drive long project lead times and low resource productivity [p. 138]

4) Process and organizational complexity compound each other [p. 141]

Interaction 1: "Exceptions" become the rule, driving process and organizational complexity

As complexity grows so too does the number of exceptions to the process. Exceptions drive work-around loops, consume disproportionate levels of resources, and significantly degrade *overall* processes performance, affecting *all* items flowing through the process.

For example, after Hurricane Katrina, a special, federally funded Community Development Block Grant (CDBG) Program was created to provide rebuilding assistance to certain homeowners whose homes were damaged or destroyed. There was much criticism of the slow pace at which funds were eventually distributed—a year after the disaster, no money had been distributed yet over 100,000 Louisianans sat on the waiting list. While there were many root causes, one was the number of "exceptions" that occurred during the qualification process.

The CDBG process had a requirement that applicants prove their ownership of the property. No one had anticipated just how many applicants would have difficulty showing title; for example, in lower-income areas, many homes had been passed on to family through generations without new title being recorded. The large number of "exceptions" consumed program staff and significantly delayed processing. Worse, processing the exceptions created a bottleneck that stopped the flow through the process, even for those homeowners who did have titles. (Eventually the program modified its eligibility requirements to accept affidavits to satisfy home ownership and other requirements, reducing the number of "exceptions" and speeding up the application process.)

Understanding the reason behind exceptions in your organization can be a key first step toward attacking process and organizational complexity. However, most process tools are not well suited for addressing exceptions (see sidebar, next page).

Interaction 2: Process and organization interactions mask the linkages across the company

As you have probably picked up by now, we prefer to view businesses and the environments within which they operate as complex systems of highly interrelated parts and processes, where actions in one area can have seemingly discon-

Why traditional process mapping efforts often fall short (Part 1)

Although we would acknowledge the value of process maps in documenting and improving process knowledge, they are less well suited to capturing some important drivers of organizational and process complexity.

First, **process maps generally favor the "standard process"** more than the exceptions to the process. For example, at one financial institution, we were struck by how readily exceptions to the process seemed to be forgotten during the mapping exercises. Individuals would explain step-by-step what to do at a point in the process, understandably focusing on the normal situation. But observing the process, it became clear that the exceptions *were* the norm.

But why do exceptions tend to go unnoticed in many process mapping exercises? Most obvious is that many people don't realize the disproportionate impact exceptions have on process performance and organizational effectiveness. They are easy to disregard as simply that, exceptions.

Also, process mapping exercises usually aim to produce clean, orderly, and understandable process maps. Exceptions are messy. They can be difficult to pin down. And when large in number and variety, they can obscure an otherwise straightforward and orderly process map. But this may be the most authentic process map, and the one of highest value, given the enormous impact exceptions have on process performance.

nected impacts in other areas (the "unintended consequences"). When these linkages go unnoticed or are left unmanaged, organizations are more likely to suffer unintended consequences and their costs.

Analysis of Interaction 2

Complexity can cause otherwise obvious linkages to become disparate and go unnoticed. For example, we worked with a government organization that dealt in the storage and distribution of supplies. In that operation, many apparently unrelated decisions and unrecognized complex linkages combined to result in almost half of its shipments flowing through distribution centers (DCs) on the opposite side of the country, when one was located within the same region as the end user. One challenge for the organization was the need to balance workload across its network of facilities. Therefore, when items were being returned from oversees for storage and maintenance, they often were sent to facilities based on which ones needed work at the time. However, months or years later when shipping these items to local users, many of the specific items to be shipped often were located on the opposite side of the country from where the user was located. By not recognizing the relationship between returns, workload, inventory positioning, and transportation, total distribution costs were overly high.

But why do many linkages go unnoticed in today's organizations? We have seen the following four reasons:

1) **They are obscured behind process handoffs and organizational silos.** Specialization has been a boon to industry. It has allowed groups to focus energy on excelling at a narrower capability or a piece of a larger process. But specialization, with all its benefits, comes with different challenges. At a minimum, specialization brings with it handoffs between functional groups (or between organizations in a network). Worse is when the focus at a particular function evolves into an organizational silo where the understanding of how the function integrates into the larger whole is lost. When processes are broken up across silos, all sense for larger linkages can be lost—and when you lose sight of linkages, you are more apt to suffer the consequences and costs of not managing them.

2) **An end-to-end view is too linear.** Companies are increasingly focused on viewing their business end-to-end—essentially extending the process map forward and backward enough to expose the linkages across functions and even beyond the borders of the enterprise. But these efforts take a linear view. In a complex system, linkages are not just forward or backward but also side-to-side. Processes are affected not just by upstream or downstream actions but also by other processes running in parallel through the same resources. **Relationships, therefore, resemble a web more than a chain.** Further, although end-to-end often means "start to finish," in a complex system the processes tend to be cyclical, the output of one generation or cycle impacting the next.

3) **An overwhelming volume of information obscures important linkages.** Many managers are rightly concerned with having a more complete picture of their business's operational environment. But they mistakenly equate that goal with having a great deal of information. And as we all know, with information, volume can impede clarity. Examples of information overload are numerous, and this is all the more likely and all the more hazardous in complex systems. Following the 1979 accident at Unit 2 of the Three Mile Island Nuclear Power Plant, investigators found that a significant contributing factor was that operators were overwhelmed with too much information, much of it irrelevant. At the onset of the accident, the operators were faced with approximately 150 separate alarms.[41] The thinking before the accident had been that the more information, the better (the plant had been designed with 800 alarms). But in the accident, the sheer volume of information masked what really mattered. With its impeccable safety record, the U.S. Navy's Nuclear Propulsion Program stands in contrast, with the number of alarms stringently limited and focused on critical pieces of information necessary to

respond to potential incidents. **What is important is to have the right information and to connect it properly.**

4) **Too often, information systems are black boxes.** Information systems that carry and format information for executive management and reporting functions often are less accessible to operating personnel (the systems are designed and implemented for the people monitoring the process more than those operating the process). For example, a professional services company moved to a system that gathered project financial information in a manner that made it easier and faster to close the books each month but that provided the project managers with less timely data. Additionally, the system required project managers to spend more time updating and verifying project information. After the transfer, project managers spent more time providing more data to have less visibility into project financial performance. Just as importantly, it is easy to lose knowledge of the complex relationships that are codified in an IT system, which then become black boxes. In many cases, these relationships comprise fundamental relationships within the business, and without this knowledge it is more difficult for individuals to develop the "structural knowledge" necessary to see and optimize how the pieces of a company's operations best fit together.

Why traditional process mapping efforts often fall short (Part 2)

A second reason process maps fall short is that **process mapping isn't geared toward showing the linkages across the company.** Process mapping efforts typically aim at precision over completeness. They map out steps, activities, and handoffs in a sequential and precise manner. But that, by nature, makes it more difficult to connect the disparate dots. Seeing the linkages requires taking a holistic but distilled view. In our work, we have often found value by forcing ourselves to "map" the organization (what it does, where it adds value, and how it works) on a single page. Obviously, this means letting go of much detail, but what this loses in precision, it makes up for in clarity.

While we certainly don't suggest you abandon process maps, they become much more helpful, and less hurtful, when you understand what they provide as well as their shortcomings.

Interaction 3: High resource utilization and high process variation combine to drive long lead times and low resource productivity

Perhaps one of the most telling process characteristics is the variation in the time it takes to perform a given task in the process: Does it generally take about the same time to complete the task day in and day out? Or does a task that gets done quickly one day take four or ten times as long another day? (Think of this as the difference between how long a task is *expected* to take and how long it *actually* takes.) Most assembly-line, repetitive manufacturing processes have very low variation (task time is about the same); more creative processes inherently have much higher variation in task time.

This variation in how long it takes to complete a task is an important factor when considering the impact of complexity since it governs the relationship between resource utilization and lead time. In some situations, an organizational policy of loading up resources with work may not affect process lead time. But in other cases, it can. Which is which?

For processes with very low variation—meaning the amount of time needed for a task or process is relatively stable—lead time is independent of the level of resource utilization. You can load up a resource (person or machine) to a high level and not impact the overall time it takes to complete the work. So if task time shows little variation, it makes sense to get the most out of your resources by loading them to rather high levels of utilization.

On the other hand, if task time *does* vary a lot, **lead times increase significantly with higher levels of resource utilization**. Further, above a certain level, the benefit of higher resource utilization is overcome, often significantly so, by increased lead time. In other words, if you load up a resource working only a highly variable task, the outcome is likely to be that you get *less* work done overall, not more.

This can be a problem because many organizations tend to develop a single, homogeneous culture that governs how the organization approaches its processes. The tendency for many manufacturing or operations-centric organizations is to approach all processes with the rigor of their manufacturing processes. Conversely, organizations focused on creative work may approach all processes with the freedom that is more characteristic of creative work.

But just about every organization has a mix of both low-variation and high-variation processes. Organizations structured for low-variation processes are easily overwhelmed if the work becomes less predictable (see the discussion of "exceptions," above). Organizations structured for high-variation processes have trouble achieving predictability when more rigor is required.

One of the most common and powerful examples of mismanaged processes that we see are creative processes resourced as assembly-line work. Think of the benefits that process rigor (such as statistical process control) has brought to repetitive tasks, namely low variation, high efficiency, and high levels of resource utilization. When applied to well-defined repetitive work the impacts on process performance can be significant, but when applied to processes that inherently have high variation in task time, the impact can be quite the opposite.

The basis for the problem of treating creative processes as assembly-line work has its roots in queuing theory, which shows that task time variation has a significant impact on overall lead time, especially at high levels of resource utilization (see Figure 35). Just as we did before, we use a factor called the coefficient of variation (COV) to represent the amount of variability. A low number reflects a largely stable process in terms of task time; higher numbers reflect a process where task time varies widely.

As shown by Figure 35, the lead time for resources working on highly variable tasks and loaded to 95% capacity is four times longer than if they were loaded to only 65% capacity. So a design task that would normally take one week for an engineer working at 65% utilization would take four weeks if that engineer were loaded to 95% utilization.

On the flipside, reducing work by a third means that the remaining work is done as much as four times faster. And the faster a project is completed, the faster another can be started. In net, **for high-variation processes, loading resources at near capacity can mean that you'll need more staff to achieve a given level of output** (this effect is addressed in much more detail in Chapter 15).

Figure 35: Impact of Variation on the Relationship between Resource Utilization and Lead Time

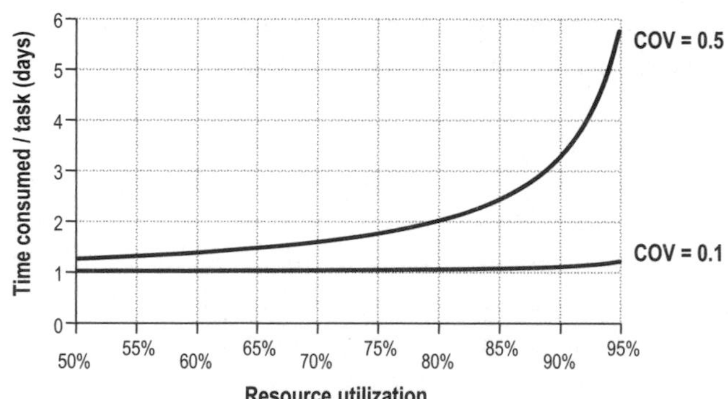

This chart shows the time consumed per task, or lead time, for a task that *on average* takes 1 day. With variation in the time it takes to actually complete the task (i.e., sometimes more and sometimes less than 1 day), when resources are loaded at higher utilization, a potentially large queue develops, increasing the overall time consumed per task (greater lead time).

We have skimmed over the details in our discussion here, but it is easy to demonstrate that improperly resourced high-variation processes can drive staffing levels to as much as twice what they would otherwise be for the same level of output. It is ironic for many organizations that in an effort to fully utilize staff, lead times grow, processes slow down, less gets done, and the number of initiatives being worked grows, as does the size of the staff working on these initiatives.

The LA freeway effect

The impact of high variation and resource utilization on lead time is often called the *LA freeway effect*, a reference to long commute times on Los Angeles freeways. As rush hour approaches, the freeways fill up. At this point, its resource utilization is very high. If there were no variation, the freeway would be full but traffic would flow smoothly and commute times would be reasonable. (Imagine the cars of a train traveling at a uniform speed down a track even if they were not connected to each other.)

However, freeway driving inherently has a great deal of variation (one driver hits the brakes while another speeds, there is a rush of cars at an on-ramp, a car switches lanes, two cars have a fender bender). The moment variation is added to the picture, the freeway slows to a standstill, with commute times of 30 minutes growing to two or more hours.

Traffic planners understand this. Ramp signals (traffic signals on freeway on-ramps to manage the flow of traffic onto the freeway during peak periods) are an attempt to reduce variation on the freeway—in this case by preventing a rush of cars trying to enter the freeway all at the same time.

Interaction 4: Process and organization complexity compound each other

Last, but not least, we discussed in Chapter 3 how process complexity begets organizational complexity and vice versa and showed the interaction via the diagram in Figure 36. As processes stretch to accommodate an increasing variety of tasks, work-arounds become commonplace, and new structures (formal and informal) spring up to support the work. Each new structure creates further specialization, which ultimately impedes visibility across functions and processes, which exacerbates process performance further. Functions, organizational structures, and IT systems struggle to support the various process interfaces.

Figure 36: Revisiting the Compounding of Complexity

Key Implications for Battle

How do you attack complexity on the Process/Organization face? The implications are very different from those for dealing with Product/Process interactions. The focus here shifts away from dealing with product portfolios and their impact on individual processes to looking broadly at how processes and organization are structured. We offer four implications for attacking complexity on this face:

1) Start with a broad, integrated view of the business
2) Ensure your resource utilization levels fit the variation in your creative processes
3) Achieve a critical mass of change through coordinated, focused actions
4) Gauge the impact of Process/Organization complexity on your ability to execute and to deploy a counterstrategy for executing your cost-reduction efforts

1) Start with a Broad, Integrated View of the Business

Many issues on the Process/Organization face find their origin in an incomplete view of the business—whether missing the meaning of process exceptions or not recognizing key linkages across your business.

Attacking process and organizational complexity starts with gaining clarity by taking a much deeper and more nuanced approach to understanding the relationships between your processes and your organization than traditional process mapping affords.

To gain that kind of clarity of view in all directions, start by considering the following questions:

- What is the volume of exceptions in your processes? Why are they occurring? What is their impact on process performance, resource consumption, and organizational design?
- What are the linkages that underlie your business? How do the various parts of your business interrelate? (It can be helpful to try to distill and represent the operation in a single page, focusing on the dominant linkages and then adding in detail.)
- Where are your systems helping you, and where are they used as black boxes, impeding your staff's understanding of key relationships and dynamics in the business? (We call this "structural knowledge," as explained in the sidebar.)
- How are you managing your processes? Are you resourcing high-variation processes as if they were low-variation processes? Have you pushed the envelope on using process rigor to reduce variation in your processes?

Structural knowledge: The best defense against process and organizational complexity

The best defense against process and organizational complexity is to develop a clear view throughout the organization of how the many pieces of the organization fit together and how this relates to the ultimate objectives of the company.

Clarity involves two things: looking externally to understand where an organization creates unique value, and looking inwardly to develop "structural knowledge" of the organization (the linkages, dynamics, relationships, and complex web of cause and effect). The former is the realm of strategic definition and relevance, the latter of process and organizational complexity.

Developing structural knowledge requires balancing and integrating top-down and bottom-up views of an organization. This means in practice that **an executive's effectiveness is often limited, in part, by his or her ability to master both detail and breadth.**

Take, for example, Clarence "Kelly" Johnson, former VP of advanced development projects over Lockheed's Skunk Works program. In the 1960s Johnson led the design of the mythical SR-71 Blackbird, which is one of the most revolutionary aircraft of all time and remains the fastest conventional aircraft in the world today. What is even more impressive is that he accomplished this in just two years with a small team and at a tiny fraction of what it costs to develop a new aircraft today.

Johnson's ability to master both detail and breadth was key to his success. He started with Lockheed as a tool designer, then mastered each area of aircraft design (aerodynamics, airframe, propulsion, flight test, etc.) as he rose through the ranks. He, therefore, had depth of knowledge across a breadth of disciplines. That gave him unique clarity about how each area interacted with the others. He spanned all silos, streamlining integration across the many disciplines involved—and created an innovative plane in record time with minimal expense.

Johnson was able to see the whole. Without such clarity, as that which comes from mastering both breadth and depth, we see the world—or the organization or issue at hand—as many pieces with unclear relationships to each other. With such a piecemeal view, process and organizational complexity will abound.

2) Ensure Your Resource Utilization Levels Fit the Variation in Your Creative Processes

We have shown how creative processes, with inherent variation, behave very differently from repetitive manufacturing processes with very low levels of variation—most notably the impact of resource utilization on lead times. The most successful organizations, whether they are operations or creative-centric, have developed a broad process management skill set and are adept at applying techniques fitting the type of process.

As we've noted, however, many companies take a one-size-fits-all approach, resourcing and managing their higher-variation creative processes as they would low-variation manufacturing processes. Those companies have enormous opportunities, especially if they have significant resources devoted to project work: By aligning resource utilization levels, they stand to reduce project lead times and increase resource productivity.

3) Achieve Critical Mass of Change through Coordinated, Focused Actions

Many issues on the Process/Organization face can gain significant inertia, with several overlapping issues reinforcing each other. You can see this by looking back at the symptoms discussed previously.

For example, a bloated and cumbersome organization will have difficulty managing trade-offs across functional boundaries, leading to lots of activity but not much outcome. That, in turn, will lead them to keep adding resources and creating still more silos in an attempt to get more work done.

Attacking these issues will often require multiple, targeted, and coordinated actions aimed at achieving a critical mass of change to disrupt the cycle and launch the organization in a different direction:

- **Multiple actions** are usually necessary because a single action rarely addresses the many interactions involved
- **Targeted actions** are needed since the actions should usually be concentrated at a combination of specific leverage points to be most effective
- **Coordinated actions** are necessary because timing can be very important; for example, there may be six actions that can break a vicious cycle when done together but that are ineffective if done at separate times

4) Gauge the Impact of Process/Organization Complexity on Your Ability to Execute—and Deploy a Counterstrategy for Executing Your Cost-Reduction Efforts

At Tesco, six organizational levels span from the board to the checkout registers, and most of the head office management team is no more than two levels from the board. This lean organizational structure ensures fast communication and decision making. In that environment, change happens fast.

But what about an opposite situation? What if, for example, your company has many management layers, diffused accountability, and cumbersome processes? If your ability to execute is impeded on a day-to-day basis by your Process/Organization complexity, then recognize that the same dynamics will likely assert themselves to derail your efforts in driving out complexity costs (absent an explicit strategy).

In the same way that such issues affect everyday execution, they also impede your ability to execute a war on complexity costs, which means addressing them may be a priority. The way past this barrier is usually to ensure adequate focus, visibility, and resources are dedicated to eliminating complexity costs. Absent a focused prioritization—concentration of force—the danger is that your existing complexity will impede your efforts to eliminate that complexity.

When Cadbury CEO Todd Stizter launched a multi-dimensional attack on complexity, he claimed that the greater alignment (what he calls a "joined-up approach") resulting from the organizational simplification was critical to successful execution of SKU reduction:

> *We have eliminated the regional layer of our management structure. The seven business units now report directly to me, and their leaders—importantly—sit on the executive committee. So we can make decisions sitting around one table and get it executed quickly.*

Recommended High-Value Battle Strategies

We have laid out in this chapter some of the key considerations for attacking this face of complexity. Part III will present a number of specific methodologies—battle strategies—that we recommend for removing complexity costs. If the symptoms of this face ring true for you, after reading the Introduction to Part III, "Taking Ground," we recommend

- Chapter 15, "Project Rationalization: Getting More Done Faster and with Fewer Resources" and Chapter 13, "Enabling Variety with Lean Processes" for additional detail and steps for reducing project lead times and increasing resource productivity
- Chapter 16, "Dynamic Operations: Optimizing Complexity Trade-offs," which explains how to identify and address mismanaged dynamic relationships in your business
- Chapter 14, "Process Segmentation: Minimizing the Effects of Variety," which offers quick solutions for segmenting your processes to minimize certain impact from interactions on this face
- Chapter 11, "Network and Footprint Consolidation" for a consideration of how to shrink organizational assets that have grown to support key processes

Conclusion

We mentioned at the beginning of this chapter that, at its worst, the interactions on this face of the Complexity Cube result in an absence of coherence—a lack of alignment between functions, goals, initiatives, resources, and so on, with portions of the organization and its processes working against each other.

On the other hand, conquering complexity on this face resembles the coherent organization. Coherence refers to alignment in purpose and action throughout the organization. Coherence starts with clarity, but while clarity is *understanding*, coherence is *action*. In a coherent organization, there is a deliberate, rational, and consistent relation of parts: All work is guided by alignment around a shared purpose. Everything that is done is done for a reason, and all efforts align with the mission, purpose, or objective of the organization.

Coherence and the Nuclear Navy

The U.S. Navy's nuclear propulsion program has a remarkable safety and operational record. The organization operates more nuclear reactors and has logged more reactor hours than any other organization in the world—and has done so without major incident. A major part of its success is the significant coherence the program has achieved, which it maintains with vigilance. For example, everything the organization and its operators do is connected to its two missions—*reactor safety* and *continuity of power*—each of which is relentlessly reinforced throughout the organization.

The program takes this further by identifying five pillars on which reactor safety and continuity of power rest. The five "Pillars of the Program" are level of knowledge, questioning attitude, forceful watch team backup, formality, and integrity. These pillars reinforce each other. A compromise of one threatens the others. The pillars define the culture and values of the organization, with operators trained, observed, and measured against them. Even minor infractions are investigated in depth and tied to a compromise of one or more pillars.

Admiral Hyman G. Rickover, the "father of the Nuclear Navy," applied this coherence throughout the chain of command. His view is "Unless the individual truly responsible can be identified when something goes wrong, *no one* has really been responsible."[42]

Chapter 7 Endnotes

40 "MIT Sloan: Behind the Scenes of a Great Turnaround." http://mitsloan.mit.edu/newsroom/2006-mulcahy.php.

41 Stephen J. Spear, *Chasing the Rabbit* (New York: McGraw-Hill, 2009).

42 Adm. Hyman G. Rickover, "Doing a Job." Speech delivered at Columbia University, 1982. Available at www.govleaders.org/rickover.htm.

Chapter 8

Where Complexity Takes Root

The Organization/Product Face

If these symptoms ring true for your company, then the Organization/Product face may be a priority target for cost reduction:

- ❑ The physical footprint is sprawling, with low or declining asset utilization
- ❑ Operations struggles to keep up with the "cats and dogs" of your product line
- ❑ The efforts of marketing and sales are diffused over an unmanageable number of products and geographies
- ❑ Your supply base is fragmented
- ❑ Third-party distributors resist efforts to focus the product line
- ❑ IT systems have become a tangled web
- ❑ Previous efforts to consolidate the network have been stymied by current needs

The "complexity of reducing complexity" is nowhere more apparent than in the interactions of the organization and product dimensions of the Complexity Cube.

As we discussed in previous chapters, complexity arises through the interaction of products and processes: It hides, unaccounted for, in the murky depths of the Process/Organization face; but it takes root—is essentially trapped—on the Organization/Product face.

This chapter will help you learn how to expose those roots. We will explore the interactions between what a firm offers of value to its customer and/or consumers and how it deploys its organizational resources—physical assets (including technology), organizational structures, network partners, and people—to deliver that value. There are three key considerations to this face:

First, this is often where complexity injects the most cost and capital. This occurs in factories and depots to support a sprawling portfolio; in external distributors, as *they* seek to keep variety while *you* keep the cost; in a fragmented supply base; in organizational structures, as functional fiefdoms assert themselves; and in technology, as IT systems are added incrementally to support a growing portfolio only to become a huge source of non-value-add cost.

Why attacking the Organization/Product face is rocket fuel for ROIC

Most readers are keenly aware of the variables that drive cash flow and value. But as a quick reminder and reference, here is the basic return on invested capital (ROIC) equation

ROIC = NOPLAT/Invested Capital

where, NOPLAT = net operating profits less adjusted taxes; and Invested Capital = operating working capital + net PPE (property, plant, and equipment) + other assets

Any improvements made to the Organization/Product face can materially increase the numerator (NOPLAT) and reduce the denominator (Invested Capital) of this metric.

As a quick and simple example, consider the impact from actions that allow you to close a distribution center (DC) that you owned and operated.

- First, NOPLAT would increase by the level of *expenses* (less taxes) incurred by that DC: salaries, utilities, office supplies, insurance, etc.
- Second, Invested Capital would decrease by the book value of the DC left on the balance sheet (Net PPE) and any other *equipment/assets* used in the DC, such as forklifts, packaging machines, etc.
- Third, the closing of a DC would most likely result in an inventory reduction (most likely nonmoving inventory). This would also decrease Invested Capital through a decrease in Operating Working Capital (in this case, *inventory*).

So, in this example, your company would enjoy both an increase in NOPLAT (the numerator) and a decrease in invested capital (the denominator), getting a much larger increase in ROIC and, ultimately, an increase in cash flow.

Second, this is most commonly where complexity takes root. Why do we use that analogy? Anyone who has ever tried to move a sapling knows that even a young tree has deep roots. And just like roots, the supporting assets of an organization are often viewed or treated as immovable (see Figure 37). Also like roots, an organization's assets will seek to optimize themselves. Roots will meander and intertwine as they seek sustenance. This can result in ever knottier, more intractable organizational complexity.

Figure 37: Complexity Takes Root

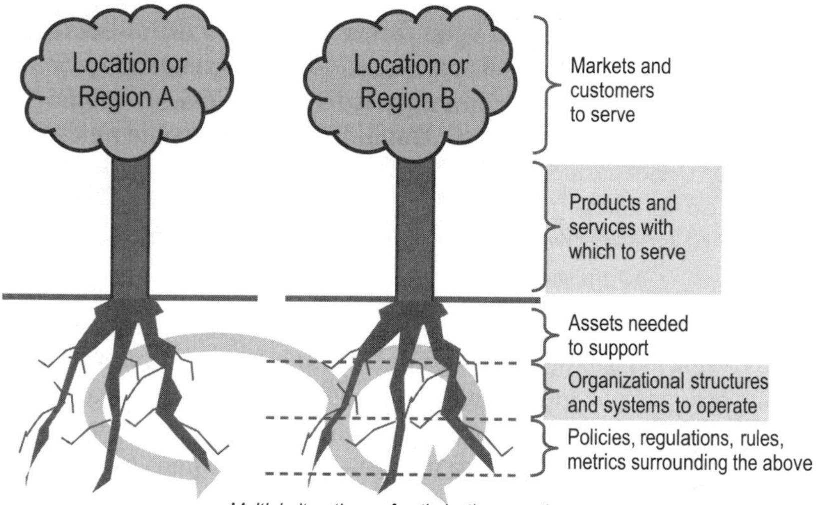

Multiple iterations of optimization over time (e.g., distribution, inventory, plant loading, capacity)

In an organization, each and every decision on assets is made with some supporting logic, somehow linked directly or indirectly in support of the products to be made and the customers to be served. But often the decisions are made in isolation from each other—*just like a root self-optimizing*. The net result is a root system that anchors an organization to one spot, even after the customers and markets have shifted. This underscores why the Organization/Product face cannot be tackled with incremental thinking and actions: the roots are too deep! Incremental change will just trigger resistance that will be nearly impossible to overcome. Think and act big in tackling Organization/Product complexity.

Consider this classic catch-22: A company cannot consider a dramatic cut to its product line because it wonders what it would do with all its manufacturing capacity; and it cannot consider closing factories because it cannot fathom how it would produce its range of products. There are many examples. The key point is that product and service variety creates anchors that bind various organizational elements to each other and vice versa. Given this dynamic, assets grow over time and complexity takes root.

Third—and critical for your efforts in taking out cost—this is where some of the biggest opportunities reside. *Because* of the "rooted" effect of Organization/Product complexity, a lot of complexity costs are deeply embedded and very hard to detect and uproot… *because* such complexity has likely been trapped by organizational and product commitments. As a result, for many organizations the Organization/Product face of the Complexity Cube represents the best opportunities for cost transformation, with impacts on both the income statement and the balance sheet.

Where chaos can collide with complexity

Jamshid Gharajedaghi, in his book *Systems Thinking—Managing Chaos and Complexity*, says that "the development of an organization is a purposeful transformation toward higher levels of integration and differentiation at the same time" (see Figure 38). The two axes are at the heart of the discussion in this chapter. We are driven as managers to make sure our company offers **differentiation** to the market, the search for differences and variety resulting in complexity and autonomy. Yet we must also make sure that our companies achieve integration, a search for coherence.

Figure 38: Integration and Differentiation

Integration	Simple	Complex
Order	Organized simplicity	Organized complexity
Chaos	Chaotic simplicity	Chaotic complexity

Differentiation

Think of the differentiation axis as the growth in what you offer (products/services) and to whom you offer it (customers/markets). Think of the integration axis as the manner in which your organization is set up to deliver that growth: the trade-offs you've made with respect to capacity, asset base, skill sets, technology, and reporting structures.

These two factors can come together in one of two ways: **organized,** in the sense that everything is aligned with your organization's purpose and priorities and they, therefore, move you toward your business goals; or **chaotic,** meaning decisions have been made ad hoc, with no attention to alignment to impact on other parts of the organization.

Many companies' starting point will be with chaotic simplicity, which means they face three choices for their next move:

- **Organized simplicity,** which can lead to insufficient differentiation and impotency
- **Chaotic complexity,** which is where many firms find themselves today; the pursuit of variety has destroyed organizational coherence
- **Organized complexity,** which strikes the balance between differentiation and integration

For many companies today, the last category is where they need to be. They need to meet the market requirements for variety (complexity), but to do so effectively they also need to achieve greater levels of integration. In practical terms, this means that **the greater the demand for market variety, the tighter and more aligned the organization needs to be in order to deliver it**—in its organization and in its processes.

Common Symptoms of Organization/Product Complexity

How will you know if the Organization/Product interactions represent a sizeable opportunity for your business? Consider if any of the following common symptoms sound familiar:

- **Your physical footprint (factories, distribution centers, warehouses, and so on) is sprawling, with low or declining utilization. At the same time, operations struggles to keep up with the "cats and dogs" of your product line.** As a result of acquisitions, rapid growth, or decisions related to geographic expansion, your footprint may have overgrown. Old plants and assets with low productivity remain because of "legacy" factors. Low-volume offerings are disproportionately eroding precious capacity that would benefit higher-volume, higher-margin products. You may even have had to buy extra capacity at the same time your own assets are deployed to producing value-destroying offerings.
- **The efforts of marketing, sales, and other functions are diffused over an unmanageable number of products and geographies.** The performance and effectiveness of your sales and marketing teams are in large part driven, and weakened, by the large breadth of offerings they need to support. Management recognizes that there are a number of core brands that generate the lion's share of profits, but internal resources are not clustered around these key areas. Salespeople cannot successfully master the details of all the products in the portfolio, and each will, therefore, sell what they are comfortable with or incentivized to sell. As there are no official efforts by the management team to narrow the range, individuals in sales and marketing take it on themselves to narrow the burden by selectively focusing their efforts on certain products and services.
- **Your supply base is fragmented; there are gaps and overlaps; it is not unusual for different parts of the organization to be sourcing the same product with different vendors.** Consider the impact of having to manage 8,000 suppliers, the fate befalling British Airways prior to its efforts to cull them by three-quarters.[43] Lack of alignment leads to proliferation of suppliers—different functions may be sourcing the exact same commodities through their own preferred vendors.
- **Your sales organization or third-party distributors resist efforts to focus your product line, citing a specific customer need.** You have tried to ratchet down the sprawling product base, but your internal sales function or third-party distributors have balked at the notion, saying that customers insist on Product A or Product B. Or consider another example that we heard recently: Even though a global technology company

deleted a low-volume laptop from its official product catalog, a sales division halfway across the world placed an order for a close customer. Rather than refuse the sale, the company restarted production on the deleted SKU.

- **IT systems have grown "organically" in response to new emerging needs to the point that they represent a tangled web.** The IT function has been viewed historically in your company as an enabler to specific strategic or market initiatives and has stretched to keep pace with growth. As a result, you may have multiple ERP (enterprise resource planning) systems patched together in a web of technology. Many key decisions are sourced with Excel spreadsheets guarded closely by individual owners. The costs to support this web grow each year, and most of the spending is dedicated to maintaining the current system, not advancing to new platforms. As *InformationWeek* reported, "Ask a CIO to name his or her main duties, and chances are manage complexity won't make the list. But that's what all CIOs do."[44]
- **Management has discussed the need for network consolidation, but efforts are stymied by current production needs.** You may have discussed issues like network consolidation many times in the past. But good reasons always stand in the way of taking action. For example, if a company has gone through a recent acquisition, there may be reluctance to embark on network consolidation for fear of disrupting integration efforts. Or there may be hesitation to consolidate because your footprint has grown by acquisition, becoming slack with capacity and with less-than-optimal configuration. But potential changes in the network are stymied or slowed by concern for ensuring postmerger integration, because specific products are made in only one certain location, and/or because management believes they've found a path to dramatically increase revenues associated with a product (thereby absorbing capacity). These could all be valid reasons for keeping the status quo. But as a management team, you need to assess when these issues are real reasons for inaction or just difficulties to be overcome in the pursuit of consolidation. There is rarely a convenient time to do footprint consolidation.

All of the above are common scenarios—sets of symptoms we have seen that indicate interactions on this face may be a company's biggest problem and, therefore, its biggest opportunity for beginning a war on complexity costs. If one or more of the above symptoms resonates, then attacking the interactions on this face may be the best place to start formulating your cost-cutting efforts. If so, it is critical to understand how organization and product complexity interact so that you can develop a robust battle plan that leverages the right battle strategies for taking ground quickly.

Major Interactions on the Organization/Product Face

Before developing your battle strategy for this face, it is wise to develop a broader view of the fundamental interactions behind Organization/Product complexity:

1) Product complexity traps organizational complexity [p. 153]
2) Organizational complexity traps product complexity [p. 154]
3) Organizational complexity creates accountability gaps and "blind spots" [p. 154]
4) Asynchronous time horizons paralyze decision making [p.155]
5) People's rootedness impedes efforts to cut organization and product complexity [p.156]

Interaction 1: Product complexity traps organizational complexity

This phenomenon of thinking narrowly is not just for factories, depots, or physical infrastructure. We see the same dynamic affecting all organizational elements: whether IT systems, functional structures, value chain partnerships, or warehouses, **organizational complexity becomes trapped by assumptions around product and service complexity.** Management believes the company has to keep all its current products and services and produce and deliver them exactly as it does today. That belief will forever trap organizational complexity into your business structure.

A European consumer goods company was looking to reduce its manufacturing footprint by half, from 16 facilities to just 8. Many of the plants had been added to the network during previous acquisitions—brand-driven acquisitions, but nonetheless asset-laden—with the result being unaddressed network complexity. So the company launched an effort to assess detailed cost and production data for each of the plants. Initial efforts were stymied, however, because of technology constraints: four main production technologies, supporting a broad product portfolio, were dispersed across the UK, France, and parts of Eastern Europe. In sum, the effort was scoped too narrowly. Without a parallel evaluation of the product line and, therefore, product strategy (and the supporting technologies), the footprint consolidation would do little more than eke out incremental gains.

Unfortunately for many companies, the lack of a sizeable gain becomes apparent only after a network assessment has been completed, when the limitations imposed by the product portfolio appear in the "constraints and roadblocks" column. By then it's too late, or at least the opportunity is diminished.

As product portfolio decisions have a life and spotlight of their own, it may seem odd to address them concurrently with organizational complexity. But as we will discuss later, by broadening the scope at the outset, we can take more specific (and often less painful) actions later to fuller effect.

Interaction 2: Organizational complexity traps product complexity

It is less immediately obvious, perhaps, that the reverse of Interaction 1 is also true: **organizational complexity traps product complexity.** Many times, plant-level or facility-level metrics are focused on goals that encourage asset utilization. Therefore, anything that could affect utilization metrics—such as SKU reduction—works against peoples' targets and objectives. On the financial side, we have seen similar dynamics where the focus was on *assigning* overhead costs as opposed to *reducing* them. In fact, we have seen internal resistance to reducing product complexity, even if it benefits the company, because

- The fuller the plant, the better the productivity numbers.
- By removing products, the remaining volume would have to absorb more overhead, triggering a potential, albeit misguided, vicious cycle. As volume is removed, the overhead is more concentrated in what remains, making the retained volume appear less attractive in a strict accounting sense.

Both objections are counterproductive, of course. You may end up with an inefficient but full plant making volume that no one wants to buy. Nonetheless, this may be a rational response to current incentives. To address complexity trapped in this way, therefore, you will have to change behavior, which will require changing those incentives.

Interaction 3: Organizational complexity creates accountability gaps and "blind spots"

With dissonance between the customer-facing portfolio and the organization elements that support it, it is perhaps no wonder that another trap for complexity is a lack of accountability or accountability at the wrong levels. If no one is in charge of costs, then no one watches costs. Unfortunately, it is not uncommon for large portions of overhead to grow unabated as a result of complexity: this is organizational cost that was once linked to former product line expansions but now has no owner.

These "stranded" costs can continue unchallenged. For example, duplicate functions such as HR and finance may arise out of the need for entrepreneurial speed and autonomy, but as the company and offerings mature, consolidation to a single point of accountability will expose waste and duplication (otherwise masked by accountability at the wrong levels or no accountability at all).

Interaction 4: Asynchronous time horizons paralyze decision making

When your product managers go home for the night, it's unlikely they switch off completely: they continue to watch and learn as much as they can about consumer behavior, knowledge they bring to work the next day. Their response time is short, and even with product development timelines, it's possible to change the size and shape of the product or service portfolio in line with evolving customer demands and tastes. Organizations, however, change much slower. Elements such as a company's supply chain network or manufacturing footprint are difficult and slow to change—akin to turning a battleship.

Hence, many firms struggle with the following disconnect: organizational structures and assets reflect what was needed to support customer requirements of the *past* rather than those of *today* (let alone *tomorrow).* Worse, the difficulty of change is itself a deterrent to change. A journey of a thousand miles starts with a single step, but how far are you willing to walk if you suspect there'll be a detour midway?

For example, the utilization of a factory may be poor today, but it is the result of decisions made years earlier. Or consider a company that wanted to catapult its IT systems to the "technology system of tomorrow." Today, its systems are a series of largely independent applications joined together creatively to cope with the increasing demands of new ventures, new products, and new strategic initiatives. In fact it is reminiscent of the following description of what goes wrong in how IT is used to support new strategic initiatives, from *Enterprise Architecture as Strategy*:

> *This process goes wrong in at least three ways.*
>
> *First, the strategy isn't always clear enough to act upon. General statements about the importance of "leveraging synergies" or "getting close to the customer" are difficult to implement. So the company builds IT solutions rather than IT capabilities.*
>
> *Second, even if the strategy is clear enough to act upon, the company implements it in a piece-meal, sequential process. Each strategic initiative results in a separate solution, each implemented on a different technology.*
>
> *Third, because IT is always reacting to the latest strategic initiative, IT is always a bottleneck. IT never becomes an asset shaping future strategic opportunities.*

So the need for change is clear. But as the company considers how to shape IT, it hesitates in the face of the ambiguity of tomorrow's needs, and given the lack of certainty regarding the future and the cost and upheaval of change, grand plans are quickly downsized. It is not unusual for firms to fall prey to a version of "analysis paralysis" as they ponder how to bridge the chasm between the immediacy of today's need with the longevity of today's decisions.

Interaction 5: People's rootedness impedes efforts to cut organization and product complexity

It is not just incentives that inspire behaviors. People seek meaning, excellence, and passion in their work as well as a sense of connectedness and community. But a side effect can be the emergence of a "root system"—recall the tree diagram from the beginning of this chapter—that can slow or impede what may be very necessary change. Sometimes it's useful to recognize the likely reactions before they emerge:

- **Assertions of independence.** A part of the business has grown into a community and an ecosystem of its own, with its own point of view and customized processes and systems. The community balks at orders of change emanating from some distant center.
- **Entrenchment.** Independence leads to a deeper entrenchment of a "this is how it's always been done" mentality, which grows stronger as time passes. It becomes harder and harder for the business unit or function to imagine a radically different future or configuration.
- **Negotiation.** Recommended changes are met with a "tit-for-tat" exchange that ignores the organizational need for improvement and, in many cases, survival.
- **Delayed decision making.** The local organization, in a bid to balance "stakeholder" interests with business needs, seeks consensus-based decision making, delaying critical actions.

A COO once told us that the major source of resistance to large-scale portfolio changes was not from customers but employees. If you embark on change, be prepared for resistance. In our time, we have heard sentiments such as these:

> *"But the customers in this region have specific requirements that cannot be met by making this in another plant."*
>
> *"This product is still profitable, and by taking it out we'd drop utilization of this plant by X%, destroying absorption and raising the costs on the other products we make here."*

> *"We have the entire distribution and warehousing system optimized; moving this to another region would jeopardize customer service levels, not to mention increased distribution costs."*

> *"Yes, we can make the product cheaper in another plant, but did you think about the tax and export/import costs that we would need to add?"*

All of these sentiments may be valid; but you cannot let any single issue, or particularly vocal group, derail a giant opportunity.

Key Implications for Battle

These interactions are real issues that need to be understood and accounted for in your war on complexity costs. For us, there are four major implications to consider that rise directly out of Organization/Product interactions:

1) Take a concurrent approach to attacking these dimensions
2) Cut deep enough to release big costs
3) Break the tyranny of the "here and now"
4) Prepare for the trade-off decisions

1) Take a Concurrent Approach to Attacking These Dimensions

As organization and product complexity trap each other, you must take simultaneous action on several fronts so you can drive benefits on both dimensions.

This is, in fact, another application of the broad-but-focused principle we introduced in Chapter 1. We want to be broad in our understanding of the issues (how the dimensions interact and where the biggest opportunities reside) but focused in execution. For example, by assessing Organization/Product complexity in its fullness—say, how the network and footprint are interacting with your current portfolio—you will get a broader sense of the issues, the key levers, and what it will take to make substantial gains. That understanding will translate into a better and more tightly scoped effort, such as focusing on a specific portion of the product line and how that currently traps specific assets.

2) Cut Deep Enough to Release Big Costs

You need to understand the chunks of cost (the fixed assets) that can be eliminated and what is required from a product-reduction perspective to get there.

That means you need to explicitly define the cost-level breakpoints up front. Do not expect costs to magically fall out. Identify exactly what, at the end of your campaign, will be different or could be different in your assets and offerings that would result in a lower cost structure: Will your footprint be smaller or better aligned? Will your portfolio be smaller and more focused? Will you be carrying less inventory? If so, how will your plan *explicitly* lead to those outcomes? But if not, where will the cost benefits come from?

The second point here is that there are no easy network or organizational restructurings. Therefore, make sure that the disruption is worth it, by identifying the big costs early and working multiple levers to release these benefits.

3) Break the Tyranny of the "Here and Now"

Given the asynchronicity of timelines, any plan needs to simultaneously work to improve the current state and ensure alignment with a potential future state. What is clear is that no company can let the tyranny of the unknowable freeze them into inaction. At the broadest level, a workable plan is to identify future state scenarios and then disaggregate them back, so that you can identify the "no regrets" decisions that will move you forward. (How to do this and how to reconcile two different timelines is the focus of Chapter 11, "Network and Footprint Consolidation.")

4) Prepare for the Trade-off Decisions

To effectively target and take out large chunks of Organization/Product complexity, your business will have to assess and manage trade-offs, such as

- **Long-term benefits versus short-term metrics.** If your metrics are set up to encourage short-term thinking, then it will take an overt management act to commit to the longer-term benefit (e.g., "Yes, we are going to accept lower utilization on our plants as we migrate to a less cluttered product portfolio").
- **Profitability versus growth (or market share).** Sacrificing market share or "hard-won growth" for profitability.
- **Local versus global.** Sacrificing global participation for more targeted local density.
- **Select customers versus all customers.** You will need to give up some "bad customers" (those who are buying products in your portfolio that are destroying profit) so you can provide better service and stronger relationships to the (fewer) "good" customers.

Your ability to extract large chunks of costs may ultimately rest on where decision makers stand relative to the trade-offs. Identify and discuss these trade-offs before launching your efforts.

Recommended High-Value Battle Strategies

We have laid out in this chapter some of the key considerations when attacking he Organization/Product face of complexity. There are a number of specific methodologies—battle strategies—that we recommend for addressing key complexity issues. We will feature a number of them in Part III of this book. If the symptoms for this face ring true for you (as highlighted at the beginning of this chapter), turn to the chapters highlighted below for more information on specific battle strategies.

We'd recommend reading the Introduction to Part III, "Taking Ground," to ensure your battle plan is meeting key criteria for success. Then,

- Chapters 9 and 10 on Portfolio Optimization in combination with Chapter 11, "Network and Footprint Consolidation," create a strong platform for concurrent action on this face. The chapters on portfolio optimization offer a definitive and step-by-step approach to SKU reduction, which, as we've suggested in this chapter, is best paired with footprint consolidation.
- Chapter 11, "Network and Footprint Consolidation," also takes into account the issue of asynchronous time horizons and provides a means of making significant cost and capital reductions in the short term while aligning with long-term strategies. The Cadbury case featured in that chapter is instructive.
- When your product complexity issues reside with parts and components, similar principles apply; see Chapter 12, "Component Rationalization and Vendor Consolidation," for details.
- Another key approach that companies underuse is Dynamic Operations. By that we mean, being able to recognize situations that lend themselves to an analytical examination of trade-offs. For example, while SKU rationalization focuses on optimizing the portfolio, Dynamic Operations doesn't seek to optimize one variable, it assesses what the best option is, given a number of variables. Chapter 16, "Dynamic Operations: Optimizing Complexity Trade-offs," explores this in more detail.

Prepare from day 1 for internal resistance and pushback

We have discussed many normal responses to attempts to uproot complexity on this face. The takeaway is do not be surprised when you hear voices of dissent, or see indications of passive resistance. The action is to communicate strongly from day 1 that this is a necessary set of actions, but also will help prepare the company for the future.

If you have issues on this face, we'd recommend that you start with these. The rest of the chapters have application too but often for later phases. For example, many companies will look to improve their processes and productivity after they have addressed footprint and portfolio issues.

Conclusion

If it was important to get crisp alignment between your portfolio and your organization in normal economic conditions, it's paramount in a downturn when ROIC is hit by falling margins and rising cost of capital—a double hit to ROIC that translates to a double hit to shareholder value. Value creation becomes ever more concentrated in a smaller portion of the business; and customer willingness to pay for features or services that are not critically value-add is further eroded, meaning a greater portion of the product line, and the supporting costs and assets, fall under the banner of bad complexity. In public companies, the willingness of shareholders to carry assets tied to value destruction becomes ever thinner. In sum, the moment of zero tolerance for Organization/Product complexity is at hand.

Chapter 8 Endnotes

43 O'Toole, "Keeping it Simple" (Chapter 14), *Airline Business*, September 1, 2002.

44 Karyl Scott, "Executive Report: Battle Complexity to Add Profitability," *Information Week*, September 14, 1998.

Summary to Part II

In this part of the book, we have taken you deep into the interactions within each face of complexity to broaden your understanding of the nature of the problem and, moreover, to help you identify the biggest areas of opportunity for your business. As you read through the symptoms and then the interactions, it is likely that one face or set of interactions emerged as the top priority.

Of course having an inkling of where to start is a long way from a project plan! But it's the right place to start. From there, you will need to formulate two or three hypotheses about target areas that may offer the biggest potential payback in your target time frame.

Augment your informed judgment with validation exercises to confirm the scope and benefits for your initial campaign on complexity costs. For example, you may recognize the symptoms and interactions of the Organization/Product face as being an area of high potential. What follows next is the management discussion—and supporting analysis—to lay out with more definition the details of the effort, which may include, for example,

- agreement as a team on what the right focus area is (say, a combination of footprint consolidation and portfolio optimization)
- how the concurrent actions on these areas will interact and integrate
- the exact scope of such an effort
- the timeline and expected benefit

Most companies are well equipped for this scoping effort—informed, we hope, by your understanding of the interactions, having studied Part II.

One gap remains: the details of the battle strategies that we recommended at the ends of Chapters 6, 7, and 8. That will be the focus of Part III.

For reference, the following tables summarize the primary symptoms, dominant interactions, key implications, and recommended battle strategies for each of the faces of the Complexity Cube.

<table>
<tr><th colspan="2">Product/Process Face of Complexity</th></tr>
<tr><td>Symptoms</td><td>❑ A large portion of products are unprofitable, weighing down profits
❑ Excessively high inventory levels are consuming working capital and adding costs
❑ Product shortages due to strained capacity are resulting in lost sales
❑ Product surpluses are leading to markdowns, waste, and additional inventory costs
❑ Long lead times are frustrating customers
❑ Frequent changeovers are eroding production capacity
❑ Service delivery, customer service, and quality levels are below par
❑ Every action seems to have a negative reaction in another part of your operations</td></tr>
<tr><td>Interactions</td><td>1) Increased product variety increases inventory levels (and lead times) in a linear relationship
2) Increased product variety erodes production capacity (in a big way)
3) Low-volume products have a nonlinear impact on inventory and capacity
4) Demand variation magnifies the impacts of product variety
5) Setup times limit a process's ability to deliver product complexity
6) A process designed for simplicity breaks down under product variety</td></tr>
<tr><td>Implications</td><td>1) Adjust for the true drivers of cost
2) Remove product variety to make what remains even better
3) Remove both unprofitable products and those that cannibalize more than grow revenue
4) Structure your processes with requisite variety in mind
5) Consider your company's ability to deliver complexity when determining the right level of complexity for your portfolio</td></tr>
<tr><td>Battle Strategies</td><td>CHs 9 and 10: Portfolio Optimization (often in conjunction with CH 11 Network and Footprint Consolidation)
CH 12–Component Rationalization and Vendor Consolidation
CH 13–Enabling Variety with Lean Processes
CH 14– Process Segmentation: Minimizing the Effects of Variety
CH 16–Dynamic Operations: Optimizing Complexity Trade-offs</td></tr>
</table>

Process/Organization Face of Complexity	
Symptoms	❑ The organization seems overly complex and bloated; no one has a complete picture of what each group does ❑ Decisions that should take days take weeks; information flows slowly through multiple layers and silos in the organization ❑ Difficulty seeing or managing trade-offs that cross functional boundaries ❑ There is lots of activity but not much outcome ❑ There are poor customer service levels ❑ Poor product availability arises as a result of poor supply chain coordination ❑ Poorly implemented or complex use of IT systems weigh down processes and impede decision making
Interactions	1) "Exceptions" become the rule 2) Process and organizational interactions mask the linkages across the company 3) Excess process variation and imbalanced resource utilization drive long project lead times and low resource productivity 4) Process and organizational complexity compound each other
Implications	1) Start with a broad, integrated view of the business 2) Ensure your resource utilization levels fit the variation in your creative processes 3) Achieve a critical mass of change through coordinated, focused actions 4) Gauge the impact of Process/Organization complexity on your ability to execute—and deploy—a counterstrategy for executing your cost-reduction efforts
Battle Strategies	CH 11–Network and Footprint Consolidation CH 13–Enabling Variety with Lean Processes CH 14–Process Segmentation: Minimizing the Effects of Variety CH 15–Project Rationalization and Resource Utilization: Doing More Faster and with Fewer Resources CH 16–Dynamic Operations: Optimizing Complexity Trade-offs

Organization/Product Face of Complexity	
Symptoms	❑ The physical footprint is sprawling, with low or declining utilization ❑ The efforts of marketing, sales, and other functions are diffused over an unmanageable number of products and geographies ❑ Your supply base is fragmented ❑ Your sales organization, or your third-party distributors, resists efforts to focus your product line, citing a specific customer need ❑ IT systems have grown "organically" in response to new emerging needs to the point that today they represent a tangled web ❑ Management has discussed the need for network consolidation, but efforts are stymied by current production needs
Interactions	1) Product complexity traps organizational complexity 2) Organizational complexity traps product complexity 3) Organizational complexity creates accountability gaps and "blind spots" 4) Asynchronous time horizons paralyze decision making 5) People's rootedness impedes efforts to cut organizational and product complexity
Implications	1) Take a concurrent approach 2) Cut deep enough to release big costs 3) Break the tyranny of the here and now 4) Prepare for the trade-off decisions
Battle Strategies	CHs 9 and 10: Portfolio Optimization CH 11–Network and Footprint Consolidation CH 12–Component Rationalization and Vendor Consolidation CH 16–Dynamic Operations: Optimizing Complexity Trade-offs

Part III

Battle Strategies to Eliminate Complexity Costs

Introduction to Part III

Taking Ground

Nothing will ever be attempted if all possible objections must first be overcome.

— *Dr. Samuel Johnson*

In Part II of this book, we took you deep into the interactions between product, process, and organizational complexity so that you will have a fuller understanding of the issues and know where best to start and how best to proceed.

We provided Part II in the spirit of "broad understanding"; we provide Part III in the spirit of "focused action." At this juncture, therefore, we assume you now have a good sense of where your biggest issues exist (which face of the cube) and are formulating what to do first to get costs out and how to go after the prize.

In the following chapters, we discuss each of our battle strategies in more depth. We should say now that the seven approaches we highlight are by no means meant to be an exhaustive list. But in keeping with the 80/20 principle, what follows is our selection of the approaches that are typically the most suitable and are often of the highest value for the task at hand.

- Portfolio Optimization (SKU reduction) (Chapters 9 and 10)
- Network and Footprint Consolidation (Chapter 11)
- Component Rationalization and Vendor Consolidation (Chapter 12)
- Enabling Variety with Lean Processes (Chapter 13)
- Process segmentation: Minimizing the Effects of Variety (Chapter 14)
- Project Rationalization and Resource Utilization: Doing More Faster and With Fewer Resources (Chapter 15)
- Dynamic Operations: Optimizing Complexity Trade-Offs (Chapter 16)

Some of the strategies are well known but in our view have been overcomplicated (such as *Lean*); others are well known but often presented and executed incompletely (such as *SKU reduction*). Others are seldom leveraged (such as *Dynamic Operations*) but are very powerful. While you may recognize some of those listed below, we present a unique and differentiated take on each of them, informed by our experience and by the ideas presented in this book. The specific combination and priority of these battle strategies will depend on the nature and location of the complexity issues in your business. While we have recommended high-value battle strategies to address issues on each face of the Complexity Cube (at the end of Part II), we recognize that every case is different and what we have laid out will hopefully *inform*, but not *define*, the actions necessary in your specific battle plan.

Developing a Battle Plan

Our focus is not on project management; we assume you have those capabilities in place. However, we have seen good and bad battle plans. And a good battle plan for taking out complexity costs generally has the following five characteristics.

1) **It has C-level leadership (or equivalent).** Given the scope of the change that is likely with any war on complexity costs (such as changes to the product line or potential organizational changes), there really is no substitute for leadership from the top. If the leadership of an organization is not on board with the potential changes coming out of your original analysis, you may have to question the value of attempting to battle complexity in the first place. Whereas other initiatives can often succeed without C-level support, complexity issues are holistic in nature and cut across traditional corporate structures, as we've shown in this book. Moreover, some manifestations of complexity resist all but the most pointed efforts to remove it (recall the discussion in Chapter 8 on how complexity takes root on the Organization/Product face), necessitating the active support of top management.

   Keep in mind, too, that C-level leadership is not just about removing obstacles. It is also about leading the way. "Even while Rome was burning, people wanted to know what the city of the future would look like." This was true, said Anne Mulcahy, former CEO of Xerox, of the organization that she helped turn around. So even as Xerox focused on the urgent day-to-day work of saving itself, cutting costs and reorienting for growth, Mulcahy helped motivate the organization by painting a picture of what Xerox would look like after the turnaround was successful.

2) **It is structured as an integrating set of work streams.** Adopting the spirit of concurrent action but not driving the battle strategies through to implementation will lead to disappointing results. It is not enough to buy in to the notion and launch efforts in parallel. You must also ensure that the work streams supporting each area actually integrate at the execution level. For example, enabling portfolio rationalization may require a detailed migration plan that involves relocating product production from one facility to another (one element of a footprint consolidation). This is

detailed planning—and lack of it will discount the value of the concurrent approach.

3) **It has Quick Wins built in.** By definition, launching a war on complexity costs is an ambitious venture with big goals. But you want to avoid going 6 to 12 months into the effort without seeing meaningful benefits. A good plan has well-enunciated opportunities for Quick Wins. You will no doubt have spotted many of these as you assessed the dynamics and opportunities in your own organization. They are an important means of accelerating the financial payback while also getting some visible "points on the board."

4) **It's framed as Phase 1 (you acknowledge there will be subsequent phases).** As we've discussed earlier in the book, as you begin to remove some complexity, your ability to see additional opportunities will increase through improved data, reduced noise, and elimination of key roadblocks. Therefore, from the outset, a good plan will incorporate the ability to adapt as you continue to learn and your vision expands. You may not know at first what will be in Phase 2, but you know that there will be a Phase 2. Moreover, this acknowledgment that some actions will be taken later will help keep the scope of the initial phase under control—bite off more than you can chew and project timelines can get extended indefinitely. For example, beyond the initial phases where you may focus on removing complexity and its costs, you will need to do some work to keep complexity costs at bay. (Strategies for keeping complexity costs at bay are covered in Part IV.)

5) **It has a solid financial case.** In Part I, we outlined the approach for sizing up the prize—the total opportunity for waging war on complexity costs. It is a deliberately top-down approach to *quickly* provide a grounded sense of the size of the opportunity. But every battle plan requires a bottom-up quantification of the financial case. The financial case will outline the expected benefits, investments, and resources required and the timeline for realizing the benefits. It will document and make transparent key assumptions (this is particularly important if your current financial systems do not currently reflect true operating costs) and consider key risks. It will also highlight likely opportunities that this piece of work will enable (potential Phase 2s). The financial case will reflect a portion of the size of the prize—the initial set of battle strategies integrated into a single campaign.

Taking Ground Against a Difficult Foe

While we present the battle strategies that follow for simplicity as individual chapters, we urge you not to forget our perspective that they are most powerful when used in combination, as part of a coordinated campaign. (Recall the example from the end of Chapter 5 in which the highest cost savings—as well as highest operating profit—were generated by combining battle strategies to reduce the *amount* of complexity in the portfolio with battle strategies to reduce the *cost* of complexity.) Working concurrently is what shifts and lifts the peak of the Whale Curve and delivers your optimal operating point by

1) Removing complexity to obtain a better position on the Whale Curve
2) Removing complexity to change the shape of the Whale Curve (capturing the same or more revenue with less complexity by ensuring each product offers incremental value)
3) Becoming much better at delivering complexity to change the shape of the Whale Curve (effectively making complexity less expensive)

Figure 39: Changing the Shape of a Whale Curve

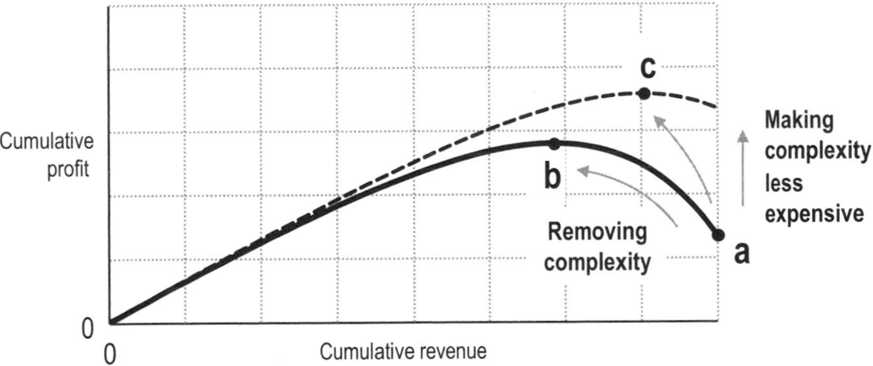

In addition to the notion of concurrent actions, there are lessons that we urge you to keep in mind as you launch your campaign:

- **Don't wait on perfect information to take action.** In an earlier chapter, we described how in *The Marine Corps Way*, the authors describe the "80 Percent Rule… which states that delaying any decision so that it can be made with more than 80 percent of the information is hesitation."[45] Likewise, here, it is usually better to move forward based on 80% of the information than to wait on full data.
- **Search for the 80/20 key levers and manage resource capacity.** We have discussed in the book the implication of too much work in the

pipeline (longer lead times). As we will discus in Chapter 15, high resource utilization also results in some unforeseen circumstances. Recognize that, in most cases, the confining resource is people's bandwidth, manage it carefully, and focus it on the highest value targets.

Conclusion

As we said in the Foreword, a war on complexity costs is about positioning a company as much to thrive in the future as to survive in economic difficulties. Part of the leaders' responsibility, therefore, is to enunciate clearly the vision for the future and, in so doing, get the team excited with the promise of what it will mean to be a cost-competitive organization—one that is lean and focused on the customer. Executing the battle strategies takes time, effort, and dedication from your team; and your campaign is more likely to succeed when the team understands the critical role each of the strategies plays within the larger war on complexity costs. But more than anything, we urge you to begin! Execution—taking ground—is ultimately what counts; and progress toward that goal is measured in your day-to-day actions. As Thomas Jefferson would say:

Act! Action will delineate and define you.

Introduction to Part III Endnotes

[45] Jason A. Santamaria, Vincent Martino and Erik K. Clemons, *The Marine Corps Way: Using Maneuver Warfare to Lead a Winning Organization* (New York: McGraw-Hill, 2004).

CHAPTER 9

Portfolio Optimization (A)

What Really Matters

Throughout this book, we have sought to broaden the discussion of complexity beyond just product complexity and SKU rationalization. But while removing product lines or SKUs is certainly not the only battle strategy, it is still central to the war on complexity costs. A twist we offer here is to focus on portfolio optimization rather than simply rationalization. The latter term is too often associated with companies that remove some portion of SKUs but fail to capture the significant benefits that rightsizing the portfolio can offer. (While this chapter explicitly addresses product portfolio optimization, the principles introduced in this chapter and the next apply just as well to any portfolio of revenue generating items, such as a portfolio of stores, dealerships, regions, and so on. For brevity and clarity, we will proceed in this chapter and the next addressing specifically product portfolio optimization.)

Does this battle strategy apply to you? It does if you answer yes to any of the following questions:

- Does a small portion of your product portfolio account for the bulk of your revenue and especially margin (as would be indicated by a more "extreme" Whale Curve)?
- Are your processes strained by the level of complexity you offer?
- Does the variety you offer make you uncompetitive with regard to product availability, service levels, and/or price?

Consider the experience of the following educational products company (which we will call "Company ABC"):

Over the years, Company ABC has brought to market a seemingly endless array of new products to satisfy customers, grow revenue, and capture more market share. Being highly responsive to its customers, the company's sales force has driven much of this innovation, with several similar or one-off products for specific customers. New product development was decentralized, with few barriers to moving a new product forward. Old products were seldom, if ever, retired.

Essentially, the thinking went that the more the company offers its customers, the happier they will be and the faster the company will grow. In fact, such customer-driven innovation was considered a competitive advantage: if a new product or variation on a product was added in response to the customer, how can it be bad?

But now, after years of responsiveness and innovation, the complexity of Company ABC's product portfolio has added costs throughout its supply chain and has reduced service levels to its customers. The company's manufacturing and supply chain processes are under strain to deliver the breadth of its portfolio. Inventory has grown fourfold and is tying up disproportionate amounts of working capital. Poor product availability, which used to not be a problem, is resulting in lost sales and potentially lost customers.

Worst of all, with the recent downturn, Company ABC experienced a contraction in its business. Still carrying the same amount of product complexity, now the costs of that complexity are compressed within less revenue, magnifying the negative impact on margin. What was once considered a competitive advantage (an ever-broadening product portfolio) has shown itself to be a distinct liability in the current environment—a luxury the company can no longer afford.

This is all the more critical as price and product availability rank high among its customers' key buying factors. The company has learned the hard lesson that what customers want isn't necessarily the same as what they will pay for. But with its high cost of complexity, the company is unable to compete on price and can't afford to invest to increase product availability; if anything, the company feels it needs to strip out capacity given the significant downturn.

How did Company ABC get into this situation, and how can it get out? It got trapped in a vicious cycle kicked off by the economic downturn, a cycle whose seeds were planted with over-proliferation in its product portfolio during better times. To break the cycle, the company needs to create some breathing room in its operations, and that requires taking out a chunk of complexity.

Does this example sound familiar to you? If after some self-examination you conclude that portfolio complexity isn't a problem in your business, then your efforts may be better spent on other battle strategies. If, however, the experience of the educational products company sounds all too familiar, or if you answered yes to the questions at the start of this chapter, then *portfolio optimization* should probably be a key battle strategy in your war on complexity costs, and we suggest you read on, as how you carry out this attack will determine how successful you are.

In this chapter and the next we will describe

- The common pitfalls of typical product rationalization efforts, including why they almost always focus on the easier but wrong metrics for SKU analysis
- What information is really needed for SKU analysis and streamlined approaches for getting that information
- The proper but counterintuitive categories of intelligent SKU rationalization (by "intelligent" we mean informed by a proper understanding of complexity and its interactions across the Complexity Cube)
- How intelligent SKU rationalization can minimize revenue loss while leading to much greater cost reduction and margin improvement than traditional approaches do
- How product portfolio optimization can serve as the foundation for revenue growth

But first, let's review what a product rationalization initiative typically looks like and identify why many product rationalization efforts fall short.

Why Traditional Rationalization Efforts Often Fail

To begin to understand why traditional rationalization efforts often fall short, it is helpful to first look at the product rationalization process, which can generally be broken down into six steps (Figure 40):

Figure 40: Steps in the Rationalization Process

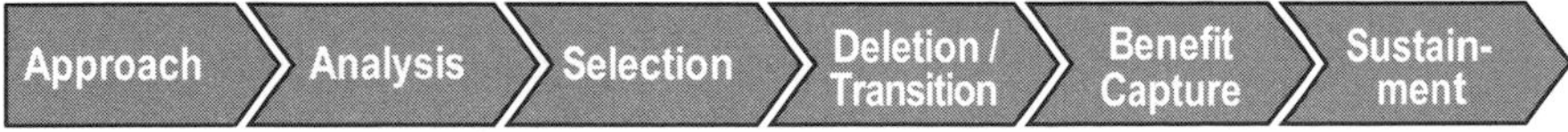

1. **Approach:** Company leadership or the project team determines the principles and methodology by which it will attack product portfolio complexity (e.g., What are the perspectives and viewpoints that will guide the effort? What are the objectives? Where will cost savings and other improvements come from?)
2. **Analysis:** Various data are collected and analyzed to establish a set of metrics—a fact base—upon which SKUs can be compared to determine which are more attractive and which less so. This is where project teams can often spend most of their time.

3. **Selection:** Based on the objectives, approach, and analysis, the project team proposes, other stakeholders push back, and company leadership approves a list of SKUs for deletion or transition.

4. **Deletion/Transition:** Execution of the plan. SKUs are deleted. Some sales are migrated to remaining products. Other sales, and in some cases customers, are lost. This is where the rubber meets the road.

5. **Benefit Capture:** Actions are taken to capture the benefits afforded by the complexity reduction.

6. **Sustainment:** The company builds and implements processes, behaviors, and discipline to keep bad complexity out.

It is important to note that these steps form a chain, meaning that failure at any one point can doom the overall effort—and we have seen product rationalization efforts fail at many different points on this chain. Success requires effectiveness across all six steps, but what we often see is product rationalization efforts that focus on some steps to the neglect of others. Typical problems we see are

- **Skipping Step 1 (Approach).** In the absence of a proper understanding of complexity and how best to attack it, many companies jump right to Analysis (Step 2). But without the proper foundation, teams typically spend precious time and resources on unproductive analysis (such as analyzing feature performance against competitor products) while often not performing the analyses really needed for Selection (Step 3).
- **Getting bogged down in Step 2 (Analysis).** In the face of uncertainty, project teams often feel most comfortable in analysis. Additional information seems to be the panacea for a lack of proper methodology, and doing more analysis makes them feel productive. However, if they come into this step without an understanding of the interactions on the Product/Process face of the Complexity Cube (something that should have been established in Step 1), teams are usually ill equipped to *understand*, let alone *quantify*, the impact of complexity and the benefit of removing specific SKUs.
- **Not cutting deep enough in Step 3 (Selection).** The apparent benefits of product complexity (revenue, resource utilization, happy customers) are much easier to tie to specific SKUs than are its drawbacks (interactions costs, strained processes performance, eroded profitability, customer overchoice). Therefore, the natural momentum to "keep the status quo" will generate resistance to selecting either particular SKUs or what will be perceived as "too many SKUs." That combined with a lack of planning for concurrent action (i.e., not understanding how complexity becomes

trapped on the Organization/Product face of the Complexity Cube, see p. 148) often leads a team to recommend smaller cuts than your company needs in order to turn the tide. And even if the team does manage to recommend a "deep" list of SKUs, they still have to overcome the problems with Step 4.

- **Fearing Step 4 (Deletion/Transition).** Fear of Step 4 is a prime cause of not cutting deep enough in Step 3. Risk aversion and pushback from stakeholders heightens when the rubber is about to meet the road. Without clarity of approach, benefits seem ephemeral while risks seem all too real. If leadership and the project team begin to focus more on the number of SKUs deleted than on the savings obtained, then the team will focus on eliminating low-risk SKUs, which may generate less benefit. We have seen many efforts declared successful (based on number of SKUs eliminated) that failed to deliver significant benefit. (Changing this mindset requires a robust understanding of the size of the prize and the actions necessary to capture it.)
- **Ignoring Step 5 (Benefit Capture).** Complexity reduction creates the opportunity for benefits, but action must still be taken to fully realize those benefits. Otherwise, the gains offered by complexity reduction can easily evaporate. (This is where the industrial equipment manufacturer introduced in Chapter 1 failed.) To lay the proper groundwork for capturing benefits, SKU-reduction efforts must clarify early on where benefits will come from (whether from, reduced headcount, lower inventory levels, or the closing of a facility, for example) and what actions will be taken to realize them.
- **Forgetting about Step 6 (Sustainment).** Portfolio optimization is less "a problem to solve" and more "an ongoing issue to manage." Without Step 6, companies often find that complexity creeps back in and they find themselves once again attacking SKUs down the road. But slashing SKUs from time to time is disruptive to the company and its customers and takes significant organizational energy. Much better is keeping the over-complexity out, which is addressed in Part IV of this book.

In short, there is a big gap between what should be a portfolio optimization exercise and what turns into simple SKU rationalization (see Figure 41, next page).

Figure 41: How Portfolio Optimization Turns Into SKU Rationalization

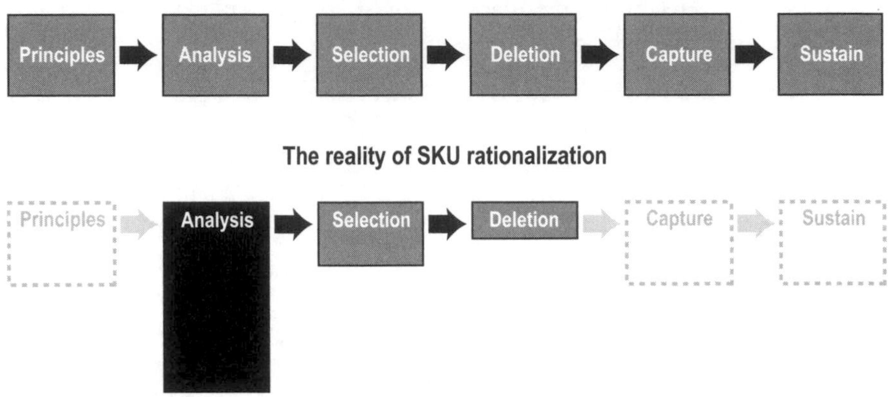

It should be clear that typical rationalization efforts that don't address the entire process risk falling very short of delivering significant and lasting impact to the company. It should also be clear that while taking the time to define your principles and methodology in Step 1 does not guarantee success, doing so facilitates and streamlines the following steps. Indeed, without that groundwork, many efforts will struggle to succeed.

Therefore, we will now turn to the proper approach to SKU rationalization, to what really matters in analyzing your portfolio. (The proper approach is based on the perspectives, principles, and recommendations presented in the previous portions of this book. In this chapter, we distill this information down to what it means for portfolio optimization.)

The Three Factors That Really Matter

Many SKU rationalization efforts focus on standard margin and sales volume, or revenue, as the primary determinants of which SKUs to remove. Other efforts, especially those in which standard margin figures cannot be relied upon, analyze what can seem to be an ever-widening variety of metrics (such as customer feedback, feature performance, parts commonality, share or market/wallet, service levels, usage patterns, and turns).

But at the end of the day, there are just three inputs that matter more than anything else:

- **Incremental revenue:** the revenue that would be lost if a particular SKU is deleted from a portfolio

- **Incremental cost:** the costs that would be released if a particular SKU is deleted from a portfolio
- **A lifecycle perspective:** a particular SKU's position on its lifecycle as compared to other SKUs and what this means for future performance

These factors are so dominant that *reasonable estimates of each of these three factors will yield much better SKU rationalization selections than will precise data on any one factor or anything else for that matter.*

While these certainly aren't the only inputs that can be considered (and particular industries will have select additions or modifiers, such as including shelf space utilization for retailers), the analysis boils down to these factors, with other helpful metrics essentially serving to make better estimates of these factors.

The "incremental" label on the first two factors is key, since the net value a SKU brings to a company is determined by its *incremental* revenue and *incremental* cost, not its actual revenue and standard cost (see Figure 42). Looking at *incremental* revenue and costs *requires considering the SKU in relation to the rest of the portfolio.* But in most analyses, SKUs are evaluated individually; and the typical measures used, such as revenue and standard cost, are at best proxies for (and often very poor proxies for) incremental revenue and cost.

Figure 42: SKU Net Value

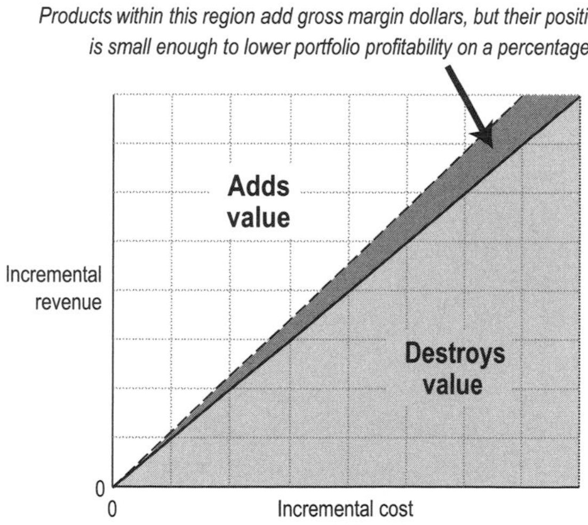

Determining the value of a particular SKU comes down to a comparison of its incremental revenue with its incremental costs. If incremental revenue is greater than incremental cost (meaning that deleting the SKU would result in greater total revenue loss than cost release), then the SKU adds net value. If the reverse is true (incremental cost > incremental revenue), then the SKU destroys value. Some products fall into a narrow region where they have a small positive net value, which makes overall profits larger on a dollar basis but dilutes profitability on a percentage basis.

Example of Evaluating "Incrementality"

Consider the example shown in Table I. The table shows two scenarios:

1) A portfolio of Product A alone
2) A portfolio of Products A and B together

Table I: Example of Incremental Revenue, Cost, and Margin

	Product A only	Products A & B			Analysis of Product B	
	A	A	B	Total	Typical approach	Incremental approach
Revenue	$100.00	$70.00	$40.00	$110.00	$40.00	$10.00
Cost	$80.00	$57.40	$33.20	$90.60	$33.20	$10.60
Margin ($)	$20.00	$12.60	$6.80	$19.40	$12.60	($0.60)
Margin (%)	20%	18%	17%	18%	17%	(6%)

This table compares a portfolio of just one product (A) to one that has two products (A and B). The incremental performance of Product B (its incremental revenue, cost, and margin) is based on comparing Product A only to the combined Product A and B portfolio. As you can see, in typical analyses that do not consider the impact on Product A, Product B looks like it has a positive 17% impact on margin. But using an incremental view, that impact is minus 6%. In short, product performance can look very different using an incremental approach (compared to a traditional non-incremental analysis) because incremental figures represent the actual impact of both revenue and cost on the company.

As shown in the table, adding Product B to the portfolio (as compared to just having Product A) raises total revenue by 10% (from $100 to $110) but also cannibalizes 30% of Product A's revenue. Typical approaches to evaluating Product B would consider its revenue of $40 and its **positive 17%** margin. But an incremental approach recognizes its incremental revenue as $10 and its incremental gross margin as **negative 6%**—quite a difference. Having Product B, as compared to not having it—which is what product rationalization is all about—destroys value, *but that fact isn't reflected in traditional revenue and margin figures.*

Adding in Lifecycle Considerations

The third input, the lifecycle perspective, must be included for two reasons:

1) Portfolio optimization aims at optimizing the future performance of the portfolio, but financial and operational data describe past performance.

2) Even more importantly, taking a lifecycle perspective is necessary for determining the sequence in which you evaluate SKUs (i.e., which product is incremental to which). If Product A is on the downswing compared to Product B, you may want to consider Product B first and look at the incremental impact of adding or keeping Product A in the portfolio. The reverse would be true if Product A is on the upswing and Product B is on the last legs of its lifecycle.

Consider the example shown in Table J, which compares a portfolio of two products to that of either product alone.

Table J: Comparison of Products Alone and Together (no lifecycle impact)

	Product A only	Product B only	Products A & B together		
	A	B	A	B	Total
Revenue	$70.00	$70.00	$50.00	$50.00	$100.00
Cost	$60.00	$60.00	$44.00	$44.00	$88.00
Margin ($)	$10.00	$10.00	$6.00	$6.00	$12.00
Margin (%)	14%	14%	12%	12%	12%

A portfolio of either product A or B alone would have $70 in revenue, but a portfolio of them together would have $100. Thus either might be said to have incremental revenue of $30 to the other, and you might mistakenly conclude that each was a poor product, possibly resulting in both products being targeted as candidates for deletion. However, in determining incrementality, it is necessary to establish **precedence** (an ordering of products from good to bad, sometimes within product families and then between product families). Once you have the ordering, you consider the incremental revenue for less attractive products against that of the more attractive products.

Precedence, therefore, is key to incrementality, and it depends on two things: **dependence** between products and relative **attractiveness** among products.

Dependence means that one product cannot exist without another product. For example, Chevrolet wouldn't offer upgraded wheels for its new Camaro if it wasn't offering the Camaro itself. Since the upgraded wheels are *dependent* on having the car, the Camaro has precedence over the wheels. (There are innumerable examples; consider the accessory sets to your child's Barbie or apps for your iPhone.) Dependence is rather straightforward and is the easier part of precedence to figure out.

Where dependence isn't a factor—meaning the products can be said to be independent—precedence is based on the relative *future* attractiveness between products. To determine future attractiveness, we have to consider a product's position along its lifecycle. This doesn't simply mean how old or new a product is, as some products can have very short lifetimes while others are much longer. It means what is likely to happen with sales of that product—stay steady, increase, or decrease—over the next several years.

Consider Table K, which adds the lifecycle perspective to the example previously shown in Table J. If products A and B have the same performance but product A is in decline and B on the rise, then it would make sense to consider product B to be more attractive and, therefore, to have precedence. Product B's incremental revenue would be $70 (incremental to not having any products); and that of product A would be $30 (incremental to just having product B alone). In this case, the net value to the company from keeping Product A in the portfolio is $2, far less than product B's net value of $10. Indeed, *incrementality and precedence combine in effect to greatly magnify apparent differences in value between products—but this is a much more accurate picture of reality.*

Table K: Incremental Analysis Added Into the Mix

	Prod. A only	Prod. B only	Products A & B together			Incremental analysis	
	A	B	A	B	Total	B (rising)	A (falling)
Revenue	$70.00	$70.00	$50.00	$50.00	$100.00	$70.00	$30.00
Cost	$60.00	$60.00	$44.00	$44.00	$88.00	$60.00	$28.00
Margin ($)	$10.00	$10.00	$6.00	$6.00	$12.00	$10.00	$2.00
Margin (%)	14%	14%	12%	12%	12%	14%	7%

This table takes Table J and adds on an incremental analysis supposing that Product B was determined to be in the early stages of its lifecycle (sales will continue to rise) while Product A is in the declining stages of its lifecycle. While both A and B seem identical in performance based on traditional metrics, given lifecycle considerations, Product B must clearly be given precedence over Product A. The added columns to the table (in the heavy outline) shows what happens when you consider having just Product B in the portfolio (compared to no other products) and the incremental analysis for Product A, which compares the *combined* portfolio (Product B + Product A) to a portfolio of just Product B alone. With this new analysis, Product B would definitely be considered a "keeper," while Product A might be a candidate for removal.

Conclusion

In this chapter we have broken out the six steps on the portfolio optimization process, pointed out why many SKU rationalization efforts fail at many points along the process, and shown which three factors matter more than anything else in evaluating the value of individual SKUs. But the devil is in the details, and the next chapter explores some of the more significant details for evaluating incremental revenue and cost for your products and how to use that information to identify which SKUs to remove, and possibly add, to optimize your portfolio.

CHAPTER 10

Portfolio Optimization (B)

SKU Analysis and Selection

Chapter 9 explained why you need to consider incremental revenue and cost, along with lifecycle considerations, to decide which SKUs to target as candidates for deletion and which to keep. In this chapter, we take you through the calculations necessary to properly analyze SKUs and describe the various categories of SKU removal and subsequent analyses that will let you pull that information together to develop a solid plan for portfolio optimization that will eliminate a large chunk of complexity costs.

Understanding Incremental Revenue

For a given product or SKU, incremental revenue depends on three things:

1) **Revenue:** the actual sales of the product or SKU
2) **Substitutability:** the extent to which the product's sales would transfer to the company's remaining products if the item were no longer offered
3) **Linkage:** the extent to which sales of other products would be lost if this product were removed

The relationship between these factors and incremental revenue can be expressed as the following equation:

Incremental Revenue = Revenue * (1 – Substitutability) + Linked Revenue

Calculating revenue should be simply a matter of pulling the right figures out of your financial records. Substitutability and linkage, however, are less commonly used, so we'll go through those items in more detail.

Substitutability

Greater substitutability means lower incrementality, since the more of a product's revenue that is transferable to remaining products (i.e., the greater its substitutability), the less it is lost upon deletion of the product—hence, the less *incremental* revenue the product actually delivers. But while substitutability and incrementality are inversely related, the two factors are not simply opposites (meaning that while high substitutability means low incremental revenue, low incremental revenue doesn't necessarily mean high substitutability).

This is an important point since it has implications for SKU selection. From the previous equation for incremental revenue, we can tell that incremental revenue can be small for two reasons:

1) Having small sales revenue (there's not many dollars in play to begin with)

2) Having large substitutability (customers will convert to other choices in the portfolio if the product disappears)

But while each reduces the revenue lost from SKU removal, they have *very* different effects on the remaining products, the Whale Curve, and thus the amount of costs that can be removed. Let's consider each reason separately.

Removal of products that have low *incremental* revenue simply because they have low *sales* revenue doesn't change the shape of the Whale Curve. If properly selected, removing low-sales-revenue products with low substitutability can reduce costs by moving the portfolio and the company to a better (i.e., higher) point on the Whale Curve, but the general shape of the Whale Curve doesn't change because the revenues of the remaining products don't change.

Therefore, the much greater opportunity lies in removing SKUs with high substitutability, *especially those with reasonably sized revenues.* At first glance, it may seem antithetical to SKU rationalization to target SKUs with reasonable revenue. But remember that it is incremental revenue that counts, and **removing products with reasonable revenue but low incremental revenue** (due to high substitutability, as shown in the previous equation) not only **limits revenue loss** but also **adds revenue to the remaining products.** We like to

Estimates of substitutability

Although a precise determination of substitutability in many cases can seem beyond reach, especially in large convoluted portfolios, don't lose heart. An informed estimate of substitutability can take you far. If you are reluctant to estimate, consider that making SKU rationalization selections based on total revenue is the same as assuming substitutability to be zero. Even a rough estimate is a great improvement.

think of this as "spreading" or "stretching" good complexity over greater revenue or, in other words, satisfying a given volume of demand with less variety, with all of the tremendous cost benefits that brings.

As shown in Figure 43, **stretching a given level of complexity over more revenue has the same effect on the complexity cost curve and the Whale Curve as making complexity less expensive.** Removal of SKUs with high substitutability, whether transferring revenue from bad complexity to good or from good to better, stretches the complexity cost curve to the right and the Whale Curve and its margin peak *up and to the right.* This not only limits revenue loss but also creates a greater overall cost-reduction opportunity, sometimes significantly so.

Figure 43: Impact of Stretching Complexity across the Most Revenue

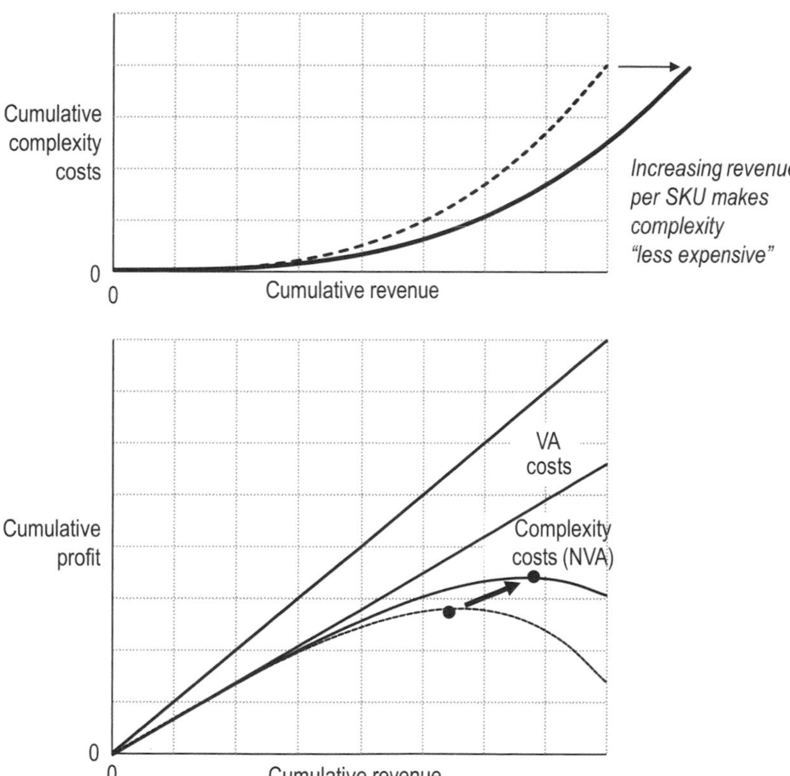

Stretching complexity over more revenue essentially stretches the complexity cost curve to the right (upper chart), which has the effect of stretching the Whale Curve up and to the right (lower chart). The new peak margin point on the Whale Curve presents greater margin (cost over savings) and more revenue than the previous peak margin point.

Revenue per SKU, an indicator of overall portfolio health

It should now be clear that a key complexity metric is the **average revenue per SKU for your good complexity.** From a complexity perspective, this is an indicator of the overall health of your portfolio, and it can be grown in three ways:

- Shifting of revenue from bad complexity to good (removal of "bad" products with high substitutability)
- Shifting of revenue from good complexity (with high substitutability/low incremental revenue) to other good complexity
- Organic revenue growth across the portfolio, which is tough in most industries in today's climate

In the current business climate, however, for many companies sales shrinkage has compressed complexity over less revenue, concentrating complexity costs with devastating impact on margin. The good news is that portfolio optimization can restore much of this in the short term (through the first two options) and lay the foundation for growth in the longer term (through the last option).

Revenue Linkage

The last factor used to determine incremental revenue is revenue linkage. For a given product, we define **linked revenue** as *revenue from the sales of other products that would be lost if the product in question were deleted.* SKUs with high levels of linked revenue are the oft-named **door openers.** Their linked revenue can often be much greater than the revenues from sale of the product itself.

However, real door openers are not nearly as numerous as they are often made to seem. In our experience, companies are much more likely than their customers to see a SKU as a door opener. Companies, therefore, must be cautious not to grant door opener status to too many of their SKUs. In fact, **the better assumption to start with is that SKUs have little to no linked revenue unless reasonably shown otherwise.** The intention in most cases is *not* to be too precise in determining the amount of linked revenue that exists. Rather, the disciplined exercise of simply estimating the level of linked revenue can serve as a forcing function to help separate the real door openers from the imposters.

Pulling these incremental revenue concepts together, consider the example of four products shown in Table L:

Table L: Incremental Revenue in Four Product Scenarios

	Product A	Product B	Product C	Product D
Revenue	**$1,000**	**$1,000**	**$50**	**$50**
Substitutability	0%	95%	0%	0%
Linked revenue	$0	$0	$0	$500
Incremental revenue	**$1,000**	**$50**	**$50**	**$550**

Product A is a high-volume product with no substitutability and, therefore, it has large incremental revenue. **Product B** has the same revenue as A, but since it has significant substitutability, its incremental revenue is significantly less than that of Product A. **Product C** has the same incremental revenue as Product B, but simply because of small actual revenue rather than high substitutability. Incremental cost aside, although products B and C have equal revenue, removal of product B would have a greater positive impact on the rest of the portfolio, because of its large substitutable revenue, than would removal of product C. Lastly, **Product D** has low actual revenue but has significant linked revenue, making its incremental revenue rather significant and larger than either Product B or C.

Understanding Incremental Cost

Understanding incremental revenue is central to SKU rationalization, as it gives a very different, more accurate picture of what each of your SKUs contributes to your top line. But the other side of the question is, what does it cost you for that incremental revenue?

For a given product or SKU, its **incremental cost** is the sum of

1) **The cost for the item itself for the portion of revenue that is incremental.** This is also called its **explicit costs,** which are the total costs (value-add [VA] and non-value-add [NVA]) that are incurred to develop, manufacture, deliver, and support the product. (In this sense, explicit doesn't refer to the costs that are clear or quantified but those that are incurred for the specific item in question.) By definition, the sum of the explicit costs across all products should equal the total cost base.

2) **The cost the product adds to other products due to its existence in the portfolio and supply chain.** These are also called **implicit costs,** which are the costs that are caused by a particular SKU but borne by other SKUs because of the complexity interactions described in Part II, primarily on the Product/Process face of the Complexity Cube (i.e., the impact adds explicit cost to the other items but is *implicit* to the SKU in

question). These costs, by definition, are NVA costs and are at the core of complexity. Although implicit costs cancel each other out—they are essentially a reallocation of costs so the sum of implicit costs across the portfolio is zero—they can have a significant impact on the true incremental profitability of an individual product and, therefore, on your ability to reduce costs through SKU reduction.

3) **The cost associated with linked revenue, if any.** This is simply the applicable cost of any other products whose revenues were included as linked revenue in determining the incremental revenue of a particular SKU. Including this is necessary to compare apples with apples when determining incremental margin.

The steps for calculating these costs across the portfolio are

1. Begin with your standard cost per unit for each SKU and separate the VA from the NVA costs
2. Reallocate NVA costs (largely overhead) according to the real drivers of these costs to determine the **complexity-adjusted standard cost** and corresponding **complexity-adjusted unit margin**
3. Determine precedence between products based on dependence and attractiveness (incremental revenue, profitability as shown after Step 2, lifecycle considerations, etc.)
4. Determine incremental revenue based on precedence
5. Establish a line in the sand for SKU deletion (based on each product's incremental revenue and adjusted unit margin from Step 2)
6. Reallocate NVA costs between SKUs to reflect implicit costs (the costs added to the good products due to having bad ones around—based on precedence and the line in the sand)
7. Add the cost of any linked revenue

The final result is the **complexity-adjusted incremental cost.** To help explain these steps, we will use an example. (More detailed calculations are in Appendix C; here we illustrate the concept and relative impact.)

Example of Steps 1 and 2

Consider the example shown in Table M. This company's product portfolio consists of one high-volume product, a medium-volume product, and two small-volume products. (Aside from differences in customer demand and production volume, the characteristics for each of the products are the same.)

Table M: Complexity-Adjusted Costing

	Standard Costs*				Complexity-Adjusted Standard Costs*				
	A	B	C	D	A	B	C	D	Total
Vol. (# units)	70	22	4	4	70	22	4	4	100
Price	$1.00	$1.00	$1.00	$1.00	$1.00	$1.00	$1.00	$1.00	$1.00
Revenue	**$70.00**	**$22.00**	**$4.00**	**$4.00**	**$70.00**	**$22.00**	**$4.00**	**$4.00**	**$100.00**
Costs/unit									
Raw materials	$0.30	$0.30	$0.30	$0.30	$0.30	$0.30	$0.30	$0.30	
Conversion**	$0.40	$0.40	$0.40	$0.40	$0.40	$0.40	$0.40	$0.40	
Overhead	$0.15	$0.15	$0.15	$0.15	$0.14	$0.16	$0.20	$0.20	
Inventory	$0.05	$0.05	$0.05	$0.05	$0.04	$0.06	$0.15	$0.15	
Total	**$0.90**	**$0.90**	**$0.90**	**$0.90**	**$0.88**	**$0.92**	**$1.04**	**$1.04**	
VA	$0.70	$0.70	$0.70	$0.70	$0.70	$0.70	$0.70	$0.70	
NVA	$0.20	$0.20	$0.20	$0.20	$0.18	$0.22	$0.34	$0.34	
Total	**$0.90**	**$0.90**	**$0.90**	**$0.90**	**$0.88**	**$0.92**	**$1.04**	**$1.04**	
Total costs									
VA	$49.00	$15.40	$2.80	$2.80	$49.00	$15.40	$2.80	$2.80	$70.00
NVA	$14.00	$4.40	$0.80	$0.80	$12.43	$4.81	$1.38	$1.38	$20.00
Total	**$63.00**	**$19.80**	**$3.60**	**$3.60**	**$61.43**	**$20.21**	**$4.18**	**$4.18**	**$90.00**
Margin									
$	**$7.00**	**$2.20**	**$0.40**	**$0.40**	**$8.57**	**$1.79**	**($0.18)**	**($0.18)**	**$10.00**
%	**10.0%**	**10.0%**	**10.0%**	**10.0%**	**12.2%**	**8.1%**	**(4.5%)**	**(4.5%)**	**10.0%**

* Some totals do not match because of rounding

** Direct conversion costs at gross production rate (i.e., not loaded for plant overhead, changeovers, or downtime)

This table illustrates reallocation of NVA costs to determine the complexity-adjusted standard costing for product portfolio with four products.

VA costs are the raw materials costs and the direct conversion costs incurred to create the finished goods. As all four products here are the same (other than demand), their VA costs are the same. Further, the company uses a typical peanut butter approach to allocate inventory and overhead costs, spreading these in proportion to production volume. As a result, the standard cost across all four products is equal at $0.90/unit, and standard margins are equal at 10%.

But, as shown in Chapter 6, **low-volume products are disproportionate consumers of capacity, inventory costs, and other overhead**. Given reasonable assumptions about product and production line parameters, correcting for the actual drivers of these NVA costs shows the adjusted standard margins to be very different—ranging from positive 12.2% to negative 4.5%. (See Appendix C for details.)

The point here isn't to launch an exhaustive activity-based costing (ABC) exercise or to conduct rigorous cost analysis SKU-by-SKU to determine costs precisely. Rather, it is to use your understanding of the drivers of NVA costs and how they manifest in your operation to make the significant adjustments that can quickly provide much better information upon which to base SKU rationalization decisions (see sidebar on revisiting 80/20 costing, next page).

Example of Steps 3 to 6

The next few steps involve determining precedence, determining incremental revenue from the precedence determinations, and then drawing a line in the sand—a demarcation line beyond which SKUs will be considered for deletion.

Returning to our example, assuming no lifecycle or linked revenue issues, it seems rather clear that Product A, with the greatest revenue and highest complexity-adjusted standard margin, has precedence, with Product B next, and Products C and D after that.

For completeness, let's assume that an evaluation of other factors suggests that Product C is preferable to Product D and hence has precedence over it. We will also assume for the moment that there is no substitutability between the products, that customers will not switch to another product if the one they want is cut. (We'll make this simplifying assumption in part so that later we can consider substitutability and show how much difference it makes.) We will also assume no linked revenue (i.e., sales of the four products are independent of each other) so that the incremental revenue is simply the actual revenue.

What do those assumptions mean for the assessment? Given the analysis so far, it seems rather clear that the demarcation line, the line in the sand, should be drawn between products A and B, which should be preserved, and C and D, which should be candidates for cutting. But before making the final call and estimating the financial impact, we can add one more refinement to the analysis by estimating the amount of NVA costs that the presence of Products C and D add to Products A and B—the implicit costs borne by products A and B that are caused by the presence of Products C and D.[46]

Details of this implicit cost analysis are shown in Appendix C. To summarize, the results show that, as low-volume products, not only are Products C and D disproportionate consumers of capacity, overhead, and inventory, but also their mere presence adds NVA costs to Products A and B. This is shown by comparing a portfolio of just Products A and B to the *complexity-adjusted standard cost* figures for the portfolio of Products A through D (from Table M) to determine the *complexity-adjusted incremental costs.* The result of this adjustment is shown in Table O. (Note that although products C and D lower overhead costs per unit by increasing absorption of overhead, their impact on the inventory costs per unit for products A and B outweighs this affect.)

80/20 costing, revisited

In principle, 80/20 costing means making the 20% of adjustments that give you 80% of the answer. Take inventory costs, for example. In calculating standard costs, most companies spread inventory costs (the cost for the warehouse, for example) evenly across the number of units that pass through the warehouse. Each unit is burdened with an equal share of the pie. But this is just as wrong as allocating inventory costs evenly between product lines, regardless of their volume.

In a typical supply chain, lower-volume products enjoy fewer inventory turns; hence, each low-volume item spends more time in the warehouse. It makes sense, then, to burden lower-volume products with a greater portion of inventory costs per unit; but how much more? Not knowing this, most companies continue to use the easy (but wrong) peanut butter approach.

By understanding process and product interactions, we are able to make a much better assumption. High-volume products typically consume more warehouse cost *in total* but less *per unit* than their low-volume counterparts. The right level of cost burden fortunately happens to be right in the middle of those two approaches (equal total cost vs. equal per-unit cost).

Take, for example, a high-volume product whose volume is 16 times that of a low-volume counterpart. In a typical environment (if properly operated), each unit of the high-volume product would on average spend about one-fourth the time in the warehouse that the low-volume product spends. The **per-unit inventory cost** of the high-volume product should, therefore, be approximately one-fourth that of the low-volume product. But since it has 16 times the volume of the low-volume product, its **total inventory cost** across all units would be about 4 times that of the low-volume product.

Table N

	Product 1	Product 2	Ratio
Volume (units)	16,000	1,000	16:1
Total inventory cost	$4,000	$1,000	4:1
Inventory cost/unit	$0.25	$1.00	1:4

Either approach—allocating inventory costs either equally between units (i.e., in proportion to revenue) or equally between product lines—misrepresents the relative inventory costs by a factor of 4 (the square root of 16, the ratio of the production volumes for these products).

This relationship provides a useful rule of thumb: **all else being equal, the ratio of inventory costs between two products is proportional to the square root of the ratio of their demands.** This rule of thumb is nearly as easy to apply as the peanut butter approach but provides a significantly better estimate of actual cost by product.

Table O: Determining Complexity-Adjusted Incremental Costing

	Portfolio of just products A & B*		Complexity-adjusted incremental costs*				
	A	B	A	B	C	D	Total
Precedence	1	2	1	2	3	4	
Incremental revenue	**$70.00**	**$22.00**	**$70.00**	**$22.00**	**$4.00**	**$4.00**	**$100.00**
Costs/unit							
Raw materials	$0.300	$0.300	$0.300	$0.300	$0.300	$0.300	
Conversion**	$0.400	$0.400	$0.400	$0.400	$0.400	$0.400	
Overhead	$0.157	$0.182	$0.144	$0.156	$0.198	$0.198	
Inventory	$0.019	$0.034	$0.035	$0.062	$0.147	$0.147	
Total	**$0.876**	**$0.916**	**$0.878**	**$0.919**	**$1.045**	**$1.045**	
VA	$0.700	$0.700	$0.700	$0.700	$0.700	$0.700	
NVA	$0.176	$0.216	$0.178	$0.219	$0.345	$0.345	
Total	**$0.876**	**$0.916**	**$0.878**	**$0.919**	**$1.045**	**$1.045**	
Total costs							
VA	$49.00	$15.40	$49.00	$15.40	$2.80	$2.80	$70.00
NVA (explicit)	$12.33	$4.76	$12.43	$4.81	$1.38	$1.38	$20.00
NVA (implicit)			($0.10)	($0.05)	$0.07	$0.07	$0.00
Total	**$61.33**	**$20.16**	**$61.33**	**$20.16**	**$4.25**	**$4.25**	**$90.00**
Margin							
$	**$8.67**	**$1.84**	**$8.67**	**$1.84**	**($0.25)**	**($0.25)**	**$10.00**
%	**12.4%**	**8.4%**	**12.4%**	**8.4%**	**(6.3%)**	**(6.3%)**	**10.0%**

* Some totals do not match because of rounding

** Direct conversion costs at gross production rate (i.e., not loaded for plant overhead, changeovers, or downtime)

This table shows how to reallocate implicit NVA costs to determine the complexity-adjusted incremental costing for a four-product portfolio.

For example, in Table M the complexity-adjusted standard NVA cost for Product A was $12.43. But as shown in Table O, in a portfolio of *just* Products A and B, this figure would be $12.33. (Product A is $0.10 cheaper when Products C and D are not in the mix.) The $0.10 difference in the cost of Product A is due to the presence of Products C and D (that $0.10 is an *explicit* cost of Product A but an *implicit* cost of Products C and D). These implicit costs are complexity costs, so they will tend to grow geometrically with the number of products; the impact can be much greater in portfolios of significant variety.

As is the case in this example, adjusting for implicit NVA costs widens gross margin differences between the products within the line of demarcation and those outside it. The impact from our analysis so far on gross margins is summarized in Table P, next page.

Table P: Complexity Adjustments on Gross Margin

Line of demarcation →

	A	B	C	D	Overall
Standard margin	10.0%	10.0%	10.0%	10.0%	10.0%
Comp. adj. standard margin	12.2%	8.1%	(4.5%)	(4.5%)	10.0%
Comp. adj. incremental margin*	12.4%	8.4%	(6.3%)	(6.3%)	10.0%

* Assumes no revenue substitutability

Notice that the complexity-adjusted cost figures—showing negative impacts for Products C and D—would lead to very different decisions regarding SKU rationalization than the standard cost and margin figures. This shows the dramatic impact of complexity-adjusted costing. (Again, we reiterate that reasonable approximations around the right factors yield much better results than a precise or exhaustive analysis that doesn't recognize the fundamental dynamics at play.)

Adding Substitutability to the Scenario

Before moving on, this is a good point to return for the moment to the impact of revenue substitutability. We have said that removing SKUs with high substitutability makes the remaining SKUs more profitable. This profit lift on the better SKUs—or, more correctly, the lack of it if the poorer SKU is kept—is another implicit cost of keeping the poorer SKU around.

If we rework the previous example assuming that the two poor performing SKUs (Products C and D) have 50% substitutability (instead of no substitutability, as we had previously assumed), then the margin gap widens dramatically, as shown in Table Q (which is an update of Table P).

Table Q: Demarcation Assuming 50% Substitutability

Line of demarcation →

	A	B	C	D	Overall
Standard margin	10.0%	10.0%	10.0%	10.0%	10.0%
Comp. adj. standard margin	12.2%	8.1%	(4.5%)	(4.5%)	10.0%
Comp. adj. incremental margin (with no substitutability)	12.4%	8.4%	(6.3%)	(6.3%)	10.0%
Comp. adj. incremental margin (with 50% substitutability*)	**12.6%**	**9.0%**	**(30.9%)**	**(30.9%)**	**10.0%**

* Revenue of $70, $22, $4, $4 for Products A, B, C, D, respectively become $72 and $24 for Products A and B alone.

Revenue substitutability has a dramatic impact on the ability to use SKU reduction to remove costs and obtain a higher-margin position (and this example assumes the same overall level of fixed assets). Table R shows the total margin and revenue before and after deleting products C and D for both no substitutability and 50% substitutability.

Table R: Impact of Product Removal

	Revenue	Margin ($)	Margin (%)
Base case (Products A, B, C, D)	$100.00	$10.00	10.0%
Removal of C & D (no substitutability)	$92	$10.51	11.4%
Removal of C & D (50% substitutability)	$96	$11.23	11.7%

Notice that while 50% substitutability in Products C and D, by definition, reduces by half the revenue lost if they are deleted, it *more than doubles* the lift on gross margin dollars in this scenario (while 50% substitutability reduces the revenue loss from $8 to $4, it increases the margin lift from $0.51 to $1.23).

Revenue substitutability significantly enhances the gains possible from SKU rationalization, and complexity-adjusted costing enables you to see what those gains may be. Proper SKU rationalization analysis, therefore, requires a view of both. It should be clear that either without the other gives a myopic result.

We will now build on the previous discussion of what drives proper SKU analysis to more directly address SKU selection.

Implications: Categories of SKU removal

Some SKUs are clearly easier to select for removal than others, but while the easiest cuts should be selected first, the more impactful ones are the deeper ones (finding SKUs that seem OK on the surface but that, after further analysis, prove to be harming more than helping the portfolio).

And deeper is important, not for releasing more "bad" revenue[47] (as we've shown, by focusing on incremental revenue, you can make intelligent SKU-reduction choices that will actually minimize revenue loss) but for ensuring you will reach significant cost-reduction breakpoints, the points at which fixed assets can be released. That, in turn, allows you to lower overhead cost across the portfolio, turning many SKUs from unprofitable to profitable—thereby reducing the amount of revenue that is "bad."

The point isn't how much revenue is cut but how far into the portfolio you really look to find the SKUs that you should cut (see Figure 44, next page) to maximize margin. And this is key. By pushing the analysis far into the portfolio, you will uncover opportunities for much greater cost reduction with greater revenue preservation.

Figure 44: Visualizing Optimization

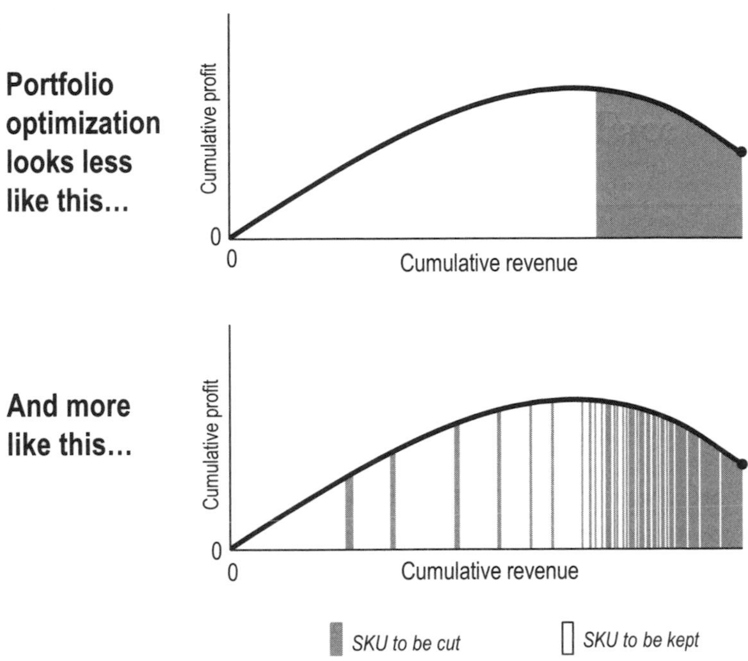

Cutting a portfolio deeply is less about how much revenue is cut, as represented by the top graph, and more about how deep into the portfolio you can look to find SKUs that you should cut, as shown in the bottom graph.

It is helpful then to outline several categories of SKU rationalization, which we list in Table S. By understanding these categories and the drivers of incrementality, you will be able to quickly add structure to your effort and achieve a rough segmentation of your SKUs before going through the entire incremental analysis.

Table S: Categories of SKU Rationalization

SKU removal categories	Types of SKUs in scope		Portion that should be removed	Characteristics of SKUs that should be removed	Nature of impact
	Profitability	Typical revenue per SKU			
"Cleaning the attic"	SKUs for which there is essentially no activity		All	All	Removes "noise"
Removing the **"small losers"**	Very unprofitable	Small	Nearly all	All*	Achieves a better position on the Whale Curve
Removing the **"sacrificial sinners"**	Unprofitable	Medium	Many	Cannot become profitable by removal of other SKUs* High revenue substitutability**	Achieves a better position on the Whale Curve *and* shifts the curve
Removing the **"silent killers"**	Profitable	Large	Some	Very high revenue substitutability**	Shifts the Whale Curve

* Except those with a promising future (i.e., are early in lifecycle) or that are true "door openers"

** Very small incremental revenue

Category 1: Cleaning the attic

The easiest category of SKUs to go after includes those that are essentially gone already. We call this **cleaning the attic.** These are SKUs that have been left in the system and product catalog but for which there effectively is no activity. Cleaning the attic creates some space, feels good, and is useful for gaining some momentum.

As we've talked about many times in this book, the hazard here is that you end up focusing on the number of SKUs deleted rather than the impact made. Companies can clean the attic—wiping out a large number of SKUs from the system—call it a great success, but have little if any impact.

Category 2: Small losers

The next category is characterized by what we call the **small losers.** They are small in volume and revenue but usually large in number, and all unprofitable. They aggregate on the right end of the Whale Curve, and—with the exception of those that are true door openers—the vast majority of these, if not all of them, should be eliminated. This is where many SKU rationalization discussions focus; but while they are worthy targets which will move you toward a better position on the Whale Curve, their removal won't substantially shift the curve itself (because their removal doesn't add significant revenue to the SKUs that remain).

Category 3: Sacrificial sinners

The third category includes SKUs that while unprofitable are not significantly so. Often they appear profitable according to company standard cost and margin figures but are shown to be unprofitable with complexity-adjusted costing. They usually have greater revenue per SKU than the small losers (see sidebar, "The 'main sequence,'" next page). This is both a plus and a minus: since more revenue is involved, there is more likelihood of resistance, whether internally or from customers. But the demand for the products also increases the opportunity to transfer revenue to other products, making those other products better and shifting the Whale Curve (shifting the peak of the Whale Curve up and to the right). Typically, many of these products should be deleted, but not all of them—as determined by revenue substitutability and the impact of that substitutability on turning some unprofitable products to profitable products.

We call these the **sacrificial sinners**, since they are unprofitable products but by their deletion they can turn other otherwise unprofitable products profitable. Within this category, those with high substitutability are the best candidates for removal since they have the lowest revenue loss and also contribute the most to making other SKUs better. However, those with low substitutability that cannot become profitable (and don't have material linked revenue) should also be removed.

Category 4: Silent killers

The last category is the most contentious, as it includes SKUs that are profitable and typically have good-sized revenues. But within this category, there can be *silent killers* in your portfolio—those with near 100% substitutability. Silent killers look good by almost any standard measure, but in reality they contribute little to no incremental revenue, yet they add cost (consuming a large amount of resources such as advertising dollars, capacity, and product line maintenance). These silent killers may be much fewer in number than the SKUs in the previous categories (the extent of silent killers will vary significantly between industries and companies), but the impact of each is much greater. By finding and removing the silent killers, you can redefine your Whale Curve and cut large chunks of cost while preserving revenue.

The "main sequence"

Low-volume products usually consume disproportionate amounts of costs; high-volume products usually are very efficient consumers of costs. Accordingly, for most companies, plotting SKUs on a revenue-margin chart will show that most SKUs fall along a "main sequence," extending from low revenue and margin to high revenue and margin—with a much larger concentration of SKUs on the low/low end than the high/high end.

Figure 45: The Main Sequence

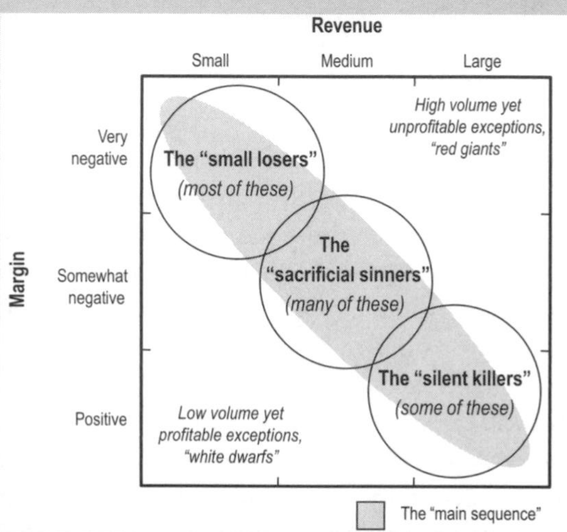

Our SKU rationalization categories fall along the main sequence. Typically, nearly all of the large number of SKUs on the low/low end are "small losers," many of the SKUs along the middle are the "sacrificial sinners," and some of the smaller number of SKUs on the high/high end are the "silent killers."

For those of you with an astronomy bent, this diagram bears remarkable resemblance to the Hertzsprung-Russell diagram of star temperature and luminosity, from which we borrow the term "main sequence." On the Hertzsprung-Russell diagram, most stars fall along a main sequence from low temperature/low luminosity to high temperature/high luminosity.

But there are exceptions, and with both SKUs and stars some fall far off the main sequence. By studying the exceptions that don't fall along the main sequence, stars called red giants and white dwarfs, astronomers have been able to gather a wealth of information about the life and death of all stars.

Similarly, exceptions to your SKUs' main sequence can offer significant information value—both as indicators of systemic issues and as guides for future growth. For example, an abundance of high-volume products that are yet unprofitable (the "red giants") may indicate systemic pricing issues in your business. Though those products are purchased in high volumes, you fail to capture that value, and pricing is often the culprit. By correcting pricing misalignments, you can move these products toward the main sequence, sacrificing revenue but potentially gaining profitability.

Also consider small-volume products that enjoy high profitability (the "white dwarfs"). By defying the typical volume-margin relationship of the main sequence, these little nuggets typically represent products of exceptional customer value—products that should be studied, emulated, and exploited.

Creating a Portfolio Optimization Plan

Cutting deep enough requires addressing all the categories outlined above. Companies will differ in the level of rigor with which they analyze and select SKUs for deletion. (Again we point out that additional rigor is helpful if it leads to a better answer but not if it prevents you from getting to an answer.) Some companies may want to conduct more rigorous incremental revenue and cost analysis to quantify these terms and actual incremental margins well for each SKU and to determine total expected benefits rather precisely before moving forward. Other companies, by understanding the drivers of benefit behind SKU rationalization, may want to jump right to the categories of SKU rationalization—in an 80/20 fashion—and look opportunistically for their small losers, sacrificial sinners, and silent killers.

In either case, you must understand what really matters (i.e., incrementality, substitutability, complexity-adjusted costs, etc.). This understanding will equip you to look deeper into your portfolio to find your silent killers and to gain the most from SKU rationalization and portfolio optimization.

However, portfolio optimization doesn't stop with simply cutting SKUs from the portfolio (remember the six-step SKU rationalization process from the previous chapter). The other side to making cuts deep enough to have a significant impact on margin is to take concurrent action, both to enable deeper cuts and to capture the benefits from them, as discussed in the sidebar, next page

By looking deep into your portfolio to attack SKUs in each of our four categories (cleaning the attic, small losers, sacrificial sinners, and silent killers), and by taking concurrent actions, you will be able to remove chunks of complexity costs, dramatically streamline the performance of your portfolio (you will not only remove the bad complexity but also make the good complexity that remains much better), and lay the foundation for revenue growth.

Growing Revenue

While the focus of this book is cost reduction, the longer-term objective of portfolio optimization should be revenue (and margin) growth. Moreover, we recognize that the fear of revenue loss has a dramatic shaping effect on a company's efforts at SKU reductions.

Portfolio optimization, led with intelligent SKU rationalization (as discussed in this and the last chapter), positions the portfolio for growth in the following ways:

- **By focusing the portfolio on what customers value.** Profitable products tend to be profitable because they offer customers what they value. Stripping out unprofitable products, therefore, strips out what customers don't value. What's left is a much more concentrated and powerful offering to your customers.

- **By concentrating scarce resources.** All resources are limited. Eliminating poorly performing products concentrates key resources (advertising and promotional spend, management attention, sales force time, etc.) on products with greater potential. Not only does this increase leverage, but "concentration of force" typically results in much greater effectiveness as well.
- **By increasing process performance.** Stripping out portfolio complexity increases process performance, improving items such as lead time, quality, on-time delivery, and order accuracy. When aligned with customer key buying factors, improvement in these metrics can drive significant

Concurrent actions that will drive even bigger gains

SKU rationalization is in large part about removing costs, and that requires also addressing the items of cost and not just the SKUs that require them (i.e., the Product/Organization face of the Complexity Cube).

Concurrent action, therefore, means putting more things into play in your SKU rationalization effort than just the SKUs themselves. It means conducting SKU rationalization hand-in-hand with network and footprint consolidation (see the next chapter), because when enough complexity is removed to remove a warehouse or a plant, large chunks of cost can be eliminated and the benefits of SKU rationalization become very significant.

This is not cutting off your nose to spite your face. The path here isn't simply to remove enough bad revenue to allow closure of a facility. It is much more powerful than that. Our approach is to execute SKU rationalization in a way that limits revenue loss while selectively removing targeted complexity that is constraining portfolio and operational performance. This boosts operational efficiencies so that fewer assets are needed. The focus is aligning your portfolio with your customers and your operations so you can *do more* with what you have (and therefore *need less* of it)—rather than simply making cuts so you are doing less and therefore need less.

This requires taking concurrent actions, bringing together substitutability and complexity-adjusted costing as described in this chapter along with network and footprint consolidation as described in the next chapter.

This also brings to point the importance of tying SKU rationalization selections explicitly to where the benefits will come from and the actions needed to capture those benefits—and we recommend this be done sooner rather than later in the SKU rationalization process. By taking concurrent actions, the link between the sources of benefits and the actions to capture them becomes clear. Many efforts, however, go after deleting SKUs and then waiting to see where the benefits will fall out. This seems to guarantee not only that cuts will be too shallow but also that the benefits afforded by those cuts will be left on the table (remember the industrial equipment manufacturer described in Chapter 1 that removed 40% of its product variations but failed to take action to realize benefits).

revenue improvement. When Motorola Computer Group cut out complexity, it saw its on-time deliveries improve as a result, from 70% to 78%. Now that customers were getting products on time, customer satisfaction also leaped from 27% to 55%. The overall result was an increase in total revenues—despite the portfolio cuts—by 40%.

- **By driving more revenue per product.** We've said before that a key complexity metric is average revenue per product. Removing products with high revenue substitutability increases the revenue per product for the products that remain. In this way portfolio optimization doesn't just release the cost of unprofitable products but also reduces the costs of your profitable products, making them more cost competitive in today's market.
- **By exposing gaps in the portfolio.** Portfolio optimization is not just about SKU reduction. Although the presumption is that there are too many SKUs, there may also be gaps in your portfolio, and portfolio optimization also involves filling those gaps. Portfolio complexity can inject noise between a company and its customers, with product proliferation resembling a shotgun approach to product coverage—with overlapping products in some areas and gaps in others. By downsizing the portfolio, you can expose these gaps. Further, approaching SKU rationalization and closing gaps in coverage together offers benefits to each: removing poor SKUs makes room for new ones, and the addition of new value-add offerings to customers can ease implementation: rather than taking away, you will be offering something in return.

Quite simply, portfolio optimization can make your portfolio much more competitive.

Chapter 10 Endnotes

46 In this case, the decision about where to draw the demarcation line doesn't change as a consequence of the implicit costs. However, determining implicit costs changes the actual benefits that can be expected, which will be important to push back on internal resistance. Also, if the implicit costs are significant, it may warrant revisiting where the demarcation line is drawn, though this is getting a bit more into the weeds.

47 Revenue associated with "bad" complexity.

Chapter 11

Network and Footprint Consolidation

Fewer, faster, bigger, better: that is the way that confectionary company Cadbury now characterizes its agenda for profitable growth. It couldn't always characterize it that way.

"Given the way the business has developed," said CEO Todd Stitzer at the outset of its complexity initiative, "Cadbury's is more complex than it needs to be: the way we're organized, our factory footprint, and the number of different product formats we produce."[48]

The company's response to this state of affairs was a multipronged effort to simultaneously consolidate assets, cut SKUs, and eliminate organizational layers. In so doing, Cadbury illustrates well the notion of "concurrent actions" that we discussed in Chapter 8. By assessing footprint consolidation in concert with SKU rationalization, a company is likely to release much larger levels of cost. Equally, assessing footprint in concert with a view of company processes is likely to lead to a more optimal supply chain, as the configuration of a company's factories, depots, and other physical assets usually plays a defining role in the effectiveness of a supply chain.

This concurrent approach also provides a secondary benefit: it requires explicit consideration of the future *market* strategy and, by definition, future *operating* strategy. Therefore, it is moving you toward the footprint of the future, not just reacting to current concerns. Companies can address the need for footprint adjustments by not just *reducing capacity* but also *repositioning for growth.*

One such company is Goodyear Tire & Rubber. With the meltdown of the global automobile business, the impact on a supplier such as Goodyear has been severe. With sales down 20%, the company's focus, according to CEO Robert Keegan, has been on "aligning manufacturing capacity with demand to reflect lower industry volume."

> *We plan to reduce manufacturing capacity by an additional 15.0 million to 25.0 million units over the next two years. We will certainly want to fully leverage these cost reduction actions when global tire markets rebound, as they inevitably will. We will intensify our focus on actions to… lower our break-even point.*[49]

It is a common phenomenon: with the economic contraction, profitability is now concentrated in a small portion of a company's business, and by extension, a sliver of invested capital is generating the lion's share of value. For many companies, the pursuit of growth has left in its wake too many factories, depots, distribution centers (DCs), organizational layers, functional fiefdoms, and convoluted IT systems. With the evaporation of revenues, most companies are

Why companies shy away from footprint consolidation

Many companies struggle with network and footprint consolidation for a host of reasons:

Now versus the future. Any change to the footprint can be expensive and difficult, with the consequences long lasting. Therefore, it's not surprising that executives pause for thought before diving into a network optimization. There's a concern that any short-term savings could evaporate in the face of longer-term strategic mistakes. As a result, analysis paralysis can set in.

Inadequate understanding of customer preferences. Companies do not always have a strong sense of customer buying behaviors and expectations in the face of product proliferation. Consequently, they gravitate toward keeping as many products as possible and worry that closing locations will adversely affect perceived customer service levels.

No one owns inventories. When inventories are spread across a value chain, with no single individual accountable for the costs, secondary behaviors kick in: sales wants to increase how much product is stocked locally at nearby DCs for faster delivery. Manufacturing may have an incentive to produce more product than what is needed (to improve asset utilization and reduce setups). When everyone optimizes their sub-metrics, companies can become reluctant to rationalize their footprint.

Budget concerns. Due to the effect on short-term earnings, finance executives are sometimes wary of making all of the required investments to close or upgrade facilities or move equipment, products, and parts from one location to another.

Restrictive legal agreements. Companies often sign long-term labor agreements, contracts with municipalities, or leases that would require large write-offs or payouts if locations are closed.

Fear of change. Management and employee concerns about change are often not addressed with a change management approach, leading to a large backlash against efforts to modify the company's footprint.

If the quest is to reposition for growth, as opposed to just reducing capacity, then footprint consolidation becomes a strategic decision. In fact, one of the key tensions we see in companies tackling these issues is between the urgent need to quickly take out capacity and cost (which often points to the more expeditious solutions) and the opportunity to dramatically improve the overall footprint for competitive advantage. Needless to say, absent a strong advocate for the latter, the urgent and expeditious usually win out.

in the same boat: they need to shrink that asset base by removing the part that is no longer tied to revenues in order to lower their own "break-even point."

Network consolidation is a key mechanism for addressing organizational complexity, the complexity in how your assets, structure, people, and technology support your business. This battle strategy is central to eliminating many of these complexity costs—the ones that "take root," as discussed in Chapter 8. The benefits, therefore, are both improved costs and the opportunity to free up capital.

While their very "rootedness" makes elimination of these organizational structures difficult, by recognizing the nature of these costs and by approaching them with the right methodology, it is possible to generate initial cost and capital improvements while also helping your company migrate to the footprint that will support your future business.

In this chapter, we will assess how we got here—how we ended up with sprawling physical footprints—and why companies struggle with network and footprint consolidation. Moreover, we will discuss the approach cited above for "taking ground" against a difficult foe and revisit the Cadbury case to understand what they did and what benefits they're seeing.

More Complex than We Need to Be

Cadbury's CEO is not alone in giving voice to the notion that *we've become more complex than we need to be.* Most executives are aware of how their supply chains have grown and stretched with the rise in consumer demand, which brought increasing complexity in upstream and downstream partner relationships.

The results are hard to miss: more and more suppliers, distribution centers, warehouses, retail stores, products, cross-regional shipments from supplier locations or company plants that uniquely manufacture certain products, and layers of management that are added over time to manage all this. So-called "lily pad" strategies that high-growth companies put in place to enable footprint development served their purpose but have left in their wake a tangled web (see sidebar and Figure 46, next page).

Most of all, a decade of acquisitions have left our footprints slack with capacity. Before the contraction, it was not unusual for acquiring companies to delay the consolidation of facilities, plants, and depots due to concern over integration. This resulted in cluttered networks. (While many deals were struck on the basis of potential market growth, each acquisition brought with it numerous physical plants and assets.)

But in the current downturn, the luxury of delay has gone. To strengthen their cost and capital position, many companies are looking to quickly downsize their capacity, as reported in *Manufacturing Outlook for 2009.*[50] According to the research group Manufacturing Insights,

Growth of complexity in the footprint

Many high-growth companies employ a "lily pad" approach to footprint development. They carefully prepare business plans that focus on the needs of targeted customers who match key demographic and socioeconomic profiles. Products or services are designed to meet those needs. Plants (or retail stores) and distribution centers (DCs) are located in a geographic region resembling a circle or lily pad, so that a company can leverage its transportation and distribution costs, advertising and marketing expenditures, and management. Over time the companies use the same approach to growth in other regions. Eventually, the companies gain enough economies of scale to offer products nationally or internationally, and their footprint fills out.

There are many benefits to this approach: as the number of DCs increases, customer service levels improve because delivery times to customers decrease. Outbound transportation costs decline as DCs, on average, are closer to each customer. Consolidated shipments of product from DCs result in fewer shipments to a given customer, further reducing transportation costs.

However, if the number of DCs increases beyond a given point, inbound transportation costs from suppliers or plants become excessive because of an increased number of smaller shipments. Fixed operating costs increase as the number of DCs rises. In addition, each DC must now carry product inventory and related safety stocks. Consequently, inventory carrying costs (e.g., theft, damage, cost of capital, and obsolescence) rise as well—and rise much more rapidly as the level of safety stocks and duplication of inventory in the network is spread across more and more facilities.

It is a good example of how growth strategies can inadvertently introduce complexity costs. We are not recommending you throw out the lily pad approach but, if you have used it, to recognize the opportunity, given a certain scale, of reorganizing the footprint for costs and effectiveness.

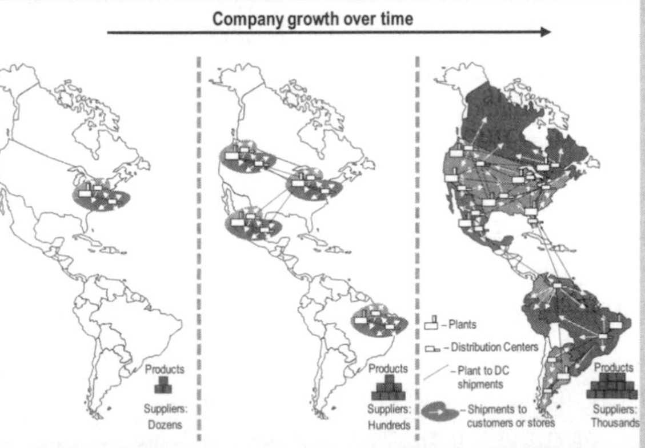

Figure 46:
The Lily Pad Effect

High-growth companies often use the lily pad approach for growth. They leverage management, distribution, and transportation costs and marketing and advertising in a geographic region (Panel 1). Then they employ the same strategy in other regions, until a critical mass is reached and they can profitably offer products on a national or international basis (Panel 2). But, as they grow, product proliferation, cross shipments, and costs increase dramatically (Panel 3). Complexity and changes in customer demand necessitate that the company's footprint or supply chain network be reevaluated at some point.

> *The coming year will be challenging to say the least. High unemployment, low consumer confidence... may get even worse before it improves. However, many manufacturing companies are viewing this pause, coming after six years of fairly steady profitable growth, as an* ***opportunity to recalibrate their business models.***

The report concludes that companies will need to "*right size*" their supply chains for profitable proximity.

Meeting the Future Halfway

For many companies, the *need* to right size will be much clearer than the best *approach* to rightsizing. Current capacity issues and footprint considerations may suggest a specific course of action with near-term benefits, but many will wonder, ***How do I ensure that the decisions I take are aligned with longer strategic goals?***

In fact, it is important to recognize that there are two convergent approaches required for successful footprint assessment:

1) Developing a detailed **current state view of the network** that assesses the intricacies of the current network and options to move forward—the fact base that is a requisite for ensuring smooth execution of network changes
2) Envisioning a **future state** that considers what the network will have to look like 5 or 10 years down the road, based on future market strategy or what the imagined endgame may be

The current state view is information rich; the future state view based on assumptions and strategy. Both are required to arrive at an effective, executable plan that is also aligned with future strategic needs. It is critical that both parts of the puzzle be completed and that the path forward be a point of convergence between the two—a path that takes you halfway to your likely future.

1) Developing a Current State View of Your Network

A current state diagnostic depends on developing a deep and quantitative understanding of the details of your supply chain. This reflects the fact that companies—manufacturers, consumer product companies, retailers, and many others—must juggle thousands of variables to profitably meet or exceed customer expectations. It is critical to build a grounded fact base not only to arrive at the best decisions on how that footprint is configured but also to successfully execute the plan—to ensure smooth migration of inventories, plant equipment, and volume, as needs be. The picture can be quite complex:

- A typical manufacturing company might purchase thousands of parts from hundreds or even thousands of suppliers. In addition to price differences per part by supplier facility, transportation costs increase as distance increases between the supplier distribution point and the company's manufacturing plant.
- Lead times across the supply chain must also be considered, especially for manufacturers adopting just-in-time production.
- Each manufacturing plant will have a different cost structure. Fixed costs will vary depending on the plant's age, location, and investment in facilities and equipment. Variable manufacturing costs per product will vary depending on the cost of labor by plant location, types of machinery used, and cost of materials. Additional investment in cost-saving technologies or equipment may reduce a given plant's cost structure.
- If customer demand for a particular product line is concentrated in a certain geographic area, then consideration may be given to locate production in the nearest plant to minimize transportation costs and reduce order-to-delivery cycle times.
- Freight to the DCs will vary with the distance from the plants producing a given product and the transportation mode. A manufacturer may own its own fleet, use a dedicated contract carrier, or rely on less-than-truckload carriers. Similarly, retailers usually stock thousands of products and supply hundreds or thousands of stores out of dozens of DCs or warehouses.
- Cost considerations must be juxtaposed against customer service levels. Some customers may demand frequent deliveries of product to support their own just-in-time production operations.
- The nature of the product may dictate costs and customer service levels. Some products may be "slow movers" that could be stocked at a master DC for delivery to a regional DC center in a cross-docking operation. For example, business customers may order shipments of slow-moving parts on Tuesday. The manufacturer would ship the parts in bulk from the master DC on Wednesday for delivery to the regional DC on Thursday. On arrival on Thursday, the bulk shipment would be "cross-docked," broken down and loaded on delivery trucks. End consumers may expect relatively short delivery times, necessitating closer proximity of a retailer's or manufacturer's distribution facility.

How a Current State Diagnostic Usually Plays Out

To understand all of the kinds of relationships just described, you will need to collect a lot of data about your organization and supply chain. Assemble a team to define the most logical approach (blueprint) to model the supply chain network. Then focus on data extraction.

The type of variables captured in the model are typically these: fixed and variable manufacturing costs, labor costs by facility by product, manufacturing capacity, DC, overhead, labor hours and costs per part or DC case, DC capacity, transportation lane costs (e.g., from the parts supplier to the plant, from the plant to the DC, from the DC to the customer or store), required delivery times to customers defined by proximity of the supply point to the customer, the number of shifts per location, and supplier, plant, DC, and customer locations.

Once data are extracted from systems, errors are addressed and assumptions are made to account for missing information. A "base case" model is run to test the validity of the model and gain stakeholder buy-in with the approach. Next, scenarios are run, such as forcing locations open or closed; requiring that some locations manufacture, repair, or stock certain products or parts; and testing different customer service levels. Often, the scenarios project demand 5 to 10 years into the future to make sure that adequate capacity remains in case facilities are closed (and tying into the future state diagnostic). Once the models are run, cost savings are compared. Many other factors are evaluated: existing labor agreements and lease obligations, expenditures to relocate equipment, availability of a skilled workforce, facility closure costs, required investments, flexibility of the new configuration to handle increased demand, and ease of implementation of a new footprint.

This current state diagnostic is intended to build a detailed understanding of the current footprint and may in itself suggest opportunities, such as redistribution of inventory, changes in the nature of distribution facilities (e.g., dedicated DCs for slow-moving stock), relocation of machinery between plants to be in closer proximity to demand, and closure of distribution or manufacturing facilities.

2) Anchoring the "No Regrets" Decisions in a Future State View

We have found that as a result of (a) a lack of confidence in the future and (b) the pain of footprint consolidation, companies need to augment their current state view with a broader future state diagnostic that anchors decisions in a more strategic context. By combining the two, companies can have greater faith that the near-term decisions they make to optimize capacity are also "no regrets" decisions in line with longer-term strategy.

The future state diagnostic grounds any potential network and footprint decision in the strategic vision of the company. What this means is that while, many times, companies consider plants and assets to be fixed, independent from, or lagging market strategy, to really reposition for the future requires a fundamental rethink of tomorrow's business and what that would mean for the footprint.

It provides companies a second lens through which to view footprint decisions—and essentially asks the question, ***What moves can we make in the near- to mid-term that will also line up with our strategy for the long-term?*** This requires a consideration of the long term, for many an uncomfortably ambiguous activity. But while no one can predict the future, framing up the two or three future state scenarios and looking 10 years out is more likely to free up the thinking, even if you then work backward to translate those insights into a more actionable 3 to 5 year strategy.

You will have completed or at least begun the current state diagnostic first, so by the time you start looking out to the future you will know the details of your current footprint and have a detailed fact base on cost, production, profitability, and capability of sites. The next step is to inject a strategic perspective, anchored by management beliefs and aspirations for the future.

For example, for Kraft one key aspiration was what they labeled a "harmonization of product variants." Instead of each country going to market with their own versions of the Toblerone bar, the future strategy was for a uniform offering delivered via more uniform production. For Cadbury, a key strategic underpinning was its desire to increase the number of advantaged brands (i.e., noncommoditized) in its portfolio. Given this, it made no sense to build a new Greenfield site designed for low-margin brands.

There are many other examples of these kinds of guiding aspirations. What you will need to do is spell out the aspirations for your company, anchored in your market strategy vision.

What's obvious at this stage is that it is impossible to inject a strategic perspective based on your aspirations into your future vision without a solid sense of the health and opportunities associated with your product portfolio—which is why we urge a concurrent view. To articulate the shape of a physical production footprint requires first articulating the production needs. Common elements of an endgame vision include

- Future state portfolio size and shape (key markets, key customer groups, target market share)
- Means of differentiation (how you anticipate winning in these markets)
- Working practices (union/nonunion workforce, labor rates)
- Organizational assumptions (integrated manufacturing organization, centralized/decentralized)

- Production assumptions (global plants, standardized formats/production, high level of automation, strategic use of outsourcing)
- Number of sites and technology associated with each
- Best-in-class costs

The bullet points above are examples of the types of themes that need to be discussed in the development of a future state vision. Many of them will require analysis, thinking, and, in some cases, informed guesswork.

No one can predict the future or anticipate curveballs, but the importance of this is to (1) inject a future-thinking perspective into this process and (2) lay bare management assumptions about the future that otherwise will color the process in a less robust manner. In fact, we often find that the discussion, and the forced alignment around the current state and direction of the company, is as valuable as any specific vision that emerges from the process. Once you're aligned on a common vision, the process of identifying sensible intermediate goals—say, three to five years out—becomes a lot more manageable.

Remember, *we're only trying to meet the future halfway*. If you're setting the endgame for 10 years out—and even if you only have 50% confidence in parts of the vision—there is likely a lot of work you can do in the first 5 years that may represent "no regrets" actions (ones that will move the footprint forward independent of new information that emerges at a later date). Identifying no regrets decisions is important, as it gives you a solid near-term future state footprint to anchor on and to build toward. This is a manageable first stage that we can move to from the current state. But it is an interim stage triangulated by grounded thought, analysis, and discussion about the longer-term needs of the business.

What this means, practically speaking, is that in a bid to reduce footprint complexity, there will likely be

- Certain facilities that offer near-term cost-savings opportunities and that are incongruent with your longer-term endgame vision
- Certain activities that make sense to get rid of, no matter what, such as elimination of process duplication
- Opportunities for strategic outsourcing that align with the future needs but also solve near-term production headaches

Together, all of these will add up to a significant stepping-stone toward your new target footprint.

Cadbury: Clearer choices, greater focus

As for the specific benefits of a concurrent approach, it is instructive to go back to the Cadbury case cited at the beginning of the chapter.

First, some more background. Following the decision to split its confectionary and beverage businesses in March 2007, Cadbury launched a new strategic plan (called *Vision into Action*) for its stand-alone confectionary business. The objective was to leverage global scale while reducing complexity and costs.

"We recognize that we can be much more profitable by simplifying the way we do things across all aspects of our business," CEO Todd Stitzer said, citing a cost model out of line with peers. "We believe we can drive a step-change in margins and returns by reconfiguring our confectionery business model."[51]

Stitzer cited Cadbury's operations in the United Kingdom as an example of complexity. Cadbury UK has a share of around 30% and annual revenues of over £1 billion. "How about this for complexity?" Stitzer said. "In 2007 Cadbury UK had 8 production/feedstock plants, 18 stockholding locations, around 6,000 employees, 30 key brands across chocolate, candy, and gum. And through the course of the year handling more than 1,000 different pack types or SKUs."

To address these issues, Cadbury structured a three-part integrated approach. In the United Kingdom that meant

1) **Footprint reconfiguration: reducing the number of distribution depots from 18 to 5.**

   In addition to cutting the number of depots, they're now reorganizing the factory base through a number of initiatives, including further automation, changes in working practices, and the movement of about a quarter of the production volume into scale manufacturing centers of excellence.

2) **Organizational simplification: moving from a siloed organizational structure where brands and categories were managed on a market-by-market basis to one with fewer layers managed along category lines (chocolate, candy, and gum).**

   The company reported that now because "each category team includes sales, marketing, production and finance," decisions are made more quickly and thinking is more "joined-up" with a more coordinated focus on revenue and margin growth. The company claimed that this allowed it to reduce general and administrative headcount by 15% and the organizational simplification was critical to successful SKU reduction.

   "We have eliminated the regional layer of our management structure," said Stitzer. "The seven business units now report directly to me, and their leaders—importantly—sit on the executive committee. So we can make decisions sitting around one table and get it executed quickly."[52]

3) SKU reduction: Cutting SKUs by 75%

Cadbury also targeted SKU complexity: "That's not an easy job in a business which aims to offer consumers real variety across a huge range of occasion," Stitzer said.[53] But cut they did—by 75% in one particular category, raising margins in line with the rest of the seasonal portfolio. (Overall across Cadbury, the company cut about 10% of SKUs in 2008.)

Conclusion

The results of Cadbury's program are so far positive. The company expects to see a 15% reduction in factories with an increase in margins from 10% to a percentage in the mid-teens, with revenues continuing to grow in the 4% to 6% range over a four-year period ending in 2011. Against that target, revenues are up 7% on a like-for-like basis, with a close to 2% improvement on operating margins. Critical to their success, however, is the fact that network and footprint decisions have been anchored both in a current state study and an understanding of future strategic direction.

What this should tell you is that network and footprint consolidation represents a big opportunity. You are freeing up precious capital and unloading cash-draining resources. It is also, for many, an essential act: no company can afford to put itself at a structural disadvantage. That is unsustainable in the long run and would put the company out of business.

Moreover, footprint consolidation can also help reposition your company for growth—particularly when you approach it with a concurrent focus on product portfolio—leveraging both current state and future state perspectives. Use the momentum of the downturn to address the footprint; the task is never easy. But done right, it will serve as a powerful springboard as demand returns.

Chapter 11 Endnotes

48 Sanford Bernstein Conference, London, September 23, 2008.

49 Goodyear Tire & Rubber Company Q4 2008 Earnings Call Transcript.

50 Bob Parker (VP of Research at Manufacturing Insights), *IndustryWeek*, February 3 (2009).

51 Sanford Bernstein Conference, London, September 23, 2008.

52 Cadbury plc. Full Year Results 2008, Analyst Presentation Script, February 25, 2009.

53 Sanford Bernstein Conference, London, September 23, 2008.

CHAPTER 12

Component Rationalization and Vendor Consolidation

with Brian Hefner

"I will no longer reinvent the wheel each time," said Harold Wester,[54] the head of engineering for Italian carmaker Fiat, who was brought in by CEO Sergio Marchionne (now also head of Chrysler) to help with the company's turnaround.

Not reinventing the wheel may be a reasonable and laudable sentiment, yet it is one frequently at odds with the experience of many companies. They find themselves doing just that: separate parts of the organization design, source, and produce versions of the same item, leading to an excess of parts, components, production, and service elements and by extension a multitude of vendors. It is a complexity double whammy—increased organizational and process complexity, all to deliver a given level of product complexity.

For example, before Wester arrived at Fiat, each of its brands was run independently, and components were designed and produced independently. Fiat's Stilo and Alfa Romeo's 149—similar sized cars with similar performance levels—didn't share any components. Only 2 of the company's 19 independently developed platforms shared the same heating, ventilation, and air-conditioning systems.

"The customer is interested in a fuel-efficient and well-functioning HVAC unit," Wester said, who is executing a plan to produce 85% of Fiat cars on just four platforms by 2010. "Whether it's the same between four cars, he doesn't care." Marchionne returned Fiat to profitability in 2006 for the first time since 2000, after less than two years at its helm.

The fact that the customer *doesn't care* (in this case that HVAC units are shared across platforms) makes component rationalization a big opportunity. As a battle strategy, this is one that is invisible to the customer; it removes NVA cost and enables additional gains through vendor consolidation and process improvement. It shares some characteristics with SKU reduction, and indeed, as we will discuss, they should often be coordinated efforts.

Brian Hefner is a partner with WilsonPerumal. He has served pharmaceutical, industrial equipment, consumer products, logistic providers, computer/high tech, and government clients. Brian started his professional career as an officer in the US Army. He graduated from the U.S. Military Academy at West Point and earned his MBA at Emory University.

Defining Component Rationalization

Fiat is a specific, tangible example of component or part proliferation and the opportunity that can exist to rationalize down the needless variety. But at a general level, we think about component rationalization as the opportunity to simplify, standardize, and reduce any element of your product or service that the customer doesn't see or doesn't care about. It is often not hard to spot these opportunities:

- **Too many parts in your database:** no one can easily find an existing item (for potential reuse), so they create a new part number each time
- **Every product design starts from scratch,** as opposed to leveraging existing components
- **Divisions and business units source their own components or sets of components,** leading to excess inventories, increased management costs, and more suppliers occurring in both manufacturing or service settings
- **Increased difficulty in managing inventory,** affecting both production and repair/service capabilities; too much of the wrong inventory, too little of the right inventory
- **Increasing complexity and inefficiency in warehouse operations,** typically leading to investments or upgrades to internal IT systems capabilities
- **A growth in engineering or procurement groups** just to manage the complexities between components, modules, and models

While product portfolio optimization or SKU reduction (the focus of Chapters 9 and 10) needs to take into account customer reactions, component rationalization is relatively free from those concerns. As a result, projects in this area can progress quickly with lower risk and quicker realization of cost savings. See Figure 47, next page, for a comparison.

Better to *prevent* component complexity

This chapter assumes a focus on the component proliferation *after it has occurred*. However, the best time to eliminate component complexity is at the point of design. Design determines 60% to 75% of manufacturing costs. Decisions about which components or platforms are to be leveraged for a specific product have a large impact on the overall product cost. (We discuss techniques for avoiding these types of issues in Chapter 17, "Curbing Product and Service Complexity").

Figure 47: Comparison of Product Portfolio Complexity Versus Component Complexity

	Product Complexity	Component Complexity (Focus of this chapter)
Orientation	• Market facing • End items • Value proposition • Profit	• Non-market facing • Modules, parts, and platforms • Quality and performance • Cost
Source of complexity	• Customer-sought variety • Market choices • Competitive response	• Internal silos • Design orientation • Sourcing issues
Levers for complexity reduction	• Product, family elimination • Region, market, customer rationalization • Fewer combinations and options	• Component standardization and substitutions • Component elimination • Design for commonality

140 Batteries and 25,000 Forecasts: A case study in component complexity

In most situations, companies need to first address the existing component complexity and then put in place strategies to prevent its recurrence. When Theresa Metty was considering joining Motorola in 2001 as head of global supply chain, she saw just such an opportunity.

"It was clear what the opportunity was," she said, citing the complexity in Motorola's platforms (100), components (140 batteries), and software (30 versions for phones). "The problem was getting the entire company energized around it, as well as talking about complexity in terms that everyone could understand."[55]

"Consider," she said, "the following situation: *Imagine 100 sales people forecasting sales for 10 products every month, each with 25 different configurations. That would be 25,000 data points to forecast each month!*"[56]

When she started at Motorola, her top two priorities reflected her early insights. First, launch a War on Complexity and in parallel focus on next-generation supply chain, two interlinking and high-impact areas.

"We affect the complexity index and efficiency of the supply chain in three key areas," stated Ralph Pini, CTO of Motorola's personal communications sector. "You need a certain level of *integration* to reduce overall part count. The [fewer] parts you have, the *simpler your supply chain* is, because you're managing less inventory. The use of industry standard parts also helps to *reduce part count*. Combined, the benefits quickly multiply."[57]

Metty also sees the benefits of attacking complexity and supply chain simultaneously: "The war on complexity and the next-generation supply chain are what I call the grand-slam home run."

The results in the first two years were significant. For example, the number of platforms dropped from 100 down to 2, battery components dropped from 140 to 30. As a consequence of many moves like these, the company saw a $2.6 billion reduction in operating/material costs, with a $1.4 billion inventory reduction. Inventory turns tripled over a 22-month period, and the company managed 40% capacity reduction, with fewer factories and distribution centers needed.

The Benefits of Component Rationalization

As the case studies above indicate, component rationalization is a powerful strategy for cost reduction. There are many direct benefits (see Figure 48).

Figure 48: The Direct Benefits of Component Rationalization

Customer	Operations
• **Greater customer value** – Increased product availability – Shorter product lead time – Improved quality levels – Reduced cost	• **Streamlined supply chain** – Increased manufacturing efficiency and flexibility – Increased supplier efficiency and flexibility (reduced lead times) – Reduced design/testing

Income Statement	• **Reduced materials costs** (greater gross margins) – Low-cost suppliers – Increased purchase volumes – Reduced obsolescence and warranty costs • **Reduced conversion costs** (greater gross margins) – Increased manufacturing efficiency • **Reduced SGA costs** (greater operating profits) – Fewer purchase transactions – Less Material Requirements Planning maintenance – Reduced distribution costs
Balance Sheet	• **Reduced inventory** (lower working capital) – Lower raw materials levels – Lower WIP levels

The benefits from an effective component rationalization are system-wide: supply chain to customer, parts and labor to balance sheet

Many indirect benefits also accrue as a result of component rationalization:

- **The ability to consolidate vendors.** Duplicate parts have likely proliferated because there is no visibility across the organization. Each area, therefore, contracts its own vendors, which increases processing and management costs and impairs the likelihood of volume discounts. *Consolidating parts requires visibility across the organization;* and doing so creates the opportunity for vendor consolidation.

- **The increased potential for deeper collaboration** through collaborative forecasting and planning, vendor managed inventory, and consignment, for example. As spending increases with specific vendors, those vendors will likely feel more compelled to participate in such programs.

Note that when we discuss *vendor consolidation*, most readers will think immediately of "Tier 1" suppliers (direct suppliers to your company). But in consolidating Tier 1 vendors, you impact the number of Tier 2 vendors as well (suppliers to Tier 1 vendors). Although going deeper into the upstream supply

How component rationalization creates deeper opportunities

In Chapter 2 we discussed the need to *shift between the faces of the Complexity Cube* as you wage the war on complexity costs. Component rationalization presents a perfect example of this idea (see Figure 49).

Figure 49: Component Rationalization Opens the Door to Additional Opportunities

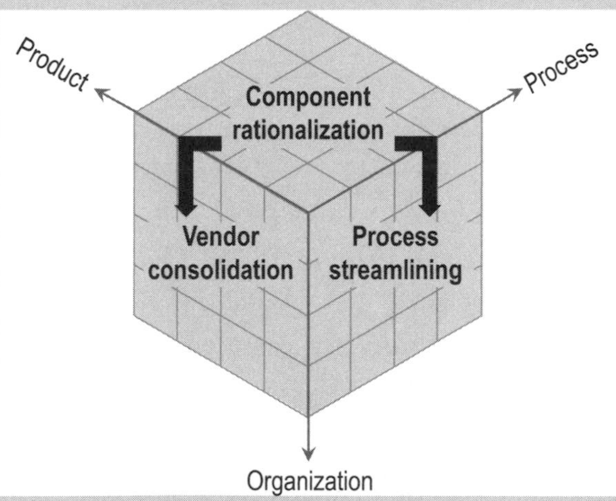

By assessing and identifying ways of finding common components, you will not only drive tremendous short-term savings in this one area but also open broader opportunities for reducing the number of vendors and stripping away organizational waste. In our cube parlance, you may start on the Product/Process face (component rationalization), but having surmounted that challenge, you may change your focus to address new opportunities on the Organization/Product face (vendor consolidation) or on the Process/Organization face (process streamlining).

chain complicates efforts, the potential for improving coordination across a broader stretch of your supply has positive impacts on inventory levels, service levels, and customer satisfaction, to name a few.

Getting Bang for the Buck with Component Rationalization

As you consider launching this battle strategy, it is important to consider how to get the most out of your investment in time, effort, and money. Here are three key lessons learned:

1) Deal head-on with the organizational elements of component rationalization
2) Anchor your efforts at the product platform level
3) Structure each component rationalization effort on a staggered timeline

1) Deal Head-On with the Organizational Elements of Component Rationalization

No matter what scale of effort you launch, companies cannot successfully complete a component rationalization without also assessing the organizational elements it touches. Given that one of the root causes of component complexity is many parts of the company doing the same thing separately, you cannot possibly hope to reap the full benefits without addressing some of these organizational problems. Addressing the elements may require new policies to standardize procurement, new structure, participation, and ownership of processes, different incentives, or improved information sharing, for example.

2) Anchor Your Efforts at the Product Platform Level

A platform is any group of elements that serves as the basis for multiple end products. As such, they share common components and subsystems. So when a company decides to take on component rationalization, the best point of leverage is at the platform level. A good rule of thumb is to consider having a single platform for any end products that share 90% of their components. If you have related products that do not meet the 90% goal, examine their components to see if you can use rationalization to achieve it.

You will still have to deal with individual components, but only after defining which platforms/modules to prioritize. This will accelerate the rationalization effort.

Once you've prioritized which platforms to consider rationalizing, you will need to examine their components. A platform is defined by its product architecture, with components and the interfaces between the components defining the functionality of the product. Typically, there are three different levels of components that go into a product:

- **Strategic** components are those components/interfaces that the company believes play an important part in its differentiation
- **Basic** are those that have no strategic value and are likely shared or used openly with competitors and others
- **Raw materials** are the core ingredients

Stratifying the components into the above categories helps delineate efforts and may require separate strategies. For example, components in the basic and raw material classification are usually easier to consolidate, and as commodities, the approach is focused mostly on cost analysis (often an area ripe for quick wins). This is not the case with strategic components, as a reliable supply may warrant a consideration of factors other than cost.

The power of reuse

Integral to all component rationalization efforts is the notion of reuse. In Chapters 9 and 10, we discussed the concept of substitutability as it applies to products and services in your portfolio. But the concept applies—and is equally powerful—to areas that are not customer facing. By focusing on substitutability as it applies to components—otherwise known as reuse—companies can dramatically reduce inventory costs, improve quality, and accelerate lead times. Platforms are a means of building commonality and thereby increasing the level of reuse of components. Between 60% and 80% of Toyota designs use existing materials, components, assemblies, and so on, which dramatically decreases costs and accelerates development times.[58] It takes discipline to focus on reuse; indeed for many engineering cultures, it is anathema to reuse when you can start with a blank sheet of paper. But engineering, like all functions, is best targeted at areas that can add differentiation and distinction. As a case in point, consider Porsche, which leverages common components and targets engineering efforts at what matters to customers: engine performance, styling, and performance.

3) Structure Each Component Rationalization Effort on a Staggered Timeline

There is a temptation with component rationalization, given the size and scale of many such efforts, to break up the work into serial phases—scoping, planning, execution—with different teams attached to each, and waiting to conclude one phase before starting the next. The problem with this sequential approach is that it can lead to a silo effect (in which work is blindly handed off from one team to the next). Treating rationalization this way stymies the natural feedback loops that help develop and refine hypotheses about the areas of opportunity. Good component rationalization efforts tend to move in waves; you find the quick wins, then the first wave of consolidations, then the second wave (informed by the success of the first) and so on. (See Figure 50.)

Not only are staggered timelines more likely to succeed but they also actually deliver benefits quicker. By focusing efforts on delivering multiple waves of benefits (vs. one big wave at the very end), companies can see cost improvements earlier. In many situations it is better to see an earlier hit (with savings accruing over time) versus a serial approach with the promise of a big hit later.

Figure 50: Serial versus Staggered Component Rationalization

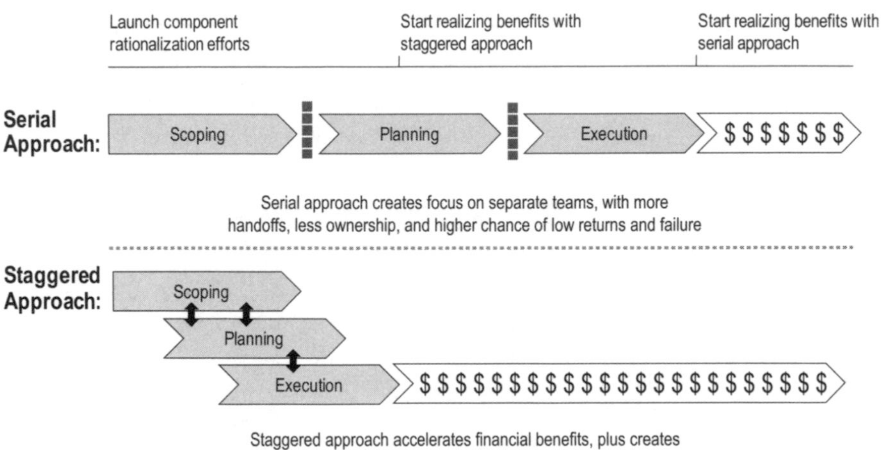

A **serial approach** creates focus on separate teams, with more handoffs and less ownership, and higher chance of low returns and failure. It defers benefits and can lead to siloed thinking. A **staggered approach** encourages more cross-team problem solving and iteration and leads to earlier accrual of benefits. It accelerates financial benefits, plus creates a greater sense of alignment, urgency, and ownership.

Learning the Hard Way: A case study

While the value of component rationalization is very obvious to many companies, how to extract the value is less so. And in fact, many often have to learn the hard way and, before they extract benefits from their component rationalization efforts, spend months laboring against organizational barriers that require senior management intervention. Consider the experience of a large, global durable goods manufacturer we will call DuraGoods. Like many companies, DuraGoods was a company that had grown organically and through acquisitions over its storied and successful history. It was a company that had strongly adopted product architecture through the management of platforms within each product family and brand. Each platform had a high number of shared modules and independent components.

Over the years, the organization to support and actively manage those platforms and modules had grown enormously. Product managers and platform engineers were the main focal points and called most of the shots when it came to making changes to products. Most of these employees were regionally focused owing to the customer/consumer tastes that differed by region. Down the product hierarchy, then, came the component and module engineers. In procurement, sourcing and purchasing professionals managed component groups regionally in some cases, globally in others.

In sum, DuraGoods had an organizational structure that was almost more complex than the number of components that made up this multibillion-dollar company. What made that fact extremely evident was when the organization decided to conduct an all-encompassing, globally scoped, component rationalization initiative (i.e., a very "broad" approach).

To get any traction or decisions made, it took a room full of 20 to 30 stakeholders across regions and functions to agree on some of the smallest component changes imaginable. Exacerbating this organizational complexity was the project plan. The company broke its effort into three distinct phases: scoping, planning, and execution. Each phase had its own team, so the scoping team for Component Group A would conduct all tasks within it. There was then a different planning team for Component Group A. And ultimately, a regional/functional engineer would own the implementation of suggested changes.

Needless to say, the early going of this effort was slow and painstaking. After six to eight months of little actual savings (or even identified realizable savings to come in the near future), senior management was getting very impatient. Several teams got stuck in the planning phase and eventually and desperately deflected off to procurement to find some sort of sourcing savings: going to a different supplier, renegotiations with current suppliers, and so on

Although these are certainly activities that produce cost savings, management was getting cynical, believing that nothing but the "squeeze-the-supplier" route was feasible.

But there finally came a point where senior management could no longer ignore the true obstacles—the how-we-do-business points of resistance, barriers, and ineffective actions. Management had to start thinking about how a number of factors influenced their ability to be successful at component rationalization: the organization's structure, participation and ownership, performance and incentive programs and policies, talent levels of employees, regional versus global management, and many more.

Eventually, the company salvaged its efforts: senior management started describing the initiative as a transformation and tackling some of the large organizational obstacles head-on. Additionally, they started reviewing how teams were organized and managed throughout the effort. And they moved toward a more streamlined team of process owners from the start, ensuring that execution and planning were being thought of even during scoping tasks. Finally after a rocky start, the company was able to extract enormous savings from the effort.

The Big Question: Broad versus targeted

Given the size of the opportunity with component rationalization and the fact that it is generally transparent to the customer, the key question is usually *how broadly* to launch an effort, as opposed to *whether* to launch an effort. There are two main scales of effort:

- **Broad:** Work ground-up, focusing on the majority of components, with major cost savings and organizational change (to ensure sustainment) as the goals; or
- **Targeted:** Work to identify targeted high-dollar opportunities, focusing on selective components with quick cost savings as a goal

Going Broad

A common approach to component rationalization, "going broad" involves a large, comprehensive look across all or a majority of components. Typically, efforts start with a baseline phase where all components are sized and categorized on a benefit/effort matrix (see Figure 51) to form priorities for the teams.

Figure 51: Evaluating Potential Component Rationalization Targets

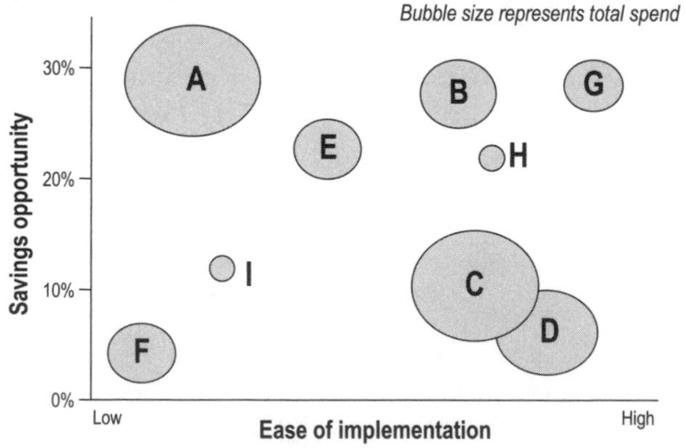

This conceptual chart shows different components (A, B, C, etc.) plotted by initial estimates for savings opportunity against how easy it would be to implement changes to those components. Ease of implementation considers variables such as data availability, degree of customization, supply base leverage, testing requirements, function of the components, and degree of standardization. You will prioritize the component groups that are the high savings/high ease of implementation.

From here, teams go into deep dives of those prioritized components to include component attribute analysis (analyzing the ways a common component is different), supplier analysis (assessing the vendors in terms of dollars spent, volume, performance, and capabilities), and low-cost sourcing assessments (given that many components are commodities, a consideration of which countries to source from becomes relevant), among others.

You then move on to the "buy-in" or feasibility stage, where you work more closely with functions including product engineering, manufacturing, and marketing functions. If component changes are feasible, the transition of ownership and implementation phase begins.

This approach can deliver large benefits. However, companies should understand its realities, namely,

- **It requires tremendous data support.** Spend analysis by supplier is the easy stuff. But finding all active components, where they are used, their functions, drawings, attribute definitions, and more, is a big task for most mid- to large-sized companies. If there is no central database already storing this information before, companies will generally need to create one when taking this approach.
- **It requires a large number of internal resources from all functions.** At first, procurement, finance, and IT are heavily taxed. Eventually, more weight is placed on engineering and marketing as well as manufacturing.
- **It will affect how you deal with external agents in your supply chain.** For example, before, it was likely that only Tier 1 suppliers were actively managed and monitored. This approach will eventually force direct interfaces with Tier 2 suppliers (which Tier 1 suppliers will probably not appreciate).

Stay Targeted

At the other end of the spectrum is the targeted approach. Instead of assessing the galaxy of components, this approach selectively targets a much smaller subset, through a hypotheses-informed approach. Leveraging management knowledge, develop your "best-guess" theories as to where to start, then validate with data. For example, are there components that have not been competitively sourced in the last X years? What are the specific parts that give production the most problems (quality, processing time, etc.)?

The emphasis on analysis with the targeted approach is on finding the shortest and least resistant path to implementation rather than on extreme precision or on capturing 100% of the total opportunity. There are several keys to making this approach successful:

- Be open minded to how the benefits will be obtained: through volume or purchase price savings, design changes, efficiency savings that come through production, or a mix of some or all of these.
- Anchor at the product platform level and from there back into which components could be priorities for cost savings. For example, if you find that one module is being updated by engineering, start with that module to determine what components and volumes might be targets for rationalization (since the module is being updated anyway).
- Be bold enough to challenge some of the strategic components from the start. It is not uncommon to find that companies stay away from these at the start, assuming that *"they are strategic for a reason… let's not touch those."* However, by challenging some of those assumptions, chances are that some of those strategic components will end up being rebranded as basic.

As opposed to the broad approach, the targeted approach really has one goal: benefits, as quick and painless as possible.

Picking Broad versus Targeted

Either approach is sound and can lead to benefits for your organization. But go into it with open eyes.

If you go broad and tackle a majority of the components, consider treating the effort strongly as a "transformation event." This, in turn, gives management the mental degrees of freedom to weave in the awareness, education, and buy-in to the overall project plan, creating a wholly positive experience for the company. In the end, component rationalization via the broad approach has two goals. First are the cost benefits that arise as a result of lower-cost components, fewer suppliers, better terms, and less overhead. Second are the benefits connected to operational improvements that will come through such a large and cross-functional initiative.

However, if time is a critical constraint, consider using the targeted approach to component rationalization, where you use a hypotheses-based approach to identify a selective group of components to tackle by prioritizing ease of implementation throughout the project.

Ultimately, if you are going to be successful in harvesting the benefits of component rationalization, then you will have to come face-to-face with the realities of the broad approach at some point of the initiative.

Conclusion

Component rationalization is a classic and popular way to reduce complexity. In terms of your war on complexity costs, with time of the essence, many companies will choose to take a targeted approach in combination with other battle strategies and soon after convert to a broader approach to mine the rest of the opportunity. Either way, recognize that no company can justify component complexity when by definition it is internal complexity and invisible to the customer. It is extra cost saddling the organization and deserves a "zero-tolerance" approach to elimination.

Chapter 12 Endnotes

54 "The Turn Around at Fiat," Money.CNN.com, May 10, 2007. Available at http://money.cnn.com/magazines/fortune/fortune_archive/2007/05/14/100031047/index.htm. Accessed July 20, 2009.

55 "Motorola's Battle with Supply and Demand Chain Complexity," *Supply & Demand Chain Executive*, April/May 2003.

56 Theresa Metty, presentation titled "War on Complexity," NECON 2006, October 2, 2006.

57 "Motorola's Battle with Supply and Demand Chain Complexity," *Supply & Demand Chain Executive*, April/May 2003.

58 Michael L. George, James Works, Kimberly Watson-Hemphill, *Fast Innovation* (New York: McGraw Hill, 2005).

CHAPTER 13

Enabling Variety with Lean Processes

Imagine that you own an electronics company that makes laptops, servers, and consumer electronics. Your margins are thin and retreating in the face of fierce global competition. Your customers want laptops customized to their needs, they want to pick from a broad selection, and they don't want to wait two months for delivery. What to do?

Neither reducing your range of offerings nor dropping customization is an option because both are customer expectations. The other option is simple: Get Lean! Remove waste, become more flexible, and minimize work-in-process so that you can deliver variety fast at low cost.

Lean reduces process costs across the board, and this is sensible improvement activity; but one often overlooked advantage of Lean is that it **lowers the switching costs of any process,** making it more flexible and thereby less sensitive to the impact of complexity.

Many books have been written on the topic of Lean, and we'd encourage further study. However, there are a few key principles particularly relevant to reducing the costs of complexity. We will cover those principles in this chapter, with a specific focus on enabling greater flexibility in your processes to accommodate greater variety.

The Basics of Lean

Lean is a management philosophy and set of process improvement tools generalized from the Toyota Production System, and it is as applicable to service processes as it is to manufacturing processes. At its core is the objective of creating more value (for the customer, and, therefore, for the firm) with less work. Lean attains that objective by removing "waste" from processes: the non-value-add activities that customers don't see and wouldn't want to pay for. (Lean sorts waste into seven categories, as described in the sidebar, next page.)

Lean represents a cultural system, a management methodology, and a complete set of tools focused on removing waste and attacking the causes of waste. What happens when you remove waste from a process can be truly transformational:

- Lead times fall by 50% to 80%.
- Costs fall as lead times are cut. The process needs less inventory and fewer people and produces less rework.
- Quality improves (yes!) because having fewer steps and less inventory in the process leaves less room for error—plus a faster process means more cycles of learning.
- Capital requirements are decreased. The increased speed of the process frees trapped capital (for example, as a result of its Lean processes and the lack of inventory clogging its supply chain, Dell no longer needs to operate any warehouses[59]).
- Customer satisfaction levels rise as your processes meet specific customer requirements faster, more consistently, and at lower cost.
- Employee engagement goes up. To drive the biggest Lean gains, process participants must understand how their process fits into the broader picture of the organization, and their jobs become less wasteful and more fulfilling.

The sum up, **Lean makes complexity less expensive.** Consider how Toyota can produce more customer value-add features than its U.S. competitors and still do it at lower cost. Toyota automobiles have consistently been at the top of quality rankings by J. D. Powers and Associates, and Lexus has become a leader in the luxury market. Yet, at the same time, the company's return on assets is eight times higher than the industry average.

The seven types of process waste

1) **Transportation:** unnecessary movement of materials
2) **Inventory:** work-in-process (WIP) or raw material in excess of what is required to produce for the customer
3) **Motion:** people or equipment moving more than is required to perform the activity
4) **Waiting and delay:** delays and waiting between when one process step ends and the next one begins
5) **Overproduction:** production ahead of demand
6) **Overprocessing:** adding more value to a service or product than customers want or will pay for
7) **Defects:** the effort needed to inspect for and fix defects

Lean also positions companies for growth: Lean companies can place more bets in the market and do so faster than non-Lean companies because they have faster lead times to market. And they understand how to leverage existing platforms to take advantage of new opportunities.

We should put this opportunity in context. In an "unimproved" process—one that has not been the subject of numerous continuous improvement projects—less than 5% of lead time is spent on value-add activities. That means 95% or more of process lead time is spent on waste or non-value-add activities, such as rework and delays. Though no process will ever have 0% waste, there certain is a lot of opportunity for improvement in that 95%. (This is in part why we say you can't rely solely on reducing *product* complexity; rather, a multidimensional strategy that incorporates tackling process complexity will likely represent a huge opportunity for most companies.)

Dabbling in Lean

Given how many companies *profess* to be Lean, or have a Lean culture, it may be surprising to an outsider that so few companies actually deliver the results of a firm like Toyota. The issue is that the essence of Lean can become lost to the minutia of Lean. It reminds us of a line from the Woody Allen movie *Love and Death*:

> *I've come up with all the little details. If I can just think of the main points, we got something!*

Jeffrey Liker, author of *The Toyota Way*, said, "Unfortunately, for many companies the essence of building in quality has gotten lost in bureaucratic and technical details.... Quality planning departments are armed with reams of data analyzed using the most sophisticated statistical analysis methods. Six Sigma has brought us roving bands of black belts... armed with an arsenal of sophisticated technical methods."

He contrasts that with Toyota, which, he says, keeps things simple. Toyota quality specialists have just four key tools:

1) Go and see
2) Analyze the situation
3) Use one-piece flow and visual controls to surface problems
4) Ask "why?" five times

U.S. companies, he believes, have focused on tools and "do not understand what makes them work together in a system." Oftentimes, management does little more than "dabble" with Lean. "There is a 'Lean production cell' here and a pull system there and the time it takes to change over a press to a new product has been reduced." But that is where the resemblance ends. The lesson: Companies should look into what their Lean efforts are delivering. If the results are unimpressive, it may be time for an assessment of how Lean is being leveraged.

It is perhaps not surprising, therefore, that Lean has been embraced with something approaching religious devotion by many and rejected, in the face of perceived near zealotry, by almost an equal number. That is too bad. The core ideas described in this chapter can and should be integrated into everyone's core management approaches, independent of the desire to adopt the Lean label.

Leveraging Lean for Step-Change Improvement: Six key lessons

In the process of helping companies deploy Lean approaches to enable variety and make significant improvements in performance, we have had the privilege of learning from those experiences. To help you cut to the chase, here are key lessons critical to leveraging Lean to enable variety.

Lesson 1: Quality and value are defined by the customer

This is easy to accept on paper, but much harder to instill across an organization, as it forces a fundamental evaluation of the work we do and how we do it. "A product is not quality because it is hard to make and costs a lot of money," writes author Peter Drucker. "This is incompetence. Customers pay only for what is of use to them and gives them value. Nothing else constitutes quality."[60]

So a "value" assessment of your processes is critical, but it requires discipline, self-confidence, and leadership to shine a bright light on what is truly value-add from the customer's perspective. Which process activities would your customers say are of value to them? **This knowledge is a prerequisite for Lean processes,** as it helps isolate the activities that will become the bones of the redesigned process. Fail to conduct this assessment, and you will end up with increased organizational costs and low productivity as your business starts to mold itself around a preponderance of "fake work" (see sidebar, next page).

Anchoring on what matters to your customers' definition of value is a big shift in mindset and a keystone for strong processes that can deliver variety with less cost. But though it must be done, achieving the shift has some challenges, such as,

- **Deciding what is value-add and what is not:** Common Lean practice is to label process activities as value-add (VA), non-value-add (NVA), or business-value-add (BVA). Definitions vary, but our recommendations are
  - **Value-add** includes activities that customers would pay for if they knew it was part of the purchase price. For example, the design work that gives Porsches their specific look is something that is of value to those purchasing that make of car.
  - **Business-value-add** is often defined as the activities that are required for the business to function but that are not value-add in the strict

Fake work: Another example of process waste

Fake work is work that may feel productive but that doesn't really add value.

In their book *Fake Work*, authors Brent D. Peterson and Gaylan W. Nielson approach the phenomenon of process waste or non-value-add activity from the employee's perspective: "*Why people are working harder than ever but accomplishing less.*"

In the book, they claim that "Fake work is misunderstood because it feels like work." By fake work, they are referring essentially to non-value-add activities. They say, "Working hard is not a barometer of fake work, so you may not even see that you are building a road to nowhere. Sometimes you do fake work because you were told to do it. Sometimes fake work is what you're rewarded for doing."

Why does fake work continue to exist? The authors suggest that "fake work thrives where old, outdated processes hang on. It thrives when companies do not clearly articulate the results they need. And it thrives when you and your managers aren't asking whether you are doing fake work."

Part of their recommendation is raising the visibility to the phenomenon. "This book is not about what is easy to see, but about the subversive and eroding aspects of organizational processes that end up creating massive amounts of fake work." We agree that fake work, as they call it, is a scourge. In our experience, the best way to attack it is by targeting the key drivers versus by chasing the symptoms.

sense of being important to customers. The trouble with that definition is that it can quickly become a catchall. In a broken process you will find scores of activities that are currently critical to the process functioning but nonetheless are NVA. But by defining them as BVA, you essentially take them off the table. Therefore, we'd favor a narrower definition: BVA is an activity that is mandated from a legal or regulatory perspective. (That will force more activities into the NVA bucket, but that's okay. When we redesign a process—and we're freed from the current sets of critical interdependencies that help the broken process function—we'll be better placed to build it around the VA activity only.)

- **Non-value-add** encompasses all activities that are neither value-add nor business-value-add. It is the work that a customer would not want to pay for. For example, a customer would not want to pay for rework or the labor associated with chasing down an order.

- **Translating vague customer input into specific process requirements:** An effective process achieves levels of speed, cost, and quality that correspond to more nebulous standards of customer satisfaction. Global grocery retailer Tesco, for example, has learned that customers waiting in checkout lines react badly when there's more than one customer in front of them. When lines build up, Tesco stores open up more registers so that they can meet the checkout speed requirements inherent with the "one-in-front" standard.

Turning vague and often contradictory customer input into actionable customer metrics can be challenging. Different customer segments will have different expectations that require different levels of process performance. For example, anyone FedExing a package has a range of options before them in terms of when exactly the package needs to arrive: it always arrives, but for some it will need to be there first thing the next day, while for others the afternoon is fine. Also, standards are never static. Customers' expectations are constantly rising: what was fast enough yesterday usually isn't tomorrow. Plus, once you start down this path, customer requirements (as defined in terms of speed, quality, or cost) can seem unattainable relative to current levels of performance. But resist the temptation to dismiss some customer requirements as *unrealistic* or *a pipe dream.* Someone will meet those requirements, and along with that take the business. Wouldn't you prefer that "someone" to be your company?

NVA relates to the process, not the people

A client once asked us if there was a less offensive term he could use than non-value-add. "It's a strong word given how hard people work here," he said. True, no one wants to feel like their work is without value; and there's a communication requirement here: people are doing what they are told or reacting to what is in their purview, so the onus should be on the process, not the people.

But the solution is not to rebrand NVA or hide it but to engage your people in building a better process. Value-add work generally is less frenetic and more satisfying; who wants to solve the same problem over and over again? People inside the process have the best visibility to the issues and are the best change agents for rooting out NVA.

Lesson 2: Work back from the customer to create a good end-to-end flow

If you know what constitutes value-add, and you know the standards the process must meet in terms of quality, cost, and speed to meet customer expectations, then you have the bones for defining a new process—or at least a substantially different and better version of the old process. That understanding of customer needs is your starting point. You then work from the customer backward, structuring an optimal flow and value stream to perform the VA activities in a way that will meet customer expectations. (Eventually, you will likely have to work backward into your supply base because the speed and efficiency of the whole supplier-to-customer chain is only as good as its weakest link.) The best processes will be structured around this "customer-back" perspective. In fact, customer-back is a foundational idea. Living that code

- Will keep your process agile, customer responsive, and ahead of the curve as customer tastes change and expectations rise
- Will drive you to constantly evaluate whether what you are doing is customer-value-add
- Focuses the organization on process inputs, activities, and outputs, ensuring a smooth flow of goods and services across the enterprise (vs. getting lost in internal debates and functional optimization)
- Puts the customer at the heart of the operation, not at the margins

For example, Tesco starts with the customer and has identified a few key metrics as customer critical requirements. We discussed the one-in-front metric earlier. Another key metric is the availability of goods. *I can get what I want* is Tesco's framing of the customer desire. This translates into fill rates on the shelf, a key competitive measure in grocery retail. Tesco works back from there: *What does our supply chain process need to look like so that our customers can always find what they are looking for in stock? And how do we ensure this process flows smoothly across functions?* Imagine for a moment that Tesco didn't begin and end with the customer. Without that focal point and subsequent knowledge about fill rates, line lengths, and the internal operations to deliver against those metrics, what are the chances that Tesco could keep customers happy and coming back for more, given the cutthroat competitive nature of UK grocery retail?

Lesson 3: You can't improve what you can't see, but don't let the mapping and measuring become an activity trap

We all use maps to help orient ourselves in a new city and get a sense of the overall geography as well as perhaps find the fastest way across town. Without that perspective, tourists walking block by block may find it takes a long time to reach their destination. Organizations, in this sense, are like large cities. They grow to their current size and shape via a significant history. They are not logical and streamlined but reflect a long stretch of organic growth. And to navigate them, you need a map—to understand the whole but also to find your way around.

One of the highest-value tools of Lean is a **value stream map** (VSM), shown in Figure 52 (next page). A VSM documents a process, end-to-end, including the inputs, process steps, and outputs, as well as information and material flow and important process data (on lead times, delays, work-in-process, etc.). It is the basis for understanding how the process *really* works and for undertaking a value-add analysis (assessing what is value-add vs. what is not).

Figure 52: A Value Stream Map for a Fruit Juice Company

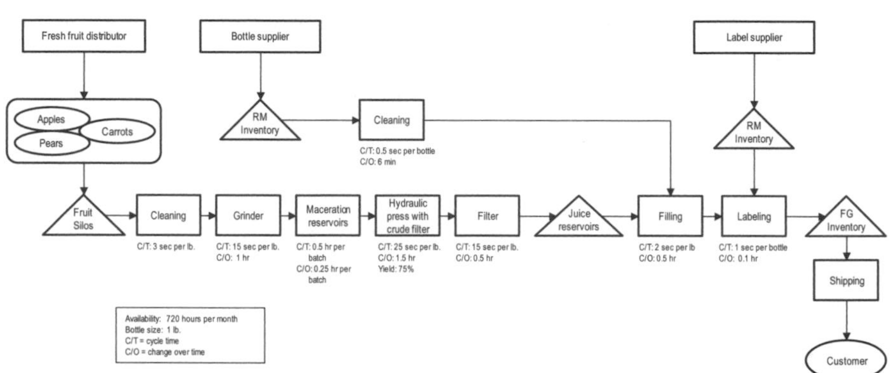

The company receives raw materials from local fresh fruit suppliers. The juice-making process starts in the cleaning area where the fruits are washed to remove dirt and unwanted materials. The fruits are cut into pieces in the grinder, then an enzyme is added for the maximum juice extraction. The grinded fruits are transferred to the maceration reservoir, then pumped into the hydraulic press. The crude filter inside the hydraulic press holds back the skins, stems, and leaves. Then the juice is filtered in the finer filter for better purification. In the filling process, the bottles are cleaned and moved to the filling location where the juice will be filled and capped. The bottles are then labeled and are ready to ship. After developing the VSM shown above, we identify that the hydraulic press is the "bottleneck" of the process since its processing time and setup time are the longest.

It can be amazingly powerful when all the participants in a process contribute to creating the value stream map and *for the first time* get a sense of how the *entire* process works. Mike Rother and John Shook wrote a book on the approach called *Learning to See*—an apt title, as value stream mapping is like removing the blinkers from the process participants. The sense of revelation is particularly dramatic in transactional processes where colleagues are often located in different places, even different countries, and though all part of the same process, blind to what is happening upstream or downstream. If no one has a sense of the overall process, then the opportunity for improvement and collaboration is capped, as most of the time the points of process breakdown are where there is a misalignment between different parts of the process.

In fact, a key lesson from Lean is that **you cannot improve what you cannot see.** But like any useful tool, value stream mapping can be overdone. Some organizations are awash with VSMs; entire departments are created to update and maintain these documents. To return to our map analogy, if you're a tourist looking to visit a museum, you'll need to pick up a guide once there showing you where the different galleries are. But first, you'll need a city map that provides a holistic view to give you a better understanding of how to get there from your hotel. Our advice: balance the value of the data-intensive drill-down value stream maps with the perspective of the broad picture.

Our version of the city map is a twist on the value stream map: construct a VSM that shows how the processes cut across functions and departments and use it to develop hypotheses about specific areas of opportunity and drill-down. For broad process diagnosis, start with this view of the organization (similar to a routing matrix, as described in Chapter 14, "Process Segmentation: Minimizing the Effects of Variety"). For process-specific insights, use a value stream map, and guard against any one approach becoming an activity trap.

Lesson 4: Processes are governed by "laws of physics"

Many people are surprised that processes are governed by laws no less absolute than the laws of physics. These laws predict process behaviors. You need to understand these laws to make step-change improvements in performance.

Law #1: The higher the number of "things" in the process, the longer the lead time (Little's Law)

$$\text{Lead Time} = \frac{\text{Amount of Work-in-Process}}{\text{Average Completion Rate}}$$

"Things" in this equation could be projects, products, components, reports, or even people. As an example, consider waiting in line at Disneyland. If there are 100 people in line for a ride, and 5 people are boarding the ride every 2 minutes, you can predict how long you'll be waiting (lead time). You'll be waiting a while.

$$\frac{\text{100 people}}{\text{5 people/2 minutes}} = \text{40 minutes}$$

Understanding the implications of Little's Law is fundamental to achieving Lean improvements. What the equation tells us is that there are two ways of improving lead times:

1) by accelerating the completion rate, normally requiring more people, machines, or some form of resources

2) by decreasing work-in-process (WIP), which we can do through Lean methodologies

In other words, **there's the expensive way** (speeding up the process) **or the smart way** (eliminating WIP).

Dell, well known for being Lean, sees WIP inventories as the enemy of speed. In fact, Dick Hunter, former head of Dell's supply chain for the Americas, said that Dell regards inventory as *a form of ignorance*. He told *Fast Company*[61] that, in his view, companies keep inventory as a hedge against poor demand forecasts and an inability to see into their supply chains. "Most companies love a big order backlog; when the semiconductor industry has six months' worth of orders, they're happy," he says. "If I've got more than three days' backlog, Michael is calling me."

As Figure 53 shows, by reducing and limiting WIP, you can get to tremendous improvements in the process, even leaving the completion rate as is.

Figure 53: Halving WIP Will Halve the Lead Time

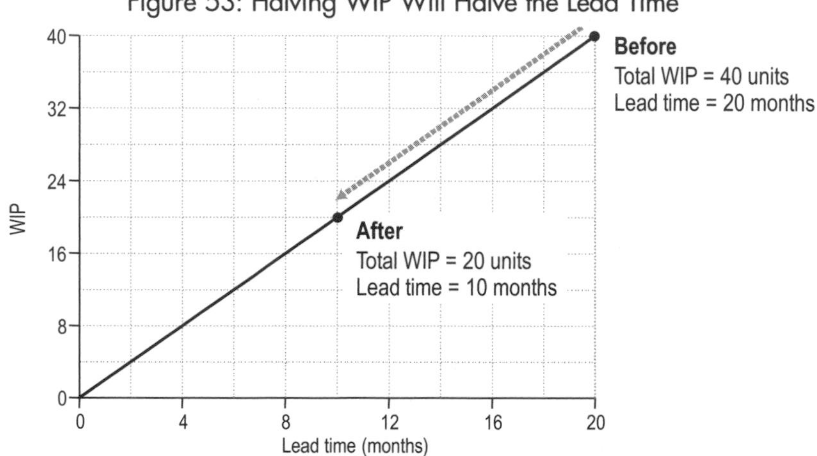

In the simplified case example above, the lead time of 20 months put the company at a competitive disadvantage, when average order lead times were 14 months. Their approach to addressing the issue was to put in place Lean initiatives to reduce and limit the amount of WIP. The result: by cutting WIP in half, they also saw order lead times cut by half, with associated improvements in cost, waste, and customer satisfaction.

Inventory reduction, therefore, is a key lever for reducing process lead times and removing waste. When WIP piles up, you get delays and lead times extend. It's logical when you think about it, but at the same time counterintuitive to how people manage their day-to-day work. If you get new work landing on your desk, surely it's better to get everything started? The answer is no: all that does is extend the completion time for everything.

Put another way, if you have no knowledge or *control* of the amount of WIP in your processes, then you have no knowledge or control of your lead times. By controlling when new work is released into a process—and keeping the total WIP constant—you will see immediate benefits. This leads to the second law of physics that governs processes:

Law #2: When processes have high variation, high utilization of resources can drive out lead times exponentially[62]

Nearly every business has some processes that have relatively predictable lead times. Those lead times may be longer than desired (hence our emphasis on removing NVA activities), but by and large those times will be within an expected range. In contrast, other processes—such as innovation, R&D, sales, and software design—will have lead times that vary widely and often unpredictably. The inherently creative aspects of many of these processes make predicting lead times very difficult. In such environments, it is critical to recognize that the normal rules governing lead time don't apply. In fact, in processes with high variation, the relationship between resource utilization and lead time switches from a predictable linearity (twice as much work = twice as much lead time) to a less predictable nonlinearity (twice as much work could equal 4 or 10 times longer lead times; see Figure 54).

Figure 54: Lowering Resource Utilization Dramatically Reduces Lead Time

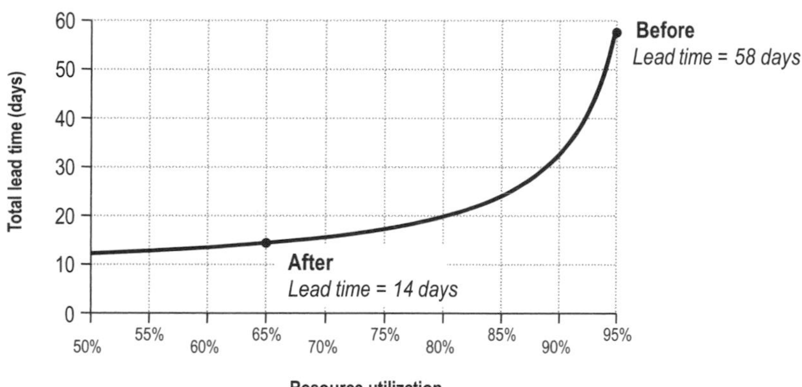

In practice, what this means is that you can't load resources as heavily in processes with high variation. It is a counterintuitive relationship. Managers are taught to watch a team's capacity and load it up with work. But one implication from this second law is that by **reducing resource utilization from 95% to 65% the manager can actually reduce task time by a factor of 4** (compare the "before" and "after" points on the graph in Figure 54).

The bottom line is that you cannot manage an unpredictable high-variation process as if it's a predictable manufacturing process (where high utilization is desirable). To improve speed of creative/high-variation processes, look to Lean practices such as these:

- Increase the levels of reuse in the process; i.e., reuse design elements as much as possible to minimize the amount of "from scratch" reinvention of a design process. Have sales staff develop best practices that will give them a jump start when they meet potential clients. Those types of actions will shorten the process cycle time and essentially reduce variation in the overall process.

- Increase cross-training so that no one part of the process becomes a bottleneck resource.

Lesson 5: Leap (don't crawl) toward perfection

Since most processes are composed of only 5% value-add activities, the opportunity for improvement is, by definition, massive. That's why one key lesson we'd pass on is to ensure you frame your efforts with enough ambition to make a difference.

One way of anchoring your efforts in the right zone is to set the bar using information regarding the value-add activity in the process. As a rule of thumb, the lead time of world-class processes has approximately 30% to 50% value-add activity in it. (Contrast that with a lot of processes that have less than 1% of value-add activity.) You can see in the example below how an appropriate stretch target can be set using this rule of thumb.

Figure 55: Eliminating NVA to Cut Lead Time

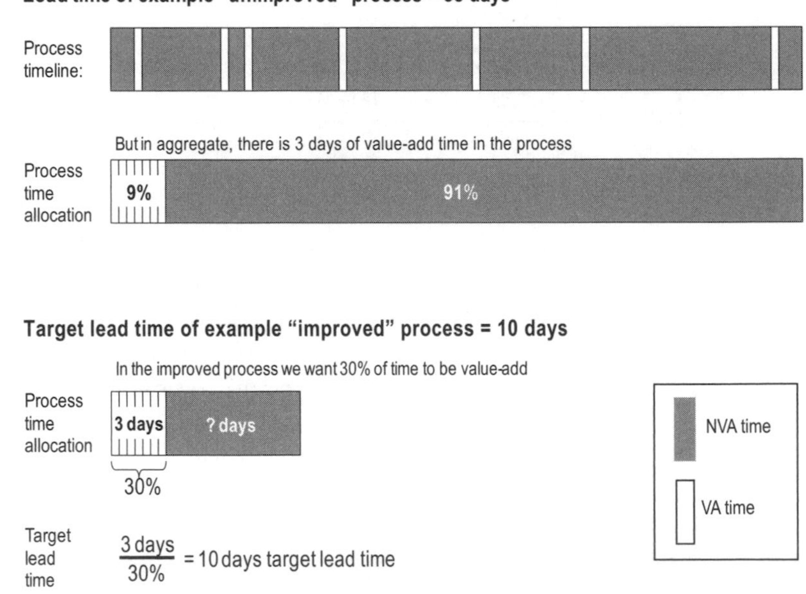

With this target, you can then ensure that your efforts are framed ambitiously enough. These types of "entitlement" targets force a rethinking of the process, not just a tweaking of the current state. Kevin Rollins, former CEO of Dell, said, "I set irrational goals, Michael and I together, to encourage our team so they don't think of conventional solutions. If we asked for a 10% or 15% increase in productivity, we'd get conventional solutions. But if we ask them to double their productivity, then they have to rethink everything."[63] Dell, in other words, establishes an entitlement goal to force breakthrough thinking and avoid incrementalism.

Lesson 6: Focus on bringing discipline to your processes (when things go well, and even more so when they don't)

One visitor to a Lean company commented that its factories were *boring*: "People were standing around." It's not surprising that it seemed like that to a visitor. Lean organizations *are* boring in that they bring discipline to their processes and manage to avoid the frenetic firefighting that characterizes non-Lean processes. When talking about process performance, *boring is good.*

But while a lot of companies have mapped and measured their processes in an attempt to take out waste, one key lesson they often overlooked is the need to bring discipline to bear *when things do go awry*. By responding to a breakdown in the process in a predictable and comprehensive way, companies can (1) correct the issue in an efficient and timely manner and (2) truly learn from what went wrong. Companies will usually focus on (1) but forget the value of (2). By understanding what *should* occur within a process (through mechanisms such as standard work and process mapping), organizations can quickly recognize issues as they occur (and when they are small). Moreover, with explicit procedures in place to capture and investigate the root cause of an issue, Lean ensures that the organization will benefit *broadly* from the knowledge generated *locally*—or as commonly said, *every defect is a treasure.*

As described in the book *Chasing the Rabbit*, the value of this done thousands of times is differentiating and extraordinary:

> *In the U.S. Nuclear Navy, when a new crew assumes responsibility for a new ship, everything it encounters—the design of the ship, the design of its procedures, the design of problem-identification and problem-solving routines, the training—is derived from the Navy's entire cumulative experience.*

How Lean Enables Variety

Lean practices obviously can dramatically improve processes. But we are interested here in how Lean enables variety: it does so by making variety cheaper. When you make variety cheaper, you can sometimes turn bad complexity (profit destroying) into good complexity (profit enhancing). Lean does this in two ways:

First, **Lean reduces overall process costs and resource consumption.** In a Leaned process, resources that were chasing down lost orders, or overproducing unneeded output, or engaged in other NVA activities in the old process can now be deployed to more value-add activities; the rework and scrap that were produced as a result of poor information flow will no longer be hitting budgetary costs. Lean processes use a fraction of the resources that non-Lean processes do, and the result is greater organizational capacity for the pursuit and delivery of variety.

Second, **Lean reduces the impact (and costs) of variety.** By definition, a process that has to handle more variety will have to switch back and forth more often than a process that handles less variety. The amount of time it takes to switch between product or components is NVA from a customer's viewpoint, meaning we have to reduce switchover time (also called setup time) as much as we can.

For example, imagine a family of products flowing through a manufacturing line. At each station, when the process needs to set up for Product A as opposed to Product B, there is a changeover. The greater the difference between Products A and B, the higher the likelihood of errors as workers struggle with multiple parameters for different products. And the longer the duration of the changeover (with nothing being produced), the greater the impact on production and lead time.

Indirectly, this changeover phenomenon also leads to higher inventories: A common response to the challenges of long changeover times is long production runs. The logic is that once you are set to Product A, produce it in high

Batch size as a function of setup time

Optimal batch size is a function of setup time according to the Optimal Batch Size Equation (described further in Appendix A):

$$B_i = \left(\frac{\sum_{j=1}^{m} \sqrt{D_j \bullet h_j \bullet s_j}}{\mathcal{S}} \right) \bullet \sqrt{\frac{D_i \bullet s_i}{h_i}}$$

B_i = Batch size of item i

D_i = Total demand for item i

h_i = Holding cost of item i

s_i = Setup time per batch of item i

$\mathcal{S}$ = Total time available for setups

m = number of products

If setup time is the same for all products, then the equation reduces to

$$B_i = \left(\frac{\sum_{j=1}^{m} \sqrt{D_j \bullet h_j}}{\mathcal{S}} \right) \bullet \sqrt{\frac{D_i}{h_i}} \bullet s$$

Which means that for constant demand, holding time, and time total available for setups, batch size is simply proportional to setup time:

$$\textit{Batch size } (B) \propto \textit{Setup time } (s)$$

volume so that you won't have to produce it for a long time, so as to minimize the switching back and forth between A and B. But of course we know from Little's Law that high levels of work-in-process generate longer lead times.

Therefore, a better approach is to reduce changeover or setup times. The closer that time gets to zero, the greater the level of product complexity the process can support, and the better you will be positioned to offer high variety at low cost.

Reducing changeover time, increasing flexibility

There is a well-proven Lean tool called "Setup Reduction" for reducing changeover times. Here it is in brief:

1) Measure and classify what consumes setup time
Watch and time the process and identify how much time is dedicated to "internal setup," activities that require all production to stop or slow down as opposed to "external setups," which are setup activities that can be done before production stops.

2) Convert internal setup to external setup (where possible)
The more setup work you can convert to external, the faster the changeover. Examine the internal activities and assess what can be done (what new information or inputs) to convert them to external.

3) Streamline internal setup
You will still have some internal setup time; assess what can be done to shorten this. For example, what NVA activities, rework, and so on are slowing you down.

4) Shorten ramp-up time
In a manufacturing setting, the ramp-up time may be the first few presses of the machine after changeover, which yield scrap and allow for adjustments. Many companies replace this trial and error by developing more accurate input parameters to help the people or machines hit the ground running after the changeover.

While Lean can enable variety, it is important to recognize its limits so that you can sensibly leverage it as part of an integrated campaign. It is usually a mistake to assume that Lean by itself can solve for complexity—and enable you to run wild in the variety you offer customers—for a couple of reasons. For one, processes are frequently overwhelmed by complexity. If your processes are flooded by variants, then the costs to make the process sufficiently Lean to cope may be prohibitively expensive. Theoretically, ideally perhaps, you could Lean out a process to deal with almost unlimited variety. But as William F. Buckley Jr. put it, "Idealism is fine, but as it approaches reality the cost becomes prohibitive." Better, then, to first reduce the amount of product complexity, then Lean out the remaining process to deal with the adjusted demand and variety.

For another reason, focusing on Lean as a panacea is often a way of avoiding a much needed assessment of the portfolio. When this is the case, you are in danger of becoming the world's most efficient buggy whip producer.

Conclusion

As we discussed earlier in the book (Chapter 3, "The Rise and Rise of Process and Organizational Complexity"), companies are facing up to the increasing challenges of customer-requested variety and process orchestration. Lean helps companies do this by creating processes that can adapt quickly and sync seamlessly with network partners. In the near term, the application of the Lean principles, as outlined in this chapter, is a high-value battle strategy to restructure processes and process costs. However, as the many companies that have followed this path know, it is more than that: it is a platform for increased agility, speed, and customer responsiveness, which in a word adds up to growth.

Chapter 13 Endnotes

59 Gary Rivlin, "Who's Afraid of China?" *New York Times*, December 19, 2004. Although its Lean processes are a key to its lack of warehouses, the company keeps stock at hand by requiring suppliers to stock 8 to 10 days of inventory no further than 90 minutes from its assembly plants.

60 Peter Drucker, *Innovation and Entrepreneurship*.

61 Fast Company, "Living in Dell Time," December 17, 2007.

62 Reference equation source.

63 "Who's Afraid of China?" *New York Times*, December 19, 2004.

Chapter 14

Process Segmentation

Minimizing the Effects of Variety

In the beginning of the book, we gave the example of a retailer that had, over the course of 30 years, continuously tweaked and improved its grocery supply chain, only to find it thrown into disarray by new emergent categories, such as flat-screen TVs, furniture, and clothing. While these categories represented a tiny (but growing) portion of overall volumes, they had a significant impact on the operations and cost of the high-volume goods, such as cans of soup.

Clearly no business wants to saddle high-volume items with the costs of supply chain disruption linked to a few slow movers. But at the same time, slow movers can have a meaningful place in the portfolio if they represent new categories that are increasingly important to customers. Therefore, when SKU reduction is off the table—as a means of reducing the variation and mitigating the impact on the high-volume items—you need a different approach.

The way to handle a mix of high- and low-volume products is by **process segmentation via value streams** in which you bracket your products and services according to their level of process similarity. *Process segmentation* assesses your product or service volume in terms of the key process paths it takes within the organization, as opposed to segmenting it by customer type or market demographic, which is common to *market* segmentation. It minimizes the effects of variety, shielding the fast movers by steering simple and predictable demand through one channel and complex, more variable demand through another—ensuring the simple demand of the former is not burdened by the higher costs of the latter.

The value of process segmentation lies in its power to make complexity less expensive. By using process segments, you can **achieve the kind of benefits you would get from SKU reduction at a local level but without impacting revenues.**

To understand why this is so, remember the interactions on the Product/Process face. The cost of complexity on this face usually results from the extra work, or processing, associated with a particular product category or feature set. When all products follow an identical path, you have something akin to an assembly line: high volume, low cost. But most product or service portfolios are not that homogenous. By separating out the volume into distinct streams, however, you can recreate the benefits of a de facto assembly line in a portion of your products, simultaneously dealing more effectively with lower-volume or higher-variation products in a separate stream.

Process segmentation ensures that your volumes flow through processes in the most effective and efficient manner possible—often requiring separate values—versus being mixed and mingled within a single value stream.

There are many benefits to process segmentation for cost reduction. In addition to being a powerful battle strategy, it is, in our experience, a valuable focus area whether you are battling complexity or not. The benefits include

1) **Cost and capital reduction.** As noted above, by segmenting process families, you get to enjoy the benefits of SKU rationalization (in terms of the impacts of low-volume offerings on high-volume offerings) without sacrificing revenue or the strategic bet that these products or services may represent. Process segmentation will also separate out the volume that has a lower associated variation on demand, benefiting the balance sheet through a reduction in required inventories.

2) **Risk mitigation.** Processes "stretch" over time to cope with an increasing variety of requests and demands placed on them, but often at a cost. Similarly, risk profiles change over time. Let's take a real example: a company that wanted to address the complexity in its order-to-pay process. As the company grew, the number of vendors and suppliers grew tremendously, as did the range of tasks now taken on by suppliers and third parties. And with that growth, some vendors became trusted partners: 80% of invoices were tied to a mere 30 organizations. But all invoices were processed through the same process, building tremendous queues but also obscuring the few that had higher risks. After process segmentation, invoices were stratified by supplier (top 30 or below), invoice amount, and risk profile (certain activities required certification before the invoice could be paid). The result: faster invoicing for trusted partners and improved risk management by isolating areas that truly warranted attention.

3) **Service enhancements.** In the example above, the top 30 suppliers frequently complained about how long it took to get invoices paid. This is predictable and typical when you inject variation into an otherwise low-variability process. Queues build up and bottleneck all the volume. Locating the volume that injects the variation and stratifying it out can have a significant impact on lead times and key service metrics. It also leads to better planning and scheduling, enabling better control of lead time performance and service levels.

4) **Better cross-functional alignment.** One of the unexpected consequences of undertaking process segmentation is the knowledge it builds in both marketing and operations, in areas that were traditionally restricted to compromise and negotiation. On the one hand, marketing can see the linkage between specific product or service attributes and process metrics: if marketing knows a promotion will cause havoc in operations and extend overall lead times, it raises a question, *Is it really worth it?* Process segmentation highlights which attributes drive unnecessary lead time and cost into a product and puts the onus on really validating whether this is something a customer values or whether there is an equivalent feature without the process implications. On the other hand, operations has a clearer view of what really matters to customers and can structure to best deliver on those requirements.

5) **Performance visibility.** In many situations, the disruptive impact that high-variety items have on low-variety items can mask or become an easy excuse for the poor efficiency of the high-volume/low-variety items. In fact, the low-variety product should be processed with higher efficiency, but only by segmenting out low- and high-variety can you gauge the potential and ensure the process is meeting performance targets.

Diagnosing Process Segments

Like many financial services companies leading up to the financial meltdown, one company had vastly increased the breadth of its products and customer segments over the past two decades. It had expanded from a few simple banking products targeted at local customers to a broader portfolio that also included brokerage, health, and life insurance products and the targeting of large national customers. But as a result of this expansion, the variety of the products was too much for the company's processes, leading to long delays and customer complaints.

In response, the company launched an effort to better understand their process segments to insulate the high-volume requests from those that were causing a lot of the variation. For example, in its insurance division, previously all requests for increased coverage had been channeled through the well-trained but very expensive medical underwriting team. But an analysis of the volume and the process flows revealed that in fact 50% of requests were routine, with no differentiating attributes, which could be easily dealt with by the less expensive account review team. The more complex requests were still channeled to the medical underwriters, but with half their workload shifted, the turnaround time also decreased, leading to happier customers and lower costs. Savings came from needing fewer underwriters and from better service levels as a result of lower lead times. In all, turnaround times were cut by 75%, and processing costs were halved.

This is a simple example, but in fact, most of the time, their approach of dividing work based on a better understanding of what is routine versus custom is one of the easiest and most effective battle strategies available for dealing with process complexity. It anchors on doing the same work more effectively by "steering" work into different channels, as opposed to overhauling the processes through which it flows. In their cases, it also allowed better use of resources, using a lower-cost process pathway for the routine and more expensive pathway for custom orders.

Sometimes process segments are obvious. If you are in charge of putting in place new plant production equipment, you have a pretty good idea of the process flow and how much of what products go through with what kind of frequency. But many times, and particularly in transactional processes, segments are neither clear nor static.

Recall the health insurer from Part I. A large proportion (95%) of enrollment requests were kicked out of the standard process and treated as custom requests (one-offs), where each was given a case number and individual attention. There was no standard process, per se, for this high volume of one-offs. But a deeper examination revealed that a large proportion of the custom requests actually shared common attributes. There was, in effect, standard volume lurking within the custom bucket. Carving out this volume as a new process family led to cost savings of $50 million. It also freed up capacity for dealing with truly custom requests because overall lead times decreased and service levels went up.

What was tricky here—and could be the same in your company—was that this was a *naturally occurring segment*. It was not designed by the company; it was a reflection of how customer tastes often settle around a common set of configurations. Whenever there is the potential for configuration in your products and services, or a highly customer-responsive culture, there exists the potential to identify and leverage naturally occurring segments.

For example, many PC makers leverage this idea to drive efficiencies while offering the potential for full customization (hard drive, battery power, memory, screen resolution, etc.). Most of us make purchase decisions based on how we intend to use a computer. So by channeling customers, based on intended use, to preconfigured machines, companies can gain scale while saving customers time. Clearly this only works if customers are channeled toward the purchase of PCs that meet their needs. And to understand what customers want often requires considerable purchase history and a lot of data. But the value of doing this, in an era that demands the option to customize, is in finding the 20% of combinations that capture 80% of the demand.

Companies often fail to identify process families because they lack an end-to-end view of their processes. As one extreme, we have seen situations where functions truly operate as black boxes: an order goes in, something is done to it,

Process stratification to build a platform for Lean improvement

While Lean has traditionally helped many make-to-stock (MTS) companies drive dramatic improvements in process performance and profitability, the opportunity is just as large for make-to-order (MTO) firms (including design-to-order and engineer-to-order [ETO] firms). In MTS firms the application of Lean tools and approaches to improve the firm's many value streams is straightforward. However, in MTO environments, where there can seem like an infinitive variety of orders—and no clear value streams—applying Lean requires a different approach, namely, process stratification. For in fact, inside most MTO environments there are usually ways of segmenting processes and volume in a way that creates stable value streams—and an opportunity for driving scale benefits and leveraging Lean improvements.

Take the example of a large and tenured equipment manufacturer that treated every order—regardless of customer—as a unique order. After analysis of its order volume, it was clear that *naturally occurring* segments did exist. Of the 150 total orders that were thought to be unique, 75 of those were actually exact duplicate orders received in the past and were forecasted by customers for the future. Within those 75, there were only 8 different versions.

Initially, the company defined itself as a pure ETO firm. After the analysis, it understood that a portion of its operations was ETO, while there was a portion that was better defined as "CTO," or configure-to-order. Managing each differently was the key in successfully applying Lean practices, such as standard work, pull systems, and continuous improvement efforts.

and the order comes out. No one quite knows what goes on in the black box, least of all the next function in the process.

Siloed thinking is a barrier to developing an end-to-end view (understanding how an order moves through the process and navigates interfaces from beginning to end). And this view is critical to developing your process segments—we're looking to find the distinctive differences end-to-end, not just within a piece of the process. For example, a special request in the sales process may lead to both specific modifications in administrative support and different manufacturing requirements; a family will link these differences together.

Also, by looking at individual functions separately, you can neither get a sense of nor create "flow." Having multiple products with different requirements run through the same process steps interrupts the flow, as operators constantly have to switch setups, materials, instructions, and so on. As a result, huge queues build in many places throughout the process. But by stratifying the processes, you minimize interruptions, thereby creating a smoother flow, which in turn leads to lower lead times, less work-in-process (WIP), and greater efficiency.

Central to process segmentation analysis is the idea of linking product and service attributes to distinctive process requirements and paths. If the goal is to splinter the volume by different processing requirements, what criteria will you use to determine which parts of the volume should go down which path?

It is important not to confuse the intrinsic complexity of the product itself with the *process complexity* that results due to the product attributes. For example, consider the toy inserts that consumer goods companies add to cereal boxes. What is more "complex"—the toy with two or more moving parts affixed to the back of the box, or a paper voucher drop-in (redeemable for free movie tickets) that is added to a subset of the boxes randomly? The answer is the latter: a company that tried that approach needed to add extra FTEs to handle the randomness of dropping in vouchers, and it was a nonstandard process. In fact, product attributes matter, but mostly in regard to the additional nonstandard processing required. This linkage is critical to developing process segments.

That's the kind of siloed thinking that allows complexity to flourish.

Feeling the pain of complexity

Key to the cereal maker's experience is the fact that the decision about using the vouchers was made by the marketing department, but they did not have to feel the pain the voucher promotion caused via its disruption to the manufacturing process.

Approach to Process Segmentation

One advantage to process segmentation as a battle strategy is that, generally, it is revenue neutral, fast, and actionable. It makes complexity less expensive. The key elements of the approach are to

1) Map the "anchor" process that cuts across the organization
2) Identify the major tributaries and sinkholes
3) Develop a straw man set of process segments (based on the flow map or routing matrix)
4) Identify product/service attributes that determine process segments
5) Begin steering the volume based on product/service attributes

1) Map the "Anchor Process" That Cuts Across the Organization

The first step is to develop an organizational view of your processes by developing a value stream map across your processes or using a routing matrix (what we use below) to assess the path that 80% of the volume takes across the organization—what we call the **anchor process.**

You want to understand what happens to the bulk of your volume: how an order comes in, what happens to it next, all the way through to delivery or service fulfillment. The best way to develop this is through one-on-one interviews with management and those closest to the process, to slowly build up the map. After you have developed the map or matrix, hold a team working session with attendees from across the organization to validate the picture you have of the organization.

A simple schematic, like that shown in Figure 56, is sufficient.

Figure 56: Anchor Process Flow

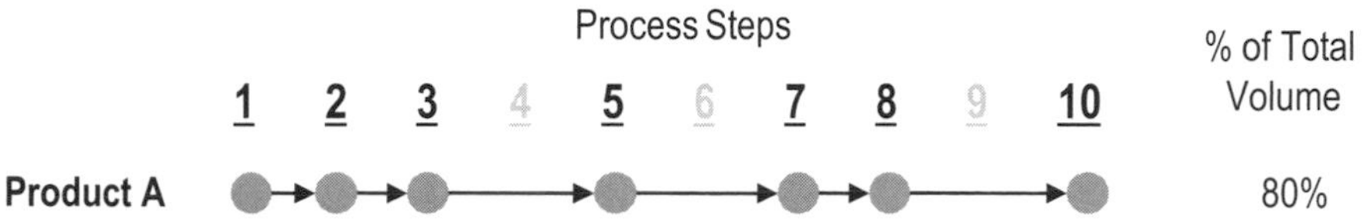

Process Steps

1 2 3 4 5 6 7 8 9 10

% of Total Volume

Product A 80%

In this simple conceptual example, Product A is the mainstay product, representing 80% of the volume. As a result, the anchor process comprises Steps 1, 2, 3, 5, 7, 8, and 10. In practice, we'd use real process names, not numbers, so don't be confused with the apparent skipping of steps (4, 5, and 9, shaded in gray). Those are simply the activities in the organization that are not required for the high-volume product but are associated with other products yet to be mapped. Many times functions creep in to support lower-volume product categories; you will want to make note of them as you plot the anchor process.

2) Identify the Major Tributaries and Sinkholes

Products or services that fall outside a certain set of attributes are diverted for extra processing, classified as custom, or bounced out of the narrow process as exception errors. But these may all be clues to major tributaries—detours that indicate a separate process family. Codifying these on the routing matrix is a key step toward process segmentation.

Figure 57: Additional Process Pathways

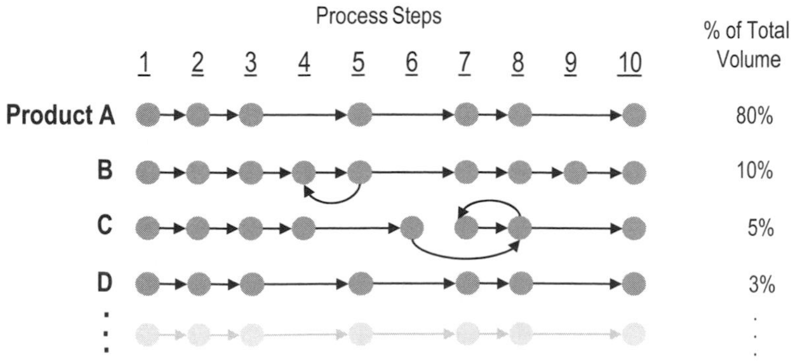

Process Steps

1 2 3 4 5 6 7 8 9 10

% of Total Volume

Product A 80%

B 10%

C 5%

D 3%

Continuing the conceptual example, here, we identified four major families and three additional steps (4, 6, and 9). B has a work loop on Steps 4 and 5. Assuming these process steps share the same resources, this definitely plays havoc with sequencing and scheduling. C is even more complicated in requiring Step 8 before Step 7. Additionally, it is the only product that requires process Step 6. However, Product D follows the same exact path as Product A. Keep in mind that, in this example, all of these products share the same resources, which means that there definitely seems to be an opportunity to segment some processes to achieve better efficiencies.

3) Develop a Straw Man Set of Process Segments (Based on the Flow Map or Routing Matrix)

The most practical way of thinking about process segments is to consider this: if you were to color code the materially different paths through the organization, how many different colored strands would you end up with? Each strand represents a different process segment: by definition each will likely have a different cost profile or have distinctive processing requirements. Focus on identifying four to eight families to not overcomplicate the analysis.

4) Identify Product/Service Attributes That Determine Process Segments

Now that you have your process families defined, consider the "shaping" attributes in your product and service volume that determine one family from another. In a manufacturing example, customers selecting certain specifications may trigger the need for additional nonstandard machining, which would require separate plant equipment, setups, and labor.

Figure 58: Identify Why Some Products Require Different Paths

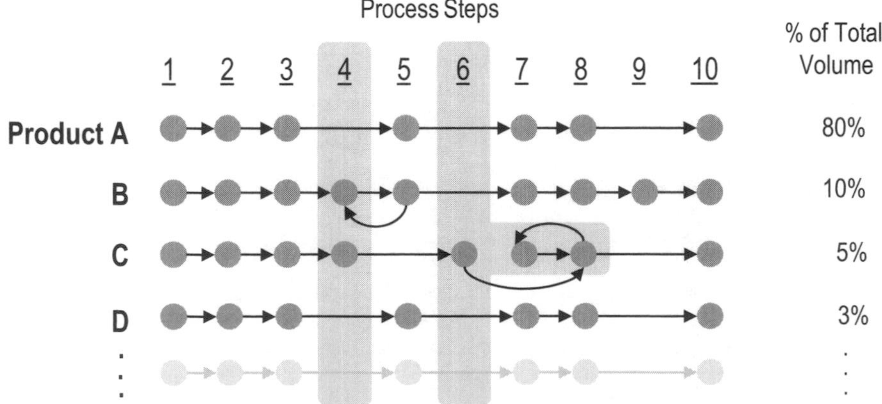

The highlighted areas (in gray) represent the process steps/product characteristics that require a deeper analysis: what are the attributes about those products or orders that require Step 4? Same question goes for Step 6 and the atypical circular loop on Steps 7 and 8 for Product Family C. What are the costs of performing those steps with shared resources (lead time and dollars)? Are those attributes something that customers are demanding, or are they "delighters" that sales and marketing introduced to drive customer satisfaction?

5) Begin Steering the Volume Based on Product/Service Attributes

Now that you have identified the defining attributes, establish a gateway mechanism to steer the volume to the right process path—matching the simpler volume to the lower cost channel. Now that we have identified the product characteristics that define whether a product belongs to Family A, B, or C or is truly custom (the remaining 5%), we can steer the volume to the right path. Figure 59 illustrates how this split would work.

Figure 59: Segmenting the Process

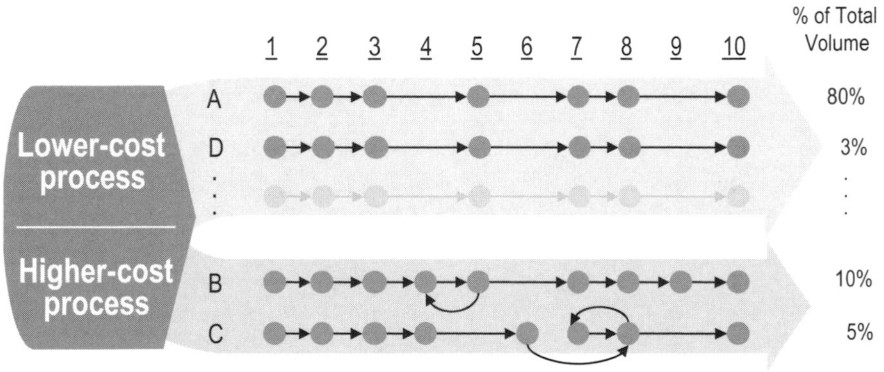

Conclusion

Process segmentation is not only an effective means of improving service and reducing costs, it also builds transparency to further opportunities. Some companies may discover, after segmenting out their processes, that a certain portion of the volume is eroding profits, even after migrating it to a lower cost channel. But greater visibility to costs helps you to assess if you can (a) serve this segment any cheaper through process improvement or (b) migrate these customers to a higher-margin option. Without this visibility, it is likely you will continue to cross-subsidize money-losing subsegments.

CHAPTER 15

Project Rationalization and Resource Utilization

Getting More Done Faster and with Fewer Resources

Upon wrapping up a project for a major healthcare company, a colleague of ours was asked by a company executive: "If there was one thing I were to change in this company, what should that be?"

Our colleague quickly recommended that the executive cut 98% of the company's projects. Surprised, the executive asked how to tell which ones to cut. Our colleague's answer: "It really doesn't matter."

Of course, 98% is no magic number, and we don't suggest that executives necessarily put no thought into which projects they keep and which they cut. The point, however, was that with far too many projects being worked, energy was so diluted that most weren't getting done anyway. By focusing on a much smaller number of projects, whether 2% or 20%, the organization would have a much better chance of getting those done and would achieve enough focus to determine whether these projects were truly important to the company. This is why it almost didn't matter which ones to cut—the more important ones would rise to the top.

This healthcare company was not alone. Nearly every company we've seen has too many projects—strategic initiatives, continuous improvement projects, new product development efforts—and overburdened resources, which practically guarantees poor results. As we discussed in earlier chapters, having a lot of "stuff" going through a process slows the organization and creates the kind of hidden complexity costs that are sapping your profits and margins. Being able to tackle this problem, to have *fewer* resources (fewer people/costs) and generate *better performance* (such as getting more products to market faster) is critical at a time when most organizations are looking for ways to take out costs.

We visited a large chemical company interested in tools to help identify better project opportunities, yet they already had over 60,000 projects on their project list. Our advice was to get better at *working* projects before worrying about *finding* better projects. Without doing the former, the latter would simply be one more car in rush hour gridlock.

What is the price of this gridlock? The answer: taking *longer* to get *less* done with *more* resources.

With such a negative impact, why do so many companies find themselves in this situation? And why do so few take the dramatic action that has the potential to reduce project lead times and time to market by as much as 50% to 75% and at the *same* time reduce project resources by as much as half? The answer: most companies don't fully understand the relationship between resource utilization and project lead time in creative processes (those with highly variable task times).

This situation is inadvertently exacerbated by many common management practices (such as trying to load up resources with work) and the chain reaction of impacts that follow. The purpose of this chapter is to make you aware of these interactions, practices, and impacts; to show how they combine to create gridlock; and to outline the steps you must take to reverse this trend.

This battle strategy will apply to you if

- You have an overwhelmingly large number of projects
- Many projects seem to just go on and on
- You have lost all confidence in project timelines
- Your management rarely ever says no to good projects
- Increasing numbers of people are working on a large and growing number of projects
- There is more and more project activity with less and less project outcome

If these sound familiar, you have much benefit to gain from project rationalization. While the benefits certainly include cost reduction, the larger benefits are greater competitiveness and revenue.

Our Approach: It all starts with fewer projects

The objective of this battle strategy is to get more projects done faster and with fewer resources. Doing this involves three things:

1) **Getting your project lead times under control.** By understanding how variation and resource utilization interact to determine overall lead time, you can reduce development times in your creative processes. Lower development time of course also means faster time to market. This has

two benefits: you gain the benefit of the impact sooner, with potentially significant impact on your competitiveness; and the sooner you finish a project the sooner you can start another, which is in part why doing less can lead to getting more done.

2) **Improving your resource productivity.** Reducing project lead times lets go of much unnecessary work. With increased resource productivity you will be able to get more done, or you will be able to get the same amount done with fewer resources, or both.

3) **Attacking variation in task time.** Variation in how long it takes to complete the kinds of creative tasks associated with most projects is at the core of why working too many projects creates gridlock. With such "creative" variation, projects take longer, which means more projects are worked at the same time, each of which leads to even more variation. With fewer projects, you will gain the visibility necessary to start attacking variation, with the benefits of even lower lead time, greater productivity, and the ability to work more projects.

We cannot overemphasize the basic principle that **achieving each of these objectives starts with working far fewer projects.** And since it may seem counterintuitive that by doing less you can get more done, and with so much opportunity for so many companies on the table, let's dive a little deeper.

Why Fewer Projects Means Much Shorter Project Lead Times

Most of us intuitively feel that the amount of time (i.e., total lead time) it takes to complete a task is inversely proportional to the amount of resources devoted to the task: If you double the amount of resources, you cut the lead time in half. And vice versa, if you cut the resources in half, you double the lead time. And aside from specific critical skill or division of labor constraints (such as that which prevents nine women from having a baby in a month), most of us operate according to this logic. Indeed, this relationship is true for tasks with no variation. But as we discussed in Chapter 7

- The level of variation is what governs the relationship between resource utilization and lead time
- Creative tasks inherently have more variation than repetitive manufacturing processes

For example, Figure 60 shows the overall lead time for a series of tasks, each with an *average* task time of 10 days and with a level of variation common to creative processes (meaning that sometimes the task will take more than 10 days and other times less than 10 days, but the average will still be 10 days).

Figure 60: Total Time Consumed per Task

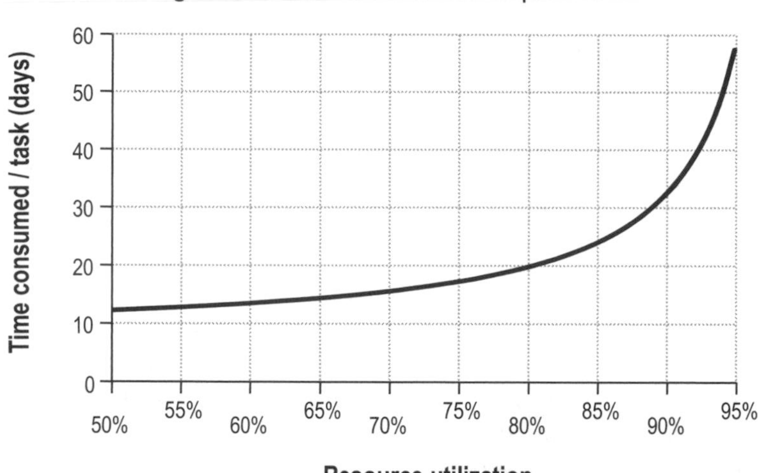

With this level of variation shown, scheduling the 10-day tasks to arrive every 11 days (95% resource utilization) means each item spends 50 days in queue, for an average total lead time of 60 days. However, scheduling the tasks to arrive every 15 days (65% resource utilization) means each item only spends 5 days in queue, for a 15-day total lead time. For the level of variation shown, *reducing resources utilization by one-third (doing a third fewer projects) cuts project lead times by a factor of 4!*

In the presence of variation—inherent in creative processes—the relationship between resource utilization and lead time points to a powerful tool for shortening your project lead times, that is, by doing fewer projects you will get those done much faster. But this is only a piece of the answer, and we must now turn to what this means for the actual productivity of your resources.

Why Faster Projects Also Means Increased Resource Productivity

The relationship between resource utilization and lead time in the presence of variation has been well established. The astute reader, however, may point out that this relationship, no matter how important for lead time, is in essence still a trade-off between resources and lead time—that even though a small reduction in work gives a dramatic reduction in lead time it is still a case of "if I load my resources with *less* work, they will get it done faster." And although shorter lead times are certainly desirable, how do either more resources or less work translate into greater productivity and lower costs? The answer hinges on what really happens with projects in most organizations.

Almost always, the queue time doesn't remain queue time but becomes filled up with "fake" work (as you may recall from p. 233, fake work is work that may feel productive but that doesn't really add value), meaning that *long project lead times become an invitation for and driver of additional work.* As project lead times grow, work expands, and true productivity, measured as the number of things that get done rather than the amount of work that is expended, rapidly declines. But where does this additional work come from and what does this really look like in an organization?

This extra work takes two forms:

- **Greater time spent on project overhead.** This is the most direct and obvious and includes the numerous project updates, steering team meetings, budget reviews, and other project admin. The volume of work consumed by project "overhead" generally grows proportionally with project lead time. For example, a major transportation company had so many projects and so much variation that projects that might have otherwise taken six months were taking years. Many of these projects reported to six or more separate governance bodies, with many project teams easily spending four days each month on steering team updates and other project overhead activities. By comparison, a six-month project would include 24 days of overhead activities. Stretching that same project over two years would require *100 days of overhead activity.* As project lead time increases, the portion of project time spent on overhead does too.
- **Increased demands on project resources themselves.** We have already mentioned the notion of mental setup time in Chapter 6. By being stretched over many simultaneous projects, which is what happens to resources when there are too many projects, resources are required to constantly shift between projects. These shifts add mental setup time and decrease productivity.

An overhead "tax" on extra projects

Think of the extra project overhead as a tax you pay each month in the form of lost productivity for each project you have underway. As the volume of projects being worked increases, the total "tax" each month increases, with resources spending a larger portion of time on overhead activities and a smaller portion of time actually working projects. Projects stretch out, more projects are worked at the same time, and the tax grows, and so on. The natural reaction in the face of growing project lead times is to have even more frequent reviews—effectively increasing the tax rate.

Additionally, in the face of variation there are many delays. Think of trying to schedule project team meetings when the team members are each also spread over many other projects and responsibilities. These delays create little pockets of queue time that often become nonproductive—what we call dead time. Think of the amount of time most employees must spend each day coordinating or waiting for other employees. Usually, employees cannot readily reallocate these small chunks of time to other more productive activities.

How Fewer and Faster Projects Means Less Variation

Variation drives lead time, which drives poor productivity. Variation is inherent in project work, but long project durations themselves create much more variation. Think about these impacts of long project lead times:

- **Greater coupling between projects.** Long lead times mean more projects are worked at the same time, which means more resources are spread over a greater number of projects, which means that each project is more coupled or less insulated from issues on other projects. This means that each project suffers from the variation across many projects.
- **Greater exposure to changes.** With longer lead times, projects will experience a greater amount of change, including changed project require-

Microsoft's 50% buffer rule

The actual relationship between lead time and resource utilization in your initiatives and development projects depends on the particular level of variation in those projects.

It is usually impractical, and likely impossible, to really measure the total variation in your development projects, but that doesn't mean that it isn't driving longer lead times and reduced productivity. Companies such as *Microsoft*, where managing creative processes has been developed into a core competency, have figured out what works for them. Brad Silverberg, a Microsoft SVP, explains his "unshakable belief in the 50% buffer rule":

> *I don't know what [buffer time] is going to be needed for, but time and time again, I know it's needed.... So, if you have two months, you'd allocate one month for a buffer. A fifty percent rule turns out to be accurate. I can't always explain why.*[64]

Indeed, it is not uncommon for variation in development projects to be such that a 50% buffer in scheduling (e.g., loading your resources at 65% rather than 95% utilization, or doing a third fewer projects) will reduce project lead time by a factor of 4 (e.g., from 60 days to 15 days in Figure 60). This means that, for example, instead of doing three projects over a year, you complete two projects in a quarter—*for a total of eight projects over a year.*

By properly managing creative processes and reducing the number of projects, *you stand to get over twice the number of projects done with the same level of resources—and with a 75% reduction in time to market.*

ments, turnover of team members, competition for resources with a greater number of other projects, and difficulty planning over the entire project lifetime. These changes present themselves as variation.

The good news is that these sources of variation ("compounded variation") are the easiest to conquer because they just require reducing project lead times.

The best way to attack variation is to start with reducing the number and duration of projects. But once that has been done and there is some stability in the number of projects and their lead times, you will be able to attack the more structural elements of variation. For example, by removing the "noise" of project gridlock, you will naturally begin to see pieces of project activity that can be treated as more repetitive. By formalizing methods for those repetitive items, you can reduce the variation in those activities and create more space for those portions that are truly creative. But first you need to get the noise down.

Doing More, Faster and with Fewer Resources

Attacking project lead times, number of projects, resource allocations, governance, and variation will certainly require coordinated action and boldness, but the prize can be great. There are four actions necessary to claim this prize:

1. Cut the number of projects
2. Get your resource allocation right
3. Strip out project overhead
4. Demand shorter lead times (but don't strip out the buffer)

For each step we'll point out key principles and some common pitfalls to avoid.

Step 1: Cut the number of projects

If you have determined that this battle strategy applies to you, the most important first step is to simply cut the number of projects in your business. We recognize this is easier said than done. If you have many projects underway and likely interconnected, stopping work on some of them can feel akin to tuning up a car while driving. To take this step, therefore, you will have to change two mindsets in your company.

Mindset change #1: Focus more on *outcome* than on activity

- When companies focus primarily on activity (*are people working hard on valuable things?*), it can be very hard to cut projects—especially projects that were determined to be good things to work on.
- By focusing on output (*what have we accomplished and how long did*

it take), it becomes easier to remove projects, since working too many projects in total ensures that few will quickly get done. Cutting projects is, therefore, no longer viewed as, for example, going from working 100 good things to working only 10 but rather as a change from completing only 5 projects to completing 10.

Mindset change #2: Learn to say no, or at least "not yet," to good things to do

- Many decision makers have a natural tendency to spread their resources across however many opportunities present themselves. The much more effective leader is able to say which of these "good things" are really worth pursuing now. (See sidebar, next page.)

Why organizations spread themselves too thin

- Unclear strategic objectives making it difficult to prioritize between projects/initiatives
- Making decisions around projects individually rather than in total, which leads to trying to pursue all "good" activities regardless of the impact on other active projects
- Focusing on activity rather than outcome, hence getting more of the former and less of the latter

It is interesting that given the choice between launching a project today that will be completed in 12 months and launching a project 6 months from now that will be completed in 3 months, many people are drawn to the former (which is the decision that is being made when too many projects are piled on). **It is much easier to *launch* a project, which feels like you are getting something done, than to *finish* a project, which really *is* getting something done.** And it is indeed unfortunate that a natural reaction to lack of outcome is to launch even more activity.

Organizations are limited in resources and, therefore, in what they actually can do at any one time. *By not deliberately prioritizing projects on the front end, you leave them to be inadvertently prioritized on the back end—likely for reasons that you wouldn't have chosen.*

It may be helpful to consider the question less in terms of *what* to do and more in terms of *when* to do it and to avoid the misleading belief that anything that is important is something you should be working now. Indeed a crude but useful approach involves rewarding project owners, leaders, and teams based on what they actually get done and the impact it has while limiting the number of projects that they are allowed to work at any one time. This is like the Netflix[65] approach: only when they are done with one project can they get another. This

The "subtle temptation" to divide one's resources

The foremost American naval historian and strategist Alfred Thayer Mahan, in his seminal work *The Influence of Sea Power upon History,* describes the temptation for commanders to divide their fleets between all objectives. In describing the Four Day's Battle of June 1666 between English and Dutch fleets, Mahan writes,

> *A great strategic blunder by the government in London immediately preceded the fight. The king was informed that a French squadron was on its way from the Atlantic to join the Dutch. He at once divided his fleet, sending twenty ships under Prince Rupert to the westward to meet the French, while the remainder under Monk were to go east and oppose the Dutch....*
>
> *A position like that of the English fleet, threatened with an attack from two quarters, presents one of the subtlest temptations to a commander.* ***The impulse is very strong to meet both by dividing his own numbers as [King] Charles did; but unless in possession of overwhelming force it is an error, exposing both divisions to be beaten separately.*** [emphasis ours]

Very few organizations have the luxury of overwhelming resources, and by spreading resources over all the projects facing them, they risk "losing" on each one. Mahan continues,

> *A hundred and forty years later... the English admiral Cornwallis made precisely the same blunder,* ***dividing his fleet into two equal parts****... which Napoleon at the time characterized as a glaring piece of stupidity. The lesson is the same in all ages.* [emphasis ours]

And we would add "...in all situations." Spreading project resources across all good project ideas is "one of the subtlest temptations" facing decision makers. Mahan concludes,

> *Granting the approach of the French, the proper course for the English was* ***to fall with their whole fleet*** *upon the Dutch before [the French] could come up. This lesson is as applicable today as it ever was.* [emphasis ours]

focuses them on finishing projects fast while protecting them from the natural tendency, or subtlest temptation, to take on too many projects.

Of course, the best approach to prioritizing and cutting projects is to evaluate all projects on a combination of criteria including

- **Strategic objectives.** What are the key things the organization needs to accomplish?
- **Timing.** What must the organization accomplish today and what can it put off until later? Which projects are closest to completion?
- **Interdependence.** Are there synergies between projects? What projects make sense only with other projects?

- **Critical skills.** What projects, or combination of projects, best match the skill sets of your available resources?
- **Budget.** Which projects do you have the budget for?

That said, if you have trouble developing meaningful criteria, do not put off the prioritization! Do what you can to set priorities, and then move on.

The best defense against paralysis at this step may be to remember our colleague's response to the healthcare executive who asked how to tell which projects to cut: "It really doesn't matter." Anything more than this is certainly better, but only as long as it doesn't prevent you from prioritization and cutting your projects.

Step 2: Get your resource allocation right

The second step involves allocating resources across your projects. (In practice, this step should be done iteratively or in parallel with the first step, since your resource capacity is the dominant input into *how many* active projects you should have.)

For the reasons outlined above and in Chapter 7, it is critically important with creative processes to load resources at lower levels of utilization. But lower resource utilization can be achieved in two very different ways:

- Adding more individuals to each project
- Using each resource on fewer projects

The first option increases variation; the second, importantly, reduces it.

For example, consider a project resourced with four people, but with each of the four also spread across three other projects. On average, each of the four persons would spend 2 hours a day on the project, for a total of 8 person-hours a day. Now compare this to having just one person fully devoted to the project. From a resource utilization perspective, these allocations are the same, but the former results in much greater variation.

By staffing the project with four people who are each on 3 other projects, the project will be impacted by the variation of at least 3 and up to as many as 12 other projects; in turn, the project will impact those projects with its own variation. But having only one person fully utilized instead of the four people partially utilized isolates this project from the variation of others, releases much coordination time, and drives greater ownership.

Hence, **the dominant principle for resource allocation is to resource projects with a smaller number of more dedicated resources** (see sidebar, next page).

Of course, dedicating resources to individual projects is not always practical. For example, specialized skill sets may not be needed on a full-time basis. But while this is not always possible, pursue that goal to the fullest extent practical.

Rather than discounting the importance of resourcing with fewer individuals, the need for specialized skills underscores the value of having resources with broader capabilities.

America's first jet fighter in just 143 days!

Toward the end of WWII, the U.S. Army Air Corps asked Clarence "Kelly" Johnson to create America's first jet fighter to counter the new jets of the Luftwaffe. *How* he did it is, in large part, by living out the principle defined here of fewer resources spending more of their time on one project.

As Warren Bennis and Patricia Ward Biederman tell in their book *Organizing Genius,*

> *Arguing that it was the only way to get the job done and done quickly, Johnson persuaded his Lockheed bosses to let him create a top-secret department within the company, staffed by a small group of hand-picked engineers and mechanics. Kelly got the go-ahead to set up a hush-hush experimental operation that sidestepped the corporate bureaucracy and was beholden only to Lockheed's top management and its customers, notably the Army Air Corps.*

Bennis and Ward Biederman continue,

> *Headed by thirty-three-year-old Johnson [they] set out to* ***design the first U.S. jet fighter in 180 days.*** *Working furiously against its deadline, the group managed to produce a prototype of the P-80 Shooting Star* ***with 37 days to spare.*** [emphasis ours]

How did Kelly Johnson lead his group *of just 23 engineers and 30 support people* to create the nation's first jet fighter in just 143 days? For one, he was certainly a brilliant engineer (folklore has it that he could "see air"), but more importantly, as the name of Bennis and Ward Biederman's book suggests, he was an "organizing genius." One of Johnson's 14 rules of management was

> *The number of people having any connection with the project* ***must be restricted in an almost vicious manner.*** *Use a small number of good people (10% to 25% compared to the so-called normal systems).*[66] [emphasis ours]

By doing with tens what many would do with hundreds, Kelly Johnson reduced variation, minimized coordination costs, and avoided the trappings of "fake" work.

Step 3: Strip out project overhead

Project overhead includes project updates, steering team meetings, budget reviews, and other project administrative activities. As mentioned before, we have seen organizations where projects report to as many as six separate steering committees and project teams spend almost a week per month on project updates and reporting. Project overhead can abound in an environment with too many projects, individual resources spread across many projects, and lack of project ownership.

We have already described how large amounts of project overhead mean that longer project lead times result in even greater amounts of overhead. Project overhead is a "tax" on a project, and it drains away precious resources.

Even more importantly, **greater project overhead tends to diminish rather than strengthen ownership.** With greater oversight, ownership often migrates upward from project leaders to steering teams that then dilute it across many members. (Remember Admiral Rickover's words: "Unless the individual truly responsible can be identified when something goes wrong, no one has really been responsible.") There is safety in numbers (e.g., many steering team members), but numbers are what kill shorter lead times. Without ownership, focus shifts from outcome to activity, work grows, and lead times lengthen. Indeed, significant project overhead usually indicates a focus on activity more than outcome, with all the negative results we have already described.

To break free of this vicious circle, **recognize that increased project oversight is a symptom of something wrong rather than of a cure**—it is a sign of lack of ownership more than a driver of accountability.

The cure, then, is to drive ownership and a focus on outcome (remember our crude but effective Netflix approach). This is not necessarily easy and may require some hard decisions, which is one reason management often takes the easier road of increased project oversight and accompanying overhead. Greater oversight becomes an easy but often ineffective response to projects taking too long. Usually there are more structural reasons that must be addressed, as we have outlined above. When those structural reasons are addressed, be sure to release the unnecessary overhead.

Step 4: Demand shorter lead times (but don't strip out the buffer)

Simply demanding shorter project lead times without making the structural changes necessary to enable shorter lead times is usually for naught. Conversely, however, making the structural changes without following through by demanding shorter lead times can be just as ineffective.

The last piece, therefore, is to demand shorter project lead times, but this should *follow* not lead the other steps. Of course, we use "demand" somewhat loosely, but it captures the spirit. It is critical, however, that demanding shorter lead times does not translate into squeezing out buffer time. From *Microsoft Secrets*,

> *It's a leap of faith for many traditional managers to see buffer space in a schedule, so a lot of times it gets beaten out of the development*

> *manager: "No, let's tighten it up. We need to ship. We can squeeze some of that buffer space down." So you have a schedule which is unrealistic.*

Here again, we are asking for change of mindset: to have you draw a distinction between plans and accomplishment. Rather than demanding short project timelines—which projects will usually miss—expect realistic project timelines and demand that people meet them. This involves a combination of expecting as well as rewarding shorter lead times, of not tolerating anything less but creating the means to achieve them. Essentially, it comes down to leadership. In the words of Admiral Rickover,

> *A major flaw in our system of government, and even in industry, is the latitude allowed to do less than is necessary.... A manager must instill in his people an attitude of personal responsibility for seeing a job properly accomplished. Unfortunately, this seems to be declining, particularly in large organizations where responsibility is broadly distributed.... No management system can substitute for hard work. The manager may not be the smartest or the most knowledgeable person, but if he dedicates himself to the job and devotes the required effort, his people will follow his lead.*[67]

Conclusion

We have outlined the steps and rationale for being able to get more done faster and with fewer resources. We have described key process interactions that you must be aware of as well as typical organizational behaviors that exacerbate the situation and specific changes in mindset that will help you overcome these behaviors and the pitfalls to which they lead.

To review: to do more faster and with fewer resources requires that you

- **Work fewer projects.** Focus on outcome rather than activity and be willing to say no, or at least not yet, to good things
- **Focus your resources.** Resource projects with a smaller number of more dedicated resources
- **Emphasize ownership more than oversight.** Streamline governance and project administration, creating clear line of sight from management to project responsibility
- **Demand shorter lead times.** Raise your expectations for excellence while making the structural changes necessary for the organization to execute

As we indicated at the beginning of this chapter, the prize for many organizations can be enormous. Imagine being able to reduce your project lead times and time to market by 50% to 75% and doing so with half the number of project resources. While not all organizations will achieve benefits this large, it may be worth asking yourself what the current state of affairs in your organization is and what might it be in light of the previous discussion.

Chapter 15 Endnotes

64 Michael A. Cusumano and Richard W. Selby. *Microsoft Secrets* (New York, NY, Simon & Schuster, 1995).

65 The movie rental service that limits the number of movies a customer may have at any one time rather than the number of movies the customer sees over a period of time. At Netflix, a customer is able to receive another movie upon returning a previously rented one. Netflix advertises "Rent as many movies as you want!" while offering plans that allow a customer to have anywhere from one to eight DVDs out at a time.

66 "Kelly's 14 Rules." http://www.lockheedmartin.com/aeronautics/skunkworks/14rules.html. Accessed July 17, 2009.

67 Adm. Hyman G. Rickover, "Doing a Job," speech delivered at Columbia University, 1982, available at www.govleaders.org/rickover.htm. Accessed July 21, 2009.

Chapter 16

Dynamic Operations

Optimizing Complexity Trade-Offs

In Chapter 6 we showed how product complexity increases inventory levels, lengthens lead times, and reduces production volumes. These impacts, however, are not independent of each other but rather are interconnected.

For example, we know that product complexity increases inventory levels, but this impact can be mitigated by giving up some production volume. Giving up production volume allows more time to be spent on changeovers, which allows for smaller production batches, which means lower inventory levels. The implication is that a trade-off relationship exists between inventory levels and production volume, and so it is with other complexity impacts.

More broadly, complexity's many impacts are interconnected with each other; by optimizing your operations across these relationships, you can reduce the cost of complexity to your business. Said another way, by understanding the manner in which complexity impacts your operations, you can adjust them and optimize the trade-offs to mitigate the overall cost of those impacts, even if you don't change the level of complexity.

Optimizing the interactions involves taking a much more dynamic view of operations, where you look at the relationship between how factors change over time and how circumstances change. A dynamic view also recognizes the many linkages between the impacts of complexity in your operations, then optimizes the trade-offs between them in light of the environment within which you operate (e.g., the cost of additional inventory and the value of additional production capacity).

Many companies, however, manage and attack these impacts independently from each other. They launch inventory reduction initiatives or lead time reduction efforts that approach each issue independently from its effects in other areas. We will show that such efforts can lead to imbalance in your operations, meaning operating in a way that magnifies rather than reduces the cost of your complexity.

Does this battle strategy apply to you? Ask yourself the following questions:

- Are you suffering significantly from a single particular impact of complexity?

- Is product complexity straining your operation yet you see little real opportunity to reduce the level of complexity?
- Have you been attacking areas of complexity impacts singly, in isolation from impacts in other areas?
- Has your operating environment changed—what matters to your customers, where your operations are challenged—yet your operations have not followed suit?

If you answered "yes" to some of these questions then you may stand to gain from identifying and optimizing your complexity trade-offs.

Awareness Is Half the Battle

The steps for optimizing complexity trade-offs in your business are best summarized like this:

1) **Recognize the situation.** Identify and understand the significant dynamic relationships and resulting trade-offs that are negatively impacting or limiting your operation.
2) **Quantify the relationships.** Determine how the various pieces of your operation interact and what drives what by how much. Analyze the trade-offs. Develop a quantitative basis for optimizing the relationship.
3) **Optimize the system for the situation at hand.** This is less about a single right answer and more about developing the "structural knowledge" (see p. 143) to optimize the relationship for the business context today as well as over various and often changing environments going forward.

Granted, the type of situations and the specific actions for doing this can be as varied as organizations themselves. Fortunately, however, identifying a mismanaged complexity trade-off in the first place is half the battle; and half of that is knowing what to look for. So to that end, our focus here is on increasing your awareness of what dynamic relationships are, the impact they can have, and why organizations often struggle to identify, much less manage, them.

Perhaps the best way to illustrate dynamic relationships and the trade-offs they engender is with a real example. The following story is based on an actual case. After going through the insights this company gained about how decisions they'd made in good faith were exacerbating their problems (because of ill-understood dynamic relationships), we will categorize different types of dynamic relationships and touch on why organizations have often struggled with them.

Case: RME Pharma, Inc.

For many years now, RME Pharma, Inc., a specialized pharmaceutical company, has held a stable share in a steadily if slowly growing market. RME Pharma has seen its product portfolio grow from predominantly a single product a few decades ago to a few major and more than 20 smaller products today. While the added variety complicated its manufacturing operations, the company's three plants were able to keep pace over the years through engineering upgrades, investments in new equipment, and improved operating practices.

But after years of straining its supply chain to meet customer demand for its products, RME Pharma found itself facing an evident production shortfall. The company felt it had already squeezed everything it could from its plants, and without capital to invest in additional capacity (RME Pharma's manufacturing plants are large capital-intensive facilities), the company felt its only option was to contract with a third-party manufacturer (TPM) to fill its production gap. (But at least having too much demand was a good problem to have.)

Unfortunately, while RME Pharma was enjoying growing demand (because of its resilient staple market), it was also facing cost pressures in three ways:

- The outsourced production came at a significant cost premium as compared to production from the company's own plants. The TPM-produced product, while still profitable, was much less so.
- While the impact on average margin was significant but tolerable in the current year, the degradation was forecasted to grow in the next and following years to potentially unacceptable levels because steady growth in demand meant that, without other changes, each year a greater portion of RME Pharma's overall production volume would be outsourced to the TPM.
- To make matters worse, RME Pharma was also hit with significant price increases in some of its major commodity inputs, further adding cost pressures and decreasing margins.

In the face of these pressures, RME Pharma decided that it needed to turn over every stone to find cost savings. As part of an aggressive effort, it hesitantly launched a complexity initiative to identify and take out a chunk of complexity costs. We say "hesitantly" because RME Pharma was reluctant to touch its product portfolio, which was where it feared most complexity initiatives pointed.

Indeed, by comparison to most other companies, RME Pharma's portfolio of about 25 products wasn't very complex. But it was much more complex than it had been not too long ago, a time when two of its three plants were designed and built. And the plants were key, because limited production capacity was the reason RME Pharma found itself having to use a TPM, at a significant cost premium, in the first place.

Therefore, a project team began by looking at the Organization/Product face of the Complexity Cube, that is, the interactions, relationships, and fit between the company's products and the plants that produced them. The thinking was that if they could better understand complexity then they could better manage it, even if not removing it. Essentially, they sought to make complexity less expensive. To be more specific, the project team was given the task of *finding additional organic production capacity without changing the product lineup and without capital investment* (and this in an operation that had been considered by many to be already pushed to the limit). That was the charge.

Step 1: Recognize the situation

Looking at the Organization/Product face, some things quickly stood out to the team. Each of the major products and many of the smaller products were produced at each of the plants. One plant in particular had clearly been designed for low-variety, high-volume production yet had many low-volume products. The team suspected there might be possible gains from reassessing plant loading: which plants make which products or how much of each product is made at each plant.

But there was some resistance to this idea, as if the team was barking up the wrong tree, and there was some rationale for this resistance. Plant loading was one area that many regarded as running very well. Some thought it was the last place there might be an issue. In fact, many years earlier RME Pharma had implemented a robust systems solution that, among other things, determined optimal plant loading.

Nonetheless, shifting to the Process/Organization face, the team quickly walked through the plant loading process, paying particular attention to interactions between the process itself and the parts of the organization involved. The team took a holistic, cyclical view, looking not only at the plant loading determination itself, but also at the inputs used to make those determinations, the sources of those inputs, and what was done with the outputs downstream (see Figure 61, next page).

Each year, net standard production rates by product and by plant were determined based on each manufacturing plant's performance over the previous year (sometimes modified for planned plant or product modifications). The standard rates were fed to finance as an input to standard costs. The plant loading group used the standard rates as an input (combined with forecasted annual demand and transportation and distribution data) to annual plant loading, that is, targets for how much of each product each plant was to make over the coming year. Then, based on the plant loading targets, updated demand figures, and inventory levels, each week the master scheduling group would establish a master schedule, specifying how much of which products each plant was to

Figure 61: RME Pharma, Inc.'s Plant Loading and Master Scheduling Process

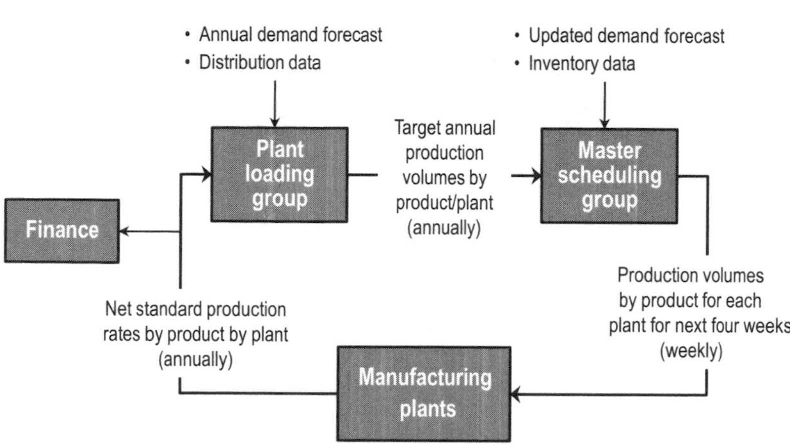

make by week over the next four weeks. The master schedule was sent weekly to each plant, where detailed scheduling (by the half hour) was done.

A couple of things quickly became clear to the team.

First, **the standard production rates** (net production rates by product by plant based on plant performance over the previous year) **were fed into the plant loading optimization application as *fixed values* when in fact they were variable** because the plant loading determination itself as well as the master scheduling that followed would affect those values. From a capacity standpoint, this was a critical dynamic feedback loop but one not captured by either the plant loading process or its system application.

By treating production rates as fixed values (i.e., "standard" rates), the systems application was unable to factor in its own impact on those rates when determining plant loading. Hence, rather than optimizing plant loading for its impact on production rates (its capacity impact), the plant loading application optimized for what it dynamically modeled, which were distribution costs; and minimizing distribution costs meant producing many products at many plants (see path "A" in Figure 62, next page). But, as the team realized, by loading select products at fewer plants, RME Pharma could achieve the positive impacts of SKU rationalization (lower inventory levels and greater production volumes) at a local level while not changing its overall product portfolio. That impact turned out to be significant.

Figure 62: Mapping of Plant Loading and Master Scheduling

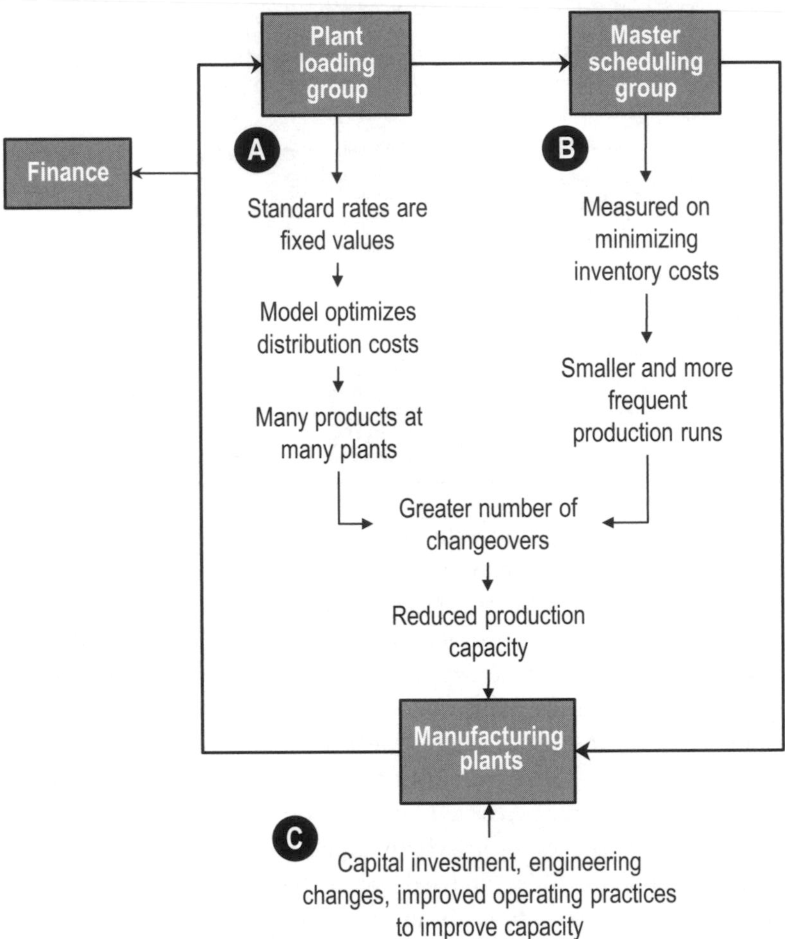

The loops on this path illustrate the unintended negative impact on production capacity that occurred in RME Pharma's plants. **Paths A and B:** By focusing on more easily modeled data and more visible metrics, plant loading and master scheduling inadvertently favored minimizing distribution and inventory costs at the expense of production capacity. **Path C:** The erosion of capacity was masked in part by capital investment, engineering changes, and improved plant operating practices. In return, the capacity erosion masked the positive impact from these investments and improvements.

The second major insight for the team was that the **master scheduling group was almost singularly measured (and focused) on minimizing inventory.** Again, the impact of that inventory focus on capacity had not been recognized, hence master scheduling leaned toward a large number of shorter product runs, allowing for less inventory but also eating up capacity with frequent changeovers (see path "B" in Figure 62).

To summarize, by taking a more complete, cyclical, and dynamic view of the production processes and the organizational structures used to operate those processes, the team found that, over the years, system and process limitations meant plant loading had structurally favored distribution costs over capacity and master scheduling had favored low inventory levels over capacity. This was a situation, not too uncommon, **where the organization focused on more easily modeled data and more visible metrics, but at the expense of more important items.**

The team now had a more integrated view of plant loading and production scheduling and their relationship with capacity, which cast new light over past trends. Capacity improvement over the years had been relegated to investment of capital and changes to engineering and plant operating practices (see "C" in Figure 62). But those actions, while helpful, masked the negative impact that the plant loading and master scheduling processes had on capacity. Further, the addition of new product lines as well as manufacturing complications (with a recent product reformulation) had their own negative impacts on production capacity. In short, there were many variables that served to mask the impact of plant loading and master scheduling on capacity.

But the answer for RME Pharma wasn't to now go too far the other way and emphasize only capacity. Low distribution and inventory costs are certainly worthwhile objectives. The issue was one of balance, and the current situation was decidedly out of balance (see sidebar on **Balance**). To achieve balance, the key was to optimize across the complexity-related, or in this case capacity-related, trade-offs involved. The next step was, therefore, to quantify these relationships.

Balance

In a complex system, balance or alignment can sometimes be more important than capability in a particular function. For example, the costly deterioration in RME Pharma's production capacity was owing to significant imbalance between its capabilities in minimizing distribution and inventory costs and its awareness of the impacts on capacity.

In fact, in this situation RME Pharma would likely have enjoyed a better situation if they had actually been less successful in minimizing distribution and particularly inventory costs! The linkages between plant loading, master scheduling, distribution costs, inventory costs, and plant capacity were more important than excellence in any subset of those factors. **Managing the interaction of the parts is often more important than becoming better at a particular part.**

Be Aware of Vicious and Virtuous Cycles

Before moving on to Step 2 and the quantification of the relationships, it is worth pointing out a particularly troublesome positive feedback loop the team identified ("positive" meaning "self-reinforcing" rather than "good"). RME Pharma's plants, as is typically the case, are subject to various uncontrollable or unpredictable inputs, parameters, and events (for RME Pharma, one such factor was atmospheric humidity). A negative perturbation (such as unseasonably high humidity levels, equipment failure, or contamination) might result in lower-than-planned production levels launching the chain of events shown in Figure 63. This is a vicious cycle, and many unforeseen impacts could and often had launched an RME Pharma plant into this cycle.

Figure 63: Production Volume Vicious Cycle

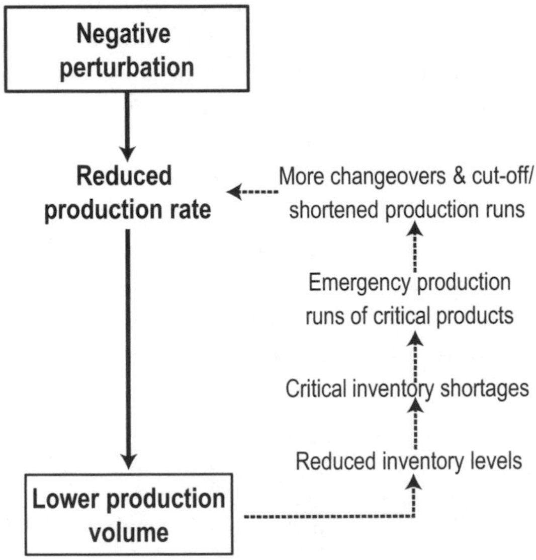

Negative perturbation

Reduced production rate

More changeovers & cut-off/ shortened production runs

Emergency production runs of critical products

Critical inventory shortages

Reduced inventory levels

Lower production volume

Typically, the vicious cycle continued until stopped by a positive perturbation. One way to prevent a vicious cycle such as this is to control for the perturbations—which can help but never completely stop all perturbations. Another trick is to build margin or buffer into the system—in RME Pharma's case by either planning with production rates that are slightly lower than normally achievable or by maintaining a greater inventory buffer (safety stock). But RME Pharma's plant loading and master scheduling process tended to minimize this margin.

On the other hand, a positive perturbation (e.g., unseasonably low humidity levels) could launch a plant into a virtuous cycle but the dynamic is not just the opposite of the vicious cycle (see Figure 64). The plant operators certainly knew that by lengthening production runs they could increase production volume, and they were always motivated to maximize production. Therefore, within the constraints of the master schedule handed them, they would develop their detailed schedule to maximize the length of production runs. By running ahead of schedule as a result of some positive perturbation, they were able to gain greater flexibility: they had more room to maximize production runs on their detailed schedule, and this had the effect of increasing production volumes, and so on. Typically, as with the vicious cycle, this virtuous cycle would continue until a negative perturbation impacted the system.

Figure 64: Production Volume Virtuous Cycle

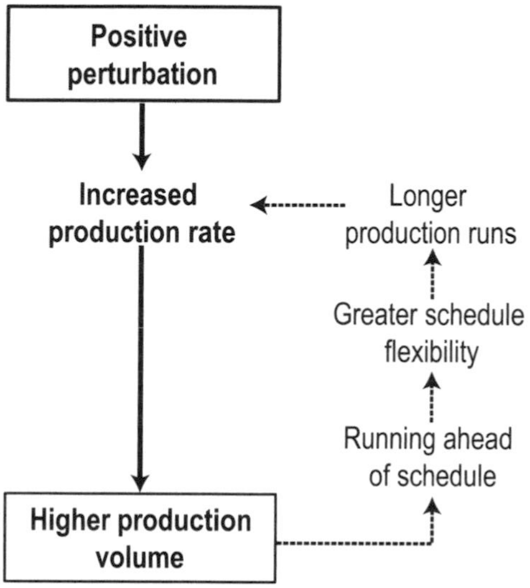

Positive perturbation

Increased production rate

Longer production runs

Greater schedule flexibility

Running ahead of schedule

Higher production volume

There are two interesting implications of these cycles: First, by managing the operation without a sense for the many linkages and these dynamic feedback loops, the plants naturally oscillated between vicious and virtuous cycles—certainly a rather disruptive operating paradigm. And maybe more importantly, *production volume increased when the plants had greater latitude with respect to the master schedule*. This was symptomatic of the unbalance within the system.

Step 2: Quantify the relationships

To quantify the trade-offs between capacity, inventory, and distribution costs, the team now turned to the Product/Process face of the Complexity Cube.

Without repeating the development here, in Chapter 6, "Where Complexity Arises: The Product/Process Face" we showed that for a given plant loading, the average overall inventory level rises with increased overall production volume—and vice versa. The team realized that key to this trade-off was the length of the production runs (commonly called the batch size or campaign length). Shorter production runs resulted in lower inventory levels but also less production volume. Longer runs yielded greater production volume but also greater inventory levels (see Figure 65). The team modeled these interactions to develop a *production volume–inventory level* curve for each of RME Pharma's plants (see Figure 66). (This curve can be developed by modeling based on the Optimal Batch Size equation in Appendix A.)

Figure 65: Impact of Longer Production Runs

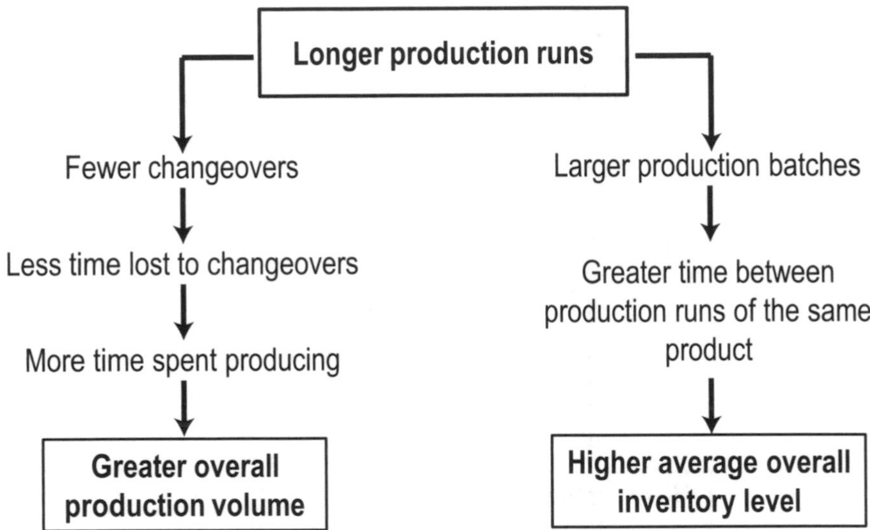

Figure 66: Example Production Volume—Inventory Level Trade-Off Curve

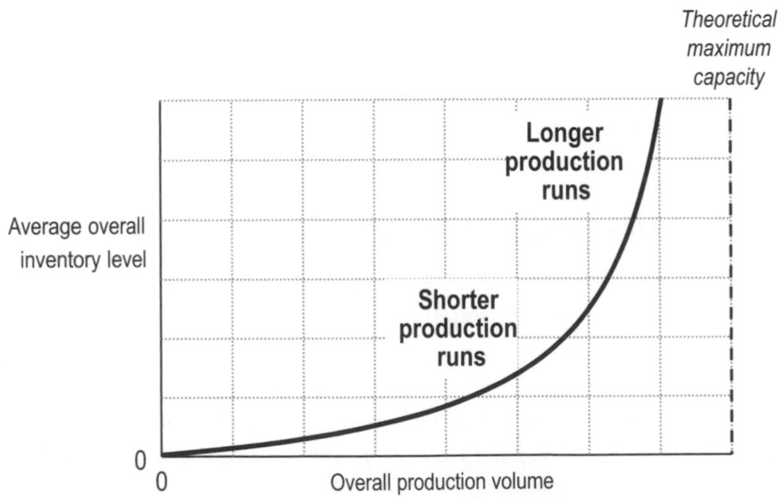

The curve in Figure 66 shows the trade-off between greater production volume and lower inventory levels. Longer production runs result in an operating point higher on the curve (greater production volume but higher inventory levels); shorter production runs, the exact opposite (operating point lower on the curve, with smaller production volume and lower inventory levels).

The team then wanted to understand the impact of plant loading on both capacity and inventory. Remember, they found that loading select products at fewer plants would achieve the positive impacts of SKU rationalization at a local level while not changing RME Pharma's overall product portfolio (see Figure 67). Quantitatively, this effect shifts the *inventory–production volume* curve downward and the optimal operating point down and to the right—*not only increasing production volume but also reducing inventory levels* (see Figure 68).

Figure 67: Impact of Producing Fewer Products at Each Plant

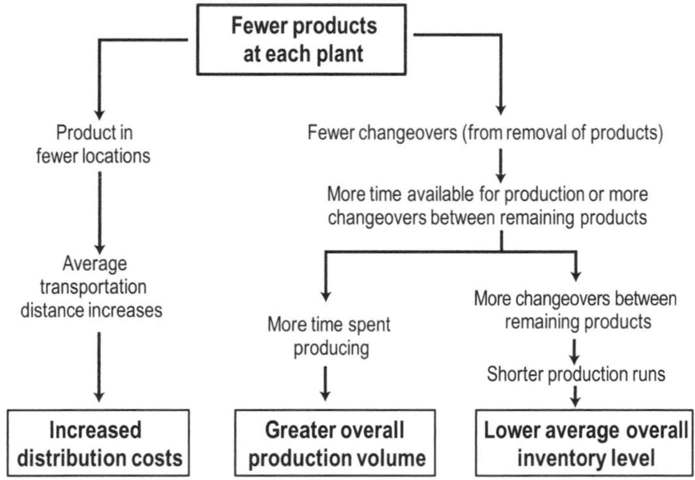

Figure 68: Shifting the Production Volume–Inventory Level Curve by Changing Plant Loading

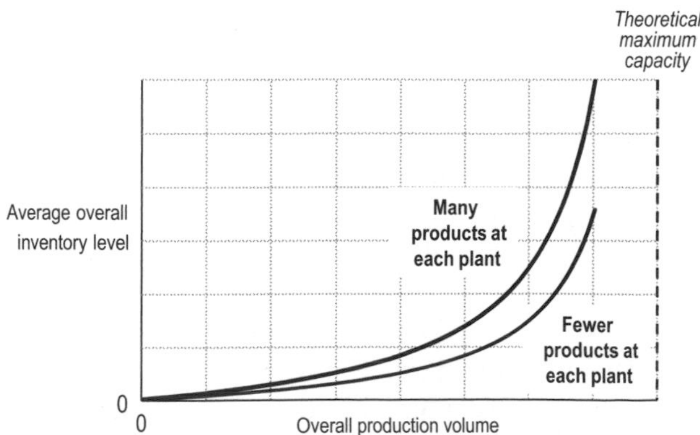

By changing plant loading to have fewer products at each plant, the production volume–inventory trade-off curve shifts down and to the right.

Further, by analyzing product and plant characteristics and by identifying and understanding key product and processes interactions, the team was able to identify which combination of products worked better at which plants. For example, one plant had particularly small storage volume between its production and filling/packaging lines. With such a small buffer volume, if the filling/packaging line went down, then the production line would soon stop because the small storage tanks would quickly fill up. Conversely, if production went down, then filling/packaging would soon stop because of having no product available to fill and pack. Production and packaging/filling were tightly coupled, with much time lost over the year.

This plant unfortunately had been loaded with two different product families that each required dedicated tanks. The product families could not share tanks; in essence that meant the storage volume between the production and the filling/packaging lines was half what it would otherwise have been. While the line was producing one product family, half of the tanks would sit empty but unavailable because they could be used only by the other product family. By removing one of these product families—and it didn't really matter which one—and replacing its volume with more of the other product family, this plant not only was able to reduce the amount of time spent on changeovers but also was able to effectively double the buffer volume between production and filling/packaging and recover significant downtime on both lines. On the *production volume–inventory* curve, this had the effect of further shifting the curve down and to the right (meaning more volume with less inventory).

With these relationships quantified, the team turned to optimizing the relationships for RME Pharma's present situation.

Step 3: Optimize the system for the situation at hand

The value of any additional production volume of course depends on the margin of that production, the company's ability to sell it, and the alternatives to producing it at the plant in question. For RME Pharma, the value of additional production was large—equal to not having to pay the TPM its significant cost premium plus absorption benefits (the impact from spreading plant overhead costs over greater volume resulting in lower overall cost per unit produced). Compared to the value of capacity, the costs of distribution and inventory were relatively small.

Hence, with regard to the capacity-inventory trade-off, the optimal operating point was high and to the right on the *production volume–inventory* curve. (Mathematically, the optimal point is where the volume-inventory curve is tangent to a line with slope equal to the value of incremental production over the cost of incremental inventory, as shown in Figure 69.) However, by focusing on inventory levels, its master scheduling group had pushed RME Pharma's actual operating point down and to the left of the optimal point. Although somewhat counterintuitive to some people, especially those who had been focused for so long on inventory, RME Pharma stood to gain cost savings by *increasing* inventory to increase its organic production volume.

Figure 69: Optimizing the Capacity-Inventory Trade-off (Master Scheduling Impact)

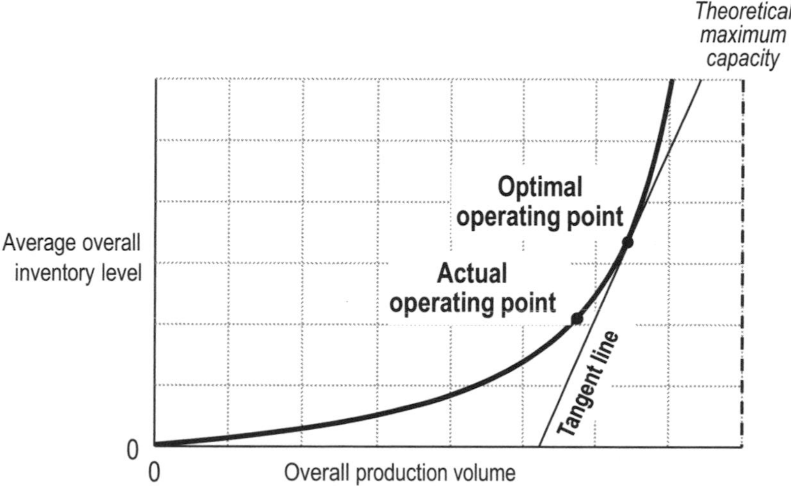

Slope of tangent line = value of incremental production / cost of incremental average inventory level

The desired operating point is where the *production volume–inventory* curve is tangent to a line whose slope is equal to the value of incremental production over the cost of incremental average inventory level. For RME Pharma's present situation, the optimal operating point was above that of its actual operating point.

To factor in the impact of changes to plant loading (the distribution trade-off), the team compared the cost savings from having fewer products at each plant to the additional distribution costs that RME Pharma would incur (as determined from the existing plant loading application). Optimizing this trade-off resulted in a new "overall" optimal operating point on a shifted *production–volume inventory* curve (see Figure 70).

Figure 70: Factoring In Plant Loading and Distribution Costs

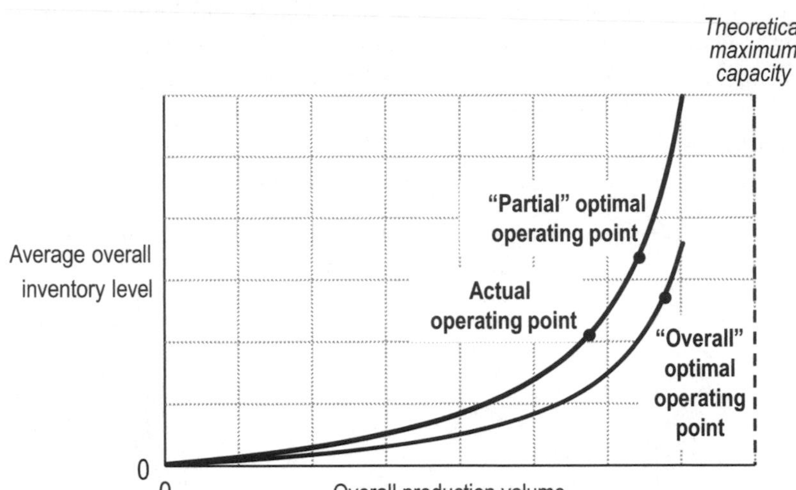

By changing plant loading to have fewer products at one plant, the production volume–inventory trade-off curve shifts down and to the right. That creates a new "overall" optimal operating point, combining greater production volume with lower inventory levels than that of the unshifted curve.

Now to some numbers: In total, by optimizing these trade-offs for its present situation, RME Pharma was able to increase production capacity at its own plants by more than 10% without changing the product portfolio and without capital investment.[68] RME Pharma did incur additional inventory and distribution costs, but the value of the additional production capacity was worth 15 times the additional inventory cost and almost 40 times the additional distribution costs. Figure 71 shows the relative annual financial impact from optimizing these capacity-related trade-offs.

Figure 71: Relative Annual Cost Savings

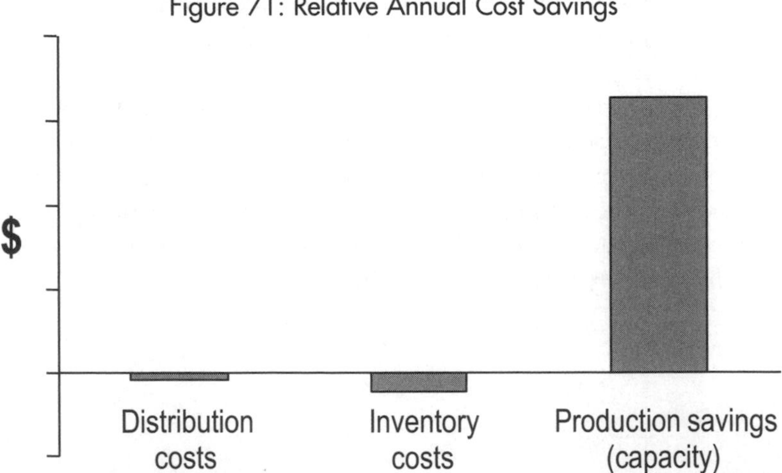

Recap of RME Pharma's Experience

By taming some key dynamic relationships, RME Pharma significantly improved on an issue critical to its business. Although the organization had thought its plants were already at max capacity (certainly enough to have had to outsource production at a cost premium), the team found opportunities to grow capacity by 10% without cutting the company's product line and with capital investment. To summarize RME Pharma's experience,

- **RME Pharma didn't remove complexity but rather made it less expensive.** Although RME Pharma did not remove any complexity (it did not delete any products from its portfolio, close any facilities, or eliminate any functional groups), it was able to better manage its complexity and, therefore, make it less expensive; it shifted its Whale Curve, making its bad complexity less bad and its good complexity better.
- **The team shifted among the faces of the Complexity Cube.** The team started on the Organization/Product face to gain insight into the issue (i.e., many small-volume products at large-volume plants), shifted to the Process/Organization face to understand the dynamics behind the issue, and then shifted to the Product/Process face to quantify the relationships.
- **RME Pharma's issues stemmed from being out of balance across some significant trade-offs.** Ironically given its situation, RME Pharma would have been better off had it done a *poorer* job of minimizing inventory levels.
- **RME Pharma found that it had mistakenly taken production capacity as a hard constraint, rather than a symptom of something that could be improved.** Because of interactions on the Process/Organization face, the organization had previously perceived its standard production rates as hard constraints rather than recognizing that those rates were impacted to a large enough degree by decisions they were making for other objectives.
- **Pieces of the solution already existed, but without an integrated solution RME Pharma had been unable to move forward.** For example, plant operators intuitively knew that lengthening production runs would increase capacity and tried to operate as such; but without being able to quantify the trade-off with inventory, the organization was unable to build this relationship into any decision making.
- **RME Pharma didn't just develop a solution for today but built capability going forward.** Rather than just prescribing a new operating point, by identifying and quantifying the key dynamic relationships RME Pharma created a new capability: the ability to optimize its opera-

tion across distribution costs, inventory levels, and capacity throughout changing business environments going forward.

- **RME Pharma found other unanticipated benefits as well.** For example, by understanding the product and process interactions and the impacts of product portfolio breadth on its manufacturing assets, RME Pharma is now able to anticipate the impact on operations from greater product complexity and input that information into its new product development process.

Moving Forward

While the particulars of this story may be somewhat unique to RME Pharma, dynamic relationships like the types we walked through here exist in almost any organization. By being aware of them, you can spot them and attack the more significant ones. To that end, it is helpful to think of dynamic relationships across three categories, each of which was illustrated in the RME Pharma case study.

- **Decisions that impact the basis of the decision itself.** In RME Pharma's plant loading process production rates were assumed fixed, but the output of decisions made upon those values changed the values themselves. This is an example of a decision that impacts the basis on which that very decision is made. By not dynamically modeling production rates, plant loading eroded capacity (big impact) to save distribution costs (small impact).
- **Vicious cycles that lead you to actions that reinforce the cycle.** Without recognizing the mechanisms behind these cycles, RME Pharma experienced more frequent and significant vicious cycles and missed opportunities to exploit the implications behind its virtuous cycles.
- **Actions taken for more "local" concerns that negatively impact longer-term or more macro concerns.** Consider RME Pharma's master scheduling group. It made decisions based on a "local" focus on minimizing inventory levels at the plants that drove negative "macro" issues, namely lowered capacity.

The Conundrum: Why do many companies struggle with managing complex systems?

Complex systems (systems with a large number of interrelated pieces) are inherently dynamic and difficult for many to manage. But given the many significant benefits to be had, why do so many dynamic relationships remain neglected? Why do so many companies struggle to manage complex systems?

The first reason is owing to the number and interrelatedness of the interactions. In *The Logic of Failure*,[69] author Dietrich Dörner explains,

> *We find an inability to think in terms of nonlinear networks of causation rather than chains of causation—an inability, that is, to properly assess the side effects and repercussions of one's [decisions]. We find an inadequate understanding of exponential development... these are all mistakes of cognition.*

As Dörner notes in the latter part of his statement, the second reason is that dynamic systems are characterized by change over time but, as many psychological experiments have shown, people have difficulty thinking in terms of relationships over time. Again, Dörner explains,

> *We cannot content ourselves with observing and analyzing situations at any single moment but must instead try to determine where the whole system is heading over time. For many people this proves to be an extremely difficult task.... That space configurations can be perceived in their entirety while time configurations cannot may well explain why we are far more able to recognize, and deal with, arrangements in space than in time.*

To make matters worse, this lack of dynamic understanding is being hardcoded into many processes and systems applications (the black boxes of your business).

Nevertheless, some companies certainly prove more effective in managing complex systems than others. What is different about these individuals? Drawing from Dörner's work,

- The amount of time they spend analyzing a complex issue depends less on time pressure than it does for less effective individuals, who are more likely to skip analyzing an issue in the face of time pressure and are more likely to overanalyze it in the absence of time pressure.
- They tend to make more multipronged/coordinated decisions; that is, they make more decisions for each objective, taking multiple aspects into account rather than just one aspect.
- They focus their decisions on what matters, identifying and attacking the most important problems first, and hold this focus over time. Less effec-

tive individuals have a greater tendency to become distracted with less important but more "interesting" or "fulfilling" endeavors, jumping from one topic to another; or they becoming overly preoccupied with one project to the exclusion of more important issues.

- They are much more likely to actually test their hypotheses, ask more "why" questions, and dig deeper into the analysis.
- They take a more structured approach to solving issues and have a greater ability to tolerate uncertainty.

The simple truth is that because companies don't know what to look for, dynamic interactions simply tend to go unnoticed. However, the good news is that you don't have to go hunting to find them: they are likely behind some of the significant operational issues or challenges you already face. You don't have to be an expert to make progress. Rather, by simply asking yourself and your organization if a mismanaged or unnoticed dynamic relationship is behind some of your challenging operational problems, you will shed much light on the issue and lay the groundwork for progress.

You should, therefore, view this battle strategy less as another thing you should go do, and more as another tool in your toolbox to help you accomplish what you already would like to do (including some things you may have given up as not possible long ago).

Chapter 16 Endnotes

68 With the exception of a $200K automatic diverter value, whose costs were negligible compared to the overall cost savings.

69 Dietrich Dörner, *The Logic of Failure: Recognizing and Avoiding Error in Complex Situations* [English translation] (New York: Metropolitan Books, 1996). The original German version was published in 1989 under the title *Die Logik des Misslingens* by Rowohlt Verlag GmbH.

Part IV

Defense Strategies to Keep Complexity Costs at Bay

Introduction to Part IV

Building the Capability to Keep Bad Costs Out

Greatness be nothing unless it is lasting.

— Napoleon

This book has been unapologetically focused on the task at hand: understanding, identifying, quantifying, and removing complexity costs. It is, as we said in Part I, an imperative of our time. Companies need to unburden themselves of the complexity costs accrued over the past decade. To that end, we have urged you to take action, with speed—to reclaim more profits, better processes, and a leaner organization relatively devoid of bad complexity.

But what now? What comes after you have taken large costs out of the organization?

In fact you have a clear choice. You can either

1) Continue as before, accepting complexity creep as a natural phenomena and then in a year or two undertake another such purge, or
2) Build new capabilities to keep bad complexity out of the business

Our recommendation, as you might guess, is option 2. For a start, it is less expensive and less disruptive to keep bad costs out than it is to wage a war against them after the fact. But there is a more profound reason: for the majority of organizations, success is directly tied less to a *one-off* breakthrough product/service or a momentary cost advantage than to having an *ongoing* capability to innovate new products and services while keeping complexity in check (and we mean on all three dimensions: product, process, and organizational).

Figure 72, next page, highlights the four arenas in marketplace competition, shaped by barriers of entry and levels of commoditization, and the need for complexity management capabilities. Many firms, to provide an analogy, are in the horse race quadrant, where the spoils go to the participant that can stay a nose length ahead over the long run.

Figure 72: The Four Arenas of Competition (And How to Compete in Them)

Commoditization? \ Barriers to entry?	Low	High
Low	**The Horse Race** • Repeatedly differentiate faster, better than competitors • Vigilantly separate good from bad complexity	**The Club** • Invest in shoring up barriers of entry • Don't let pursuit of operational efficiency distract you
High	**Commodity Hell** • Relentlessly strip out complexity to achieve low-cost provider status	**The Mafia** • Focus on preserving barriers to entry, often through regulatory means

The nature of competition in your market determines what matters most. For many companies, competition is a horse race that requires ongoing capabilities to stay a nose length ahead in bringing products to market and in operating and managing and reducing complexity to make room. Also, note that many companies are in multiple fights, with different parts of the business operating with higher or lower barriers to entry, requiring a nuanced approach to assess the nature of competition and what matters most.

In their excellent book *Competition Demystified: A Radically Simplified Approach to Business Strategy* (which the authors seem to offer as a useful update to Michael Porter's 1980 classic *Competitive Strategy*), Bruce Greenwald and Judd Kahn explain that barriers to entry are the dominant force affecting the competitive environment.

> *We agree with Porter's view that five forces—Substitutes, Suppliers, Potential Entrants, Buyers, and Competition within the Industry—can affect the competitive environment. But, unlike Porter and many of his followers, we do not think that those forces are of equal importance. One of them is clearly much more important than the others. It is so dominant that leaders seeking to develop and pursue winning strategies should begin by ignoring the others and focus only on it. That force is barriers to entry—the force that underlies Porter's "Potential Entrants."*

Consider a company selling differentiated products into a noncommoditized market. Many would consider this an attractive spot to be in, as the company has the opportunity to earn premium prices and superior returns. But absent sufficient barriers to entry, superior returns will attract new entrants, increasing the intensity of competition.

In the face of intense competition, differentiation as a lasting competitive advantage is an illusion. Competitors and new entrants will effectively copy successful differentiation. Absent true barriers to entry, true and lasting *competitive advantage* isn't the differentiation itself *but the ability to differentiate faster, more effectively, and less expensively than competitors.*

Separating good complexity from bad complexity is paramount if you want to win the horse race. Why? First, because bad complexity is complexity that adds more cost than value—in other words, it destroys value. Good complexity is the reverse: creating more value than cost. Bad complexity adds costs, eats up margin, and destroys the value gained by good complexity. Good complexity is a step forward while bad complexity is a step back.

The only path to superior returns is to consistently take more steps forward than back, and to do so demands you become attuned to what is good complexity and what is bad. Companies that can't do this risk achieving commodity level returns but with a whole lot more effort.

What this all means is that for companies in the horse race, the purge of complexity costs is a necessary but insufficient *first* step. The *next and critical* step is to develop the capabilities to prevent or manage complexity on a sustainable basis (see sidebar).

Viewing complexity management as a *partner* to innovation and other capabilities

Managing complexity is not the only capability required to win the horse race, although it is often one that can put the most distance between you and the competition.

Companies need capabilities across a variety of disciplines (such as innovation) to repeatedly differentiate. But the one usually missing from the "capability portfolio" is complexity management.

In our experience, if you were to rank capabilities by need and by existing skill gap, the ability to manage complexity would clearly top the list. Companies are often very good at introducing new products and services to market but very poor at deleting or removing them. Likewise, companies have often invested time, money, and effort at improving processes, but these efforts often stop short of getting to grips with the more difficult cross-functional issues that are inherent with process complexity. So while you need to improve *all* the key differentiating capabilities in your business, the first step is making sure that complexity management is included in the mix.

What Complexity Management Capability Looks Like

We use the term *capability* broadly here to mean the right structures, metrics and information, behaviors, and skills. Capability will look different for every company, not just in terms of what's required but also in terms of where you're starting from.

In Chapter 17, "Curbing Product and Service Complexity," we'll be examining how product and service complexity creeps into organizations with a view to creating an environment that discourages its proliferation. The difficulty is that it creeps in from many different directions. For example, it is not uncommon for an innovation process to be the center of SKU proliferation, as companies often overestimate the value of incremental products and underestimate the cost. We'll discuss the keys to keeping product complexity at bay including

- Putting in place the enablers, such as better information around the costs of complexity and incremental value, for example
- Pursuing a number of specific strategies that leverage this information as a focal point for preventing product (and component) complexity

In concert with this, many organizations will need to focus on preventing process and organizational complexity, which we will discuss in Chapter 18, "The Lean Operating Model: Creating a Structural Barrier to Process and Organizational Complexity." This is a big topic and worthy of a book in its own right, but we will lay out the case for the Lean Operating Model as a key part of the answer.

The *Lean Operating Model* inhibits process complexity (and the ensuing organizational complexity) by aligning the organization along standard ways of working. Complexity is simply not allowed! Done right, the Lean Operating Model is a holistic organizing framework for focusing the organization on what matters in its marketplace and driving continuous improvement at the right level. It also serves as the critical backbone for the effective deployment of new technologies, such as enterprise resource planning (ERP), investments in assets, and broad-based continuous improvement initiatives.

Where to start exactly will be largely informed by what you've learned thus far: by attacking complexity costs as we've recommended in this book, you will also have diagnosed the major drivers and sources of complexity in your business.

Before we get into the two battle strategies, however, we want to take a short trip with a Deep Dive on setting up a complexity metric that can help you monitor complexity at an enterprise level—which gives you the ability to set targets and see if the actions you're taking are driving complexity in the right direction.

If you have followed through on our approach to attacking complexity costs, you will now be in a considerably improved cost position, with better service metrics and a stronger platform for future growth. You will likely also be ready for a rest. However, we'd urge you to push forward to consider what you can do at this juncture to keep the bad costs out. Hopefully, as we've tried to show in this book, anything you can do to keep bad costs out is good for business.

DEEP DIVE #4

A Corporate Complexity Metric

Tracking Progress at the Macro Level

Parts I and II of this book emphasized the need to take a two-prong approach to attacking complexity:

1st Prong: Reduce the overall amount of complexity in the business by removing complexity that adds disproportionately large costs to the business

2nd Prong: Reduce the cost impact of each "unit" of complexity on the business by becoming much better at managing and delivering it

In other words, winning the war on complexity is not only about reducing the amount of complexity in your business but also about making complexity less expensive. Given that organizations will likely need to work both levers in their focus on eliminating bad complexity, what is the best way to track progress?

For this we recommend the **Complexity Cost Ratio (CCR)**, a good metric to assess a company's health. The CCR is simply a ratio of non-value-add (NVA) costs to value-add (VA) costs:

$$\text{Complexity Cost Ratio} = C_{NVA} / C_{VA}$$

Recall that a useful gauge for the impact of complexity in a business is the percentage of the company's total cost base that is non-value-add (NVA)—and remember that, by definition, NVA costs and value-add (VA) costs add up to your total cost base. For many companies, NVA costs can be as high as 70% to 80% of their total costs. While this is an easy way to look at complexity costs, for many companies a more useful way to express complexity costs is in terms of the ratio of NVA to VA costs. For the majority of companies, CCR will be greater than 1, meaning that their NVA costs are greater than their VA costs. The CCR is the number of dollars in NVA costs the company spends for each dollar of VA cost. Many companies will find they are spending between $2 and $4 in NVA costs for each $1 of VA cost.

A company's CCR is an overall indicator of how much complexity is costing them. It represents the "overhead" incurred to deliver value to the customer as defined by the consumer. The CCR provides a very different view of complexity. Rather than focusing on complexity's inputs, such as the numbers of SKUs, vendors, systems—those things can be measured easily—it measures, if less precisely, the impact of those things on the business.

As a company becomes more complex, its CCR will tend to rise. Conversely, as complexity is stripped out or better managed the CCR will tend to fall. The lower the ratio, the more streamlined and lean the business. However, the CCR will never be zero. In practice, attacking complexity means removing chunks of NVA costs to improve the CCR.

While this may seem a very different way of looking at complexity and its costs, it is not without precedent or rationale. Lean separates overall lead time of a process into VA and NVA portions, and uses PCE (the percentage of total lead time that is VA) as an indicator of the overall health of the process. These are holistic parameters used to characterize the performance of a process. Similarly, the CCR is a holistic measurement to characterize the overall impact of complexity in a business.

It is important to remember that there is good and bad complexity, though all complexity adds cost to a business and impacts its ability to deliver. A high CCR isn't necessarily bad, but it does mean that the business is paying a high price for the complexity it's carrying. Periodically assess your CCR to understand corporate-level progress toward improving levels of complexity costs. And for companies looking to keep complexity at bay, use it to provide an assessment: are our collective efforts in keeping complexity costs at bay paying off?

Conclusion

The pursuit of a better CCR is never ending as organizations grow and flux, creating new opportunities for complexity to creep in. And complexity *will* creep in, but you can make it much harder for it to do so and put in place the simple steps that will capture the lion's share of benefits. To what degree it creeps in will largely depend on how you approach the next phase: building capabilities in your organization.

CHAPTER 17

Curbing Product and Service Complexity

While the mantra of "more is better" used to summarize most companies' approach to product and service variety, that is changing. With shifts in consumer behavior and the economic contraction, many retailers are realizing that "less is more."

"All that go-go 1990s where we were adding items in and people wanted more, more, more, more choice... just didn't pay off," said Catherine Linder, Walgreen's divisional vice president for marketing development.[70]

To that end, keeping product and service complexity in check is a top priority for organizations. Companies of all stripes are now asking: *Once you have taken out the big costs and adjusted your portfolio, how do you keep bad complexity at bay?* The answer in brief is **manage complexity as a complete system and drive accountability through governance:**

- With governance comes the accountability for looking cross-functionally and for considering the systemic nature of complexity
- With accountability comes the demand for the information, metrics, and capabilities that help sustain a strong portfolio

We will discuss the framework for developing a systems view of complexity and driving accountability and governance in the rest of this chapter.

Roles of a Chief Complexity Officer

Before continuing, however, we need to make it clear that accountability will be effective only if it is housed within a single role. We'll refer to that role as the Chief Complexity Officer (CCO), although the duties could reside with any senior level executive. Therefore, we will discuss our approach to preventing complexity creep through the lens of there being a CCO whose job is to manage complexity as a system (the only way it truly can be managed). More specifically, the CCO has two primary roles:

Role 1: Managing the level of complexity in the business

Role 2: Building the organizational capabilities required to manage complexity

CCO Role 1: Managing the level of complexity in the business

At the outset, the CCO will need to monitor and manage three areas:

1) The rate at which new complexity is added to the portfolio (e.g., new products and services)
2) The rate at which that complexity is removed
3) The total level of complexity in the business

The astute reader will recognize that the third area depends on the first two: if complexity is added faster than it is removed, then the total level of complexity in the business rises. And, vice versa, the overall level of complexity can only be lowered from current levels if more complexity is removed than is added.

You might want to think of the addition and removal rates as the inputs to the complexity system and the *level* of complexity as an output. But that distinction isn't quite right. Many firms focus on the rate of addition and possibly the rate of removal, without much of an eye to the total level. In fact, **without an eye to the proper total level of complexity for the portfolio** (which will change as conditions change), **you cannot determine the proper rate for adding or removing complexity.** Thus the total level of complexity must be treated not just as an output but also as an input into determining the proper addition and removal rates.

Why does product complexity creep in? The impact of incrementality on new product development

In Chapters 9 and 10, we explained that what really matters in SKU analysis are **incremental** cost and revenue (in addition to evaluating lifecycle issues). But most companies typically consider only total revenue and *unadjusted* cost figures, meaning their profit projections for new products *often overestimate their profit impact and underestimate cost impact.*

The profit overestimation occurs because there is almost always some level of cannibalization—a new product "steals" revenue from existing products. So total revenue figures are almost always greater than *incremental* revenue figures, which evaluates both how much profit a new product adds and how much it takes away from other products.

Also, since adding a product adds costs to other products, cost figures *not* adjusted for complexity costs underestimate true incremental cost.

Overestimating revenue impact while underestimating cost impact explains why products that appear (in isolation) to be winners can destroy value in aggregate. It echoes the view of Gerard Arpey, president and CEO of American Airlines, who says, "Complexity creeps into organizations incrementally, and each additional decision is, by itself, almost always justifiable."[71]

We have previously discussed the surge in product and service complexity over the past decade; the flood gates were wide open. But while new products were being added, few of the old or stale products were being removed. For many companies, the situation resembled Figure 73 (next page), where the number of products in the portfolio (the bucket) continued to increase with the flow of new products driven by innovation, product line extensions, and acquisitions.

The level of complexity as a rate equation

The relationship between adding and removing products can be represented by a simple rate equation:

(Addition rate) – (Removal rate) = (Net rate of change in the total amount)

This straightforward equation is useful not only for gauging the direction and rate of change in the level of complexity in the portfolio but also for gaining a sense for the equilibrium or steady-state level of complexity toward which a company may be heading—not necessarily a *desired* level of complexity, just the level you'll end up with if nothing else changes.

By "steady state" we mean that the level of complexity in the product portfolio is rather constant (the net rate of change of product complexity is approximately zero). You can see from the above equation that this results when the rate of adding new products equals the rate of removing old products:

At steady state: (Addition rate) – (Removal rate) = 0

(Addition rate) = (Removal rate)

If a company typically adds 100 new products a year and removes 10% of the total portfolio a year, then the steady state or equilibrium level of complexity in the portfolio would be 1,000 products:

At steady state: (Addition rate) = (Removal rate)
100 = 10% × (No. of products in the portfolio)
No. of products in the portfolio = 100/0.1 = 1,000

But if instead of removing 10% of the portfolio each year the company removes only 1%, while still adding 100 new products a year, the steady state number of products in the portfolio would be 10,000:

At steady state: 100 = 1% × (No. of products in the portfolio)

No. of products in the portfolio = 100/0.01 = 10,000

Clearly, the removal rate, which is often ignored, can have a significant effect on the size of the portfolio.

Figure 73: Unconstrained Addition of New Products

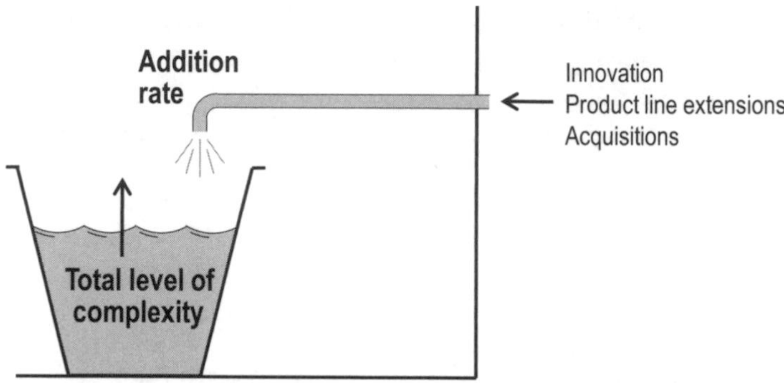

As the rate of new products continues unrestrained, portfolios "fill up." Some companies, such as Motorola, have implemented mechanisms to discourage complexity creep (see sidebar). This approach resembles adding a filter to the inlet of the product development pipeline, as shown in Figure 74.

Figure 74: Filters Can Keep Some Bad Complexity Out, but the Level of Overall Complexity Still Rises

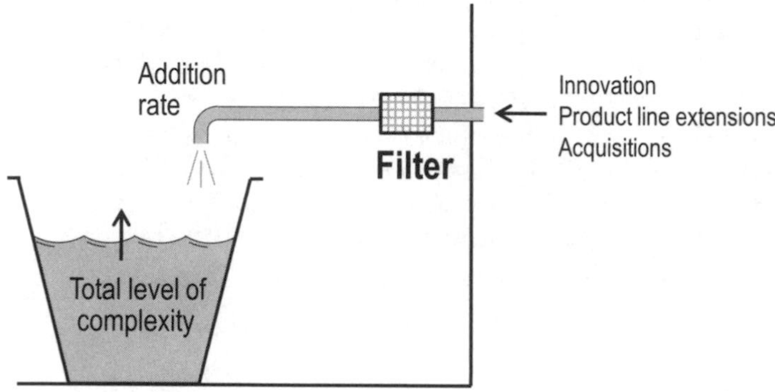

Examples of such filters include

- A **library of acceptable designs** for product engineers to pull from. They must first confirm that an existing design/component will not suffice before adding anything new to the portfolio.
- A **minimum reuse threshold** that all new products must meet. For example, new products must have 80% of their components in common with other products in the family.
- **Escalation guidelines** that demand that changes beyond a certain limit be "escalated up" to senior management. That way it becomes a strategic decision of whether value of the increased complexity supersedes the cost of that complexity.

A filter has the benefits of keeping some of the crud out and reducing the rate of complexity addition. But without complexity removal as well, the overall level in the bucket will still continue to rise. A filter approach may make the problem of increasing complexity levels seem less urgent, but it does not eliminate the problem.

The Complexity Index: Motorola's mechanism for discouraging component complexity

An example of a filter mechanism to control overall levels of complexity is Motorola's **Complexity Index** (which is similar in intent to the Complexity Cost Ratio described in the previous Deep Dive). Designed to discourage product complexity, it scores every new product for factors such as average part count, test time, assembly time, mechanical and/or software postponement, use of industry standard parts, and component reuse.[72]

Theresa Metty, formerly head of supply chain for Motorola, recalled, "In my fourth staff meeting I posed this challenge to the product launch team, which works hand-in-hand with engineering when they're designing a product: *Can you come up with an index that tells us how complex every product is relative to other products in our portfolio and relative to competing products?*"

Metty explained that each factor carries a various weighting. "With each product we measure the complexity on those factors, weight them, add them up and that's the index for that product," she said. "A product that has an index of 1.7 is not great; we don't want products like that. An index of 1.0 is best-in-class by our competitors, and products rated at a 0.7 or 0.8 are better than the best out there. We want all of our products to come in under a 1.0 complexity index. That way we'll know they are truly best-in-class."

The value of such indices is that they are easily communicated through an organization and provide a tangible point of measurement. They encourage discussion around how complexity creeps into organizations and highlight areas for improvement. And a metric such as Motorola's is relatively easy to implement as it works within a large corporate culture—everyone can assess their own ratios. But as is clear from the framework in this chapter, such metrics are only a part of the answer. And they do not make serious headway with some of the issues at the crux of complexity costs—the systemic, cross-functional issues.

You will see that the rate of complexity removal has, of course, a dramatic impact on the level of complexity in the portfolio. In an attempt to maintain or limit their overall level of complexity, a few companies have implemented portfolio management processes that essentially require that a product be removed for another to be added. This configuration is illustrated in Figure 75, where we have added a drainpipe to the bucket and where the inlet and outlet flows are matched to maintain a constant level in the bucket.

Figure 75: The "One In, One Out" Approach to Limiting the Level of Complexity in the Portfolio

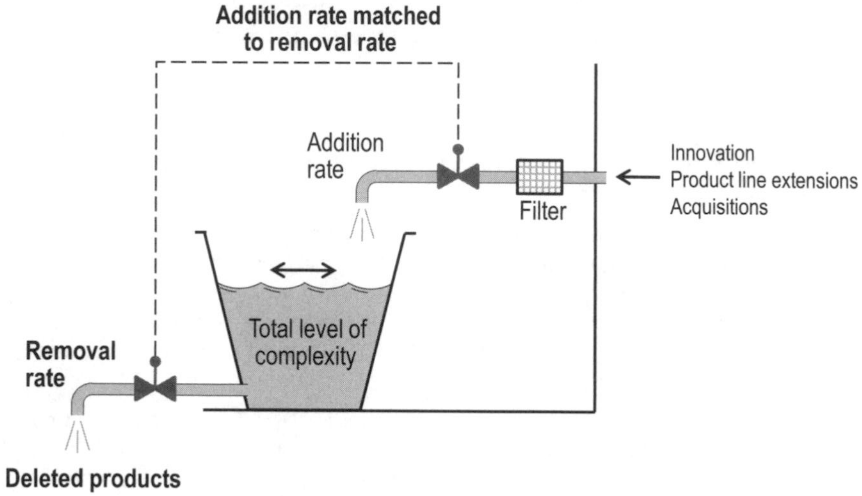

Determining the "Right" Level of Complexity

This approach of trying to manage complexity by matching the removal rate to the addition rate is usually more aspirational than real in practice, something executives profess an interest in but fail to make the hard decisions to enact. Without a more holistic perspective, and in the face of pressure or a desire to add new products, keeping or removing products can be seen as arbitrary—and indeed it may be if you assume the current level of complexity is the right one. Reasons are often found to circumvent cutting enough products to balance additions to preserve or develop products thought to be "must haves." When that happens, the complexity management system can easily revert to the configuration shown in Figure 74, in which overall complexity still rises.

But even if a one-in/one-out practice is maintained, it falls very short of true and effective complexity management because, while in theory it can put a brake on complexity growth, it ignores two important questions:

1) What is the right level of complexity in the portfolio in the first place?

2) How should this level change with changing market or economic conditions?

We have shown already in this book that the right level of complexity depends on many things, including the following :

- **Scale: the amount of revenue in the company.** As revenue contracts, the impact of complexity on profits increases (see Complexity Costs' Impact on Profitability in a Downturn on p. 38). A decrease in revenue means that your company can afford less complexity. On the other hand, growth means your company can afford a greater level of complexity.

- **Customer/market behavior.** Today, companies are adjusting to shifts in consumer behaviors as a result of increased savings rates, the so-called new normal. The level of complexity to offer in your portfolio depends on what customers value in terms of variety, features, cost, and service levels (lead time, on-time delivery, and so on). Companies need to be mindful of variety that may overload customers (see sidebar) or pricing shifts in their key markets. For example, market commoditization increases the pressure on companies to remove complexity from their portfolios.

Avoiding or compensating for overchoice

One factor in deciding the optimal level of variety to launch on the market is to understand customers' ability to deal with it. When there is too much variety—or the variety triggers a negative response from customers—we call that **overchoice**. We may all have faced it before: too many choices in the grocery store or trying to delineate between an overwhelming number of financial investment plans. According to Wharton marketing professor Barbara Kahn, the key to assessing what is just right is assessing the customer's level of expertise.

"The more people become experts, the more they articulate their preferences—and the more they have a consumption vocabulary and know what the relevant attributes are, the more variety they will be able to take," says Kahn. She also suggests "arranging [product] assortment in such a way that consumers just see what it is they want and they don't have to see all that they don't want."[73]

By providing customers with choice, but presenting it in a way that they can easily compare options (i.e., good, better, best), companies can deliver on what might seem like an impossible premise: deliver a lot of variety in a way that doesn't overwhelm customers.

- **Ability to deliver complexity.** Improving the ability to deliver complexity essentially makes complexity less expensive, meaning that your company can afford to carry a greater level of complexity in its portfolio.
- **Capability relative to competitors.** Your ability to delivery complexity relative to your competitors impacts your product strategy, which in turn impacts the level of complexity you should choose to carry in your portfolio. For example, if you lag competitors in your ability to deliver complexity (due to inefficient processes) yet compete on product variety, you will be competing at a cost disadvantage. Alternatively, you might choose to pursue simplicity and compete at a cost advantage but give up

the value of variety. Competing head-to-head where you are at a disadvantage will lead to poor results.

- **Product and portfolio performance.** The true performance of the portfolio itself is the strongest indicator of what level of complexity you should carry in your portfolio. However, as a lagging rather than leading indicator, relying on portfolio performance means you could have wasted a lot of money on complexity that isn't generating value before you know there's a problem.

Because of the factors above, complexity cannot be managed by simply placing (a) constraints on the addition of new products, or (b) requirements on the deletion of bad ones. Each action needs to be part of an integrated strategy that is driving you toward the desired level of complexity in the portfolio.

In contrast to the methods described previously, Figure 76 illustrates the holistic management of product complexity. This configuration keeps the inlet and outlet pipes, the control valves, and the inlet filter from the other models. But there is also a determination of what the proper level of complexity should be for the portfolio, with the inlet and outlet control valves integrated but functioning separately to manage the right level and mix of complexity in the portfolio. For example, revenue contraction or market commoditization would warrant more severe and rapid removal of products from the portfolio and possibly at the same time a throttling down or tighter filter on the addition of new products. Conversely, significant growth or improved process or organizational capabilities may allow increasing the rate at which new products are added to slowly raise the level of complexity in the portfolio.

Figure 76: Holistic Complexity Management

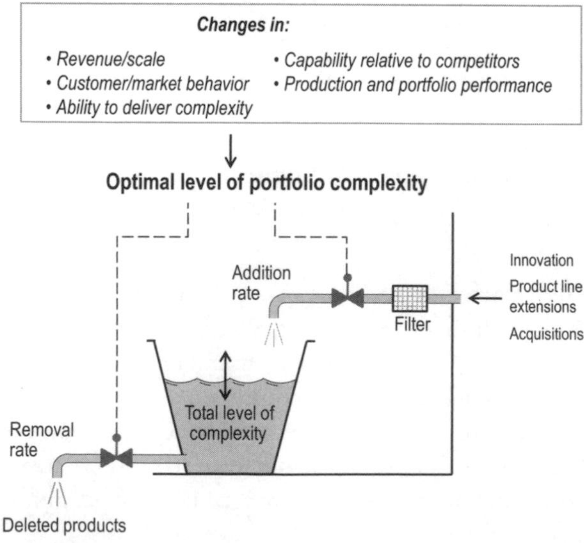

This combination of deep understanding, a broad perspective, and an integrated set of actions is the best defense for keeping bad complexity at bay.

Mike McCallister, CEO of Humana, sees this balancing trick as an acute challenge for large companies. He said,

> *You have startup companies that are totally innovation driven. That's pretty straightforward and pretty simple. We've had companies in our space that just stayed consistent with their old approaches, and that's pretty simple. The trick is when you start putting them together and managing all of the organizational implications, as well as having a reasonable focus: What are you all about as a company, and how are you going to approach the market?... I think that management's job is to balance all those horses, keep the organization pointed in the right direction.*[74]

CCO Role 2: Building the organizational capabilities required to manage complexity

The second critical CCO role is building the organizational capabilities required to manage complexity. The "building" is needed because many, if not most, organizations lack some or many of the capabilities, processes, and metrics required to succeed in continuously optimizing the variety in your portfolio:

- **Processes as described under Role 1.** This would include the capabilities needed to reduce SKUs, which are described in Chapters 9 and 10, as well as other battle strategies. Most companies do some sort of SKU reduction, but efforts are often incomplete. Complexity is one of the least understood of common corporate ills today. We've attempted to remedy that with this book, but there is no substitute for focused training and education—to build a common language and new skills and approaches as well as improve capabilities in the battle strategies of Part III.

- **Capabilities in customer insight.** As we discussed above, many times companies overestimate the revenues associated with new products as well as overlook opportunities for substitutability. We see this formalized in many innovation centers—instead of disruptive, differentiated innovation, you have SKU proliferation driven by internal biases. Kevin Werbach, Wharton professor of legal studies and business ethics, gave the example of consumer technology product makers that tend to "overfeature" their innovations. "These are geeks who want to add the latest new thing and historically have a tendency to make their products too complex," he says. "They are technology experts, and their tendency is to build the product *they* can use, which is not the mainstream product."[75]

- **Redefined incentives.** A key driver of bad complexity is misaligned incentives and metrics. Absent balancing measures, revenue-driven organizations can end up with bloated portfolios, as salespeople will modify an existing product (creating a new SKU) for the additional sale, unaware or unworried about the consequences. Therefore, one of the priorities for the CCO is assessing and aligning metrics—and at the very least, making the impacts of the current incentives system transparent.
- **Support systems and information.** As we saw with Deep Dive #3 in Part II ("The Juice Dilemma"), it is important to capture the true costs of complexity. Unfortunately, most costing systems are inadequate in this regard. Similarly, good support systems—for example, a navigable parts database—will avoid some complexity creep associated with a lack of visibility to current components and parts.

Conclusion

When companies ask us what predicts success in managing complexity, we respond with a series of questions to assess whether or not they have in place processes or focus areas that replicate the three key areas for managing total complexity. *Even if a company has just undertaken a purge against all complexity costs, an absence of capabilities to prevent complexity creep is an indicator of problems ahead.* As we've discussed, many of these capabilities begin with a single point of accountability. Absent that role—which we've referred to as the Chief Complexity Officer in this chapter—building these capabilities will take second place to areas that *are* being championed by strong executive leadership.

Retailers have been sensitive to the issue of product proliferation for decades—faced with limited shelf space but at the same time dedicated to providing customers what they want, when they want it. According to *The Wall Street Journal*, "Retailers have talked about slimming down variety for several years, but that move was riskier when consumers were spending more." So up until recently, retailers were reluctant to limit choice—to pull back from the 88 kinds of Pantene shampoo, conditioner, and styling products typically available in a Target store or to assess the incremental value of each of the 50 or so versions of the Oreo cookie.[76] But as credit conditions tightened (and retailers needed to reduce inventories and hang on to cash) and customer buying habits changed (with an onus on value vs. variety), the equation changed. Now retailers are seeing the benefits, according to *The Wall Street Journal*, with "lower labor costs, fewer out-of-stock items and an increase in their ability to squeeze vendors for better deals."

Not to mention a boost to revenues: Wal-Mart analyzed data for its stores and found that shoppers spent an average of 22 minutes in a Wal-Mart and, moreover, that wider product variety led to fewer items in the shopping basket.[77] Customers have a finite amount of time: the time is allocated to *choosing* or *purchasing*. Wal-Mart adjusted its range to increase sales.

Recognition of this shift is important to the discussion of keeping complexity at bay, because it offers a departure from a decades-old back-and-forth between marketing that sought to increase the breadth of the portfolio and operations that struggled to deliver the variety and was skeptical of its value. In fact, customers want variety, but the right kind; and in many situations, the service levels and right price (a consequence of lower complexity) are just as critical as product attributes in their purchase decisions. The impact of the "new normal" is that it mandates a clean break from the received wisdoms of old: everyone needs to assess anew just exactly what the customer is seeking and what that means for what's in the portfolio.

Chapter 17 Endnotes

70 "Retailers Cut Back on Variety, Once the Spice of Marketing," *The Wall Street Journal,* June 26, 2009.

71 Michael L. George, Stephen A. Wilson, *Conquering Complexity in Your Business* (New York: McGraw-Hill, 2004).

72 Cherish Whyte, "Motorola's Battle with Supply and Demand Chain Complexity," *Supply & Demand Chain Executive*, April/May 2003.

73 Available at Knowledge@Wharton, "SmartGrowth: Innovating to Meet the Needs of the Market Without Feeding the Beast of Complexity." Accessed October 25, 2006.

74 Available at Knowledge@Wharton, Podcast, "Humana CEO Mike McCallister: Letting the Consumer Drive Innovation." Accessed July 17, 2009.

75 Available at Knowledge@Wharton, "SmartGrowth: Innovating to Meet the Needs of the Market Without Feeding the Beast of Complexity." Accessed October 25, 2006.

76 "Retailers Cut Back on Variety, Once the Spice of Marketing," *The Wall Street Journal* June 26, 2009.

77 "Retailers Cut Back on Variety, Once the Spice of Marketing," *The Wall Street Journal* June 26, 2009.

Chapter 18

The Lean Operating Model

Creating a Structural Barrier to Process and Organizational Complexity

As you know by now, the cost of complexity stems only in part from the number of products in your portfolio. Often the bigger generators of waste and cost lie in your processes and organizational structures. And just as you have to prevent product complexity from creeping back post-rationalization (as discussed in the previous chapter), you have to be proactive in preventing process and organizational complexity from reestablishing a foothold.

One of the most effective ways of battling complexity creep is through deploying a **Lean Operating Model**, a set of practices that create a structural barrier to process and organizational complexity. Doing full justice to this topic is beyond the scope of this book; however, our goal in this chapter is to give you an introduction to this important approach for keeping complexity at bay. We'll discuss what a Lean Operating Model is, how it works, the seven steps to putting it in place, and a specific case study of a company that has used this approach to control costs in a cutthroat industry and focus the delivery of customer value.

A Lean Operating Model helps stymie process and organizational complexity in a number of ways:

- It standardizes work, therefore eliminating non-value-add variation in how processes are performed, and helps to address what to standardize (to execute quickly) and what *not* to standardize (to adapt quickly)
- It enables end-to-end clarity through appropriate governance and "super key performance indicators (KPIs)" that span functions
- It helps align assets and organizational structure, defeating organizational complexity and avoiding workarounds because of misalignment

Achieving these ends helps you

1) **Inhibit complexity** by adhering to agreed-upon ways of working

2) **Align the organization** through a commitment to a way of operating

3) **Reduce cost and waste** through ongoing improvements at the right level and in the right place

4) **Provide a greater range of strategic options and greater speed and agility** for tactical endeavors

5) **Deliver true sustainable advantage** because while a competitor can copy a strategy, it is much harder to replicate an integrated set of capabilities

In brief, a Lean Operating Model allows you to build simplicity, transparency, and continuous learning into your operations by aligning the organization around delivering its most important value (as defined by customers) while leveraging standard ways of working.

Project "One-Company"

All organizations function under some sort of operating model by definition—a structure exists to get things done to the benefit of customers. But often the model is implicit, not explicit.

Imagine trying to build a house without an *explicit* blueprint; no one would know what to do. Workers would pick up tools and build a one-room shack, then add another room, and another, and so on, until you are left with a strange-looking ramshackle house.

The same thing happens with companies that fail to define an operating model. As they grow, processes are added ad hoc in response to customer requests. Functions become siloed; they coordinate but only via a mess of workarounds. Separate IT systems are introduced, eventually becoming a web. Management focus is diluted across hundreds of initiatives. The company is not acting as one but as hundreds of independent entities.

We often come across corporate initiatives labeled under the banner "One-*insert-name-of-company*." These initiatives are a testament to the costs that the *lack* of consistency imposes on an organization. The management insight to move toward whole-firm performance—via "One-Company" initiatives—is spot-on. Our contention is that the underlying model should be based on the Lean Operating Model described in this chapter. Developing an explicit operating model gives you time to pause and look up occasionally, to make sure the house you are building is structurally sound. No one wants the roof caving in.

Why the term *Lean Operating Model?* As discussed in Chapter 13, the term *Lean* applies to an improvement philosophy focused on removing waste (non-value-add activities and costs) and inefficiency from processes. Lean encompasses a broad range of practices that establish discipline around process performance and process management, including developing standards where needed, making changes only when data show a new standard is better, eliminating all forms of waste, and so on. By *operating model*, we mean how an organization's people, processes, and technology interact to deliver goods, services, or other organizational ends.

Combining the two concepts gives us a Lean Operating Model, a management approach that is

- Anchored on an understanding of value, as defined by the customer
- Supported by an organization aligned to this definition of value
- Sustained by a focus on learning and continuous improvement

A Lean Operating Model is the means by which a company can *best* configure its people, processes, assets, and technology to *maximize customer-value-add* (reflected in customer satisfaction and revenue) while *minimizing non-value-add activities* (reflected in productivity, speed, and, ultimately, profitability). The relationship of these objectives is shown in Figure 77.

Figure 77: Aligning the Organization with a Lean Operating Model

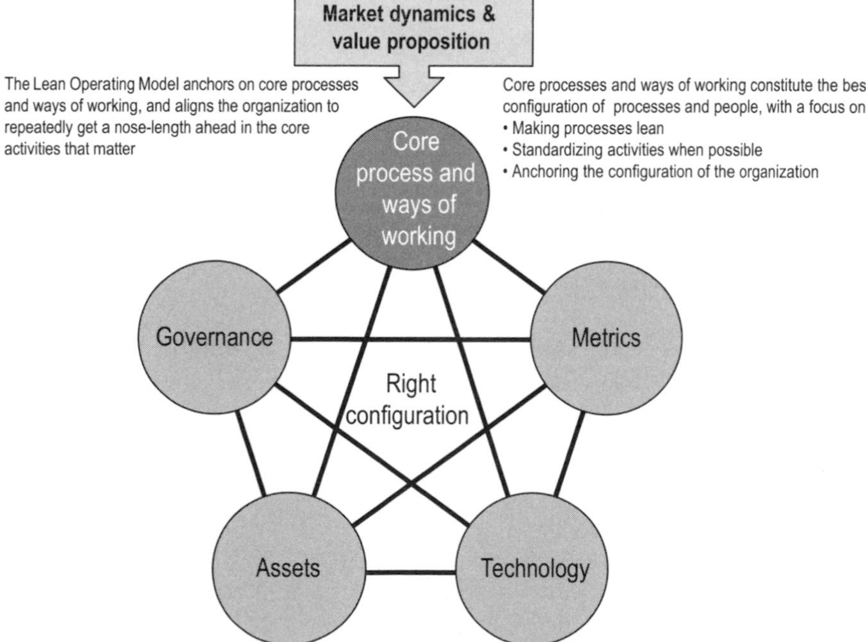

The Lean Operating Model integrates and aligns key organizational elements to repeatedly win in the ways that are key to customers

Done right, the Lean Operating Model is a holistic organizing framework for focusing the organization on what matters in its marketplace and driving continuous improvement at the right level. It also serves as the critical backbone for the effective deployment of new technologies, such as enterprise resource planning (ERP), investments in assets, and broad-based continuous improvement initiatives.

In this chapter, we are not describing a deployment methodology for Lean continuous improvement programs. While Lean is integral, the Lean Operating Model has a purpose that is broader than supporting continuous improvement, that of attaining competitive advantage by orienting the firm on what truly matters in the marketplace.

The Seven Steps to Developing a Lean Operating Model

Developing a Lean Operating Model is a major commitment to competing in a specific way to beat the competition. The pieces of the puzzle that you want to align are shown in Figure 77. Here are the seven key steps to creating your own Lean Operating Model.

1. Identify what it takes to win in your arena of competition
2. Anchor on core processes
3. Align the organization with end-to-end metrics
4. Focus Lean improvements where it counts
5. Standardize ways of working
6. Establish a structure of process ownership
7. Develop a culture of learning

Each of these steps can be a significant initiative in its own right. They also may run concurrently in many cases. We discuss each of them below.

Step 1: Identify what it takes to win in your arena of competition

As we discussed in the Introduction to Part IV, success depends on first recognizing the arena of competition in which you're playing. Companies in a "horse race," for example, know the spoils go to companies that can repeatedly differentiate faster and better than competitors (see the matrix on p. 289).

It is our experience that for a vast number of companies, success depends not on a one-time strategic initiative but on their ability to do a few things well day in and day out. Winning looks less like a decisive, dominant blow and more like a long series of rapid, small victories. Companies must equip and train to win battle after battle—and to do so requires speed and vigilance. They must execute and adapt quickly, and this is enabled by the Lean Operating Model.

Step 2: Anchor on core processes

Likewise, in most businesses, there are a few key core processes that define success. In grocery retail, for example, in spite of technological advancements, new customer demands, and changing environments, the basic structure remains relatively constant.

As Figure 78 shows, this grocery retailer's success is defined by its ability to locate real estate and build stores, select and buy range, and coordinate the distribution of goods from suppliers to stores and the marketing and in-store processes to sell the goods.

Figure 78: Core Processes of a Grocery Retailer

Core processes: Build → Buy → Move → Sell

The real picture is, of course, more complicated than a series of four or five boxes laid out in sequence: For example, each core process will be supported by a number of subprocesses and people, which together constitute your organization's "ways of working." Some subprocesses, such as support processes like IT, will span a couple or more of these core processes. New strategies may dictate different demands placed on your core processes, for example, ensuring distribution channels can handle higher volumes or a different mix.

But no matter the situation, it is critical to explicitly identify which core activities will add up to success in your marketplace. Your core processes may be obvious and already internalized; but that is not always the case. Do what you have to do to identify and agree on the core processes as the anchor points for your company's operations. Doing so will let you

- Catalog all your processes and start to evaluate areas of focus for improvement and standardization.
- Assess where assets are aligned or misaligned. For example, are your functions supporting these key processes or is there divergence in interests?
- Plan for technologies that can span end-to-end in the organization as well as provide utility for the long term.
- Establish or refine metrics and governance for end-to-end performance and continuous learning and improvement.

Step 3: Align the organization with end-to-end metrics

Once you have identified your core processes, you can align on customer value and establish end-to-end metrics that motivate positive behaviors. For example, while many functions may work to optimize their own inventory levels, what really matters in the end are the total inventories the company carries, not just that carried by any one specific function. Efforts to minimize inventories in the factory, for example, may push more to distribution, increasing overall levels.

Step 4: Focus Lean improvements where it counts

Anchoring on core processes can also reveal the biggest opportunities for improvement. You can thus focus your Lean efforts on a more targeted, higher-leverage set of issues. For example, many companies may divide their improvement efforts across the company somewhat evenly by department or function. But, in fact, a better outcome would be to concentrate them on the few key issues that will move the needle on factors affecting a critical-to-customer metric, only visible through an end-to-end view.

Step 5: Standardize ways of working

Some executives initially resist the notion of "standardization." Indeed, in a recent *Harvard Business Review*,[78] Joseph M. Hall and M. Eric Johnson declared, "The movement to standardize processes has gone overboard." The authors conclude that some processes "require an artist's judgment." We'd agree insofar as we believe the debate should be less about *whether* or not to standardize processes and more about *which* processes should be standardized.

In fact, we'd turn it around and pose it this way: the key is to identify which processes should **not** be standardized. Two factors define the latter group.

1) When the costs of standardization outweigh the benefits
2) When customers value distinctive or unique input (for example, it would be difficult to standardize all parts of an instrument-building process if the musicians you serve assert a preference for having different, distinctive sounds)

Processes with variable inputs can still usually be standardized or partially standardized by stratifying the process—in essence providing a fork in the road that will split according to process inputs.

And remember this: it is better to standardize *portions* of a process than nothing at all—essentially creating standardized building blocks that can be put together in a myriad of ways and allowing for more responsive and efficient flexibility. Such modularization adds up to increasing the amount of reuse in the process—duplicating common procedures wherever they occur. For example, while surgery is a high-skill, high-variability process, the post- and pre-op procedures could be standardized because there is more similarity in patient care at those points.

However, more often than not, the debates about whether and what to standardize are at the margins. A Lean Operating Model formalizes the organization's repeatable, high-volume tasks, which are usually the preponderance of work. It helps avoid the rework—and subsequent process complexity—of reinventing the wheel. This is the liberating concept that allows companies such as Tesco to then adapt quickly to market conditions, to scale efficiently, and to continually improve its processes.

It is important to understand how **the pursuit of standardization at the micro level can improve flexibility at the macro level.** And the macro level is what matters for results.

In the book *Enterprise Architecture as Strategy*, the authors cite the paradox in which standardizing core business processes makes the *individual* processes less flexible but makes the *company* more agile.

> *A great athlete will have muscles, reflexes, and skills that are not easily changed. But these capabilities give athletes a tremendous ability to react, improvise and innovate in their chosen sport.*

Likewise, when companies are no longer concerned with the mechanics of their "order-to-pay" process, they can focus instead on *anticipating* customer trends and putting more energy into strengthening their company for tomorrow versus struggling with firefighting today.

In fact, the reason for a company's lack of agility is not usually standardization or formality but the lack of it. In *Enterprise Architecture*, the authors reflect on the internet boom,

> *Which exposed the inflexibility of many companies' technology and process environments, which led to an inability to adapt to new channels. This inflexibility was not the result of a digitized foundation for execution. It was the result of systems so complex that any change required individually rewiring systems to all the other systems they connect to.*

In sum, standardization at the micro level allows flexibility at the macro level. And as counterintuitive as it may seem, standardizing priority, repeatable work—keeping out process and organizational complexity—creates the kind of organizational flexibility that can give you an edge in the marketplace.

Step 6: Establish a structure of process ownership

By orienting around the key processes that define success in your marketplace, you are implicitly acknowledging the need to be process-centric. But to enhance and sustain a Lean Operating Model requires an explicit move toward process ownership—a form of governance that assesses, monitors, and improves those core process areas critical to the business.

For some firms this is a radical mind shift; for many others it is a formalization of something they do implicitly already. Commercial functions echo many of the key processes critical to companies: sales, manufacturing, distribution, and so on. However, there are some distinct differences between traditional operating practices and a process-ownership model—including a number of benefits from the latter:

- **Explicit identification of the linkages between major processes:** functions can be inward looking while processes by definition have inputs and outputs and are, therefore, outward looking.
- **Explicit anchoring on the customer:** being process-centric is really being customer-centric. It all starts as the customer and processes align to support customer preference.
- **Greater definition of the role of the "process owner":** a process orientation forces you to both simplify and standardize the roles for the "owners" of the targeted areas. At a high level, the role of process owners can be characterized as
  - Assessing the overall health of their process and linkages to other processes
  - Monitoring performance against critical process metrics
  - Sponsoring efforts to close performance gaps and constantly improve

A useful model for considering the role of the process owner is Toyota's concept of a chief engineer, a role that has been pivotal to their success in product development.[79] Many companies disperse the development process between multiple functional departments, with the result that no one individual is responsible. But at Toyota, the chief engineer is that point of accountability: not just a project manager but a leader and technical systems integrator, with a strong sense for what customers want and an impeccable technical pedigree. Or as Toyota would say, "Engineers who have never set foot in Beverly Hills have no business designing a Lexus."[80] In fact Toyota avoids the trade-off between functional excellence and end-to-end coordination by ensuring the chief engineer is a technically oriented integrator rather than a program coordinator.

Step 7: Develop a culture of learning

Humana's CEO Mike McCallister said, "One of the things we've tried to develop around here is a learning organization. When we first started that process, I got reactions like, 'I don't know what you're talking about—a learning organization?'"[81]

The term is used in different ways. The specific meaning we have in mind is **an organization that is capable of learning specific lessons from its mistakes and process "noise" and incorporating those insights into an existing standard.**

In the book *Chasing the Rabbit*, the author discusses what happens when companies don't learn:

> *In low-velocity organizations, people suppress those indications that the work processes are inadequate and have to be modified. When they run into obstacles, they treat them as the normal noise of the process, its unavoidable perturbations, around which they must work. They get the job done, but they do not increase the chance that the next person will have a higher chance for success and a lower chance for failure.*

Standard work (Step 5) creates the platform for learning. If you treat a process as a "one-off" each time you perform it—the implicit result if you lack standard methods—then you will have no basis for identifying early warning signs and no platform for incorporating learning.

Pratt & Whitney, a company that designs and builds commercial and military jet engines, did just that through a program called "engineering standard work" (ESW) that laid out workflow maps, codified design criteria, and created activity pages that described the best methods known for specific design work.

According to *Chasing the Rabbit*,

> *These were all mechanisms for capturing and sharing knowledge. There was also a mechanism for building knowledge. When someone encountered a problem while using some element of ESW—a workflow map, design criteria or an activity page—there was an owner of that element who could be called in to investigate. When the root cause was discovered, the ESW was modified, increasing the likelihood that the next person to depend on that element of ESW would succeed.*

Clearly not an overnight task, developing a culture of learning differentiates many firms and is something that is enabled by the previously discussed six steps.

The U.S. Navy's Operating Model

The U.S. Navy provides a useful analogy with regard to how it approaches operations—and illuminates many of the key elements of Lean Operating Models. In the Navy, operations is separate from strategy and is distinct from tactics (think of *operations* as the engine room, *tactics* as how you fight the ship, and *strategy* which fight you are in), but there is nothing secondary about operations. In fact it represents a clear domain of leadership within the Navy and is central to the Navy's ability to fight and win battles.

Operations is very different from *strategy*, which is also different from *tactics.*

- **Strategy:** Strategy defines how you deploy scarce resources. Do you fight on one front or two? Which markets are you in? It sets the playing field.
- **Tactics:** Tactics refers to how you fight the battle (in Navy terms, what separates tactics from strategy is once "contact" has been made). What maneuvers do you deploy to win the given battle? This is *not*, as many companies believe, the domain of the "low-level" thinker; this is often confused, in fact, with strategy.
- **Operations:** Operations are ongoing disciplines that enable tactics and strategy through integrated systems, processes, infrastructure, and people.

Naval operations is highly standardized, with detailed operating procedures and protocols rigorously followed for starting up a propulsion plant, launching an aircraft, submerging a submarine, communicating information, and so on. Tactics, on the other hand, has been marked by imagination, improvisation, flexibility, and adaptation. But the Navy's tactical flexibility relies on a foundation of operational rigor. By streamlining the elements of operations—having defined and standardized ways of operating—the naval commander is better equipped to fight the battle.

Each distinct area requires different capabilities but also possesses different dynamics. The "turn rate," or rate of change, of operations is different from the turn rate of strategy (see Figure 79).

Figure 79: Tactics, Operations, and Strategy Meshing Together

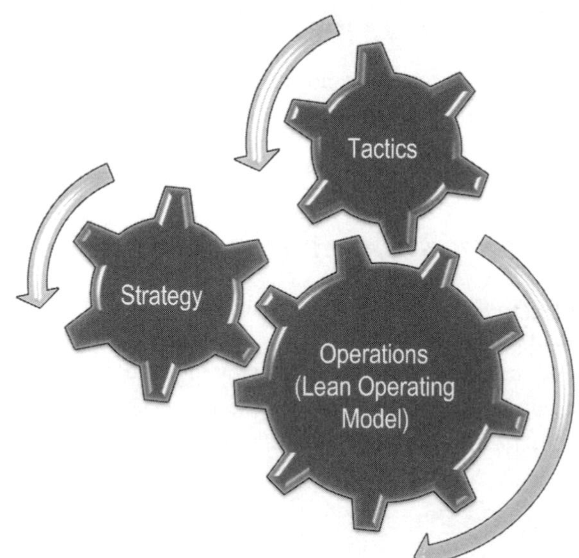

Working in sync though with different turn rates, the elements of the Lean Operating Model enable strategic breadth and tactical speed.

Strategy, tactics, and operations need to work in sync, though the rate of change of each is different. Having them meshed together, though, through a Lean Operating Model, enables strategic breadth and tactical speed.

Without clear distinctions and delineations, you're left with the worst of both worlds: strategy and tactics that move only at the speed that operations evolve; and operations that are continually turned upside down by new strategies. Unfortunately, this is the position that many companies find themselves in. When companies struggle with "strategy-to-execution," it is often a symptom of poor definition and subsequent lack of appropriate remedies. "Strategy-to-execution" becomes a euphemism for getting something done **in spite of** the organization.

The second big learning from the Navy is the focus on standardization. Everything that can be standardized is standardized in operations, which means that (a) waste and complexity are not allowed to creep into the organization because of input variability and (b) the organization is fast and disciplined, so that when new strategic or tactical opportunities emerge, the Navy can respond.

Finally, the standardization provides a basis for learning. While there is zero tolerance for procedural noncompliance, the Nuclear Navy in particular does not expect—in fact it doesn't tolerate—unthinking compliance (a "questioning attitude" is one of the five "pillars" of the program).

As questions are raised, they are evaluated and, if warranted, reincorporated back into the standard ways of working. This captures the value of the new insights and leverages it across the entire fleet, while preventing the chaos of a thousand people independently changing processes. This is an imperative in the Navy and most organizations today because it is very hard for one person in her or his specific function to forecast the impact of a change elsewhere in the organization.

Why ERP Deployments Go Wrong and the Need for Lean Operating Models

Often the first time a company starts seriously thinking about the issues we're discussing in this chapter is during the deployment of an ERP system. ERP is a set of IT systems used to manage and coordinate resources, information, and functions in a business using shared data. ERP deployments, however, can take on a life of their own: with big teams of company personnel involved, and often large teams of external consultants in support, the program can become an all-consuming focus, enormously expensive and, as a result, driven and shaped by the timeline as opposed to the business needs.

ERP deployments often start life under the banner of transformation, and with good reason.

- First, given the resources applied to these programs and their high-profile nature, it can be the ideal opportunity to align the organization on how the business is expected to win in the market and what that requires of the organization's processes and IT. As an extension of that, it is a rare opportunity to tame decentralized multiunit organizations where every unit "likes to do it their way" (based on the belief that their business is somehow fundamentally different from every other business unit). The need to standardize or at least simplify processes for ERP enablement raises the bar on what is acceptable. ERP can legitimize a discussion about moving to standard work.
- Second, ERP requires a thorough review and baseline of your processes. Part of the review focuses on what is core to the business (which is at the heart of a Lean Operating Model), and this review can help you redefine how your firm wins in the marketplace and what the core capabilities are that enable you to stay a nose length ahead of your competition.
- Third, at a process level, the spotlight can provide the impetus to make "a major push" on improving processes, making them lean and removing waste and opportunities for failure. This requires some thinking ahead—decoupling the improvements from the technology—and with planning, is the right lead-in to technology deployment.
- Finally, given the organizational nature of ERP, it is also the right time to assess how assets, functions, metrics, and people currently support the core processes. Similar to the first point above, executives should use this as a point of transforming the organization.

Unfortunately, however, despite the opportunities they present for transformation, many ERP programs retreat into being just ERP deployments. The reality of meeting deadlines squeezes out the opportunities for improvement. Decisions are made based on expediency, not on overarching process strategy.

For example, consider a global consumer company that launched a global ERP rollout. In the lead-in to the deployment, they did many things right. They framed it in a broad vision and strategy for the company. They identified the core processes and assigned process owners against them. But they failed to construct their own Lean Operating Model, which led to gaps, such as,

- Insufficient understanding about how their core processes enabled them to win in the market and no metrics attached to these core processes. This led to a lack of clarity about how the ERP investment would derive a return. (This kind of gap is not uncommon: companies define a broad corporate strategy but fail to enunciate how they intend to win the fights needed to achieve strategic goals.)

- Insufficient focus on becoming Lean. While the company discussed process improvements, management did not allocate resources nor did they incorporate such efforts into the timeline, so they could not drive significant process improvements in advance of process automation.
- No documentation on how the organization was aligned or not aligned in support of its core processes, which led to a divergence of interests: the ERP team driving forward on implementation and the rest of the organization intent on self-preservation (or the preservation of the status quo).

Since it did not explicitly frame how the firm could efficiently engage with the market to meet customer demands (which is what a Lean Operating Model will do), this company's ERP program retreated to become an effort in which

- Technology took precedence over customer needs (and the activities that matter to the customer).
- Core processes became defined by existing biases or industry standards; core points of differentiation were lost or trampled. (In general, efforts that lack a driving operating model identify "best practices" that, at best, are an amalgamation of competitors' processes and, at worst, may have no relation to the context of the business.)
- Results were a mere shadow of what they could have been had the effort been addressed with Lean process improvements.
- Drivers of process and organizational complexity were "locked in" through technology and automation, impairing cost-competitiveness and hindering future efforts to take out complexity costs.

The specific message is clear: if you are considering an ERP system in the near future, start now to address the business-critical questions and build your Lean Operating Model. If you are currently in the process of deploying an ERP system, then ensure that the timeline demands do not trample the business-critical questions that warrant discussion.

More generally, the lesson is that having a well-defined operating model can help avoid enormous waste: it will provide you with a powerful mechanism for controlling complexity and puts in place a platform for leveraging technology.

Case Study: Winning the retail wars with the Tesco operating model

If you're looking for an example of an industry in which execution matters, the grocery segment in the United Kingdom is a prime candidate. In her book *Trolley Wars*, author Judi Bevan describes the UK grocery market evolving "as a result of protracted, ongoing and often ruthless conflict between the big chains. Beneath the seductive camouflage of smiling here-to-help faces, celebrity endorsement, generous offers, slick slogans and the mantra of 'healthy competition,' the fight to win the hearts and wallets of the British shopper is never ending."

For global retailer Tesco, its decision to move to a Lean Operating Model was as much about seizing a global growth opportunity as it was about driving out waste and cost. The retailer, which in 2008 had global revenues of £47.3 billion,[82] operates more than 4,000 stores across 14 countries, including the United States since 2008 under the name Fresh & Easy Neighborhood Market.

Dominant in the United Kingdom (where it accounts for 30% of the grocery market), Tesco has spent the last decade focused on growing its international business, its store formats, and its range. It has expanded from the traditional grocery range into home furnishings and electronics, for example, and has moved beyond the traditional store format to small inner-city stores and suburban megastores. And it has launched operations in the United States, continental Europe, and Asia. To accommodate this growth, the company realized it needed a more scalable solution and one that was not overwhelmed by the increasing complexity of its operations.

The company describes its model—called the Tesco Operating Model—as a "common set of back-office and retail processes, systems and operating capabilities which we can develop once, and use many times across the countries where we trade and when we go into new markets."[83] (We would describe that list as defining the core processes that Tesco needed to anchor on to achieve its strategic goals.)

Figure 80: Tesco's Process for Updating Its Business Model

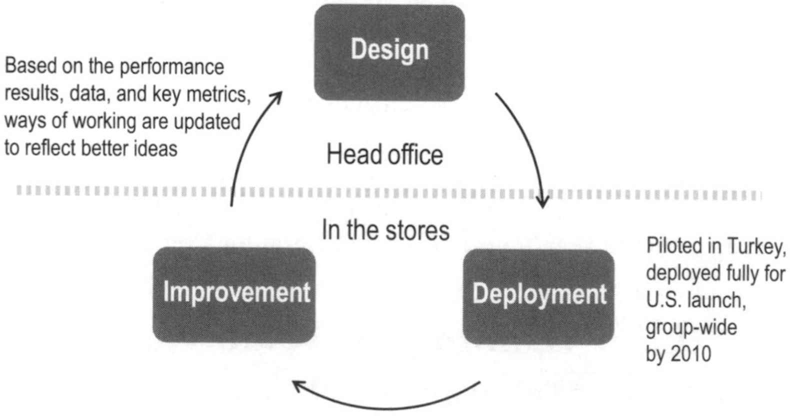

Design

Based on the performance results, data, and key metrics, ways of working are updated to reflect better ideas

Head office

In the stores

Improvement

Deployment

Piloted in Turkey, deployed fully for U.S. launch, group-wide by 2010

The Tesco Operating Model strives for scale and continuous improvement. As the model is deployed, it generates new insights about, e.g., continuous replenishment and store ordering.[84]

Tesco has thus standardized a single way of working for a large number of defined processes, such as listing products and suppliers, setting prices, ordering, distribution, keeping track of finances, and payroll.

Interestingly, given the discussion of ERP systems above, Tesco's move in this direction began as a model for IT systems (called "Tesco in a Box"). It then evolved, said Mike Yorwerth, Tesco's director of group technology and architecture, into "not only a set of IT systems but also a set of business processes. It describes planning and building stores, deciding on markets, selecting products, getting through the supply chain to selling to the customers in the shops."[85] As Tesco expands into new markets, instead of reinventing the wheel—or in this case the grocery store—it leverages a common set of processes, management frameworks, and supporting IT systems. Says Yorwerth,

> *It's a very compelling vision because it's a model we can then roll around the group and it brings all the key performance indicators with it that we can continually improve.*
>
> *In the UK we've got what we think is a world-leading continuous replenishment system, sales-based ordering and very sophisticated forecasting. But when Tesco develops a better way of forecasting, that will get incorporated back into the model.*

In this way, Tesco's model underscores well a key element of the Lean Operating Model—as a framework for capturing learning and improvements.

The Relentless Pursuit of Perfection

According to one study, companies with "a foundation for execution supporting an operating model reported higher operational efficiency (31%), customer intimacy (33%), product leadership (34%) and strategic agility (29%) than companies that had not developed a foundation for execution."[86]

In fact, there are a number of external dynamics that are increasing the need for companies to embrace the ideas behind the Lean Operating Model:

- **The pace of change** is raising the bar for whole-firm performance (in which the parts of the business act in a synchronous manner). For a company to act and seize on new market opportunities, companies require greater cohesion, agility, and speed—all elements of the Lean Operating Model.
- **New technologies** represent opportunities that you or your competitors will leverage—but to deploy them requires a stable platform of processes and longer-term vision, which is only possible through a commitment to a way of working.

- **Increasing complexity** in what customers want and when they want it is putting enormous stress on operations. Operations that were "getting by" through workarounds are at their breaking point.
- **Global competition** means there is no longer a hiding place for non-value-add cost or waste. The intensity and scale of global competition is forcing companies to focus on what is valuable to customers and purge the organization of what is not (waste).

To borrow the former Lexus tagline, the Lean Operating Model is the best means for focusing an organization on the relentless focus and improvement required to win in today's market. This discipline prevents complexity from creeping in and recreating a mess of cost and poor processes.

In an ongoing battle for short-lived advantage, companies need capabilities and a common framework of processes for rapid execution, fast innovation, operational efficiency, and complexity reduction. When the advantages of differentiation are transient, then the real advantage belongs to those with the embedded capabilities to *repeatedly* get a nose length ahead.

Chapter 18 Endnotes

78 "When Should a Process Be Art, Not Science?" *Harvard Business Review*, March 2009.

79 Originally the role was pioneered in the Japanese aircraft industry.

80 James M. Morgan and Jeffrey K. Liker, *The Toyota Product Development System* (New York: Productivity Press, 2006).

81 Available at Knowledge@Wharton, Podcast: "Humana CEO Mike McCallister: Letting the Consumer Drive Innovation." Accessed July 17, 2009.

82 Tesco, based on reported Group Revenues (excluding value added tax).

83 Tesco Annual Review and Summary Financial Statement 2008.

84 Based on an interview with Mike Yorwerth, featured in IT World Canada.com, "Tesco-in-a-Box Spearheads UK Grocery Giant's U.S. push…."

85 *ibid.*

86 Jeanne W. Ross, Peter Weill, and David C. Robertson, *Enterprise Architecture as Strategy* (Boston: Harvard Business School Press, 2006).

APPENDIX A

Optimal Batch Size Equation

The Optimal Batch Size (OBS) equation[1] is a closed-form formula that provides the batch sizes and production frequencies, for all items, that will minimize inventory holding cost and lead time while meeting demand (so long as the total production time does not exceed the available time).

The optimal batch size equation can be used to estimate the appropriate production schedule and also to quickly access the impact from changes in key parameters, such as a change in demand or introduction of a new product, on the production performance such as WIP and lead time.

Given the demand for each product, available machine hours, holding costs, and setup times, the optimal batch size equation is defined as follows:

$$B_i = \left(\frac{\sum_{j=1}^{m} \sqrt{D_j \bullet h_j \bullet s_j}}{\mathcal{S}} \right) \bullet \sqrt{\frac{D_i \bullet s_i}{h_i}}$$

Where,

B_i = Batch size of product i

D_i = Total demand for product i

h_i = Holding cost or penalty cost associated with the size of the batch of product i in the evaluation period

s_i = Setup time per batch of product i

$\mathcal{S}$ = Available setup time

m = number of products

The production frequency or number of batches in the evaluation period (for product i) is $n_i = \frac{D_i}{B_i}$

From the equation above, the first ratio is constant between products; therefore, the size of the batch varies by the ratio of the square root of the product of total demand and setup time to holding cost.

---

[1] The equation was developed by Dr. Nithiphong Vikitset of Wilson Perumal & Company, Inc.

Numerical Example

The monthly demand and production requirements for five products produced on the same line are given in Table A1.

Table A1: Monthly Demands and Production Requirements

	Product 1	Product 2	Product 3	Product 4	Product 5
Processing time (hours / unit)	0.4	1.5	0.2	0.8	1.8
Setup time (hours / batch)	4	5	5	8	10
Monthly demand (units)	50	40	40	200	200
Monthly holding cost (per unit)	5	5	10	15	4

Total processing time required to produce all given demands are 608 hours. Therefore, if there are 720 machine hours available in a month, the available setup time are 720 – 608 = 112 hours. Using optimal batch size equation, the optimal batch sizes and cycle-time intervals[2] (CTIs) are shown in Table A2.

Table A2: Optimal Batch Sizes and CTIs

	Product 1	Product 2	Product 3	Product 4	Product 5
Batch size (units)	19.90	19.90	14.07	32.49	70.34
CTI (days)[3]	11.94	14.92	10.55	4.87	10.55

The results in Table A2 mean, for example, that Product 1 would be produced in a batch of about 20 units every 12 days, whereas Product 4 would be produced more frequently (almost every five days) and in larger volumes (batches of 32–33 products each time it is made). This combination of batch sizes and production frequencies across all products, determined using the OBS equation, will minimize inventory holding costs[4] and lead times while meeting demand.

---

[2] For a given product, its cycle time interval is the time between the start of one production cycle and the start of the next production cycle of the same product.

[3] The cycle time interval is calculate by $CTI_i = \frac{B_i}{D_i}$

[4] The average inventory levels for each product equal half its batch size, based on a typical sawtooth inventory profile, excluding safety stock.

Appendix B

Detail for Product-Process Interactions

This appendix provides additional detail and explanation for the following two Product/Process interactions described in Chapter 6, "Where Complexity Arises: The Product/Process Face":

Interaction 2: Increased product variety erodes production capacity

Interaction 3: Low-volume products have a non-linear impact on inventory and capacity

Interaction 2: Increased product variety erodes production capacity

To better understand the relationship between product complexity and production capacity, it is helpful to consider for a moment the relationship between inventory and production volume. As we showed in Chapter 6, the average overall inventory level for a product is proportional to its batch size. Therefore, inventory levels can be reduced by running smaller batches, but smaller batches mean more frequent setups/changeovers which eat up production capacity (see Figure A.1, next page).

Figure A.1. Impact on Production Capacity and Inventory from Reduced Batch Size

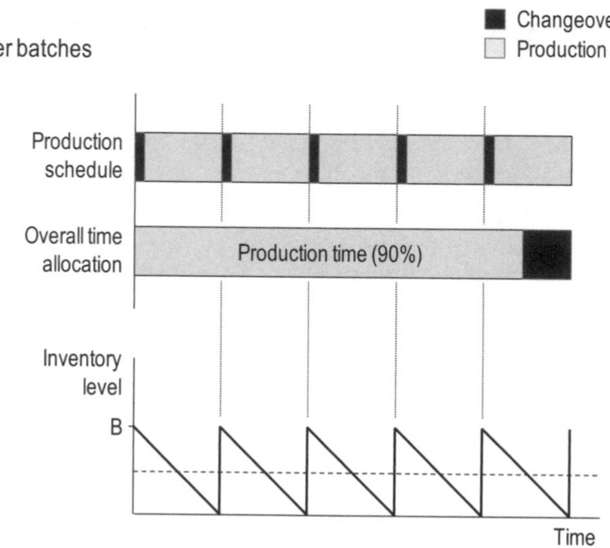

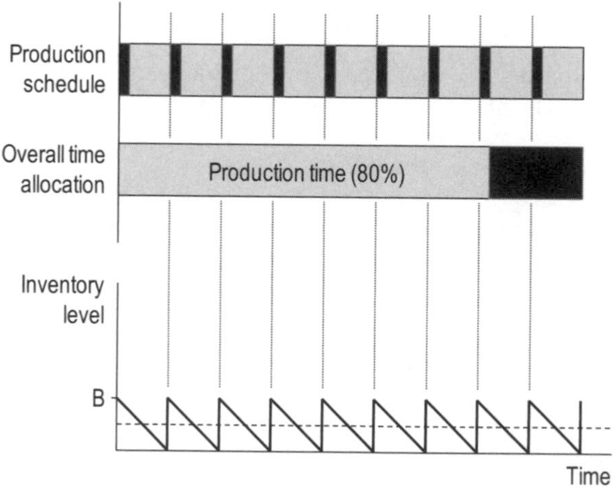

Reducing batch size reduces average inventory levels, but also increases the frequency and number of changeovers. The batch size and inventory levels in (b) are about half that in (a), but production volume has been reduced by approximately ten percent since more time is spent on changeovers—time that is not longer used for production.

Looked at another way, as production volume is increased in a plant, a greater portion of time is spent producing which allows less time for changeovers. Less time for changeovers means fewer changeovers; fewer changeovers mean larger batches; and larger batches mean greater inventory (and greater time between production runs of a given product).

As production volume approaches the theoretical maximum (a theoretical but typically unreachable limit where all of the available time is spent producing and non on changing over the line) batch sizes and inventory will grow asymptotically as shown in Figure A.2. This curve represents a fundamental relationship between production volume and inventory levels. While poor operating practices can result in being above and to the right of this curve (more inventories with less production volume) this curve represents the best case relationship between inventory and production volume (given our simplifying assumptions).

Figure A.2. Relationship Between Inventory and Production Volume

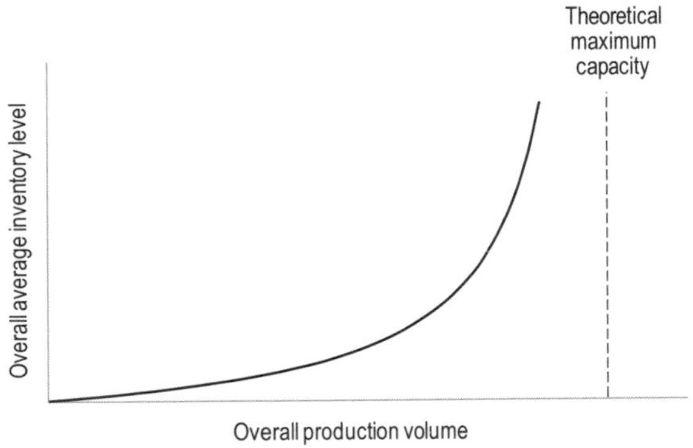

Overall inventory levels increase as production volume approaches a plant's capacity. Increased production volume reduces the time available for changeovers. Less frequent changeovers means larger production batches (longer production runs) which increases inventory levels. As production volume approaches a theoretical maximum (where all time would be spent on production) inventory grows asymptotically. A company's desired place on this curve depends on the relative value of additional production volume compared to the overall cost to the business of additional inventory; a company's actual place on the curve depends on production scheduling.

So where does product complexity come in? We have already shown that for a given level of overall demand inventory levels increase proportionally with the number of products. This means that, given the same simplifying assumptions we made before, the *inventory/production volume curve* simply scales up proportionally with the number of products (see **Figure A.3**). Note that at any selected production volume a doubling in the number of products doubles the overall inventory level. This effectively shifts the curve upward and to the left, representing a combination of more inventories and lower production volume, as the number of products is increased.

Figure A.3. Impact of Product Complexity on Inventory Levels (Constant Production Volume)

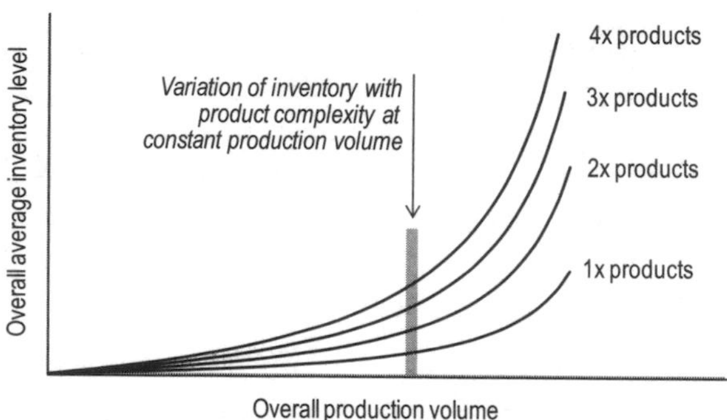

Mathematically, the inventory – production volume curve scales up proportionally with the number of products. At given production volume, the level of inventory for 4x products is twice as high as that for 2x products—this is the same linear relationship between inventory and number of products shown in Figure 29 (p. 116).

To now understand the impact of product complexity on production capacity alone, consider the relationship between multiple *inventory/production volume curves* (each corresponding to a different number of products) at a given level of overall inventory (see **Figure A.4**). If the overall inventory level is kept constant, then the impact of increased product complexity is felt entirely on production capacity. This relationship, which shows how production capacity decreases with an increasing number of products (with the level of overall inventory held constant), is shown in Figure A.5. As you can see in the figure, *increased product complexity erodes capacity*. It most situations the impact is felt as a combination of decreased production capacity and increased inventories.

Figure A.4. Impact of Product Complexity on Production Volume (Constant Inventory Level)

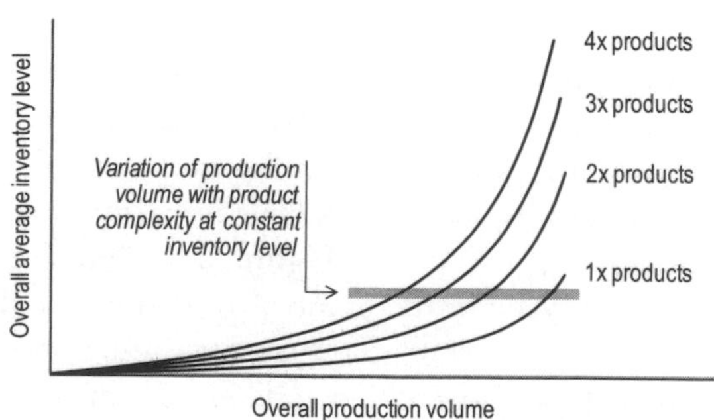

At given level of inventory, production volume declines with increased number of products.

Figure A.5. Impact of Product Complexity on Overall Production Volume (Constant Level of Inventory)

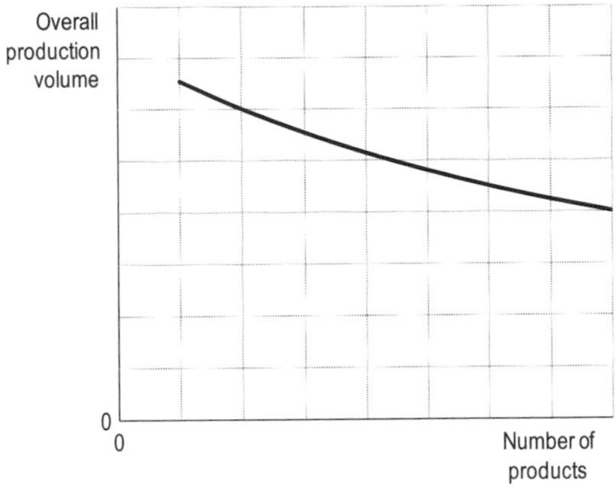

Production volume is inversely related to production complexity (number of products). Spreading production across a greater number of products reduces overall production volume (for a constant level of overall inventory).

Interaction 3: Low-volume products have a non-linear impact on inventory and capacity

Small-volume products eat up disproportionate capacity and contribute disproportionately to inventory and lead time. Starting with a simplifying example and building from there, first notice that for a given product the production volume is simply the batch size multiplied by its frequency of production:

Production volume = Batch size × Production frequency

Assume a small-volume offering was to be produced at the same frequency as an offering with twice the volume (see **Figure A.6**). The batch size of the large volume product would accordingly be twice that of the smaller volume offering, but each would incur the same overall changeover time (assuming the products shared similar product characteristics other than volume). The setup to run-time ratio for the low-volume product would therefore be twice that of the high-volume product, and on a per unit basis the small volume offering would "erode" twice as much production capacity.

Most operators know this—instinctively at least. Typically, production runs of low-volume products will be less frequent than that for their high-volume counterparts. To bound the issue on the other side, consider an alternative approach where the batch sizes are equal but the low-volume product is run at half the frequency of the high-volume product (see **Figure A.7**). With equal batch sizes, the setup to run-time ratio and the per unit erosion of production capacity are the same for each product. But while the volume of the low-volume product is half that of the high-volume product, their overall average inventory levels are the same. In other words, the inventory level per unit for the low-volume offering is twice of the high-volume offering. On a per unit basis, low-volume products tend to drive much more inventory than high-volume ones.

Most operations operate somewhere in between, *with low-volume offerings eating up more capacity and driving greater inventory levels, on a per unit basis, than their higher-volume counterparts* (most accounting systems, however, spread these costs in a peanut butter fashion, often by number of units, which is why small-volume products are almost invariably under-costed).

Figure A.6. Comparison of Products with Different Volumes at Same Production Frequency, Different Batch Sizes

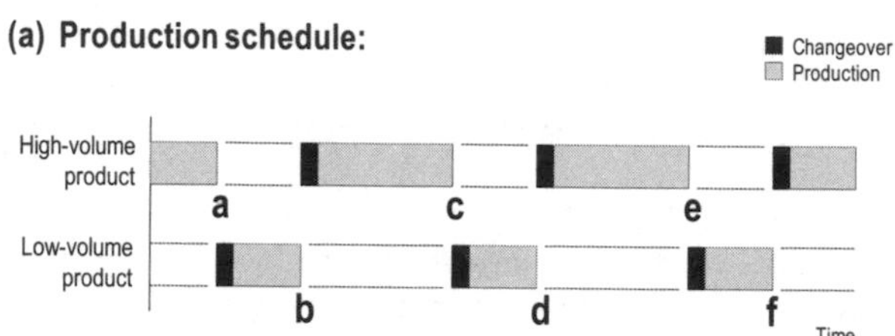

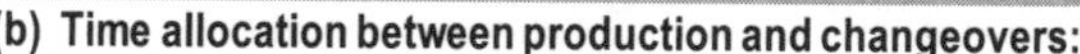

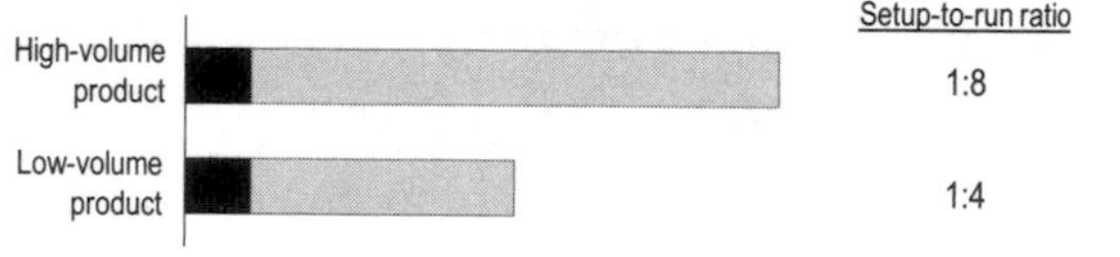

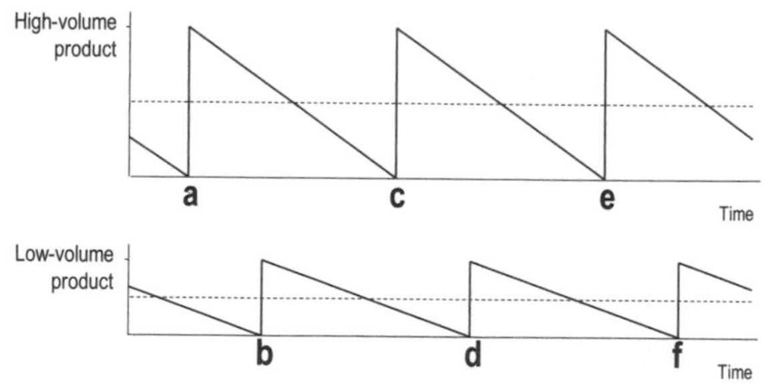

A higher-volume product is shown with twice the volume of a lower-volume product (the products share the same characteristics such as production rate, setup time, etc). If produced at the same frequency, as shown, the changeovers for the lower-volume product will consume twice the capacity per unit than that of the higher-volume product. (a) The production schedule alternates between the products, with a batch of the higher-volume one being completed at times a, c, and e; and that of the low-volume one at times b, d, and f. Since they are produced at the same frequency each production run of the lower-volume product is half as long as that of the higher-volume product. (b) Over a given amount of time, the products have the same cumulative changeover time but very different production volumes. The setup to run-time ratio of the lower-volume product is twice that of the higher-volume product. (c) Since the batch size for the lower-volume product is half that of the higher-volume product, its average inventory level also half that of the higher-volume product. But it also has half the volume meaning the inventory cost per unit produced is the same for the two products.

Figure A.7. Comparison of Products with Different Volumes at Same Batch Size, Different Production Frequency

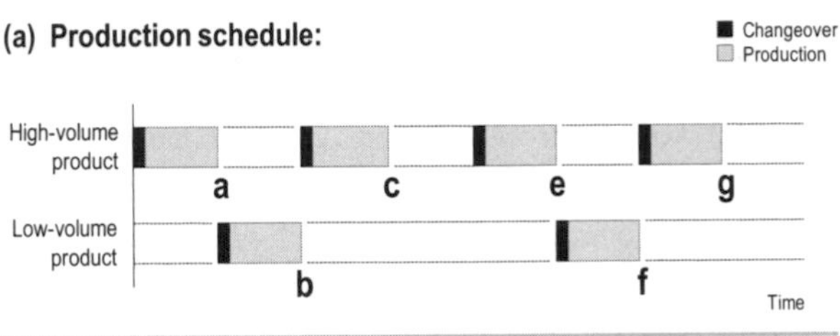

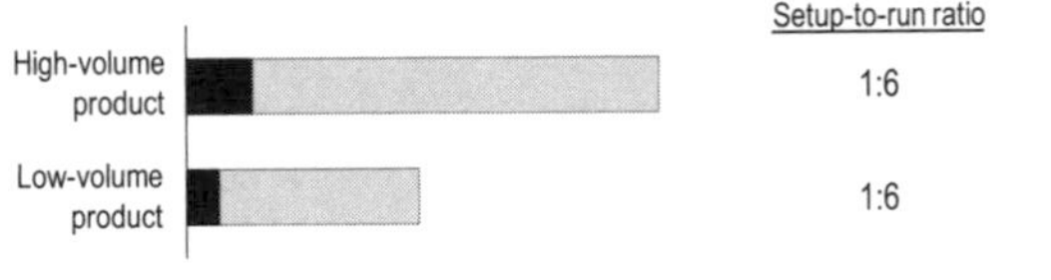

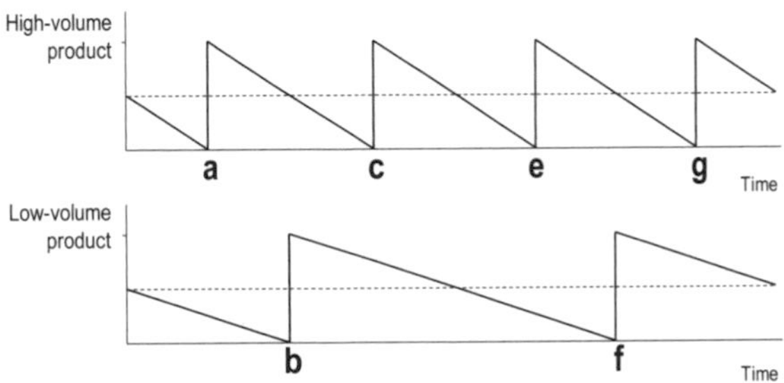

A higher-volume product is shown with twice the volume of a lower-volume product (the products share the same characteristics such as production rate, setup time, etc.). If produced with the same batch size, as shown, the average inventory level per unit produced will be much greater for the lower-volume product than the higher-volume product (in this case twice as much). (a) One batch of the lower-volume product is produced for every two batches of the higher-volume offering. (b) The setup to run-time ratio for each product is the same, meaning they have the same impact on capacity on a per unit basis. (c) The average inventory level of the lower-volume product equals that of the higher-volume product, but since it has half the volume of the higher-volume product, its average inventory cost per unit produced is twice that of the higher-volume product.

Appendix C

Backup Calculations for Chapter 10 Tables

The tables in Chapter 10, "Portfolio Optimization (Part A): SKU Analysis and Selection," used to explain complexity adjusted incremental costing and the impact of substitutability on margin were based on the simplified production plant example shown in this Appendix. The analysis makes use of the Optimal Batch Size equation described in Appendix A.

In these spreadsheets, the highlighted numbers tie to numbers in the referenced tables in Chapter 10.

Backup calculations for Table M on page 189:

Plant information:

Total time available (hrs):	720
Overhead cost ($):	15

Product production parameters:

Product:	A	B	C	D
Processing time (hrs/unit):	6	6	6	6
Setup time (hrs/batch):	6	6	6	6
Inventory cost ($/unit-mo.):	$0.69	$0.69	$0.69	$0.69

Calculations:

				INVENTORY			PLANT OVERHEAD				
Product	**Demand (# of units)**	Proc. time (hrs)	Batch size (# of units)	Avg. inv. M. (# of units)	Cost of inventory	**Inv. cost per unit of demand**	Number of batches	Total setup (hrs)	Total plant time (hrs)	Overhead allocation	**Overhead per unit of demand**
A	**70**	420	7.14	3.57	$2.45	**$0.04**	9.81	58.86	478.86	$9.98	**$0.14**
B	**22**	132	4.00	2.00	$1.37	**$0.06**	5.50	33.00	165.00	$3.44	**$0.16**
C	**4**	24	1.71	0.85	$0.59	**$0.15**	2.35	14.07	38.07	$0.79	**$0.20**
D	**4**	24	1.71	0.85	$0.59	**$0.15**	2.35	14.07	38.07	$0.79	**$0.20**
Total	**100**	600	N/A	7.27	$5.00	**$0.05**	20.00	120.00	720.00	$15.00	**$0.15**
		= Processing time per unit x Demand	*Determined using the Optimal Batch Size equation from Appendix A*	*= 1/2 Batch size*	*= Inventory cost pr unit x Average inventory level*	*= Inventory cost/ Demand*	*= Demand /# of batches*	*= # of batches x setup time*	*= Total processing time + Total setup time*	*Plant overhead costs allocated by total plant time consumed by product*	*= Plant overhead allocation /Demand*

Time available for setup: *120*

Backup calculations for Table 0 on page 192:

Plant information:

Total time available (hrs): 720
Overhead cost ($): 15

Product production parameters:

Product:	A	B	C	D
Processing time (hrs/unit):	6	6	6	6
Setup time (hrs/batch):	6	6	6	6
Inventory cost ($/unit-mo.):	$0.69	$0.69	$0.69	$0.69

Calculations (All 4 products):

				INVENTORY			PLANT OVERHEAD					Total
Product	**Demand (# of units)**	Proc. time (hrs)	Batch size (# of units)	Avg. inv. M. (# of units)	Cost of inventory	**Inv. cost per unit of demand**	Number of batches	Total setup (hrs)	Total plant time (hrs)	Overhead allocation	**Overhead per unit of demand**	**NVA cost per unit**
A	**70**	420	7.135	3.568	2.453	**$0.035**	9.810	58.861	478.861	9.976	**$0.143**	**$0.178**
B	**22**	132	4.000	2.000	1.375	**$0.062**	5.500	32.998	164.998	3.437	**$0.156**	**$0.219**
C	**4**	24	1.706	0.853	0.586	**$0.147**	2.345	14.070	38.070	0.793	**$0.198**	**$0.345**
D	**4**	24	1.706	0.853	0.586	**$0.147**	2.345	14.070	38.070	0.793	**$0.198**	**$0.345**
Total	**100**	600	N/A	7.274	5.000	**$0.050**	20.000	120.000	720.000	15.000	**$0.150**	**$0.200**

Time available for setup: *120*

Calculations (Products A & B only):

				INVENTORY			PLANT OVERHEAD					Total
Product	**Demand (# of units)**	Proc. time (hrs)	Batch size (# of units)	Avg. inv. M. (# of units)	Cost of inventory	**Inv. cost per unit of demand**	Number of batches	Total setup (hrs)	Total plant time (hrs)	Overhead allocation	**Overhead per unit of demand**	**NVA cost per unit**
A	**70**	420	3.902	1.951	1.341	**$0.019**	17.942	107.650	527.650	10.993	**$0.157**	**$0.176**
B	**22**	132	2.187	1.094	0.752	**$0.034**	10.058	60.350	192.350	4.007	**$0.182**	**$0.216**
Total	**92**	552	N/A	3.044	2.093	**$0.023**	28.000	168.000	720.000	15.000	**$0.163**	**$0.186**

Time available for setup: *168*

Backup calculations for Table Q on page 193 (spreadsheet 1):

Plant information:

Total time available (hrs):	720
Overhead cost ($):	15

Product production parameters:

Product:	A	B	C	D
Processing time (hrs/unit):	6	6	6	6
Setup time (hrs/batch):	6	6	6	6
Inventory cost ($/unit-mo.):	$0.69	$0.69	$0.69	$0.69

Calculations (All 4 products):

				INVENTORY			PLANT OVERHEAD					Explicit
Product	**Demand (# of units)**	Proc. time (hrs)	Batch size (# of units)	Avg. inv. M. (# of units)	Cost of inventory	**Inv. cost per unit of demand**	Number of batches	Total setup (hrs)	Total plant time (hrs)	Overhead allocation	**Overhead per unit of demand**	**NVA cost per unit**
A	**70**	420	7.135	3.568	2.453	**$0.035**	9.810	58.861	478.861	9.976	**$0.143**	**$0.178**
B	**22**	132	4.000	2.000	1.375	**$0.062**	5.500	32.998	164.998	3.437	**$0.156**	**$0.219**
C	**4**	24	1.706	0.853	0.586	**$0.147**	2.345	14.070	38.070	0.793	**$0.198**	**$0.345**
D	**4**	24	1.706	0.853	0.586	**$0.147**	2.345	14.070	38.070	0.793	**$0.198**	**$0.345**
Total	**100**	600	N/A	7.274	5.000	**$0.050**	20.000	120.000	720.000	15.000	**$0.150**	**$0.200**

Time available for setup: *120*

Calculations (Products A & B only):

				INVENTORY			PLANT OVERHEAD					Explicit
Product	**Demand (# of units)**	Proc. time (hrs)	Batch size (# of units)	Avg. inv. M. (# of units)	Cost of inventory	**Inv. cost per unit of demand**	Number of batches	Total setup (hrs)	Total plant time (hrs)	Overhead allocation	**Overhead per unit of demand**	**NVA cost per unit**
A	**72**	432	4.732	2.366	1.626	**$0.023**	15.215	91.292	523.292	10.902	**$0.151**	**$0.174**
B	**24**	144	2.732	1.366	0.939	**$0.039**	8.785	52.708	196.708	4.098	**$0.171**	**$0.210**
Total	**96**	576	N/A	3.732	2.565	**$0.027**	24.000	144.000	720.000	15.000	**$0.156**	**$0.183**

Time available for setup: *144*

Backup calculations for Table Q on page 193 (spreadsheet 2)

	Portfolio of A & B alone			Portfolio of Products A, B, C, & D					Incremental analysis				
	A	B	Total	A	B	C	D	Total	A	B	C	D	Total
Volume	72	24	96	70	22	4	4	100	72	24	2	2	100
Price	$1.00	$1.00	$1.00	$1.00	$1.00	$1.00	$1.00	$1.00	$1.00	$1.00	$1.00	$1.00	$1.00
Revenue	$72.00	$24.00	$96.00	$70.00	$22.00	$4.00	$4.00	$100.00	$72.00	$24.00	$2.00	$2.00	$100.00
VA costs	$0.700	$0.700		$0.700	$0.700	$0.700	$0.700						
Explicit NVA costs	**$0.174**	**$0.210**		**$0.178**	**$0.219**	**$0.345**	**$0.345**						
Total unit cost	$0.874	$0.910		$0.878	$0.919	$1.045	$1.045						
VA costs	$50.40	$16.80	$67.20	$49.00	$15.40	$2.80	$2.80	$70.00	$50.40	$16.80	$1.40	$1.40	$70.00
Explicit NVA costs	$12.53	$5.04	$17.57	$12.43	$4.81	$1.38	$1.38	$20.00	$13.12	$5.50	$0.69	$0.69	$20.00
Implicit NVA costs									-$0.59	-$0.46	$0.53	$0.53	$0.00
Total cost	$62.93	$21.84	$84.77	$61.43	$20.21	$4.18	$4.18	$90.00	$62.93	$21.84	$2.62	$2.62	$90.00
Margin ($)	$9.07	$2.16	$11.23	$8.57	$1.79	-$0.18	-$0.18	$10.00	$9.07	$2.16	-$0.62	-$0.62	$10.00
Margin (%)	12.6%	9.0%	11.7%	12.2%	8.1%	-4.5%	-4.5%	10.0%	**12.6%**	**9.0%**	**-30.9%**	**-30.9%**	10.0%

Note: The Eplicit NVA costs in the second spreadsheet are pulled from the last column of the first spreadsheet

Index

About WilsonPerumal

WilsonPerumal is a strategy and operations consultancy that helps companies compete in a complex world. We partner with our clients to help them reinvigorate their Market Focus, Strategic Clarity, and Operational and Organizational Alignment in order to outpace their competition. We bring a unique point of view, one that is grounded in rich experience, distinctive thinking, and a deep understanding of the issues challenging companies today.

We combine strategy expertise with a deep heritage in operations and Lean thinking to develop complete solutions for our clients. While many firms help clients with the individual pieces of their business, we are unique in our focus on integrating and aligning the pieces for whole-firm performance. WilsonPerumal partners have led major transformations and key initiatives in clients across a diverse set of industries and segments, including Retail, Consumer Goods, Industrial Goods, Technology, Financial Services, the Federal Government, and the U.S. military.

www.wilsonperumal.com